FLYING BLIND, FLYING SAFE

The Former Inspector General
of the U.S. Department
of Transportation Tells You
Everything You Need to
Know to Travel Safer by Air

D0008935

MARY SCHIAVO
with SABRA CHARTRAND

AVON BOOKS ◆ NEW YORK

All of the information in this book has been compiled from the most reliable sources, and every effort has been made to eliminate mistakes and questionable data. Nevertheless the possibility of error always exists. Neither the authors nor the publisher will be held responsible for any errors or omissions contained herein.

AVON BOOKS
A division of
The Hearst Corporation
1350 Avenue of the Americas
New York, New York 10019

Copyright © 1997, 1998 by Mary Schiavo
Cover photo courtesy of The Ohio State University
Visit our website at **http://www.AvonBooks.com**
ISBN: 0-380-79330-X

First Avon Books Paperback Printing: April 1998
First Avon Books Hardcover Printing: May 1997

AVON TRADEMARK REG. U.S. PAT. OFF. AND IN OTHER COUNTRIES, MARCA REGIS-
TRADA, HECHO EN U.S.A.

Printed in the U.S.A.

WCD   10   9   8   7   6   5   4   3   2   1

For my children,

Larissa Fackler Schiavo and Alexander Fackler Schiavo,

my husband, parents, and sisters

and all loved ones you have ever watched board a plane

ACKNOWLEDGMENTS

Sometimes even though you know you must do something, the best of intentions never come to fruition without the help and encouragement of others. I had the assistance of more people than I can mention here, some of whom must remain anonymous to keep their jobs. My thanks to all who helped me. I especially wish to thank Sabra Chartrand, *New York Times* reporter, for her assistance in writing this book, Patricia Lande Grader and the other folks at Avon Books who worked to make this book a reality, and Suzanne Gluck, at International Creative Management, my excellent agent.

Of course this book would not have been possible without my six years of experience as Inspector General of the U.S. Department of Transportation. I wish to thank former Deputy Inspector General Mario A. Lauro, Jr., for his assistance while we were at DOT and thereafter on this book, and the staff of the Office of the Inspector General, U.S. Department of Transportation, 1990–1996. They served the American people with dedication and courage. Thanks to those U.S. senators and representatives, and their staffs, who supported my work as Inspector General, and to the Federal Bureau of Investigation, which helped my office in many investigations. Thanks to the employees within the FAA who tried to improve the safety of avia-

tion, sometimes at the peril of losing their jobs, both while
I was Inspector General, and thereafter.

I am grateful to Ohio State University, which taught me
to fly, taught me the meaning of public service and gave
me the opportunity to pass on the lessons to others as the
Enarson Professor of Public Policy; as well as to my first
flight instructor, James L. Nielsen, now an airline captain,
who said, "You fly the plane, don't let the plane fly you,"
a lesson which extended to most things in life.

Thanks also to my family and friends who assisted me
in ways too numerous to list, especially my husband, Alex
Schiavo, my parents, Harland and Nina Fackler, and my
children, Larissa and Alexander.

Finally, thank you to the hardworking, government-
trusting American people. God bless us all.

CONTENTS

INTRODUCTION	The ValuJet Tragedy	1
CHAPTER ONE	Who Does the FAA Work for, Anyway? Not You.	37
CHAPTER TWO	The Plane Truth	53
CHAPTER THREE	The Tombstone Agency	64
CHAPTER FOUR	Business As Usual	73
CHAPTER FIVE	See No Evil: Bogus Parts	97
CHAPTER SIX	Cash Cows: Where Your Airport Money Went	122
CHAPTER SEVEN	Relative Truth: CULT-ure at the FAA	128
CHAPTER EIGHT	The Second Greatest Thrill	141
CHAPTER NINE	Who Watches the Manufacturers?	177
CHAPTER TEN	TWA Flight 800	191
CHAPTER ELEVEN	1997, 1998 . . .	206
CHAPTER TWELVE	There's No Such Thing As "Safety" at the FAA	233
CHAPTER THIRTEEN	Airplanes	240
CHAPTER FOURTEEN	U.S. and Foreign Airlines	270
CHAPTER FIFTEEN	Airports	327
CHAPTER SIXTEEN	Straighten Up and Fly Right	345

CHAPTER SEVENTEEN   **Flying Healthy**   366
CHAPTER EIGHTEEN   **Weather**   374
CHAPTER NINETEEN   **When You Have to Fight**   383
CHAPTER TWENTY   **Silencing the Watchdog**   392
EPILOGUE   **If We Really Want**
                     Change . . .   397
                     Help Yourself   408
CHAPTER NOTES   411

INTRODUCTION

The ValuJet Tragedy

When the call came that would trigger alarm bells over ValuJet, I wasn't thinking about airlines at all. In early February 1996, my desk, always buried under a mountain of government paperwork, was stacked with folders holding evaluations of security at the biggest airports around the country. As Inspector General of the Department of Transportation, I had ordered tests to see how protected airports really were against terrorists or saboteurs. Now the dismal results lay before me. Teams of normally mild-mannered auditors from my office and the Federal Aviation Administration had posed as bomb-carrying and gun-toting passengers and, to my dismay, had wandered unchallenged through airports, in cargo areas and even onto airplanes, all over the country. I wasn't completely surprised; we had run the same investigation in 1993 and gotten worse results. I was discouraged to find that, three years later, the airlines and airport managers had barely improved their slapdash security. When my phone rang, I was engrossed in writing budget testimony that included an account of how easy it was to slip past security at every major airport. I reached absentmindedly for the phone and immediately heard the voice of an aviation journalist who called frequently to quiz me about airlines and the FAA. This time she didn't start with a question.

"ValuJet just had another one." It was Elizabeth

Marchak, a reporter for the *Cleveland Plain Dealer*. She didn't need to explain. "Is the FAA going to do anything about it?"

Sighing, I felt a familiar, frustrating disappointment flood through me. ValuJet, a small discount airline that had grown extraordinarily in popularity and size in just a couple of years, was like an unruly teenager with indulgent parents. Lots of people wanted to see it brought into line, but most of them had given up on looking to the parents for discipline. I felt like the principal of the school to which the kid went—not again, I thought, not another hassle with this troublemaker. Marchak's voice echoed my weariness. Neither of us was the least shocked to hear about another ValuJet accident.

I reached for a note pad. What happened this time?

Landing gear collapsed on a plane coming down into Nashville; the same plane's landing gear had collapsed in December. When the plane hit the ground this time, the right main landing gear collapsed, the belly slammed onto the concrete, the crew lost control, and the aircraft skidded off the end of the runway. Was the FAA going to do anything about it? Marchak repeated.

"I don't know," I answered. "But I am."

Even after five years as Inspector General at the Department of Transportation, I was still unnerved by the news of a plane accident. Dismayed, I realized I'd come to believe that a certain number of crashes were inevitable. As I put down the phone, I wondered—did that also mean I believed it was only a matter of time before a planeload of people was killed? With a jolt, I forgot about the airport security report. ValuJet had had a string of accidents in the past year, including a fire that had left passengers shaken, terrified or injured, but still alive. This newest one in Nashville hadn't killed anyone either, but it filled me with dread nevertheless. Picking up the phone again, I called three of my top staff. One—my deputy, Mario A. Lauro, Jr.—had been raising red flags about ValuJet for months. Now it seemed clear that the accidents were going to continue, that ValuJet could not fix whatever was wrong. Common sense said ValuJet was headed for a disaster worse than the accidents already plaguing it.

Experience from five years of working inside the Federal Aviation Administration told me that the FAA was probably doing nothing to stop it.

Surely the FAA, the only branch of government with authority over the aviation industry, knew everything my office did about ValuJet's problems. In fact, they had to know more—after all, their inspectors had access to ValuJet's fleets, hangars, training records, log books and management offices. So what *was* the FAA doing about it?

As Transportation's Inspector General, I had a duty to keep an eye on how the FAA and the rest of the Department of Transportation did their jobs. I had no authority over the airlines. I could evaluate safety practices and make recommendations, but my office couldn't set or enforce new regulations for the aviation industry. Only the FAA and the Secretary of Transportation, with powers to check and balance enshrined in federal statutes, had that authority. I was the watchdog of the FAA. The FAA in turn stood guard over the airlines. But that role could be interpreted two ways—as policing the airlines to ensure safety at all costs, or as protecting the airlines from any opposition or criticism. After five years, I had come to realize that the FAA believed the statutes ordered it to champion the aviation industry. The FAA's duty, the Federal Aviation Act said plainly, was to promote commercial aviation. Safety was important, too. But nowhere did the statutes explain how the FAA was supposed to reconcile this dual, conflicting mandate. Within the FAA, few believed there was even a conflict at all. From its creation in the 1950s, the FAA had (until 1997) been led by men experienced in the world of aviation—former military pilots, aircraft manufacturing executives, airline senior managers. They were steeped in flying and private business, two cultures that prized and thrived on independence and freedom to act. Government regulation—even in the pursuit of safety—was little more than interference.

It didn't take much insight to guess how these officials viewed ValuJet. In its 1996 Strategic Plan, the FAA had said ValuJet was a model others, including the FAA, should emulate. A wildly successful start-up, the airline seemed to embody the future of modern aviation. The

FAA supported such winning business propositions and was reluctant to enforce restrictions that might hobble growth. What I saw, however, was an apparently troubled airline with ineffective FAA supervision. The combination could be lethal.

I had worked with two of my top staff members, Ray DeCarli and Larry Weintrob, for five years. My deputy, Mario Lauro, Jr., was a tall, soft-spoken professional known for considering all sides of an issue in our staff meetings. He had come with me to the Office of Inspector General in 1991 from my last job at the Department of Labor. As I waited for Congress to confirm my appointment, my staff listened to me talk about ideas for Inspector General projects—I wanted to look first at aviation safety, then at Federal Rail, the supervisors of the railroad system. (I later learned that to save money on inspections, when Federal Rail officials checked out trains, they would look at only one side of the cars.) I was interested in bridges— I remembered that even the Brooklyn Bridge had gone up with second-rate materials that later had to be reinforced— and in safety threats from badly made and poorly installed highway guardrails and bridge components. I had jurisdiction over all these transportation areas. That meant I could examine whether safety was really ensured, or whether money and effort were simply being wasted in department programs. Once I began the job, however, aviation safety became paramount. Dozens of investigations left me writing dozens of reports. Each was loaded with recommendations for safety improvements. Each was a lesson and an exercise in FAA crisis management.

But it was Ray DeCarli, the Assistant Inspector General for Audits, who taught me my first lesson. Only a few weeks into my new job, I told DeCarli I had been asked to investigate charges that the FAA was interfering in a prosecution of Eastern Airlines for falsifying maintenance records. One of my first jobs after law school had been as a federal prosecutor, and I was used to organizing large-scale criminal investigations and working with the Federal Bureau of Investigation. The detective work was invigorating, and the safety questions raised by the allegations against Eastern were critical. I told my new staff to expect

more of these assignments: I wanted to be an active Inspector General, to make aviation safety our office's number one priority.

DeCarli spoke up cautiously.

"The previous Inspectors General didn't touch safety
issues," he warned. They audited how the FAA spent its
money, or whether it followed personnel regulations. But
checking up on the agency's enforcement of safety just
wasn't done.

"Why not?" I was incredulous. "If you don't touch
safety, what do you do?"

Over the next five and a half years, we plunged into safety
issues, investigating, auditing and inspecting FAA practices that for decades had been left to the agency to manage as it saw fit. In almost every area we examined—FAA
methods of inspecting airplanes and airlines, supervising
airplane parts manufacture, examining airline mechanics,
redesigning critical air traffic control systems, ensuring airport security, certifying new jet designs—we found frightening gaps in FAA competence, thoroughness and
judgment.

Gradually, I came to a disheartening conclusion: the
agency was its own worst enemy. It was just too close to
the aviation industry to see its own job clearly. Over time,
I learned to speak my mind about the safety lapses I saw
all around me. It took a threat to my own life to make
me lose my reluctance to rock the boat. In 1992, two days
before the presidential election, I was stricken at work
with serious internal bleeding. I had had surgery the week
before, and something had gone very wrong with my recovery. I didn't feel well in the morning that November
day—but went to work anyway—and at noon, my blood
pressure plummeted to 60 over 20. I keeled over in my
office. I needed an ambulance. It took the emergency medical technicians only a few minutes to load me onto a
stretcher and into the ambulance, then rush me to the nearest hospital. A light rain helped revive me as I was
wheeled out of the Department of Transportation. "Stay
with us," they pleaded. But then I heard them say, "We're
losing her." All the way to the hospital I worried about
my family hearing the same words.

Later, after I was stable, I learned I had lost over half the blood in my body through internal bleeding. It took more than a month for me to recover. During that entire time, I thought about how tenuous life could be. I decided then: everything I do from now on has to make a difference. It does not matter what else anybody thinks.

I also remembered the concern for my family and the strong feelings about them that went through my mind in those minutes in the ambulance. I also thought about things left undone, and I prayed. Later, when I would hear about a plane crash, I would wonder what the passengers thought of in their final moments. So on that February morning, when I mused about ValuJet's troubling accident rate, I knew my office had to do something. The FAA was simply not up to it, I told my staff as I briefed them on the latest landing accident.

"Let's get someone down to Atlanta to find out what's going on with ValuJet," I said, not feeling wise or clairvoyant, just afraid. "There's something wrong, and we've got to find out before someone dies."

The next day, Weintrob and two other officials from the Inspector General's office walked into the Atlanta office of the FAA, vexing the cautious inspectors who worked there and triggering a chain of events that would not be fully revealed or understood for months. It would take the deaths of more than a hundred people aboard a ValuJet plane that burst into flames, smashed into the Florida Everglades and sank in a murky swamp to expose chronic weaknesses in the FAA. The 110 souls on that flight probably never knew what caused the fire that took their lives. At first, government investigators could not pinpoint the reason for the disaster, either. But the tragedy would expose what the FAA had long known—that ValuJet was primed for a major crash, that its maintenance was slipshod, its quality control dismal or nonexistent, that it had an accident rate fourteen times worse than its equals, that its managers were out of their league and that, according to an Inspector General report, the FAA's own inspectors, one of whom had falsified credentials just to get the job, had wanted ValuJet shut down months before the Everglades disaster.

In February, however, my staff and I knew only that ValuJet *looked* like trouble.

ValuJet was a phenomenal success story. In just three years it had leapt from two planes on eight routes between Atlanta, Jacksonville, Orlando and Tampa, to fifty-one planes with 320 itineraries. Founded in 1993, it saw its revenue soar to $368 million in 1995. I'd heard that original investors who'd pumped $200,000 into starting the company were now sitting on stock worth $20 million. *In three years!* Travelers loved ValuJet because it was cheap, and it forced other airlines to offer competitive fares. ValuJet kept its prices down by cutting out frills. Passengers were offered no meals, no seat reservations, no printed tickets or city ticket offices, no airline clubs or frequent flyer programs. Employees got no discount tickets and executives got no benefits like company cars; corporate offices had no fancy furniture. Pilot captains earned about $42,000; flight engineers took home $28,000; flight attendants, around $14,000. But pilots were paid only for flights they completed, a policy that encouraged them to fly rather than delay or cancel flights for maintenance or bad weather. Year-end bonuses supposedly made up for poor salaries, but they depended on annual profits. ValuJet bought used or reconditioned planes for cheap—nine from Turkish Airlines, ten from SAS, eighteen from McDonnell Douglas (planes which had been previously owned by Delta Airlines) and ten others from various sources. Five spare engines and about 4,000 parts were bought from Turkey, too. All maintenance was farmed out to repair stations, freeing ValuJet of the need for costly repair facilities, parts bins and mechanics of its own. Cutting frills and keeping capital expenses down made ValuJet a barebones operator with a lot of cash in reserve. And it meant ValuJet could offer steep discounts in its fares.

There were many start-ups like ValuJet in the 1980s and 1990s. Lean and hungry, they represented a new breed of airlines like People Express, Northeastern Airlines and Air Florida—start-up carriers that scavenged the aviation boneyards of the world for planes and parts, and farmed out their maintenance to the lowest bidders. These discounters offered cheap flights to the seemingly endless

numbers of people who wanted to fly. Many outfits came
and went within a few years of their first flights. I knew
that Lewis Jordan, ValuJet's president and Chief Operating
Officer, liked to say that ValuJet's prices enabled people
of modest means to fly. He touted statistics, put forth by
the Department of Transportation in a promotion piece on
low-cost carriers, that showed one of every seven passengers flew only because of discount carriers. Competition
from these discounters forced fares down across the board,
saving consumers $6.3 billion in 1995. ValuJet was a *valu-
able* service to students, the elderly, families with children
and small-business entrepreneurs, its owners said.

It was also a money tree for them. In early 1996, Valu-
Jet had hundreds of millions of dollars in cash reserves.
ValuJet's Chairman, Lawrence Priddy, told *Business Week*
that "every other start-up wants to be another United or
Delta or American. We just want to get rich." ValuJet
had no qualms about shortchanging its employees. Pilots
had to pay for their own uniforms and, more important,
their own training. *The Wall Street Journal* reported that
Jordan boasted, "There is not a gun big enough to make
us give a higher base pay and higher bonuses" to flight
attendants.

Jordan was the quintessential aviation industry man, a
pilot and former Continental Airlines executive under
Frank Lorenzo when Lorenzo's ill-fated Eastern Airlines
bought Continental. In my years as Inspector General, I
met dozens of industry leaders like him—at Boeing, at the
airlines, in the Air Force, in the government complex
where I worked. They were always men, and they belonged to a unique fraternity of lifelong aviators. Some
were invited to join an exclusive club called Los Conquis-
tadores del Cielo—Conquerers of the Sky. It was a career,
a technical skill, a hobby and a fascination—all together,
for these men, a way of life.

I had grown up around pilots in Ohio, on a farm not
far from where Orville and Wilbur Wright were born and
first tinkered with their idea of a flying machine. When I
was nine, my father took my mother, my sisters and me
on a flight over our farm and tiny hometown as a surprise
Easter present. My sisters and I jostled to peer out the

window and competed to pinpoint the specks of our house and barn on the ground. Tornadoes had swept through our county the week before, and we kids were awed to see houses and buildings that had been torn apart and flattened by the storms. I felt the little plane take on a life of its own. It wanted to fly; it wanted to bounce and soar and veer over our town so much that we crisscrossed Pioneer, Ohio, and the flat farmland around it many times with ease. On that day I knew: I wanted to be a pilot. The bird's-eye view also taught me an early lesson about the potentially destructive power of weather—the same strong winds that ripped farmhouses apart could toss a little plane around like an empty tin can.

At eighteen, I earned my license in a small Beechcraft Musketeer that rolled down the runway at Ohio State University's School of Aviation and lifted into the air on a design and principles not vastly different from those perfected by the Wright Brothers decades before. My instructors were pilots who had taken up teaching just to be able to fly for a living before eventually moving on to the airlines. It was 1974, and they were not used to seeing women behind the controls of an airplane. A few made it clear they did not think I and the one other woman in aviation school had any business hauling on the yoke of a plane. Some deliberately made our initiation difficult— like the instructor who ordered me to check my plane's oil on a day so windy no one had any intention of flying. He and other instructors watched and laughed from a window in the one-story brick building that served as our ready room as I struggled with the dipstick in the wind, oil splattering Jackson Pollock–like across the front of my clothes. The instructors and student pilots often sat around that room, drinking coffee, smoking and trading flight stories. I never felt entirely welcome there. Mostly I told myself that between my jobs as a dorm secretary and a psych lab assistant, I didn't have time to hang out with the guys.

But there were instructors and professors who treated me as a student pilot, without regard for gender. They lectured us in class and climbed into the cockpit with us, talking all the while about avionics, flight instrument rules, weather patterns, mechanical schematics, the physics of wing design, the grace and beauty of flight, the thrill of takeoff and landing.

Years later, I would find my life filled with this fraternity of aviators once again. After law school, after an early career as a federal prosecutor in Kansas City, after a turn as a White House Fellow that would lead to an appointment under Elizabeth Dole as an Assistant Secretary of Labor, I joined the Department of Transportation. It was 1990, and my pilot's license had long been collecting dust. My eyesight had proved too poor for me to even consider a job as an airline pilot, and my work and my own family had left me little time to check out the community airports where a pilot could rent a plane for a few hours. But my love of flying hadn't faded. Finally I could combine my work with my interest in aviation. As soon as I started my job I began to meet FAA officials, air traffic controllers, pilots, aircraft company managers and airline executives. Their world was comfortable and familiar. We talked shop, and it was a language I thought I understood perfectly.

Very quickly, I discovered there was a controlling facet to aviation I had never encountered before—the *business* of flying. Flight is at the core of a powerful, wealthy industry of companies worth billions of dollars. These corporate giants employ tens of thousands of people and support the economies of entire cities, buy products and supplies from thousands of smaller businesses and import untold foreign money into the U.S. Their research labs keep the U.S. on the cutting edge of aviation, space and military technology. Their marketers satisfy millions of customers every day, rising to meet the increasing demand for air travel, keeping up with trends so Americans can enjoy a kind of travel freedom our grandparents never even considered.

ValuJet was a star in that universe—but with the dispatch of Weintrob to Atlanta, it soon became apparent that closer scrutiny of this phenomenon was long overdue. There were plenty of signs that ValuJet was cursed by its own success, its growth straining its management and organizational structure. ValuJet executives just had not

been able to keep up. This had already alarmed experts
with greater skill and experience than I or my staff had.
In 1995, when ValuJet bid for a contract to ferry Department of Defense personnel, Defense specialists had scrutinized ValuJet's books, inspected its facilities and talked
to its pilots, mechanics and managers. The Defense Department had complaints about virtually everything: it decided the airline did not measure up in management,
personnel standards and quality assurance, or in maintenance facilities, training, inspections, records and manuals.
It concluded that the jobs of mid-level managers and supervisors were "ill-defined" and those managers "lacked
a clear sense of their duties and responsibilities." Quality
assurance and internal audits were a problem; tool testing,
records and documentation were a mess. Inspectors did
not get proper training. Even more alarming, the Defense
Department said, "There is no proactive process for day to
day evaluating and correcting repeat aircraft discrepancies.
Temporary corrective actions were accepted rather than
seeking a permanent fix." *Discrepancies* was a nice way
of saying breakdowns, malfunctions, pilot deviations, and
accidents. The Defense Department's report was breathtaking in the scope of its condemnation. The answer: no contract. ValuJet is not good enough to fly our people.

"The company does not yet meet the DOD Commercial
Air Carrier Quality and Safety Requirements," it said. Valu-
Jet could not be trusted to fly government workers, but it
was free to ferry thousands of innocent passengers every
day. And though the Department of Defense wrote a scathing rejection of ValuJet, the report was deemed for internal
use only. The public was not privy.

ValuJet could blame its own practice of scattering maintenance to some fifty different contractors at eighteen companies on the fact that it could not control repairs and
upkeep on planes. Its emphasis on keeping planes in constant service to maximize its earnings doomed maintenance and thus safety to second place. The immature
airline got too big for its britches, and no one seemed to
be watching it closely, except a few journalists. If the FAA
had properly regulated ValuJet, its rapid growth might not
have led to disaster. But that February, all that seemed

clear to me was that the Federal Aviation Administration simply did not know what to do with ValuJet. The airline's safety record had deteriorated almost in direct proportion to its growth. ValuJet pilots made fifteen emergency landings in 1994, then were forced down fifty-seven times in 1995. (I didn't know it yet, but that record would be surpassed within months with fifty-nine emergency landings. From February through May of 1996, ValuJet would have an unscheduled landing almost *every other day*.)

Stories about emergency landings had accumulated in my office for months. Many of them were amazing predicaments that passengers could hardly dream had occurred as they sat flipping through magazines during a flight. Mere weeks had passed since ValuJet's last mishap. On a trip to Nashville the previous December, the crew had tinkered with safety equipment to avoid abandoning their flight plan. Right after takeoff from Atlanta, cockpit alarms erupted to warn the pilots that the landing gear would not retract. Instead of turning back, the crew disconnected a circuit breaker to silence the alarms, thereby fooling the plane's computer into sensing that the landing gear had been retracted. They flew to Nashville with the wheels extended. As they got closer to their destination, the crew reconnected the circuit breaker, prompting the plane to deploy its wing spoilers and slow its speed. The landing was treacherous—the plane's tail hit the ground, and then the nose banged into the runway. When the tail hit, the impact tripped two circuit breakers and knocked out the plane's radio link with the air traffic control tower. The pilot was forced to abort the landing. Since he no longer had communications with the tower, the pilot declared an onboard emergency, swung around 270 degrees and landed on a nearby runway.

The accident could have been worse had the pilot lost control of the plane. What caused it? Poorly maintained landing gear? An inexperienced pilot hired for cheap? A crew more concerned with making their flight plan so they'd get paid than with safety? Or all of the above?

I knew from my own maneuvers over a runway that takeoff and landing are the trickiest part of flight. Even the best pilot with the finest plane cannot control Mother

Nature. My stomach still tightens when I remember bringing my plane down in college just as a fierce gust of wind caught the left wing and rolled the plane to the right. The plane and I hung in space, halfway into a cartwheel, for long, stupefying seconds. Only the vagaries of the wind saved me from tumbling—the gust died down as suddenly as it had arisen, my wings leveled and the plane glided onto the runway. But the ashen look on the face of my instructor when I returned to the ready room told me just how lucky I had been.

ValuJet's problems could not be dismissed as aberrations. As I probed, I learned that FAA inspectors had looked at ValuJet planes nearly 5,000 times in the three years it had been flying, yet they had never reported any significant problems or concerns. What were the odds of that? I wondered. It seemed much more likely that ValuJet had fallen into the void created by the FAA's split personality. I had been Inspector General long enough to know that the FAA couldn't reconcile its conflicting duties, and that often it supported the business of aviation at the expense of safety. I was beginning to suspect that no one— not even the Department of Defense in its examination of ValuJet—had linked the string of accidents at scattered airports around the country into a comprehensive picture of safety at ValuJet. The airline had not come under any real public scrutiny.

But the danger signs were too strong to ignore, and they were uncomfortably similar to the chronic problems suffered by another airline that had grown too quickly for its own good. Now one of the nation's largest, most successful and stable carriers, American Airlines in 1985 was the pariah of the aviation industry. That year, American paid a $1.5 million fine for shoddy maintenance practices like using plastic wing parts on three planes for months because a mechanic misunderstood a manual, using a car part to fix a transmitter, failing to remove a pin that locks nose gears in landing position, three times testing a plane with an engine that wouldn't accelerate properly without solving the problem and then sending it aloft for a fourth test loaded with passengers, and neglecting a torn O-ring in a toilet seat. In that case, four gallons of fluid leaked from the toilet, froze on the exterior of the plane and then broke away in chunks of ice that smashed into the engine, knocking it off. The O-ring cost $2; the new engine, $2 million. Aviation, safety and government experts said American's problems stemmed from its explosive growth—it had increased operations 20 percent in 1983 and 1984, adding hundreds of planes to its fleet. The FAA found that the rapid growth stretched American's maintenance program too thin, until the airline was putting off or making incomplete critical repairs. The company was more concerned with making its schedule than with having equipment meet performance standards, the FAA said.

The similarities were too eerie for my comfort. I decided to follow a simple adage I had heard countless times on the farm from my mother: better safe than sorry.

When Weintrob and his colleagues walked into the Atlanta office of the FAA in February, the FAA field staff did not know what to expect. But there was really only one major question: what is the FAA doing about ValuJet? The FAA field staff had the power to evaluate the airline and shut it down if necessary. Ironically, on that day only forty-five of the forty-seven planes ValuJet had in service at that time were up and running; the other two were in the shop after recent mishaps. Weintrob wasn't surprised, and he pressed for details about the recent spate of accidents. The reply stunned him: confused, the FAA inspectors asked—what spate? The inspectors admitted they didn't know how many accidents there had been. Taken aback, Weintrob and his team laid out the details: in its short life, ValuJet had had more than its share of accidents and mishaps. Its planes repeatedly overshot runways and suffered from collapsed landing gear. Emergency landings were a weekly occurrence. A plane burned after an engine exploded. Planes took off in weather that kept pilots of other airlines on the ground. In the case of the engine explosion, shrapnel spewed into the fuselage of a plane, piercing the metal and injuring seven people inside. One was a flight attendant who was severely disfigured in the subsequent fire.

Some of the stories, Weintrob recalled, had been too outrageous to believe at first. ValuJet put a plane back in service with a hole in its engine housing and let it make eight flights that way; an emergency chute inflated inside a cabin, pinning a flight attendant to a wall; a cockpit microphone shorted out, so the pilot couldn't talk to Air Traffic Control; a plane landed with too little fuel left in the tanks; crews on a jet complained about a broken weather radar system thirty-one times before it was fixed; when a Boston flight had stuck landing gear, the plane was diverted to the Washington, D.C., area, but on the way, the landing gear started working again, so the crew continued to fly without taking the plane in for service; a plane cabin suddenly depressurized during flight; mechanics used duct tape to patch planes; a mechanic wielded a hammer and chisel to fix a sensitive engine part and later, that engine had to be shut down in flight.

The faults were not always on different aircraft—some ValuJet planes had chronic problems. It would not have been difficult for the Atlanta inspectors to go over ValuJet records and trace these persistent breakdowns. A random selection might have pinpointed a used DC-9-32, serial number N904VJ. For months, beginning in January, that plane would suffer a string of mishaps: a malfunctioning fuel anti-ice valve, faulty gears, a loose oil cap causing a drop in oil pressure, smoke and fumes seeping into the cabin during taxiing, loss of pressure during an emergency landing, landing gear that wouldn't retract after takeoff, broken piston rods, leaking tail seals.

Instead, the Atlanta inspectors seemed unimpressed with Weintrob's summary: the number of accidents and incidents were not "disproportionate," they said. There was no common link between them. The FAA had no special plans for ValuJet. Though not the one they wanted, this was an answer. Weintrob returned to Washington. What he didn't know was that a few days later, the Atlanta FAA staff wrote a memo to their headquarters. For eight pages they described accidents and poor FAA surveillance until reaching an inevitable conclusion so startling and obvious that it should have changed history—except that it was also a conclusion so threatening to ValuJet and contrary to FAA habit that the memo was immediately buried, secreted away until disaster forced it into the open.

When asked by reporters about the airline that February, FAA officials insisted they had found no "significant safety concerns" at ValuJet.

Then, in an abrupt about-face, the FAA suddenly took action—it announced a white-glove review of ValuJet. That meant inspectors from outside Atlanta would spend 120 days scrutinizing the airline. Had the agency responded because we were poking around in their backyard? Whatever the reason, the FAA action was downplayed. Consumers choosing ValuJet for their travel plans were still largely unaware that the airline had a poor maintenance record, inadequate quality control and pilots with less experience than those flying for other airlines.

Near the end of February, I was in the Secretary of Transportation's office suite for a regular weekly meeting with his Chief of Staff. Briefings with Ann Bormolini were usually friendly and casual, and this week presented us with no special agenda. At the end of the meeting, however, Bormolini looked over at me and said, "Oh, by the way, I have a close personal friend who is a lobbyist for ValuJet." The friend had called, Bormolini said, because she wanted to know why the Inspector General's office had sent people to Atlanta to look at ValuJet. What, Bormolini asked lightly, should she tell her friend?

The question floored me. The friend worked for a law firm that contributed hundreds of thousands of dollars to political causes and parties. Only the FAA knew we were looking at ValuJet. If the airline had learned of our inquiry, then it had a direct pipeline through the FAA and straight to the Secretary's office. So—ValuJet apparently had clout beyond its years. Certainly, I knew that in the past the FAA had told airlines, manufacturers or airports about our investigations. But I had never experienced the involvement of someone so close to the Secretary of Transportation.

If the FAA had wasted no time in warning ValuJet that we were looking at its record, then the discount airline had wasted even less in dispatching a lobbyist. Speechless for a second in Bormolini's office, I couldn't help but think the money spent on the lobbyist could just as easily have been invested in improved maintenance or better parts.

"ValuJet has had a great number of accidents and incidents and I sure wouldn't fly them," I replied, choosing my words carefully. We wanted to know why they were so plagued, I explained, and were gratified to see that our initial probing had resulted in the FAA's special white-glove program. Bormolini nodded, a pleased, guardedly blank expression on her face. No need, then, to call my friend back, she assured me. But as I left the Secretary's office, I assumed Bormolini and the ValuJet lobbyist were already burning up the telephone lines.

I had learned something from my experience as a lawyer—the value of putting events in writing. Back at my desk, I wrote a brief memo to Bormolini, outlining my staff's actions on ValuJet and those of the FAA. I cautioned her not to tell the ValuJet lobbyist. I didn't want there to be any doubt that Bormolini knew exactly what was going on—and knew that I knew, too.

By March, the FAA inspectors sent to Atlanta had staked out their position: in a memo to their headquarters that summarized the white-glove review, they said: "Valu-Jet is an unconventional carrier" obsessed with low overhead and controlling expenses. The inspectors were concerned about "a significant decrease in experience level of new pilots being hired by ValuJet as well as other positions such as mechanics, dispatchers, etc.," and "continuous changes of key management personnel."

Finally the FAA warned ValuJet.

"ValuJet is not meeting its duty to provide service with the highest possible degree of safety," the FAA warned the airline. "It appears that ValuJet does not have a structure in place to handle your rapid growth, and that you may have an organizational culture that is in conflict with operating to the highest possible degree of safety."

Instead of taking serious action, like grounding the airline, the FAA quietly told ValuJet that from then on, it needed FAA consent before buying any more aircraft or setting up any new routes. The voice might have been soft, but such a restriction was rare in the era of airline deregulation. At the time, we did not realize this was a diversionary tactic.

As if to make amends, a few days later, at the end of February, Secretary of Transportation Federico Peña was booked on a flight on ValuJet. Peña, the former mayor of Denver, had little expertise with the aviation industry and even less with safety regulations. His closest dealings with the FAA had come from presiding over the planning and construction start-up of a new Denver airport. His reward for supporting Bill Clinton and serving on the new President's transition team in 1992 had been the cabinet post of Transportation Secretary. But now, apparently, he had decided to take a stand. His Delta reservation from Atlanta to Washington was canceled, and he flew ValuJet instead, apparently to demonstrate his faith in the discount airline. It seemed to me he was also sending the airline a message: there is nothing to fear from the FAA or Transportation's Inspector General. Unlike me, he could say, "I have flown ValuJet."

On April 2, 1996, the FAA advised my office that there was no pattern to the ValuJet accidents and incidents. One month later, on May 11, Marchak called again. It was a Saturday afternoon, and in an uncanny coincidence, I had just finished writing a column for *Newsweek* magazine, inspired by the reports crossing my desk in the ValuJet investigations and a host of other investigations and audits revealing the holes in the safety net. The piece warned that all airlines are not equally safe and passengers should know how to pick and choose the most secure. I had seen a Department of Transportation report condemning discounters, and I had ValuJet, Tower Air, commuter airlines (small operations that fly regional routes) and air taxis (planes for hire) in mind as I wrote, but I mentioned none by name. Now, again, Marchak was calling about ValuJet, but this time her voice shook with emotion. She was on her way to Miami, where a DC-9 had just slammed into the Florida Everglades. Flight 592, headed for Atlanta, had smashed into the swamp, killing both pilots, three flight attendants, and all 105 passengers. Apparently, right before the crash, the crew reported to Air Traffic Control that there was smoke in the cabin and cockpit.

I felt queasy and sick; the crash struck nauseatingly close to home. The nightmare I had theorized about with Mario Lauro, Ray DeCarli and Larry Weintrob was unfolding in front of me, as real as the conversations we had had and the column I had just finished. The idea of so many lost lives filled me with horror. I wondered again at my own sense that the accident was inevitable.

Government officials began appearing on television to reassure the public that discount airlines were safe to fly. Top officials at the Department of Transportation shifted quickly into crisis-management mode. Secretary Federico Peña drew on his own experience flying ValuJet to reassure the public on national television: "I have flown ValuJet. ValuJet is a safe airline, as is our entire aviation system." One of the FAA's top Associate Administrators, Anthony Broderick, assured reporters that in its inspections "the basic result . . . was that we found no significant safety deficiencies." Peña insisted that ". . . if ValuJet was unsafe, we would have grounded it."

The FAA Administrator, David Hinson, echoed their assurances. Many people admired Hinson as one of the most effective Administrators to lead the agency in many years; I was among them. When he came to the FAA in the summer of 1993, he wasted no time in admitting the agency had bungled several major projects and set out to salvage what he could of the programs and the money spent on them. Under his watch, the disastrous, over-budget Air Traffic Control replacement plan was halted and reorganized. In April of 1996, he canceled a nine-month-old contract for a new navigational system because mismanagement had caused cost overruns and delays. I was impressed; it was unheard of for the FAA to act so decisively on an out-of-control program. He oversaw the rewriting of the FAA's cumbersome personnel rules, cutting the guidelines from 1,069 pages to 43. In January 1995, Peña and Hinson led the FAA contingent at a two-day "safety summit" with about 1,000 leaders of the airlines and aviation industry to brainstorm ideas for airport security and airline operating requirements. The conference

came up with seventy recommendations for improved air
safety—many of which had already been rejected or dismissed by the FAA. They called for better pilot and maintenance training, faster installation of new equipment like
airplane de-icing equipment, and anticollision radar. The
attendees also announced a goal of "zero accidents" and
declared they wanted to see one standard of safety for
carriers. That would mean eliminating the distinction between those commuter airlines whose planes seat sixty or
fewer passengers and the major carriers. Under Hinson,
the FAA followed through on this goal in 1996, when it
decreed that planes with between ten and thirty seats had
to live up to the same flight-time limits, pilot training and
rest requirements, and safety programs as the major carriers. The new regulations affect dozens of commuter airlines that serve 70 percent of the communities in the U.S.

A former executive at Midway Airlines and McDonnell
Douglas, Hinson had always seemed genuinely determined
to streamline the FAA and address safety as well as commercial interests. Yet I knew he had to have seen one of
the reports that had alarmed me. It was the agency's own
account of the differences among air carriers—the one that
concluded that ValuJet had fourteen times the problems of
others. Hinson had to realize that within a few days of the
disaster, records had revealed that the crashed plane was
the used DC-9, tail number N904VJ, that had been plagued
with faulty equipment and emergency landings since January. Watching Transportation and FAA officials, I realized
there was no charitable way to characterize what they were
doing—they were simply lying to the public about Valu-
Jet's record. It was not the first time I had seen the department react to a plane crash with a blitz of political spin
control. But this time their overstatement and vehemence
left me outraged. The audience for these distortions and
misrepresentations was unsuspecting people who might
fly ValuJet.

My anger was tempered somewhat by the certainty that
the department's facade would eventually crumble. I knew
from years of taking whistle-blower complaints on the Inspector General's hot line that there were countless honest,
hardworking people at the FAA who would find it impos-

sible not to come forward with what they knew about
ValuJet. Inspectors in Atlanta, managers in Washington—
eventually one or more would call a hot line, talk to a
reporter, complain to a superior. Somehow the truth about
the department's reports on start-up and discount airlines,
the truth about ValuJet's accident record, the truth about
how it subcontracted maintenance, the truth about its high-
handed policies toward pilots and flight attendants, would
surface to prove that the airline's standards were not equal
to those of some other discounters or the major carriers.
There were just too many people who knew better than
what Peña and Hinson were saying on television. That was
the flip side of how Washington worked—there were always leaks. This ship of state is the only vessel that leaks
from the top. I was sure this time would be no exception.
That certainty helped me feel that I didn't need to mince
words, either. The truth would come out, whether I said
it or not.

The night after the crash, Hinson and I appeared on a
national news program to talk about ValuJet. The *Nightline*
music rose and fell. I respected Hinson and didn't want
to duel with him on national television. But I was wary
that he might want to use this popular national show to
patronize the public. I stiffened involuntarily as I heard
his words.

"The airline is safe to fly. I would fly it," Hinson insisted, looking gravely into the television camera and at
millions of Americans still stunned by the fiery Everglades
crash. He seemed to be saying there was one level of
safety whether people flew a major carrier or a discount
airline.

Calm, intelligent, with the authority of a government
official, Hinson served up exactly the reassurance most
Americans wanted to hear at that moment—all airlines are
created equal. FAA spin control was at full tilt. But I knew
better, and I couldn't keep it to myself.

I had read the FAA's own evaluation of discount airlines. Clearly all airlines were not equal. "You can pass
the exam with a C or you can pass with an A." I was
sticking to my guns.

"It's not my job to sell tickets on ValuJet," I noted,

hoping Hinson might get the message. I was alarmed that he seemed to be doing just that—encouraging people to continue flying ValuJet before anyone had definitively determined what was wrong with the airline. How did we know those passengers were safe?

That was not what people wanted to hear—but certainly what they needed to know. Yet the FAA was more concerned with moving forward—it didn't want to be forced to backpedal on its longtime position on discount airlines, on the argument that all airlines are equally safe, on the idea that people are less at risk if they fly than if they drive their cars on treacherous highways. I had heard these arguments countless times before, at speeches made to industry groups by Hinson and high-ranking FAA officials. It was particularly dangerous when the agency used television to spread myths about safety. That was just what Hinson was doing on *Nightline*.

Insistence that all airlines are equally safe, that there is one standard for safety that, once met, is always satisfied, serves a multiple purpose: to protect the FAA from having to explain its failures, and to preserve its cozy relationship with the airline industry. But after ValuJet, I had heard it enough. Staggered by the Everglades crash, I could not believe that Secretary Peña and his underlings were not as upset as I was. They seemed concerned only with protecting ValuJet. Yet they knew the truth—and whether the crash would prove to be from a mechanical fault, a pilot error or hazardous cargo—they *all* knew those threats had existed for months. I advised them, and they had been contacted by a lobbyist—more than once, as was later revealed. The FAA had done little to correct the threats.

The FAA very likely would have continued with their charade if not for a phone call at my home late in the week after the ValuJet crash. An anonymous FAA employee tracked me down through a reporter. The caller would not give a name, and said the call was being made from a public phone outside FAA offices. I needed to know, the voice said nervously, that in the days after Weintrob had grilled the Atlanta inspectors about ValuJet, the Atlanta staff had taken a good look at the airline. Ten days later, they put their fears in writing to Headquarters.

Did I understand? the caller demanded. The field staff in
Atlanta had recommended *in February* that ValuJet be
grounded. They had put it in writing. Someone had
quashed the memo. The person on the other end of the
line left the FAA building specifically to call and tell me
that certain FAA officials, including a Mr. Anthony Broderick, were meeting at that moment to discuss the secret
memo. They had the memo with them right now, the
caller insisted.

Quickly, I dialed the Inspector General's investigations
office. "Send an investigator with a subpoena over to the
FAA," I demanded. For once, government wheels turned
quickly, and the investigator rushed to the FAA. But the
meeting was already over, and FAA officials said they
knew nothing about any memo.

Discouraged, I hoped for another chance, another call
from the informant. The opportunity came from a most
unexpected source: suddenly, the next morning, the FAA
called a press conference to offhandedly release a tall stack
of ValuJet documents. Buried in the middle was the innoc-
uous-looking report from the Atlanta field staff. I practically lunged at the copy handed to me. The tone of the
memo was sharp. The field staff said they were concerned
about "the quality of maintenance inspections performed"
and "the management of repetitive discrepancies." The
FAA was seeing the same problems the Department of
Defense had spotted six months before.

Skimming several pages describing ValuJet's troubles,
I stopped short at the field inspectors' bombshell: that
"consideration should be given to an immediate FAR-121
recertification of this airline." Official FAA jargon, yes,
but the meaning was clear: ground ValuJet. Clearly, back
in February the FAA Atlanta inspectors had developed
serious doubts about the carrier. They wanted ValuJet
banned from the skies. But the drama had ended there.
The memo was deep-sixed, and ValuJet was not evaluated
for recertification, not grounded. Still, the memo was out
now. Once it was in daylight, the questions were fast and
steady. In the days that followed, I picked up the newspaper or switched on the television to find explanations from
Anthony Broderick, the FAA's point man with the media.

He quibbled with the *interpretation* of the memo. What was the meaning of "recertification," after all? Broderick argued that it was unofficial jargon, a term that simply meant the FAA should keep a close eye on an airline, a process largely involving paperwork. But the FAA itself ordered "recertification" when it grounded another airline, Arrow Air. And in June, when the FAA finally ordered ValuJet to cease flying, it said, "ValuJet may not recommence *certified* operations, not advertise such service until its fitness to do so has been re-established by this office."

For me, revelation of the memo caused events of the previous February to become crystal clear. Everything fell into place: On February 7, Weintrob had warned the FAA in Atlanta about ValuJet's lousy record. Just over a week later, on February 14, some of those same FAA inspectors wrote the memo recommending that ValuJet be grounded. The airline was alerted and dispatched a lobbyist, who contacted her friend, the Chief of Staff over at Transportation. The next thing anybody knew, the FAA announced a white-glove review of ValuJet. It never mentioned that the review would replace recertification. Any ideas about grounding ValuJet were scuttled. And then suddenly, on February 22, Secretary Peña's Chief of Staff was asking me what she could tell her ValuJet lobbyist friend about the Inspector General's investigation of the airline. The following week, Secretary Peña's flight was changed from Delta Airlines to ValuJet. And by February 28, the FAA had finished with its special review of ValuJet.

Washington at work.

ValuJet should have been grounded, at least temporarily. Its high accident/incident record was not the only red flag. The passengers who bought ValuJet tickets had the bad luck to choose an airline that embodied the flawed way the FAA did its job.

For days after the plane smashed into the swamp, Hinson told the press that "ValuJet is safe."

A couple of days after that, the FAA released its own internal review of ValuJet, acknowledging that "some critical surveillance activities did not receive much attention." That cautious language blurred the fact that for two years, the FAA had not conducted any structural inspections of ValuJet's growing fleet of used DC-9s.

Anthony Broderick explained that the FAA had taken ValuJet in hand right after the Everglades crash, making sure that it was safe—including a daily inspection of all fifty-one planes. "You either meet our standards, or you don't. If you don't meet our standards, you don't fly."

But in June, after stonewalling and hedging, the FAA could no longer hide the fact that its daily spot inspections of ValuJet were finding so many problems that the airline had to cut its flight schedule in half because of grounded planes. Soon after, the whole operation was grounded and Hinson admitted that "serious deficiencies" in ValuJet's maintenance led to its shutdown. In one of the understatements of the year, he added: "Yes, we bear some responsibilities in this case."

Broderick boldly claimed that "a number of things confirm the concerns our people had when they initiated the special emphasis program in February," referring to the white-glove test of ValuJet that the FAA chose over grounding.

"There are a number of things that show ineffective control and procedures," Broderick added. Soon everyone was singing a new tune. Secretary Peña reluctantly went further: "The FAA looked itself in the mirror. It found that organizational and management changes were needed." Appearing before Congress that month, Hinson shifted position and said that "over time, the airline's organizational capabilities appear to have become outstripped by the logistical difficulties of assuring the quality of maintenance work performed on its behalf at so many facilities by so many vendors . . .

"I think we should have better understood the effects of rapid growth on this airline," Hinson admitted carefully. "It is apparent now that the extraordinarily rapid growth of this airline created problems that should have been more clearly recognized and dealt with sooner and more aggressively. We also should have better anticipated and addressed proactively the many difficulties that virtually complete outsourcing of its maintenance can present to an airline in meeting its ultimate responsibility to assure the safety of its aircraft.''

Then ValuJet President Lewis Jordan took the microphone at the same hearing. In spite of the crash, revelations about ValuJet's accident record, and the grounded planes that forced the airline to slash its schedule, Jordan insisted his airline was safe.

''I can state, without any doubt, that ValuJet is a safe airline. Let me repeat: ValuJet is a safe airline. I would have grounded the airline myself if I thought otherwise.''

In the end, the ValuJet crash would be, in my mind, the most heinous example of taking action only after people have died. The passengers didn't know what killed them. But it didn't take the National Transportation Safety Board, the agency responsible for investigating accidents and recommending safety procedures, long to figure it out. In fact, they were already too familiar with what they were looking for.

''Preliminary evidence indicates that five cardboard boxes containing as many as 144 chemical oxygen generators . . . had been loaded in the forward cargo compartment shortly before departure,'' the NTSB wrote in a memo to Hinson just two weeks after the crash. ''The forward compartment of this aircraft was a class D compartment, which had no fire/smoke detection system to alert the cockpit crew of a fire within the compartment.''

Anger and dismay radiated from the memo; inter-agency letters are seldom so strongly worded.

''. . . a fire should not be allowed to persist in any state of intensity in an airplane without the knowledge of the flight crew,'' the NTSB memo said bluntly. ''A fire detection system should be required in class D cargo compartments.''

As a report from the House Committee on Transportation and Infrastructure would later state, the recommendation was ''rejected by the FAA because they believed the gain in safety would not justify the cost of requiring all aircraft to install such systems.''

The NTSB wasn't just making theoretical arguments. In 1973, a Pan Am 707 flight out of John F. Kennedy Airport in New York was diverted to Logan Airport in Boston when the crew reported smoke in the cockpit. Dense smoke blinded them as they tried frantically to land. They failed. The plane crashed short of the runway, killing all three crew members. The source of the smoke was never precisely pinpointed, but the NTSB believed that it started when a cargo of nitric acid packed in sawdust began leaking. Over ten years later, in August 1986, a McDonnell Douglas DC-10 flew from Honolulu to Chicago, landed, and its passengers and crew filed off the plane. Minutes later, a fire started in a cargo compartment, burned through the cabin floor, spread through the entire plane and destroyed the plane. The NTSB declared that "the fire had been initiated as a result of a mechanic's improper handling of a chemical oxygen generator." It began urging the FAA to ban hazardous material cargo from commercial airlines. The FAA always replied that it did not feel the threat was great enough to justify the inconvenience such a ban would cause the airlines.

Over the years, the NTSB continued to nag the FAA about cargo-hold smoke and fire detectors. In 1986, the FAA decided the way to address the problem of fires in cargo or baggage compartments was to require airlines to test the compartments and *make sure that their liners could withstand a fire*. Make sure the fire cannot burn through the cargo-hold liner, airlines were told. But the FAA rejected a requirement for fire detection systems in class D cargo compartments. The agency said the danger of a cargo fire was "beyond the scope of its rulemaking notice."

Two years later, the FAA's solution to cargo-hold fires didn't help passengers on an American Airlines flight.

On February 3, 1988, an in-flight fire erupted on an American DC-10 flying to Nashville. Flight attendants "notified the cockpit crew of smoke in the passenger cabin. The NTSB found that hydrogen peroxide solution (an oxidizer) and a sodium orthosilicate-based mixture" had been shipped and loaded into the mid-cargo compartment of the airplane. After the hydrogen peroxide leaked from its container, a fire started in the class D cargo compartment. In defiance of the FAA's new rule, the fire eventually breached the cargo compartment, and the passenger cabin floor over the mid-cargo compartment became hot and soft. Luckily the plane landed, and everybody got off safely.

". . . further, when investigating the accident on American Airlines flight 132, the Safety Board noted that because the cargo compartment was not equipped with [a] fire or smoke detection system, the cockpit crew had no way of detecting the threat to the safety of the airplane until smoke and fumes reached the passenger cabin. After smoke was detected in the passenger cabin, the cockpit crew had no means to identify the location of the fire."

Eight months later, in October 1988, the NTSB once again urged the FAA to require a fire and smoke detection system in all class D cargo compartments. "Consider the effects of authorized hazardous materials cargo in fires for all types of cargo compartments," the NTSB pleaded, "and require appropriate safety systems to protect the aircraft and occupants."

Yet in 1992 and 1993, two fires broke out on planes carrying chemical oxygen generators that were being shipped without being declared as hazardous material. Fortunately, nobody was killed. The fires didn't inspire the FAA to reconsider its insistence that fire and smoke alarms in certain cargo holds were unnecessary. (Federal Express cargo is valued enough to be protected by smoke and fire detectors. In September 1996, just months after the ValuJet crash, fire broke out on a FedEx flight from Memphis to Boston. The detectors went off, and the pilot made an emergency landing in Newburgh, New York. The only injuries came to the crew of three when they got rope burns from sliding down an escape rope.)

In August of 1993, *five years* after the 1988 American flight fire, the FAA responded to the NTSB safety recommendation. It told the NTSB that "it did not believe that fire/smoke detection systems would provide a significant degree of protection to occupants of airplanes," making the $350 million cost to the airlines entirely unjustifiable. The safety files were marked "Closed—Unacceptable Action."

Until three years later. The oxygen generators stowed

next to tires in the cargo compartment of ValuJet flight 592 erupted, and with no fire or smoke alert system in the cargo hold, the pilot and crew of the plane apparently had no warning until smoke engulfed them in the cockpit.

Two weeks later, on May 24, 1996, the Department of Transportation's Research and Special Programs Administration temporarily prohibited the transportation of chemical oxygen generators on passenger aircraft. It was a hollow victory for safety. Too many people had died for a few changed lines in the regulations. At the same time, after dallying for years, the FAA issued an incongruous emergency notice of its own: any person who tried to transport or get someone else to transport oxygen generators as cargo aboard passenger aircraft would be subject to *swift enforcement action*. It said nothing about requiring airplanes to have smoke and fire detectors in cargo compartments.

Secretary Peña did not repeat his confidence-building gesture of flying ValuJet when he traveled to Miami after the plane smashed into the mucky swamp. By that time, he had in his possession the internal FAA report that plainly stated that ValuJet had a mishap rate fourteen times that of the major carriers—the report that singled out Valu-Jet and Tower Air as the airlines with the worst safety records. But still, Peña did not admit knowing that for four days, until he was confronted with the study during a television interview. Only then did the Department of Transportation release the report to the public.

On June 17, 1996, the FAA shut down ValuJet.

The next day, Secretary Peña and Administrator Hinson announced that Anthony Broderick was opting for early retirement.

The same afternoon, Hinson said the FAA would initiate new procedures for inspecting airlines like ValuJet.

The aviation industry had fought ValuJet's grounding, arguing that thousands of jobs were at stake. But public pressure grew as reports of ValuJet's safety record surfaced. The FAA's part in allowing ValuJet to fly with inadequate supervision and inspection humiliated the

agency and forced it to take action it usually avoided like
the plague—penalizing a profitable airline.

All through the summer of 1996, a grounded ValuJet
scrambled to convince the sudden swarm of FAA inspectors crawling through its hangars, planes and offices that
it had gotten maintenance under control. The FAA boasted
that its oversight was the most detailed scrutiny the agency
had ever given an airline—sixty inspectors working around
the clock performed the equivalent of four years' inspection activities in four weeks. The proud officials seemed
unaware of the tragic irony in the fact that just shy of
its fourth anniversary, ValuJet was getting the quality of
inspections it should have had all along. The airline was
subjected to re-creations of stuck landing gears and cabin
fires—the same mishaps that had happened, repeatedly,
earlier in the year. Intense pressure from Congress, from
the aviation industry, from investors and from ValuJet bore
down on the FAA in favor of giving the discounter the
okay to fly again. At the same time, *Aviation Week and
Space Technology* reported that "gaps in records effectively disqualified ValuJet pilots, instructors, check air-
men" (or pilots who judge other pilots)—just as ValuJet
was poised to start flying again. The flight attendants'
union had sought to keep the airline grounded, and to
prohibit Jordan and Priddy from having any control over
the carrier. They failed.

On September 26, 1996, a mere four months after the
Everglades crash, the Department of Transportation announced that ValuJet would be allowed to resume flying
fifteen aircraft. President Jordan immediately announced
that the airline would change the way it paid salaries—
eliminating the bonuses offered for profits and bringing
maintenance and engineering supervisors onto full-time
staff. It also named an executive position it had never
thought it needed before, Senior Vice President of Maintenance and Engineering.

In December 1996, ValuJet was again in trouble with
the authorities. The airline had sold 15,000 tickets for
flights between December 19 and January 6 without the
FAA's safety approval to operate. In January 1997, the

FAA reported it had again found problems in ValuJet's safety.

ValuJet limped along. It bragged that it had a new fleet of airplanes *on order*—but delivery was not scheduled until the distant future, and many orders in the airline industry are quietly cancelled or indefinitely postponed. Then in September 1997, ValuJet announced it would merge with Air Tran Airlines, a 1994 start-up carrier with less experience than ValuJet. ValuJet would change its name to Air Tran; that way the passengers could easily be fooled about who they were flying with.

"It's something else!" was its slogan—but what?

The strategy of hiding a tarnished reputation and a history of crashes and accidents is not a new one. When I was a federal prosecutor, we had just such a strategy for mobsters who got in a jam and turned government witness. The Federal Witness Protection Program would give the mobsters a new name and a new life in their new identity as far away from their old lifestyle as possible.

One airline which had a spectacular fiery crash in Miami in 1997 was in so much trouble for all sorts of violations that there was a congressional hearing in 1991 and the old carrier ceased operation and Fine Airlines emerged. Not so fine was the fact that all the planes were transferred from the old carrier—all but one new executive plane to carry the airline's brass.

ValuJet should not have been flying that day in May. Inspectors at the FAA had recommended the airline be grounded. It should not have been carrying oxygen generators. The NTSB had repeatedly recommended that such cargo be banned, and ValuJet had no authority to carry them anyway. It should not have shipped the generators in a compartment with no fire or smoke warning system. The NTSB had, over and over, urged the airlines to install such basic safety equipment.

But ValuJet can't bear the blame alone. The airline complied with the law. The FAA told them they could keep flying, didn't stop them from shipping hazardous materials like oxygen generators, didn't force them to install smoke and fire detectors in their cargo holds, didn't force them to hire quality control inspectors.

Anthony Broderick may have said it best, right after he was forced into retirement because of his role in the ValuJet fiasco. He explained to *Aviation Daily* that ValuJet would not have been shut down without the post-crash media frenzy that prompted high-level demands to take action.

"We would very likely not have seen the same solution," Broderick said, referring to grounding. ValuJet was already trying to put the brakes on its excessive growth and get its maintenance problems under control. "Things would have been allowed to change in a more measured way."

Ironically, Broderick still seemed unable to grasp that the conditions for the Everglades crash were allowed to fester while those "measured" steps poked along. Even worse, he had contradicted his own words to another reporter the previous February, when he had vowed that he would "not hesitate to do everything in my power" to ground ValuJet if safety were at stake.

What Broderick and other FAA officials did appreciate is that small, independent airlines like ValuJet are vital to the continued growth of commercial aviation. Around Miami International Airport, where ValuJet flight 592 took off, one in five jobs in Dade County is in aviation. It is a big business, and there is a lot at stake. Just months after the ValuJet crash, the FAA proved that it had learned little if anything from its humiliation.

Another small start-up, Mesa Airlines, suffered maintenance and training woes strikingly similar to ValuJet's. Mesa's own pilots, staff and passengers complained so much that the FAA finally investigated the airline in 1996. But the agency found no serious problems and issued no reprimand or penalty. It seemed no action would be taken against Mesa until Senator Ben Nighthorse Campbell raised the complaints at a hearing before Congress. He had gotten too many letters from Coloradans afraid of Mesa.

"I'm convinced this is an airline looking for a place to crash," Campbell thundered in the hearing. A few weeks later the FAA reversed itself and took enforcement action against Mesa. Still other airlines were reprimanded only after exposure of questionable maintenance practices or accident rates in the press—a series of articles in the *Cleveland Plain Dealer* compelled the FAA to ground Rich International, for example.

Airlines continue to insist to the FAA that they have a "business" right to fly, and the FAA clearly remains reluctant to police them. The FAA seemed to believe that in the case of ValuJet and Mesa. Certainly, ValuJet seemed determined not to take any responsibility for the safety of its passengers. While the airline was still grounded, President Lewis Jordan told employees and investors that they had to work with the FAA to get ValuJet back in the air. But then he added: "It's important to note that much of what has happened to us is beyond our control. . . ."

The reaction of the media and the public to the ValuJet crash gave me hope that in the glare of the spotlight, the FAA would be forced to take stock of itself. A growing chorus of voices condemned the FAA's dual mandate to promote the aviation business while regulating safety, and demanded that the first duty be dropped. Finally, in the summer of 1996, Secretary Peña asked Congress to delete the provision that charges the FAA with promoting aviation. In the glare of the ValuJet spotlight, the chances for action in both the House and the Senate looked good. We seemed, finally, to be on the right track.

I turned my attention once again to completing my report on the gaping holes in airport security. The reviews written by Inspector General and FAA agents who posed as gun-wielding or bomb-carrying passengers and wandered unchallenged through some of the biggest airports in the U.S. were staggering. The investigation was a repeat of one done first in 1993, when plainclothes agents walked through metal detectors, around departure lounges, through unlocked doors onto planes, into cargo holds, onto loading docks and onto the tarmac with guns, knives and a hand grenade. In 1993, they were caught in off-limits areas of airports only 25 percent of the time. The FAA and the airlines vowed to improve their security arrangements. So we waited. In 1995 we sent staff back to the same airports, this time with more fake explosives and marzipan candy dressed up to look like plastic explosives. In 1995 the agents were able to get onto planes, into cargo areas and all through airport facilities without being stopped or questioned 40 percent of the time.

Glancing at the papers scattered on my desk, I saw proof that Kennedy International Airport in New York was a security nightmare. But so were many big airports—Chicago, Los Angeles, Miami. They were simply sieves. I flipped through the pages, shaking my head—any terrorist with an ounce of gumption and a little bit of advance planning could plant a plastic explosive in a hundred different critical spots at an airport, including in checked luggage or an airplane cabin. These findings could not be dryly summed up in a dull report and filed away at the Department of Transportation. I had to deliver these revelations not only to the Secretary, but to the White House and Congress as well. Surely this time we would all see eye to eye.

But if I expected the Secretary and the FAA to embrace my concerns about airport security, I was disappointed. The Secretary, for his part, wouldn't even see me or attend the briefing. Apparently after learning that my 1996 report condemned airport security as being almost as lax as in 1993, Peña bowed out of a scheduled briefing. Though I knew the FAA officials who remained wouldn't greet me happily, nothing could have prepared me for what they planned to do with the report. They could not contest its results, because their own agents had posed as suspicious passengers. Instead, they wanted me to bury the report indefinitely. The 1996 Summer Olympics were approaching, and the Department feared our findings would frighten athletes and tourists flocking to Atlanta for the international games. Afraid of a "copycat" bomber, they did not want me to issue the report and told me not to send it to the White House or Congress. We can't risk it, they argued—someone might leak it to the public.

No one at the briefing denied the possibility of an attack on aviation or a bombing during the Olympics. But it wasn't smart to tell the public about the dangers at airports and then do nothing about them. So it was better all around to keep the report under wraps.

Except that I could not leave the room with that report

on my conscience. I simply could not take responsibility
for hiding it from Congress, the White House and especially the public. But the Department had the ability to
postpone the report's release, and to try to limit whom to
send it to. So we sat around the conference table calmly
discussing the likelihood of a bomb and negotiating over
who might see the report. They were adamant that it not
go to Congress. They refused to send it to the President.
I insisted that it had to be delivered to authorities beyond
the Secretary. I refused to bury it indefinitely. Finally we
compromised—the report would be relayed immediately
to the White House National Security Advisor, Anthony
Lake. We would withhold it from the general public until
after the Olympics by dragging our feet if anyone submitted a Freedom of Information Act request to see the report.
But in the meantime it would be sent to Congress.

Two days later, on July 3, as I was rushing to get the
report out before the long holiday weekend, I got a call
from Jackie Lowey, an assistant to the Deputy Secretary
of Transportation. Lowey wanted me to hold off on sending the security report to the White House. The report is
going to be classified, she announced. Dumbfounded, I
explained that the department's classifying office had already approved it for release—besides, much of the information had been made public in the 1993 report. That
didn't matter, Lowey said; the department was requesting
classification, anyway. She insisted she was working alone
in the office and didn't want the report issued in the Secretary's absence. So I should just sit on the report. When I
argued that it should at least be sent to Congress, Lowey
wanted to know only one thing: what if someone on the
Hill leaks it to the media? She was afraid to warn Congress about airport vulnerabilities because the information
might seep out to the public and the press.

Clearly, the department didn't care whether the report
would qualify for classification or not. By the time the
decision was made, the Olympics would be over. The department would have what it wanted, and to get that, officials there were willing to ignore their own conviction that
the terrorist threat was real.

Once again, the FAA's loathing of any action that might

cost airlines money (or alarm paying customers) had prevailed over safety. After nearly six years of investigating safety practices, of issuing reports, of talking to reporters, of testifying before Congress, of watching planes crash and people die, I was no closer to changing that truth than on the day I started my job. That was how it happened with ValuJet, and how it might happen with airport security. The FAA would act only after a disaster, only when forced by public scandal and humiliation.

I knew then that the truth about aviation safety and security had to be presented directly to the public. Without a government filter. Without the FAA to whitewash reports and then spin their meaning through the media. Without the Department of Transportation to ''classify'' findings it didn't like; without aviation lobbyists to persuade members of Congress to reject our studies as a waste of time. It was obvious from the way people reacted when I appeared on news shows and interview programs that they were desperate for information, concerned about safety and shocked to hear what I knew. Yet what I had to say about an airline like ValuJet shouldn't have been news to people, and it should not have gotten attention only in the aftermath of tragic crashes. It should not have taken the deaths of passengers to break down the wall of propaganda and silence erected by the aviation industry, the FAA, the Secretary of Transportation and powerful members of Congress—a wall designed for no other purpose than to keep the flying public out of the business of flying.

I decided to go over that wall, carrying what I knew with me in my head. I resigned my job, determined to speak publicly about the rot at the core of the FAA and the attendant dangers to the flying public. This made powerful figures in Washington unhappy. On July 17, I was called before the Senate to explain my intentions. I was six months' pregnant and the day of testimony was long, frustrating and marked by attacks from Secretary Peña and several Senators. That night, exhausted, I fell asleep in the early evening, only to be shaken awake just before nine o'clock by my distraught husband.

''There's been another crash,'' he whispered hoarsely. ''It doesn't look good. A TWA jet crashed into the ocean.''

CHAPTER ONE

Who Does the FAA Work for, Anyway? Not You.

The letter was addressed to the United States Attorney General. The top of the crisp white paper bore the seal of the Department of Justice. The bottom held a scrawled signature. In between, a harsh, blunt warning leapt off the page.

"As you know, this office recently completed a nine-month grand jury investigation into the maintenance practices of Eastern Airlines," the New York U.S. Attorney wrote. "This letter is to express my concern regarding the FAA's handling of this matter in particular and its ability to police the airline industry, in general." The FAA, he continued, had interfered in the investigation of Eastern.

But the most shocking revelation concerned headquarters officials. "FAA officials in Washington, for as yet unexplained reasons, inhibited and limited the scope of the New York based investigation, which would have uncovered the widespread nature of the illegal practices discovered by the grand jury investigation had the inspectors been permitted to follow the investigative leads. . . . [I]t was apparent that the FAA was unduly influenced by Eastern executives in this matter. . . . [I]t would appear the regulatees were regulating the regulators! I fear that this relationship may not be unique to Eastern and am concerned generally about the effects of the influence the industry exerts on the FAA.''

Startled, scanning quickly, I searched for an explanation. Sam Skinner leaned back in his desk chair, watching my reaction. Like me, he was a pilot and a lawyer. He loved flying, and was a former investigator who enjoyed a good mystery. He rarely shied away from a fight. We shared a personality that made us natural prosecutors, values that earned him the nickname Sam the Hammer and me Maximum Mary, and a temperament that inclined us to be pleased with those titles. Prosecution had originally brought us both to government. Now Skinner was Secretary of Transportation in the Bush Administration. I had just been appointed the Inspector General. The U.S. Attorney's complaint had been forwarded to him.

''I've been saving that for you,'' he said, a cryptic smile seasoning his words. His grin didn't ease my mind. It was October 1990, and Congress had not yet even confirmed my appointment. Curiosity spurred another glance at the letter. It seemed unreal. I had worked for Attorney General Richard Thornburgh, and he wasn't one to take risks. But he wanted the department to deal with this complaint. Was he pushing some hidden agenda? If any government agency could be called noble, the FAA, as the branch of the Transportation Department responsible for regulating aviation, seemed to be it. It served an important, practical purpose. From the age of eighteen, I had owned a well-thumbed paperback called *FAA Regulations for Pilots,* its dog-eared red-and-gray cover opening to dense text with diagrams, formulae and charts, its pages ornamented with a yellow highlighting pen and my college-freshman scribbles. I had memorized every regulation in that book for the FAA's written and flight tests. My instructors at Ohio State University's School of Aviation had instilled in me and my classmates a healthy respect for safety, pilot discipline and the uncertainties of flight. Ohio State was proud of its aviation school, of the tidy, organized airfield and the fine-tuned fleet of immaculate planes. Faculty were cautious to the extreme with the health and safety of young

student pilots. But the drills on safety and responsible flying were not intended only to keep up the image. We were
warned that when it came time to earn a pilot's license,
the FAA would be tough, expecting students to meet the
highest, strictest standards of performance and safety. Our
instructors wanted us to know that the FAA was a force
to be reckoned with.

I wore out the pages of that regulation manual. The
book was my first encounter with the FAA, and until I
joined the Department of Transportation, it provided my
lingering impression of the agency. I believed that the
FAA served aviators and the public well, regulating air
traffic, keeping flying safe and insisting the airlines account for their actions. Surely Skinner was poised to tell
me that the Attorney General had an ax to grind?

"Now do you see why I wanted you here immediately?" he asked instead, getting up to roam his office.
The letter troubled him. Whom could he trust it to? Certainly not the FAA, and not a mid-level staff member who
might leak it to the press. A consummate Washington
player, Skinner knew that if the Attorney General had
asked Skinner to look into this complaint, then somebody
had to act. It was, he believed, precisely the reason Inspectors General were appointed. The letter would lead to my
baptism by fire.

"Find out what's going on and report directly to me."

Questions and new doubts about the FAA ricocheted
around my head. Surely the Attorney General was mis-
taken? Clutching the letter on my way out of Skinner's
office, I felt confident it would amount to little more than
political hyperbole. I never imagined that as I went out
the door, I stepped unknowingly onto a stage that had just
been set for my relationship with the FAA. Finding out
what was going on would turn into a six-year journey that
would leave me dismayed, disillusioned and afraid for the
flying public.

Yet I had leapt at the chance to be Inspector General
because the job combined the four things I loved most—
investigations, law, aviation and public service. Truthfully,
the office was tailor-made for me, and I was happy to quit
my post as Assistant Secretary of Labor in charge of keep-

ing union elections honest. If I'd had any doubts, they
were allayed by the colleagues and friends I had turned to
for advice. Everyone encouraged me to take the Inspector
General job—but only if I intended to do something
with it.

In August 1990, I had walked into Elizabeth Dole's
office at the Department of Labor. Dressed in slacks, wearing her glasses, Dole was hard at work on a hot Sunday
afternoon. The building was quiet—in fact, the whole city
was quiet. Congress was not in session, so there was little
activity around town. I told her I was thinking about leaving her department.

"That would be a very interesting challenge," Dole said
of the Inspector General job. "You could do some good.
But be sure you know what you're getting into."

I thought I knew what she meant; only later would I
fully understand her warning.

I asked for advice from friends at the Federal Bureau
of Investigation, too, because I knew that as Inspector
General I would work with them again. Charlie Parsons,
an official in Washington who later became the head of
the FBI office in Los Angeles, urged me to take the job:
"The only way to do a decent job is to stick with it for
several years. Fight for reform. Make your mark."

I knew I could probably keep the Inspector General job
for as long as I wanted it. Though I was appointed under
President George Bush (and at the time, it looked like he
was sure to be reelected), Inspectors General are usually
spared the politicking that goes on with other presidential
appointments. The office is supposed to be independent,
and for the most part had been treated as such by the
White House and Congress.

Dissatisfaction with my job at the Labor Department
also influenced me. Part of my job as an Assistant Secretary of Labor was to supervise and certify union elections.
That meant making sure that union elections were honest
and fair, and that union members had free and equal
chances to vote. My employees manned union polling stations and guarded ballot boxes. Sometimes this work was
tricky—a lot of my staff were women, and often they
were called on to guard ballot boxes overnight in seedy

warehouse districts. But there were even more unpleasant aspects to the job. When we had to get tough, union officials complained that the administration was anti-union. And they rejected any attempt to question the validity of an election. I grew to despise the politicking and deal-making that went on after virtually every decision. Lobbyists and union groups constantly tried to influence my work. The final aggravation came when I declared an election in Panama invalid, and my conclusion was overruled after the union protested. The decision seemed justified to me—the election for officers of a maritime union that worked the Panama Canal had taken place during the U.S. military action in Panama. It seemed clear that union members had not had a fair opportunity to vote because there was a war on election day. The Panamanian mail system was at a standstill, so voters could not have even filled out mail ballots. When my decision was reversed, I realized I wanted a different job.

As an independent Inspector General, I could accomplish so much more. I had loved flying from childhood. Every summer, my father, who dreamed of becoming a pilot but never had the time or money for lessons, would take my sisters and me to Wright Patterson Air Force Base for the air show. My vivid memories of crowds milling around planes on bright summer days are enhanced by a series of home movies my father made over several years. Each quirky, blurry film features comical shots of planes zipping across the sky—tiny blips zooming back and forth, absolutely indecipherable to the hand-held camera a mile below. These shots are interspersed with close-ups of me or a sister grinning and patting the side of one plane or another. There were many firsts at that air show—one year, the sleek SR-71 Blackbird spy plane was a great hit. It made its public debut by taking off from the airbase and flying to California and back before most people were ready to go home.

My sisters and I spent many weekends roaming through the Dayton Air Force Museum, too. Its first exhibit featured Icarus, whose hubris overrode his regard for safety. He flew too close to the sun and died. Vintage planes filled the museum and grounds. I particularly loved the

enormous B-52. Its wings were so long and heavy that
they drooped to the ground at the ends. Each trip, after
we finished visiting our favorite planes and clambering
through the big bombers, we begged our parents to take
us to the gift shop. We knew they wouldn't buy anything,
but we couldn't resist gazing at the pennants, airplane
models, little planes on sticks, toy planes on wheels, plastic model kits, and military hats and garb. Somehow, when
I was eleven years old, I talked my frugal parents into
buying me a tiny silver B-52 charm. I wore the tiny plane
on a chain around my neck until the silver paint wore off.

I dreamed of carving a profession from combining law
with flying. I envisioned being one of the first women Air
Force pilots, and then having a second career as one of
the first female commercial airline pilots. I scored high on
Air Force admissions tests but backed out of enlisting in
1973 because the recruiter pressed me to sign up for six
years—he said only men could enlist for three years because the military had no worries they would become pregnant and drop out—and because he would only put me on
a waiting list for flight school but couldn't say when pilot
training would open to women. I went to Ohio State University and then to Harvard instead, my ambitions to fly
for an airline intact until—while in the midst of qualifying
for a commercial license—my eyesight proved too poor
for the "big rigs." Nevertheless, when *Glamour* magazine
chose me as one of "ten outstanding college women" for
1975, part of the prize was a lunch with anyone I wanted
to meet. Most of my fellow honorees chose famous artists
or musicians, ballet dancers or other celebrities. I asked
to meet some of the board of directors and lawyers of Pan
Am. We lunched in the executive dining room on the top
floor of the landmark Pan Am Building in Manhattan—
nineteen-year-old me and half a dozen slightly amused
middle-aged men, a sweeping, glittering view of the city
encircling us. I wore my Ohio State University pilot's
wings pinned to my suit.

The *Glamour* magazine award was indirectly responsible for driving me back to the Dayton Air Force Museum
for the first time in years. Producers for the television
game show *The $64,000 Question* saw the magazine and

asked me to compete with aviation questions. I went back
to the Dayton museum hoping to learn everything there
was to know about aviation. And I came pretty close—
after several rounds of play on the game show, I won a
Buick. Of course, the object was to advance to the isolation booth and the $64,000 question. To get there I had
to bet the car—on the name of the author of *Winged Defense*. I said Billy Mitchell, but then instantly regretted it.
No, I added, changing my answer, the author was Eddie
Rickenbacker! Naturally the correct answer was Billy
Mitchell, my first instinct. I lost the Buick, and my shot
at the isolation booth. But I won a year's supply of pepper-
mint patties and Chap Stick.

Growing up on a farm meant a practical, frugal but
comfortable lifestyle. "Waste not, want not" was a fact,
not a concept. My parents raised soybeans, corn and wheat
on 341 acres, and my sisters and I were expected to work,
too. At harvest time, when bushels of corn were transferred
from the field wagons to the grain elevator, it was our job
to sweep up anything that fell on the ground. We knew
better than to sweep up dirt at the same time. In the spring,
it was our job to chop down the uninvited corn stalks that
sprouted in the rows of soybeans. In the winter, between
crops, we helped pick rocks out of the fields that had been
brought to the surface by plowing. Our tiny town of Pioneer, Ohio, is a mandatory instrument flight rule reporting
point for many east-west flights in the U.S., but otherwise
it's a dot on the map with only a thousand residents. People lived within their means and were fiercely proud of
avoiding debt or bad budgeting. My parents agonized
every time they accepted credit at the local feed store or
had to borrow money to get through a season.

I carried those principles to my job as a federal prosecutor in Kansas City and then to Washington, believing they
applied to government, too. Wasting, abusing or fraudulently spending taxpayer dollars doesn't have to be an
inevitable part of governing—not if someone is willing to
account for the money. I hate to see tax money squandered
on ridiculous projects or badly managed programs. Thus
the Inspector General job appealed even more—I could
police the Department of Transportation's spending habits.

Though the letter to the Attorney General that Skinner handed over surprised me, I was not entirely naive about the FAA. Over the years, anecdotes about safety lapses had drifted my way—my own flight instructor once took a night-flying job with a cargo delivery airline, and he regaled me with harrowing accounts of being forced to fly broken-down planes in severe weather just to keep a schedule. He often wished aloud that the FAA would shut down his employer for safety violations. Finally he quit because he feared for his life.

Astonishing safety lapses happened directly to me, too. Once on an Eastern Airlines flight, I looked out my window just in time to see mechanics binding the engine cowling with duct tape. When I complained, the flight attendant brushed me off; the mechanics surely knew what they were doing, she said. Only when fellow passengers overheard my protests and added their concerns did Eastern agree to get us another plane. Then, astoundingly, the wing flaps of that replacement plane appeared stuck in opposing positions, and the same passengers and I watched incredulously as mechanics used a ball peen hammer to try to force the flaps into place. We demanded another plane for the second time in one day.

As Inspector General, I knew I could check into the FAA's supervision of flying requirements at small cargo carriers or maintenance at big airlines. For me, the job was perfect. With its independence and forceful mandate, it could be tremendously effective—if the person in the job knew how to organize a formal investigation, work with different agencies and law enforcement, and was willing to turn a paper audit into a criminal case, if the evidence demanded it, or take results public when necessary. As a lawyer, prosecutor and investigator, I'd had years of that experience. And I loved those projects—developing cases, following leads, putting the pieces of the puzzle together.

What I did not anticipate was the fortitude I'd need to be able to live with making enemies. I knew there would be opponents outside government. But, in fact, the most forceful came from inside the Department of Transportation, where the instinct to promote the free enterprise of

commercial aviation stood in stark contrast to the need for
government regulation of the skies.

The root causes of the FAA's divided loyalty stretch
back to the pioneering days of flight and are hopelessly
tangled with the origins of commercial aviation. The
agency's identity, its character and its raison d'être formed
over decades, so that the jet age began with a government
agency keenly interested in fostering the business of flying.
The FAA did not spring up overnight. The agency wasn't
even established until more than fifty years after the
Wright Brothers' first successful flight. The roots of its
mission go back to aviation's first real champion, the military, and its first business partner, the federal government.
For decades the military, the government and aviation
grew and prospered together, fostering one another, pursuing the same goals, speaking with one voice.
Airplanes fly because Wilbur Wright studied buzzards.
In the 1890s, the Wright Brothers ran a bicycle repair shop
in Dayton, near my hometown. Self-taught mechanical ge-
niuses, they became interested in flight when Wilbur read
about a German, Otto Lilienthal, who had successfully
built and flown a glider. At that time, inventors had been
tinkering with flying machines for over twenty years. Earlier designs used flapping wings and balloons. In the fif-
teenth century, Leonardo da Vinci designed an elegant
helicopter he called an "ornithopter." The Wrights, however, wanted to perfect powered flight. But they knew they
had to be able to control an engine-driven plane. By
watching buzzards, Wilbur realized that the birds controlled themselves by twisting their wings. He figured out
that for a plane to bank, turn left or right, climb or de-
scend, or fly in combinations of the three, it needed the
same three axes that Mother Nature so perfectly crafted
in birds. That meant a plane's wings had to twist, too—
so that one side of the craft could provide more lift than
the other and thus allow the plane to turn or stay level if
buffeted about by winds. The Wrights adapted those principles to their flying machine, and in 1903, it lifted off
and flew for twelve seconds at Kitty Hawk, North Carolina. Though it was airborne for less than a quarter minute,

the Wright Flyer was engine-driven and pilot-controlled. It was the beginning.

Flight was born in an era when innovation, testing and experimentation were uncontrolled. No licensing procedures, permit requirements, regulations or laws governed the early days. Aviation as a moneymaking business was born then, too, with two 1909 transactions—the Wright Brothers sold their patents to a French company and then won a U.S. Army contract to build "aeroplanes" for a skeptical military. Then war truly boosted the aviation industry. During World War I, the military seized on this fantastic new weapon, built hundreds of planes, made rapid technical improvements in aircraft and gave the public a new romantic action hero—the ace fighter pilot.

In 1914, the first commercial airplane service in the U.S. began with a flight between Tampa and St. Petersburg, Florida. Although it was one pilot and one passenger in a flying boat on a twenty-two-mile journey, the passenger paid, and thus the first scheduled heavier-than-air passenger operation was born. It was an economic failure.

At the time, there was one U.S. airplane manufacturer.

After World War I, passenger airline service sprang up immediately in Britain, Germany, France, and Holland, which started KLM in 1919. In the U.S., we had 1919's Aero Limited from New York to Atlantic City. During Prohibition it moved to Miami to ferry Americans to watering holes in the Bahamas. Booze was also the driving force behind Aeromarine Sightseeing and Navigation, as Americans ferried between dry Miami and wet Havana, starting in 1920.

After mail delivery took to the skies, flight routes sprang up across the country throughout the 1920s. Their operators, usually former military pilots, knew these routes could be used for much more. Aviation had vast moneymaking potential, even if the pioneers couldn't imagine a plane able to cross the U.S. or the ocean in one hop.

Predictably, since there was no air traffic control system, the first midair collision between airliners on scheduled flights also happened in the Twenties—April 7, 1922. The two planes were finding their way by following a road—in opposite directions.

In 1926, the nascent aviation industry began pressing Congress to set safety standards. Without such legislation, the industry believed, the business of carrying passengers would never take off. In May 1926, the Air Commerce Act was passed; it would be the first of many government actions to promote the aviation industry. It decreed that the Post Office could hire private fliers to carry mail. The winners of those contracts became the pillars of the aviation industry. William Boeing, a Seattle lumber supplier, won the contract for the Chicago-to-Oakland mail run, and began building his own planes to serve the route. Flying companies won contracts for other segments of the mail run, and with success transformed themselves into United, American, TWA and Pan Am airlines.

But the real significance of the Air Commerce Act— evident in its title—was its commitment to promote the development and stability of commercial aviation. The act created a culture that the FAA, decades later, would slip comfortably into. It made it the duty of the Secretary of Commerce to encourage air commerce by attracting capital, creating appropriate laws, and establishing civil airways and navigational facilities.

Over the next three decades, diffuse, conflicting and overlapping laws would be put in place. Initially, the Post Office inspected aircraft, and set up a preventive maintenance course for pilots. Eventually, individual states passed laws that planes had to be licensed and registered. They added a patchwork of safety requirements. But no federal safety program existed. It wasn't until 1958 that broad authority to regulate aviation would be concentrated in one entity. Like many of the aviation laws that would take effect from the 1960s through the 1990s, strict regulation came about only after disaster. As commercial air travel boomed following World War II, crashes and accidents also increased. So, emerging airlines promised that each stewardess was also a nurse. Aircraft manufacturers built planes that overcame the barriers to night flying, high-altitude flying and blind flying—flying without being able to see where you are going. Airlines were founded to encourage the purchase of planes "made in America." They began competing for world routes. In the 1950s, a former general, Dwight D. Eisenhower, became President. He firmly believed that the aviation industry was critical to national security—that a powerful airplane manufacturing base and airlines with vast fleets and control of the skies could be deployed in time of war for national defense. As a result of all this, so many planes were taking to the air that they were literally running into one another. Finally, more than a decade after the end of the World War II, the aviation industry was desperate for the government to do something about the growing chaos. So Congress created the agency that would become the Federal Aviation Administration.

Three decades later, the aviation industry was deregulated, competitive and wildly profitable. And by the mid 1990s the FAA, Boeing and the rest of the industry could reliably predict an increase in air travel because business was booming. Even a dreadful slump in the early 1990s could not slow record demand from consumers. After losing $4.8 billion in 1992, at the peak of the recession, the airlines earned profits near $3 billion in 1996. Immediately they began buying new planes. In the fall of 1996, Boeing announced $7.5 billion in new orders, a lot of them for its dazzling, computer-flown new 777 mid-size jet. ''Load factors,'' or how full planes are for each flight, shot up in 1996. Experts predicted the airlines would need bigger jets. Boeing forecast nearly five hundred orders for planes that can carry five hundred or more passengers, and Airbus said it would probably sell closer to a thousand. Demand for seats was so great in late 1996 that the airlines were able to raise prices several times without the higher fares making a dent in reservations. Travelers were just willing to pay more.

This, naturally, was music to the ears of the airline industry. It proved that if left alone, business met consumer demand and eventually everyone would make money. But it also furthered an unwillingness at the FAA to impose regulations on the industry. When times were bad, the FAA didn't want to add to aviation's burden. When times were good, it didn't want to hobble growth. As a result, the FAA regularly reduced safety issues to their operating costs.

At its core, safety isn't cost-effective. Recommendations for changes in airline practices, for new equipment, for improved safety rules were evaluated not in terms of how many accidents they might prevent or lives they might save, but in terms of how many dollars they would cost the airlines, aircraft builders, parts manufacturers or fleet maintenance companies. When the National Transportation Safety Board first advised in 1991 that all planes should have black boxes with advanced recording technology, the FAA wanted to know how much it would cost the airlines in lost revenue while planes were pulled out of service for retrofitting. The FAA had the same response when the NTSB clamored for new fire safety measures—how much would it cost the carriers to buy and install fire and smoke detection systems for cargo holds? How much would it cost to recall all propeller blade models suspected of faulty cracks? To extend the de-icing boot on the wing of ATR planes? To require aircraft manufacturers to run actual tests of safety features on new planes? How much would it cost to require child safety seats, or smoke hoods for every passenger?

In the years right before I became Inspector General, the Department of Transportation, the airline industry and the FAA had resisted recommendations to add fire-resistant upholstery, cabin-floor emergency lights for crash evacuation and improved fire extinguishers and smoke detectors to planes. In 1985, Representative Norman Y. Mineta, chairman of the House Subcommittee on Aviation, blasted the industry for its safety complacency and accused it of "actively resisting and trying to thwart" simple improvements like lighting and fire extinguishers as "not being worth the cost.

"Mind you," he added, "we are not talking about redesigning a wing or a cockpit panel. We are just talking about some lights." He was on target when he said the agency's "natural instinct is to ignore problems that are staring people in the face until there is a crisis of some sort, or the public concern and attention get to such a level that their inaction looks patently ridiculous."

With black boxes, propellers, de-icing boots and cargo smoke and fire detectors, the FAA declared that the cost was too high to impose on the airline industry. Too high considering the low statistical likelihood of a fatal crash from fire in a cargo hold, a cracked propeller or ice on an ATR wing. Too high to require of the airlines and aircraft manufacturers when these accidents just were not happening on a large scale, too high for the rate of return in safety. In other words, it wasn't worth it.

There is valid reason for the aviation industry's position, an honest concern about expenses and profitability. They have every right to argue in favor of keeping costs down. But once inside the department, I wondered why the FAA was arguing for them. It's a federal agency, funded with taxpayer money, charged with advocating safety. The aviation industry could be expected to maintain that it couldn't afford to implement new procedures, install new equipment, pull planes out of service. But why was the FAA advocating for them? The FAA regularly told the NTSB that it couldn't have anything on its wish list of safety measures because of cost considerations. It regularly told the same thing to the Inspector General, Congress, even the White House. It reassured the public with the mantra, "Accidents are not happening, planes are not falling out of the sky."

The reluctance to require the airlines to spend money is extended even to simple, low-tech safety devices like child safety seats and smoke hoods. The FAA refused to require either one, even though studies indicated that smoke hoods would add less than a nickle to the price of an airline ticket—less than a pack of peanuts or a sip of soda. The FAA refused to order smoke- and fire-detection and -suppression systems that cost less than fifty cents per passenger. On the other hand, when it is forced to issue new safety regulations, the FAA seems to extend the airlines every courtesy. When flammability standards were finally set, the carriers were given two years to upgrade seat upholstery to fire-resistant materials. Then they were told they could delay even longer by postponing the new upholstery until each plane's next major mechanical overhaul—often many years away. When fuselage corrosion cracks were discovered, the FAA told airlines and maintenance companies they could just drill a hole near the end of the crack to stop it from spreading and then go ahead and fly the plane until the craft could be returned to a major maintenance bay. The FAA tries to accommodate airlines in other ways, too. It regularly extends the flying time of aircraft, allowing planes that are due for a 50,000-hour overhaul to continue flying their routes. It routinely waives medical conditions that its own regulations say should disqualify a pilot.

The FAA can rightfully argue that it is just doing its job. Except that contrary to popular belief, it doesn't work for the traveling public. It works for the aviation industry. This would probably surprise most Americans. But that is because most don't make a habit of reading obscure congressional acts from the 1950s. Even when the policy makes the nightly news, it is often overshadowed as the FAA promotes its image as a safety and regulatory agency. But the truth is, Congress declared in the Federal Aviation Act of 1958 that the FAA's primary purpose is to ". . . provide for the regulation and promotion of civil aviation . . ." Air safety is low on the act's list of policies. The first priority is to promote the business of aviation.

"The encouragement and development of an air-transportation system properly adapted to the present and future needs of the foreign and domestic commerce of the United States," the statute says. If that's not enough, the policy is even more specific in its third goal. "The promotion of adequate, economical and efficient service by air carriers at reasonable charges. . . ." The law obligates the head of the FAA to champion the "promotion, encouragement and development of civil aviation." It's quite clear: "The Administrator is empowered and directed to encourage and foster the development of civil aeronautics and air commerce in the United States and abroad."

The FAA's dual mission did not leap out at anyone in 1958—or in most of the years following—as a glaring paradox. In those days, aviation was heavily regulated. The government controlled prices, routes, even the purchase of airplanes. The aviation industry thrived under the care and nurturing of the government. The government and the military were intrinsic to the development of aviation; the same people guided and assisted aviation on both sides.

The aviation industry urged Congress to pass the very legislation that created the FAA. The FAA's mandate was essentially a national industrial policy designed to foster commercial aviation.

But with deregulation in 1978, the industry was free to take advantage of all that technology, competition and huge numbers of new passengers had to offer. But there were unforseen downsides, such as destructive competition. When I became Inspector General more than ten years later, it was clear there was something else no one planned for—the FAA watchdog simply could not keep up.

CHAPTER TWO

The Plane Truth

I settled into a chair at the horseshoe table as the FAA people passed out a series of charts and graphs neatly printed on white paper. I only glanced at the diagrams—dry-looking stuff. The papers seemed to show rather dull projections for rates of airline travel for the next few years. But soon I was leaning forward in my seat as others murmured in alarm to their neighbors. At the front of the room, the FAA officials began to drone tonelessly. Shortly after the turn of the century, they declared, aircraft accidents will increase dramatically. I looked intently at the suddenly sobering papers in my hands. These charts prove this assertion, the officials said matter-of-factly—if demand for flights from travelers increases at present rates, if the growth of discount airlines continues at this pace, we can expect a major crash every week or so after the turn of the century. Only then did their passion rise. This was proof, the officials said, that the FAA needed more money for inspectors, more money for air traffic control programs, more money for equipment. A dreadful onslaught of crashes is just around the corner, and we're hard at work ensuring that safety won't be compromised, they said. But we need more resources.

When the pitch was over, the FAA officials diligently collected the charts from each of us. But as they went around the room, they warned us: no news of these terrible predictions should be made public. People would only be scared away from air travel, forced into their cars and killed on the freeways, they said as they gathered up the charts, packed them carefully and took them away. Stunned, I wanted to study the data. Where had it come from, how had it been interpreted and substantiated, and what were the airlines planning to do about it? More important, what did the *FAA* plan to do to prevent all these new crashes? But the presentation was over. No strategy was mentioned or explained at the meeting; the FAA's efforts were all focused on increasing its budget. If I had been worried about the FAA efficiency because of the letter to the Attorney General, now my fears were bolstered: how could the FAA be good at safety oversight if it knew about this impending threat but had no plan to confront it?

Determined to have my own copies of those charts, I asked the FAA to send me the graphs and any supporting research. The reply was swift: no such data existed, I was told. No charts or graphs like that in our offices, the FAA said. In fact, no such research had been done, no such conclusions reached. But I'd seen them, I argued; I'd held them in my hands! That didn't matter; suddenly, none of the officials knew what I was talking about. Over the next few years, I came to learn firsthand that, sadly, withholding information was routine for the FAA. Fortunately, the Boeing Company made similar statistics public. The manufacturer published a study that said ". . . if, as we expect, air traffic is to double in the 1990s, we need to reduce by half our accident rate just to hold our own." After that, the cat was out of the bag. A consultant's report for the FAA warned that "even if today's accident rates were sustained or slightly improved, the growth in air travel is projected to be so significant that the absolute number of accidents would be so high and so frequent that people everywhere would react in horror!" The Flight Safety Foundation said, "If the accident rate continues at its present low level, in twelve to fifteen years we will be experiencing twice as many accidents as we have today, or even more. Some predictions indicate that this could mean a major aircraft incident somewhere in the world every two weeks.''

Like millions of Americans, I believed it was the FAA's job to keep an eye on the aviation industry and ensure that flying was safe. After all, air safety made up 60 percent of the Department of Transportation's business. But after the briefing on future crashes, I began to wonder whether the FAA was up to the task. The confidential complaint to the Attorney General about Eastern Airlines and the FAA seemed proof that it was not. In spite of Ray DeCarli's warning that Inspectors General had never before delved into safety, I was determined to fill the gaps apparently left by the FAA. From the outset, I had proof that the FAA sometimes simply looked the other way.

Eastern Airlines was a venerable institution, an East Coast carrier that had expanded to include national and international destinations. But like many airlines, it began having financial trouble in the mid 1980s. Eastern laid off staff, trimmed flights and ultimately declared bankruptcy. Gradually, reports began to circulate that in its last days it had also cut corners on maintenance, reporting partial repairs and repairs that hadn't been done at all as having been completed. The U.S. Attorney's office in New York had been tipped off that many maintenance records in Eastern's New York facility had been falsified. The prosecutors decided to take a look at the allegations. Immediately they were startled to find hostility and resistance from the FAA. Eventually the U.S. Attorney decided the FAA was actually interfering, trying to thwart the investigation and protect Eastern. FAA officials leaked confidential agency and grand jury documents to Eastern, including secret investigation reports. It tried to replace two inspectors working on the case after Eastern complained about them. The lawyers complained to the Attorney General in Washington, who in turn asked Secretary Skinner to intervene. Skinner asked me to take a stab at sorting out the conflict between the FAA and the U.S. Attorney.

Obviously, the first step was to get everyone together. A meeting was set up with lawyers from the Justice and Transportation departments, the FAA Deputy Administrator and his staff, and junior field officers who regularly worked at Eastern and had seen the suspicious maintenance records. As Ray DeCarli and I walked to the meeting, we strategized how we would get the two sides to talk out the dispute, work through the misconceptions, explain points of view; after all, we all worked for the government.

Once the meeting was under way, the FAA's Deputy Administrator, Barry Harris, sat still and quiet as the federal prosecutors laid out their complaints in cautious language. I watched him for a moment—before the meeting, I had heard he was from Kennebunkport, Maine, and his family was friendly with President George Bush's family. A tall, thin, patrician man, Harris looked stern as an official from the New York FAA field office that supervised Eastern agreed with the prosecutors: there seemed to be some irregularities in the airline's maintenance. Suddenly, Harris bolted forward in his seat and erupted. Chins jerked up and heads pivoted in astonishment. Eastern was a safe airline. He was unconvinced by evidence of poor maintenance or falsified records. He knew, he barked, because he flew home on Eastern every week. He commuted between Washington and Florida, and so did his family. Would he put his family on Eastern if it was not safe? Harris argued vehemently.

The room fell into a stunned silence. The rest of us waited as the Deputy Administrator stopped. But he said no more—he offered no evidence to contradict the federal prosecutor, just a passionate loyalty to Eastern. I sat immobilized by the outburst. There was an uncomfortable silence. Harris had barked his defense of Eastern in front of the FAA junior field staff. Now, shrinking back in their seats, they seemed to want to disappear. I knew I would have felt foolish and alarmed if I had presented a case and my boss had argued so vehemently against it. How could these inspectors not feel they had been disloyal to the FAA? They had sided with the enemy. For the first time, I saw for myself how difficult it is for FAA employees to speak out against an airline or take a position contrary to the management line. Certainly these field officials would never blunder like that again. Harris's message was plain: loyalty to the airline industry was more important than getting to the bottom of Eastern's maintenance mess. The FAA itself would later acknowledge that this attitude made it inappropriate for the agency to be involved in the Eastern case in any way. Rather than change its attitude or policy, FAA headquarters simply removed itself from the Eastern investigation. Ultimately, the airline pleaded guilty to conspiring to prevent the FAA from determining whether it was falsifying its maintenance records. In July 1991, it faced a fifty-three-count criminal indictment.

Others beside Harris told FAA employees that an airline's interests were paramount. The FAA's decades-old management structure had calcified into an inefficient bureaucracy that let the aviation industry set its pace. A significant part of the problem was a lack of dynamic leadership at the top.

Harris worked for Administrator James A. Busey, a ramrod-straight retired admiral. There was no mistaking Busey's posture or gait as he made his way through agency offices. From our first meeting there seemed to be a deep rift between our expectations of my duties. Busey made it clear he didn't like people who failed to respect the chain of command. If the Office of Inspector General had a report to submit or recommendations to make, the appropriate paperwork should wend its way through the correct supervisory levels but not find its way to the public. If I had something to say, Busey wanted me to say it to the relevant managers at private meetings and keep the bad news in-house. If our office did something he didn't like, I got a handwritten note asking, "Where's our spirit of cooperation?" In my first months on my job, I rarely saw him, and this lack of access distressed me until I realized that it happened because Busey simply wasn't in his office very much. A political appointee, he spent lots of time networking with industry leaders or attending to ceremonial duties. In between, he was preoccupied with piloting himself from one event to another on an FAA jet. He left the agency to get along as it always had, run by career civil servants who paid scant attention to the comings and goings of their leader.

FAA administrators are always appointees, men (they were always men until 1997) who for decades built contacts in the upper echelons of the military or the aviation industry, ties that eventually led them to believe they deserved to rest on their laurels for a couple of years at the FAA. And why not? The salary was good, the title lofty, the responsibilities few and the perks munificent. The Administrator, for example, always had a butler. The white-jacketed steward would quietly shuffle into the FAA leader's office with trays of fine china stamped with the FAA seal, pots of steaming coffee, and pastry. His quiet fussing around the edges of many meetings and his unobtrusive slipping in and out (''I'll get my boy to bring that,'' I heard one administrator say) with papers or to collect dishes sometimes made me feel as if I had stepped into a scene from the British Raj. It was puzzling—government officials are not allowed to have personal-service employees. No one below the level of Deputy Secretary can have a personal driver, but the Administrator did. And *no one* is supposed to have a butler. But the FAA Administrator had this steward—in my office, we nicknamed him ''the houseboy''—a gofer who brought breakfast in the morning and fetched throughout the day. His presence seemed to reflect a military style of management—the retired Army and Navy men who came to the FAA were accustomed to having junior officers who served as stewards.

But then the FAA Administrator headed a veritable fiefdom from his enormous office. His comfortable suite, with a large salon area for entertaining guests and an adjacent conference room, was the gateway to the FAA for industry executives, lobbyists and politicians. The office always looked impressive and ceremonial; his underlings' desks could be collapsing from the weight of paperwork, but the Administrator never had anything on his large, gleaming table except matching leather desk sets and expensive models of airplanes soaring toward the ceiling. The message was not lost on anyone—the Administrator was not there to administer, but rather to act as an emissary.

My earliest impressions of FAA administrators were quite different. That was because I had never met one. I'd come close, however. A favorite aviation professor at Ohio State University, J.J. Eggspeuhler, was considered for the

Administrator's job right after Administrator Alexander Butterfield was fired for revealing the existence of the Watergate tapes. I admired Eggspeuhler tremendously. His advanced aviation course lectures were always stimulating and challenging, his style bright and interesting. He had the gift of making learning fun. He treated students as equals, expecting them, among other things, to think for themselves, exchange ideas, test his knowledge. He taught classes on flying in adverse weather, weather patterns, instrument flight techniques, flying advanced aircraft, advanced avionics and navigation. Unlike the curmudgeonly airport manager who gruffly told me women should not be in the aviation flight program, Eggspeuhler encouraged women to take up flying. He treated me and the one other female student pilot in the school no differently than his male students; Eggspeuhler expected nothing short of brilliance and self-reliance from us, too. I visited him whenever I returned to Columbus after leaving OSU for Harvard.

When the FAA tried to lure Eggspeuhler to Washington, I thought the faraway agency must recruit the very best people. Eggspeuhler would have been an admirable administrator—but only later would I understand that he would have been unique, too, for his devotion to aviation safety. (He went on to found his own company dedicated to researching aviation safety.) Many times over the years I thought longingly of the difference an administrator like Eggspeuhler might have made, someone without the military and industry ties of all the others. In the end, after considering commuting from Ohio to Washington, Eggspeuhler turned the job down. He told me it was because he didn't want to uproot his family. Now I wonder if it wasn't because he understood the real truth about the FAA long before I did.

Candidates for administrator knew the FAA was essentially a flying club. Immediately upon joining the FAA, they found themselves commanding their own fleet of aircraft. Administrators are usually pilots themselves, and most are eager to maintain or increase their flight "ratings" or their licenses to fly different craft. Suddenly they

are faced with an opportunity to earn a license on a
Gulfstream or a Lear jet, or on a helicopter—for free.
Once certified, they then fly themselves around on private
jets. Keeping that license up-to-date in turn becomes the
rationale for zooming around the world on FAA jets.
Watching Busey's jet-setting schedule, I wondered how an
administrator could attend daily meetings and keep up with
FAA business if he was always on the way to the airport.

The Deputy Administrator's invective at the Eastern
Airlines meeting revealed his priorities in a manner he
probably never intended. By shouting that he knew Eastern
was safe because he flew home to Florida every week, he
disclosed that he'd developed a close, cozy relationship
with the airline, and inspired me to take a closer look at
the free flights he was getting from Eastern. Many weekends he used an FAA free pass to ride home to Florida
in a jump seat usually set aside for flight crew. When he
wasn't riding Eastern, he would get to Florida by arranging
FAA-paid work trips to cities near his home and thus
claim further free flights. In fact, he took business trips
that left him in or near his home many different times, at
a cost of $35,986 to the government. All of these trips
involved circuitous routing and weekends, and on some,
FAA planes were used to boot. These work trips seemed
to have another purpose—getting the Deputy Administrator home at government expense. Shortly after the Eastern
meeting, the Deputy replaced Busey as Administrator.

The commuting left the vivid impression that for Deputy
Administrators or Administrators, leading the FAA had
never been a full-time commitment. They spent a lot of
workdays racking up flight hours and earning licenses to
fly new aircraft. They frequently served as pilot in command or second in command on flights that were entered
into logs as necessary for "maintaining currency," or
keeping up-to-date. Transportation, of course, was only
secondary. The FAA requires an occasional pilot to have
twenty-four flight hours in a year. But one Deputy Administrator's flight hours were many times that. In fact, he
flew so much in FAA aircraft that the bills became staggering. Over the course of fourteen months, he spent
$108,185 on trips that would have cost the government

$11,225 if he had just bought a ticket on a regular airline. At the same time, by monopolizing those planes, he may have prevented other pilots who hadn't earned their minimum flight hours from getting the time in the air they needed. But the freebies didn't stop with airplanes—he went after helicopters as well. He spent hours in flight training and ground school that the FAA paid for—hours and days that he was away from his desk. Training that extensive is normally reserved for full-time FAA pilots, aviation safety inspectors and others whose jobs demand they fly helicopters. He had flown helicopters years before, but didn't have any recent experience. He wanted to update his license, and the FAA had choppers in its fleet. It just seemed like a good way to do it, he told my office when we questioned him.

That Deputy Administrator was hardly the only FAA employee who took advantage of perks. Nevertheless, the FAA's top brass, of all people, should avoid even the perception of fraud or abuse. My predecessor thought so, too. In 1989, then-Inspector General John Melchner, in looking at how the FAA spent money, had questioned about 50 percent of flights in FAA planes made by pilots who claimed they needed the hours to keep up their licenses. Those pilots already had more than the twenty-four hours that they needed. Like the various administrators, about 5 percent of the pilots flew over ninety-six hours, while 61 percent didn't get their minimum flight hours. My predecessor estimated that $1.2 million could have been put to better use in giving flight time to people whose jobs required them to fly. The Inspector General's office recommended that the FAA set a new rule: only pilots short of their minimum hours can make free flights. The agency didn't rush out and establish a new policy, though it did say it would "strengthen" its control over the flights.

However, the strengthened controls clearly did not apply to the Administrator. Certainly he had important destinations—giving speeches, cutting ribbons and attending banquets at a whirlwind of aviation conventions and seminars, adorning international meetings in Mexico and Belgium, baptizing countless new aircraft and showing a keen interest in experimental aircraft exhibitions and, of course, the

annual spring Paris Air Show. Naturally someone else had
to run the FAA. The Administrator generally displayed
little knowledge about the inner workings of the FAA,
anyway, and the Deputy Administrator even less. Thus the
Administrator's duties fell to the career FAA officials who
were around before him and would be there after he left.
For their part, the FAA staff were confident they rarely
had to defer to or consult with the Administrator. This
became clear at staff and agency meetings in my first year,
when the Administrator would frequently sit with folded
hands, no papers or reports in front of him, waving questions of facts or figures off on assistants. When the Administrator testified before Congress, an underling was always
sitting nearby so he could lean away from his microphone
to get the right answer.

The FAA is not alone in being headed by political appointees. Many agencies in Washington are headed by
friends and fans of presidents, people to whom favors are
owed. Even cabinet posts are filled for those very reasons.
But though it was a fact of political life in Washington,
it made working with the FAA sometimes very difficult.
For all intents and purposes, the FAA is a corporation
with 50,000 employees and a $10 billion annual budget.
It is responsible for a major economic product. Yet its
chief executive officer is essentially a goodwill ambassa-
dor, a figurehead who knows little about its daily business,
spends the majority of his time slapping backs at conventions and cannot get attention or respect from his underlings. Management is not expected of the head of the FAA.
A desire to promote aviation is essential, however, and the
Administrator's job is filled, performed and judged purely
on his success at ensuring harmony between the agency
and the industry. Administrators like Hinson needed no
convincing—they came to their jobs devoted to promoting
commercial aviation. Another problem for administrators,
however, was the temporary nature of their jobs—most
kept the appointment far less than four years. Since they
knew they'd be moving on soon, they rarely kept on top
of the issues. Perhaps the most painful episode came after
David Hinson had been at the FAA for two and a half
years. By December 1995, Hinson openly told me that he

couldn't do everything he wanted because he "had less than a year to go." I was discouraged by this blatant admission of impotence. He had to know he was essentially washing his hands of any leadership, and that the message would quickly filter down to the "troops." Once again, staff and field employees could just sit back and wait out the Administrator. I watched as he routinely ordered "a study" of some of our most disturbing findings of abuse. "Studies" meant nothing would get done. An FAA official assigned to Vice President Gore's task force to "reinvent" government confirmed the FAA's policy of inaction. In speaking to a group of Inspectors General, he laughed and said, "You know what the FAA does with your reports? We study them for a year and the issue goes away."

I can't remember when I started calling these men the "Kidney Stone Administrators," but I do know that it became apparent to me early on that they were tolerated only because everyone at the FAA knew it was merely time before they would pass. That was why everyone assumed that the Associate Administrator for Regulation and Certification, Anthony Broderick, was the real power behind the throne—he set the FAA's agenda, decided the FAA's position on safety and acted as a filter between the Administrator and everyone else. So perhaps he said it best when he was finally forced out of his job: "Who is setting aviation policy, making budget decisions and being out front on major policy issues? I do not think you would point to the FAA Administrator."

CHAPTER THREE

The Tombstone Agency

The Bible may teach that human life is priceless, but we all know the value of the body's minerals is about eight dollars. In my early years as Inspector General I learned that the FAA assigned a worth to the average passenger who might die in a plane crash. In its cost-benefit analysis, cost estimates for which were frequently provided by the airlines and the industry, which could grossly exaggerate the cost and minimize the value of life lost, the FAA easily determined that the value of those lives didn't amount to much compared with the hard, cold billions that saving them would cost in aircraft safety devices, in beefed-up monitoring of planes, pilots and air traffic, and in airports hermetically sealed against bombs and hijacking.

Curious, incredulous at the macabre implications, I frequently asked about these elusive valuations, and talked to many people who had heard about them or knew someone who knew someone who had heard about the numbers on any particular project, yet I never met anyone who had actually seen the official figures, much less helped compile them. But in many meetings, FAA officials argued as if they had those figures on the tips of their tongues— "losses," they would explain patiently, from the small number of crashes and even smaller number of attacks on planes just did not justify vast airline investments in safety and security. After all, as the FAA's security chief, Cathal

Flynn, would tell me, the terrorist bombing of Pan Am flight 103 over Lockerbie, Scotland, cost $1 billion. Trying to prevent another Pan Am 103 would cost $5–$10 billion over ten years. Couldn't I understand—the numbers just didn't add up. "Besides," he added, "if we do too good a job, we will subvert the threat and [terrorists] will attack Amtrak."

"We regulate by counting tombstones," an FAA official told a journalist a few years ago. The nickname's origins are unknown, but by the time I joined the Department of Transportation, even people who worked for the FAA cynically called it the Tombstone Agency. Within the Washington beltway, agency officials, government bureaucrats, staff on Capitol Hill, aviation lobbyists, airline representatives and journalists all understood the poignant irony of this nickname. The FAA will not do anything until people die. It was a sad, bad, inside joke. Only the public never knew how much truth was in it.

If outsiders viewed the FAA as encumbered by a divided loyalty and hamstrung by its dual mandate, the FAA didn't seem to share that confusion. The tombstone mindset made plain its loyalty to the cost-conscious interests of the aviation industry.

Anonymous travelers are not the only victims. In 1993, the Governor of South Dakota flew on an MU-2 turboprop plane equipped with blades made by Hartzell Propeller of Piqua, Ohio. The blades had a manufacturing flaw—cracks that caused the propeller to disintegrate and break up in motion. One such accident had already happened, so in 1992 the NTSB demanded a recall of the propellers. But the FAA didn't think one crash was enough to warrant that. The blades were not dangerous, the agency insisted, and it would cost air carriers too much to pull the propellers off each plane. However, my office had just started work on what I came to call the "black hole" study—exploring what happened to FAA reports of service and maintenance difficulties and airplane accidents. What kind of follow-up existed? We would discover that many of the reports disappeared into a void where they got no further attention. I thought the FAA should at least alert airlines and private pilots about possible problems so they could

examine their aircraft. The FAA usually declined—that
would upset the manufacturers in question, and cost the
aviation industry time and money. So people using those
planes had no way of knowing that at least one craft had
crashed because of a blade flaw. By April 1993, the NTSB
had repeatedly recommended the inspection of all such
propellers. But six weeks after the last request, a cracked
Hartzell propeller spun into pieces and brought down the
South Dakota Governor's plane. Only then did the FAA
issue a recall (two crashes constituted a "trend," the
FAA declared).

Yet the case was not unique, the Governor's death being
the sad price for a lesson finally learned.

Countless small mishaps that don't cause death or even
injury happen all the time. The FAA knows these "incidents" will outweigh the "accidents," that skidding off a
runway or having to shut down one engine in flight doesn't
make headlines or the nightly news. Even if a jumbo jet
skids off a runway, even if the skid is caused by a faulty
repair, an unqualified pilot, an overlooked safety inspection—if no one was hurt or killed, then it's just an incident, not an accident. Only with a major crash, only with
people dead and sobbing survivors filling television
screens, does the FAA step up to the plate and make
changes. I found the FAA's complacency toward accidents
difficult to accept. Just because people weren't dying in
huge numbers didn't mean safety was at an acceptable
level. I remembered the way a small coal mine accident
would mobilize the entire Department of Labor when I
worked there. Far fewer people were injured or killed in
mine accidents than in aviation incidents and accidents
every year. But each one was a significant event at the
Labor Department. My union-elections work had nothing
to do with mines, but when there was a mine accident, I
stood around in the hallways with everyone else, waiting
for the hourly bulletins that told us who was injured or
killed. No one talked about anything else on those days.
When someone died, folks in the Department of Labor
were visibly upset—they felt the system, or they themselves, had failed the victim. So it was strange to feel the

abstract, clinical attitude FAA workers seemed to take toward the numbers of people injured or killed on planes.

Time and again my office uncovered practices that led to incidents with a frightening regularity that would shock the public—sloppy inspections of planes, perfunctory review of pilots, lax oversight of airline procedures, disregard for bogus airplane parts, sievelike security at airports, antiquated air traffic control systems. Many of these affected other government agencies, too, though they often responded very differently from the FAA. The Coast Guard, for example, has a vast fleet of planes, enormous spare parts bins, countless pilots and dozens of airports and landing facilities under its control. So many of our investigations applied to them, too. But where the FAA could be counted on to fight Inspector General recommendations, the Coast Guard would simply correct what it could. The Coast Guard always seemed as short of money as every other government bureaucracy, yet they managed their fixes without extra budget.

Rarely did my reports, or similar studies from the General Accounting Office and investigations by the FBI, get such cooperative and expedient responses from the FAA. Its reluctance to take action in the absence of tombstones was an ingrained, almost knee-jerk response. Unfortunately, too often the FAA eventually got its graves as incidents turned into accidents.

In 1994, sixty-eight people died when an Avions de Transport Régional (ATR) plane crashed into a soybean field in Roselawn, Indiana. A peculiar design flaw made the French-Italian plane become suddenly, violently uncontrollable in cold weather. Pilots and aeronautical engineers knew what the problem was: the de-icing "boots" on the ATR wings were not big enough. Those were the rubber sleeves on each wing that could be expanded to crack sheets of ice. But the FAA determined that lengthening the boot would cost too much money. It took three plane crashes, the third one scattering human remains and debris over eight acres of Indiana farmland on Halloween, before the FAA relented and ordered extension of the de-icing boot and limits to ATR flights in icy weather.

It took a fatal plane crash for the FAA to heed years

of evidence that the distance between planes landing at an airport should be increased. I agree, because once I had been on a plane that was flying closely behind the jet ahead of it. In 1985, I was riding on an MD-80 that was about to land in Dallas when the jet suddenly rolled sharply to the right. Passengers screamed, but the plane leveled off before anyone was injured. Immediately the pilot came on the intercom and apologized for the jolt. ''Whoops,'' he said. ''Sorry about that, folks. We got too close to the plane ahead of us and hit their vortex.''

He was referring to the spirals of wind that flow backward from a jet's wing tips. Essentially, they create small tornadoes. If a second jet is too close and hits those wind vortexes before they disperse, they can knock a plane right out of the sky. The fact that we hit one on our way into Dallas was not the pilot's fault—he had followed the landing instructions he was given and had taken his place in line with the proper spacing. Except, for years the NTSB had been telling the FAA to increase the distance between jets, especially behind heavy jets. The Board had investigated fifty-one accidents caused by wake turbulence between 1983 and 1993. Twenty-seven people had been killed, and forty planes damaged or destroyed. In those years, the NTSB had repeatedly asked the FAA to set new rules, but the FAA refused. The agency also ignored a NASA study recommending the same. The airline industry didn't think increased spacing was necessary, and didn't like the idea because greater distances between planes meant fewer landings every hour, thus fewer money-earning flights.

From December 1992 to December 1993, a Cessna Citation jet, a Westwind jet and a Cessna propeller plane crashed after hitting the wake turbulence of Boeing 757 jets ahead of them. Thirteen people were killed and several were injured in those accidents. Finally, the FAA began to act. In December of 1993, immediately following the crash of the second jet, it sent out a letter warning pilots to be careful of wake turbulence from Boeing 757s. It would be three years more before the FAA ruled that the separation between heavy and lighter aircraft had to be increased.

The faulty propeller blades and wake-turbulence crashes

demonstrated that the FAA's "tombstone" policy hadn't changed since 1988, when the roof of a nineteen-year-old Aloha Airlines 737 peeled off in-flight. A fuselage crack caused the jet to come apart, and a flight attendant died when she was sucked out of the cabin. Only then did the FAA set new guidelines and a deadline for the upgrading of aging aircraft. Years later, reading about Aloha Airlines, I was struck by the multiple possible causes of the accident: an old plane, poorly maintained by its mechanics, sloppily inspected by the FAA, belonging to an airline that didn't get the oversight it should have had.

"Since the tragic Aloha accident in 1988, the FAA has put in place new and aggressive programs to respond to this issue, to ensure that aging aircraft are adequately inspected and maintained," Anthony Broderick said to Congress in 1991, essentially closing the barn door after the animals had escaped. What about before the Aloha disaster? What had the FAA's inspections accomplished?

Perhaps the FAA could argue that no one foresaw the top of a plane being stripped off like the lid of a sardine can (except that it had happened to a 737 overseas, and Boeing was already warning airlines, including Aloha). But what the FAA inspectors missed, two passengers saw upon boarding the plane. Unfortunately, they didn't report the crack in the fuselage near the main cabin door.

The FAA could not make the same argument for flight data recorders—those miraculous black boxes. Since 1982, the NTSB has urged the FAA to order airlines to install better black boxes, or, as the government jargon puts it, "Flight Data Recorder Expanded Parameter Recording." By 1995, improved black boxes were the number one item on the NTSB's annual most-wanted list of transportation safety improvements.

Like me, most pilots have no experience with black boxes. Small, general aviation planes don't have them. And like me, most pilots hope never to deal with those recording devices, since their prevailing image is as mangled debris retrieved from a crash site.

All the NTSB wanted was black boxes that can continue recording for fractions of a second beyond a catastrophic explosion or massive electrical failure aboard an airplane.

European airlines have used such advanced black-box technology for years. That means that many American planes flying to Europe have the advanced boxes. But the FAA does not want to *compel* airlines to put in these better boxes. No, the agency declared, the new technology would cost the airlines too much money. With that, however, the FAA made pretty broad assumptions about cost versus safety. It seemed to automatically conclude that retrofitting entire fleets with new black boxes would be prohibitively expensive. The NTSB, however, felt very strongly about the need for the new technology. It not only wanted the boxes replaced on old planes, it sensibly demanded that new aircraft rolling off the assembly line and those built in the future get them in the first place.

"We are at a serious safety disadvantage without such modernized recorders . . ." NTSB chairman Jim Hall said in April 1996. The NTSB was especially keen to have the boxes installed on Boeing 737s, since these planes' rudders had been suspect in several crashes and hundreds of reports of rudder trouble that investigators couldn't pin down—crucial pieces of the puzzle were missing from their primitive recorders.

"There have been two accident investigations involving B-737s—Colorado Springs in 1992 and Pittsburgh in 1994—that have been seriously hampered by the lack of this information," Hall said. "The potential for recurrence remains."

In both accidents, the planes' flight data recorders measured up legally. But they weren't good enough to tell investigators what they really needed to know about rudder positions during the crashes. The NTSB suspected the rudder pedals or rudders because thirty-nine other pilots had described similar problems with 737s. None of the 737 black boxes tracked the rudder mechanism, or "flight control inputs" and "control surface positions" including positions of rudder, wing and tail controls. Fortunately, in the other thirty-nine emergencies, the pilots wrestled their planes safely to the ground. But it was obvious that not every pilot would be so lucky, or that something else might make the situation worse and drive the planes into the ground just as they had been in Colorado Springs and

Pittsburgh. More crashes could happen if the NTSB didn't figure out the mechanical problem and get it fixed.

"What adds to our frustration is that we feel the B-737 retrofit is within the economic grasp and maintenance scheduling capabilities of the aviation industry without serious disruptions," Hall said. The military had no problem ordering a retrofit of all its aircraft, which had never had flight data recorders, with black boxes. It learned its lesson after a terrible crash took the life of Commerce Secretary Ron Brown and thirty-four others in Croatia. (Hall immediately wrote a letter to the Department of Defense, urging it not to install the traditional black boxes, but to get the better, newer ones.)

The FAA was not as quick to respond as the Pentagon. Once again, the bottom line was money.

"According to the FAA, the major impediment to the retrofit of Boeing 737s . . . is cost," Hall wrote in an angry letter to FAA Administrator David Hinson in April 1996. Upset at the FAA's insistence that the airlines could not afford better black boxes, Hall sent his own people out to investigate the project.

"Industry has suggested that a major portion of the cost to retrofit the Boeing 737 is due to the need to hold airplanes out of revenue service while the installations were made," Hall wrote to Hinson. NTSB people immediately saw the real problem—"industry" didn't even try to make retrofitting cheap. It assumed there was only one, costly way to retrofit the planes, and never looked for a cheaper alternative.

". . . it has been assumed that aft lavatories must be removed to allow wires to be routed from the tail to the recorder, a time-consuming process," Hall explained. That was an expensive undertaking. But when NTSB staff talked to Boeing, maintenance workers and airline employees, they discovered that the wiring could also be threaded through access ports on a lower part of the bulkhead. The bathrooms would not need to be removed, saving about 150 hours of labor. Adding the new black boxes with the rudder sensors could be done during ordinary checkups.

Instead of pressing the airlines to find an economical way to install new black boxes, and instead of sending its own investigators to challenge the airlines' assessment of the cost, the FAA had simply embraced the carriers' argument that the project would be too pricey. So, the 737s kept flying without the ability to record potentially life-saving information.

"Had the FAA and industry begun the implementation of this recommendation in March 1995," when the NTSB originally made the request, Hall said, "most Boeing 737s would have been retrofitted with an acceptable, short-term improved recording capability by this time. The lack of FAA action to date is unacceptable."

Over a year later, in the days after TWA flight 800 crashed into the Atlantic Ocean, the public, politicians, investigators and grieving family members waited tensely while scuba divers searched for clues. Everyone hoped the divers would find the plane's black box, intact, bearing some clue to what had happened to the plane. Eventually the recorder was found, its body remarkably undamaged. But it played back only a millisecond of a mysterious loud noise. The box was one of the old models, and didn't have the extra capacity to record in the midst of a catastrophe like TWA flight 800.

Because of FAA refusal to require the advanced black boxes, the exact cause of the TWA flight 800 center fuel tank explosion remains a mystery.

Ironically, the FAA's protection of the airlines backfired. People are refusing to fly on old 747s because the source of the spark causing the explosion is still unknown and because the FAA will not order interim safety measures to make the center fuel tank less dangerous. TWA had to get rid of its old 747s or lose its customers.

In 1997, the FAA raised the value of a human life to $2.7 million, at least for 1999 fiscal year purposes.

CHAPTER FOUR

Business As Usual

A long and damning paper trail should have followed ValuJet flight 592 into the Florida Everglades. Weaknesses in the airline's safety record that might have shut it down before the crash should have been boldly etched in black and white on FAA inspection reports. In ValuJet's three years of existence, FAA inspectors had scrutinized the airline 4,858 times. Yet they found very little worth writing down during any of those inspections, and no infractions serious enough to trigger alarms. After the tragic Everglades crash, spurred by the gruesome deaths and public outrage, the inspectors examined ValuJet's own books, and discovered so many egregious violations that the carrier was grounded within weeks.

The resulting consent order between ValuJet and the FAA listed thirty-four separate violations going back three years, breaching every possible type of regulation: plunging cabin pressure caused an emergency descent; equipment, storage facilities and records at two contract fueling agencies were not inspected for months in 1995 and 1996; pilots didn't sign off on training and qualification records; mechanics ignored a broken main cabin door; a hole in a main engine cowl was designated a low maintenance priority; flight crews complained thirty-one times about one plane's broken weather radar before the system was fixed;

cables were crossed on the left gear flaps of at least three planes.

ValuJet agreed not to fight its grounding and, in June 1996, paid $2 million toward the FAA's cost of reinspecting its planes. It was not a penalty; in fact, with that money, the airline bought itself a virtually clean slate. "The FAA agrees that, except for violations of regulations concerning hazardous materials and civil aviation security," the consent order said, "it will not pursue any civil penalty for any violation of the regulations known by FAA as of the date and time of the execution of this agreement."

How could it? ValuJet had already been inspected for those violations nearly 5,000 times and given a tidy bill of health for three years. The FAA could hardly go back and find all the faults without admitting that it was to blame for missing or ignoring them in the first place.

Yet I knew the FAA was to blame; my senior staff agreed and Congress had certainly heard from us that this was the case. But we also knew ValuJet was not alone. Shoddy inspections were a plague at the FAA. Exposing them had occupied me since my first year on the job.

In 1991, as we tied up loose ends on the Eastern Airlines investigation, I also tried to tidy up a review begun by my predecessor. Bleak reports describing the mediocre performance of airline inspectors who worked in the FAA's Southwest Region filled my reading hours in the early days of my job. The FAA is responsible for certifying and then continually examining aircraft design, airline operations, airplanes, pilots, mechanics, repair stations, aircraft parts—essentially, every stage of commercial aviation. The agency does this with one basic tool: inspections. Probing each level of this inspection authority was a critical part of assessing the FAA's dedication to safety. In the FAA's Southwest Region, inspectors did an abysmal job of examining the nation's aircraft operators. Countless required or recommended inspections were never conducted, while others were carried out so perfunctorily they were meaningless, and still more revealed problems that went unreported just to spare the airlines any inconvenience. Inspections of planes, pilots, mechanics and repair stations were so unreliable as to be virtually useless. Fortunately, most of the time savvy and diligent airlines filled the gap. But it was inevitable that the inspections process would eventually break down at an airline like ValuJet, creating the perfect conditions for a deadly crash, exactly the cause of the crash the NTSB would find six and a half years later. So the reports troubled me. However, I had learned as a prosecutor to form my own opinion and then go with my instincts. The only way to move forward with safety evaluations was to pick an issue and get started. For that, I needed to see the inspection guys in action myself.

American Airlines cycles its fleet through its Dallas hub, a part of the FAA's Southwest Region, so in January of 1991, I went there. Inspectors are supposed to spend 35 percent of their time actually looking at aircraft, and I hooked up with an FAA agent who planned to work in the field the day I was in town. I tagged along with him to American, chatting with the inspector about the long years he'd spent overseeing the airline. His familiarity with the airline and its workers was evident as he strode through the airport, past boarding gates and out onto the tarmac. He considered himself on the same team with his friends at American. He spotted an MD-80 parked off to one side. The plane was idle, so it was convenient to inspect. Curious, I asked how he chose the plane. As we walked toward the craft, the inspector seemed puzzled. The answer should have been obvious—the airplane is here, so it gets inspected. There were no hard and fast rules about which plane to inspect, he told me. Often he checked out planes for no reason other than that they happened to be at the gate, passengers getting on or getting off. We strolled under the MD-80, the inspector craning his neck. He did not have a checklist or a rule book; did he have the requirements memorized? I'm just looking for anything unusual, he told me, a dozen feet below the giant belly, you know—leaks, parts hanging from the plane. My eyes followed his, though I could not make out much detail. Dripping fluids or giant cracks might leap out, but anything less would be hard to detect from the ground. Distracted, I suddenly realized the inspector was moving swiftly toward steps leading into the plane. Apparently we were finished with the exterior. Once inside, we moved quickly through the cabin, the inspector ahead of me, tapping seat backs as he went. He stopped to check a flashlight. We returned to the cockpit; the inspector glanced through the logbooks in case the crew had any complaints. Nothing. Good, he said; we're out of here. The entire inspection had taken less than fifteen minutes.

Like all of the FAA's nearly 3,000 inspectors, the staff working out of Dallas/Fort Worth, Texas, were the main link between the government and the airlines, and it was their job to make sure the carriers operated within the law. They were supposed to stay on top of the airlines, verifying that planes and pilots were in shape to fly. If they checked pilots, then they were supposed to be pilots themselves, licensed to fly various planes so they could scrutinize other pilots, ride with cockpit crews on routine flights and read through pilot logbooks. Some were meant to be trained experts in aircraft engineering and mechanics so they could inspect planes at airports and go through records at maintenance facilities and understand that there is no machine more complex, or exposed to more extremes in temperature, pressure and dynamic loads, than an airplane. It's a hands-on job, one that pays from $40,000 to $70,000 a year. To do their work properly, inspectors should follow detailed checklists and keep up on training. But most of all, they needed motivation, a sharp, diligent eye—and impartiality. In Texas, my confidence sank as my suspicions rose. Nothing even close to that was going on in the Southwest.

When I got back to Washington, I thumbed through my predecessor's report again, concentrating on the conclusion over and over—in thousands of inspections of planes and pilots, the inspectors had found virtually nothing wrong, nothing worth writing down or reporting. The numbers were stunning: from 1988 to 1990, 833,000 inspections turned up fewer than 4,000 violations. The inspectors issued few warnings or fines, and rarely tracked cases or followed up on inspections. What were the odds that all those planes and pilots would have such consistently clean bills of health? Inspections are the backbone of the FAA, and clearly they were being grossly mishandled.

That was obvious because special inspections—white-glove reviews—often found problems at the airlines or facilities that had passed conventional muster. The key seemed to be that the special inspectors were from out of town. They weren't the same buddies who inspected an airline day in and day out, and they conducted much more than a mere walkabout on the ramp. Yet there was nothing illegal about FAA inspectors developing long-standing close relationships with the airlines they inspected, not even about FAA inspectors having authority over airlines they used to work for. Because no laws were broken, the FAA didn't see a problem.

Was the FAA undercutting its own ability to ensure safety, diminishing its own power to make the aviation industry obey the law? This was undoubtedly not just a Dallas/Fort Worth problem. The FAA has nine different regions, from Alaska to the Great Lakes to the South. All told, the agency was required to conduct hundreds of thousands of inspections every year of commercial airlines, commuter carriers, air taxis and helicopter operators. Suddenly, what seemed like another item on the list of Inspector General projects—review the FAA inspection process—became a pressing need. We had to find out whether inspections across the country were as poorly handled as they had been in Dallas/Fort Worth. We had to repeat what I had done in Dallas—attach ourselves to FAA inspectors as they went about their business. Then we'd comb through old records to see how they had done their jobs in the past.

My concern turned to dismay before we really even got started. The first thing our field agents discovered was FAA staff courtesy—it was their habit to call aircraft operators, repair stations or maintenance contractors and let them know that an inspector would be coming over on such and such a day. There were no surprise inspections of airlines in general, other than which plane to choose for a cursory ramp inspection. We followed, our auditors amazed, as the inspector showed up with a list of questions that he was under no obligation to pursue. He could ask

one question, any combination of questions or none. The
Dallas inspection became a baseline for the whole country:
to scrutinize an aircraft, inspectors would drive to the airfield, walk out to the ramp and inspect whatever aircraft
happened to be parked on the tarmac at the time. If an
inspector looked at one aspect of an aircraft or at hundreds
of parts, he completed the inspection just the same. If he
only walked around on the tarmac under the plane looking
for leaking fluids, his stroll counted as an inspection. The
whole process was left entirely to the inspector's judgment, or mood. It was madness that truly had no method.

Inspectors didn't complete their suggested task lists
(they were only suggestions, after all), they didn't record
the actual time they spent on inspections, they didn't verify
recorded work when reviewing airline maintenance records
and they failed to report deficiencies they found or follow
up to see if they were corrected. That they routinely chose
not to report violations was the most egregious practice
we saw. How could safety be enforced under such a system? Our findings were frightening: landing gear, oxygen
systems, engines and engine controls were checked in
fewer than half of the inspections. The engines themselves
were ''inspected,'' perhaps only with a glance, only 52
percent of the time. Yet the FAA insisted it completed
hundreds of thousands of inspections every year. How
many were thorough? And what about those that were
not completed?

In 1990, eighty-four aircraft operators were inspected
between 200 and 18,000 times. We knew inspections were
haphazard, but some of the examples were simply ludicrous: Eastern Airlines collected 18,000 inspections, all
during the time it was fudging its maintenance; one Eastern Airlines jet was inspected 200 times in one year, and
not one violation was found during any of those exams;
another 1,900 aircraft operators who were due for inspections never got them. None of that should have surprised
me, given the inspection technique I witnessed firsthand
in Dallas. The major airlines have better safety records
and images than small carriers—in part, perhaps, because
FAA inspectors concentrated on the big guys: in 1995,

Delta Airlines planes underwent nearly 13,000 inspections—but received only seven violations.

Embarrassed at the blatant discrepancies we found, the FAA took action—it decreased the "required" inspections from 103,000 in 1990 to 44,000 in 1994. Instead, it told inspectors to increase discretionary inspections from 168,000 to 267,000. Then it boasted of a better record for required inspections.

In truth, the inspectors on whom the flying public and the airlines relied were frequently undertrained, inexperienced and unsupervised. One described being sent to inspect a plane whose door he didn't even know how to open. Another logged 200 hours of inspections as he sat on a flight to London—a flight that took less than ten hours. Inspectors who had been trained to examine small planes were sent to inspect jumbo jets. They were charged with passing judgment on pilots who flew planes that 52 percent of the inspectors themselves weren't qualified to fly. Others completed paperwork for in-flight inspections without ever being on the flights in question. The FAA waived training updates for hundreds of inspectors—sometimes just because an inspector said he or she was sick that day—while at the same time, the overall number of inspections each was supposed to do increased. The inspectors rarely did the paperwork necessary to follow up on the few problems they uncovered: in 1991, inspectors found ninety-two violations, but they failed to enter seventy-one of them into the computer database. Instead, they marked them down as "satisfactory" or "informational." In other cases, inspectors told two airlines about five violations, but they failed to report them. So later, neither the inspectors nor their supervisors remembered to follow up on the violations. When we insisted on seeing what had happened to those planes, the FAA found several cases where the airlines had not made the repairs. Two aircraft had to be grounded because the airlines hadn't fixed a problem discovered in a ramp inspection. Under ordinary circumstances, no one from the FAA would have pursued those cases.

The FAA tried to monitor inspections through a computer database—even though the agency itself admitted that the database was poisoned by incorrect and incomplete data. Still, it was all they had, and all we could use, too. The data seemed like gibberish—an indecipherable collection of numbers, abbreviations and acronyms that forty-two people from seven regions of the Inspector General's office approached with despair. After grueling analysis, we found that in 1989, 23,000 required inspections simply weren't done (but 225,000 discretionary inspections were). The FAA liked discretionary inspections because they made it easy to meet the requirement that 35 percent of time be spent on inspections without committing to the more difficult, higher-risk required inspections. In many cases, this was because the FAA regional offices just didn't plan well—they made timing and scheduling mistakes, allotting time for too few or too many inspections. Nearly 9,000 required inspections were canceled—even though we argued, in all seriousness, that inspections should be canceled only if a carrier went out of business. Actual inspections took up only about a quarter of inspector time on the job, though we found inspectors who logged more than eight hours of surveillance a day, miraculously without working any overtime. Amazingly, eighty-two inspectors said they logged between one and five weeks' worth—that's 40 to 204 hours—of inspections in a single eight-hour day. Of those, 40 percent focused on two easy inspections: ramp checks (looking at the plane as it sits at the gate) and in-flight inspections (observing crew en route). To make matters worse, the ramp inspections appeared to be totally arbitrary. Thus fourteen planes were inspected more than one hundred times in 1989, while others were overlooked entirely. And despite the fact that the inspectors seemed mostly concerned with meeting quotas and turning in paperwork, even there they failed at their jobs. Review of airline maintenance records was notoriously superficial. At one airline, we found records showing twelve cases of oil filters being changed on a plane. Yet there were no corresponding records that new filters had been issued for that plane. It was impossible to know whether the filters had really been changed—but had the inspectors picked up on that?

A big part of the problem was FAA supervisors—they

simply didn't do their jobs. In seven district offices, they failed to consistently review or approve inspections. Most supervisors never went into the field with their inspectors. They never insisted that staff meet the 35 percent time requirement. A General Accounting Office report agreed with our audit: on average, inspectors spent only 23 percent of their time checking out planes and pilots.

The FAA didn't fall down just on ValuJet. It was incompetent at virtually all of its inspection responsibilities. It failed to watch over the examiners who certified aircraft mechanics; it was sloppy about inspecting aircraft parts; it gave up altogether on surveying foreign factories that manufactured airplane engine and body components; it paid lip service to thousands of airplane checkups and pilot tests. The agency offered plenty of excuses: foreign inspections cost too much; domestic aircraft builders inspected the parts they bought; part suppliers knew they had to promise quality control or lose their government permits; planes were not falling out of the sky because of bad parts or bad mechanics. They were content to leave it at that.

Yet between 1990 and 1996, my office issued ten reports on the FAA's inspection system, all of them critical: aircraft operators, parts manufacturers, repair stations, designated mechanic examiners. Every investigation or audit was a battle, accomplished only after crafting strategies to outwit the FAA. My office made seventy recommendations to intensify FAA inspections. Yet none of these shortcomings were news to the FAA—ten years before, a Senate committee had haggled over many of the same defects. We weren't alone this time, either. When I started to peel away the layers of safety inspections in 1991, a Government Accounting Office report already warned that "ineffective inspections were a contributing factor" in six airline crashes in the 1980s. The GAO told Congress that the FAA had to do something about "several fundamental and deeply embedded problems in its airline inspection management and oversight." The accounting office was blunt: "FAA's inspection program has not ensured that airlines comply with federal safety regulations," it said, and if that wasn't enough, added: "FAA's routine inspections have been ineffective in identifying serious safety problems.''

The NTSB weighed in, too, even before ValuJet, pointing out that a 1988 crash that killed twelve people might not have happened if the FAA had more meticulously inspected the airline and its pilots. Unfortunately, slipshod review of aircraft is the norm, not the exception. The entire inspection system is so haphazard that a passenger can fly round-trip on a major airline, riding one way on an airplane that has been checked hundreds of times in the space of a few months, then flying home on a plane that has not had a single visit from an FAA inspector. The FAA blames its spotty inspection program on money. Like most government agencies, it doesn't have enough. So it has allowed its inspection program to deteriorate across the board, rather than instructing inspectors to pick and choose their targets carefully. Common sense dictates that the FAA focus on inspections where safety is at the greatest risk. Common practice is almost entirely arbitrary. To be sure, the FAA has a plan—in 1991, it announced a flashy new computer system to analyze safety performances. But it was not scheduled to go on-line until sometime in 1997 (and it did not pan out even then)—and FAA officials said they hadn't figured out how to use the information to schedule and adjust inspections. Even without those qualifications, a long shadow of computer illiteracy darkens the FAA, an agency notorious for mismanaging information technology. Certainly it uses computers to store, organize and report aviation data. It tracks and analyzes aircraft malfunctions, rules violations, accidents, pilot medical exams, security violations, airline safety inspections and aircraft and pilot registrations. So the systems are crucial. Yet in a 1991 report, the GAO criticized the FAA for bungling the management of its computer systems and said the agency couldn't do its job because its computer systems were plagued with unreliable data.

Rumblings of objection emanated from the FAA even before our final report was complete. Anytime an office like the NTSB or the Inspector General sends findings and recommendations to the FAA, the agency is supposed to answer in writing. This time the FAA dragged its feet, clearly reluctant to even acknowledge that we'd investigated its inspections practices. But however much the FAA might have wanted to procrastinate, time was not on its side. The fact that thousands of planes were uninspected was too alarming for the press, the public and Congress to ignore. Almost immediately, news of our findings began circulating on Capitol Hill. My phone rang constantly with congressional staffers asking questions about the inspections in their bosses' districts. Finally, Representative James Oberstar, the chairman of the House Subcommittee on Aviation, announced he would get to the bottom of the inspections controversy through hearings on Capitol Hill. His office asked me to testify.

I looked forward to meeting Oberstar. He had led the House Aviation Subcommittee for years, and his many hearings and bills on aviation issues had earned him the nickname "Mr. Aviation." He was respected for his activism—he wasn't afraid to call hearings and investigate issues. There was no doubt that he understood a great deal about the aviation industry, and, more important, about safety regulations and the FAA. Not long before the hearings, his staff asked me to brief them on my investigation. I was impressed with how quickly Oberstar's aides had grasped the issues. They expressed great concern at the poor caliber of airplane inspections.

I spent days preparing my testimony—first, an official statement that I would submit for the *Congressional Record*, and second, details and statistics that I might be asked about in a question-and-answer session with the members of the subcommittee. It was exciting—I felt honored to be taking part in the legislative process, and thrilled at the prospect of helping shape what I hoped would be new laws. And I enjoyed the briefings, the exchange of information and ideas, with the Capitol Hill staffers. It was like being a White House Fellow again.

Shortly before the hearings, Anthony Broderick paid me a visit. We had never met, but I knew who he was. Broderick, the FAA Assistant Administrator for Regulation and Certification, was the real power behind the throne at the agency. Across the aviation industry, the name "Tony" meant only one person. Broderick had nearly twenty years at the FAA, a manager with an intimate knowledge of aviation and every vagary of FAA practice and policy. He was a favorite of airline executives, aircraft manufacturers and industry trade groups.

If Broderick was at all upset about our findings he hid it; in fact, he was charming and friendly. He seemed to agree with the findings and just wanted to reassure me that the FAA would take our recommendations into consideration and make the necessary changes. Moreover, I could tell Congress he'd said so. I was stunned, but quite pleased. Our study was solid, we had pages of reviews of shoddy inspections and now Broderick was acknowledging the thoroughness of our work. Mostly I was pleased that because Broderick was high enough on the FAA ladder, his decisions would be enacted. It seemed that my first year, my first safety project, was going to lead to real change.

So that was just what I told Congress. I proudly described our investigation, our findings and our results—and then assured the politicians and the public that everything was okay because the FAA was cooperating and would work with us for improvement.

"There are changes being made, and there have been some new procedures promulgated since our audit," I told the panel. "We are also discussing our findings and work with Mr. Tony Broderick and the FAA and they have assured us they will work toward resolution."

Then Broderick came forward. The discrepancies between the Inspector General and the FAA were merely technical, he said—our results were skewed by the way we interpreted the numbers. "We have," Broderick told Congress, "an accounting problem, an audit problem, not a substance problem."

No inspectors certifying pilots are unqualified for the work, he insisted. It was all in what you knew about the inspections process. Say an inspector licensed only to fly small planes gets sent to check out the crew on a 747. You might conclude that the inspector is unqualified to check out that pilot. But look closely. It could turn out that the inspector was really there that day to check out the flight engineer, whether it was for an oral test or a written exam. And flight engineers are not fly-rated for a 747, either. So everybody is okay.

"Again, we have an accounting and audit problem," Broderick reassured Congress, the public and the reporters in the hall. He was adamant that inspection failures were not the dramatic safety problem we made them out to be. He chose frivolous examples to make his point, describing one airline that appeared to have a pattern of inspection problems. Upon scrutiny, Broderick testified, it turned out that "they kept finding that there were fire extinguishers that were loose on the airplane. . . . The Velcro was coming undone. That's the kind of thing that's not a critical issue, but when we saw the pattern, we showed it to the airline and they replaced the Velcro with metal clips. . . . We don't want them to go out every day and check to make sure that the Velcro on that particular fire extinguisher is still good. That's not a critical item.

"If we're now going to burden the system," Broderick warned, "the taxpayer, the traveling public with following up and closing out, in a paperwork sense, each one of these items which the professionals doing the inspection don't deem are important . . . we're going to be spending a lot of resources that are better spent, I think, on inspections."

As for following up on violations, Broderick announced that that weakness was now resolved because the agency had developed a computer game in which an inspector was presented with a series of tasks. The trick to winning the game was to punch in follow-up procedures. If the inspector didn't do the correct follow-up, a little accident would fill his screen.

"This stresses the importance of follow-up," Broderick proudly told the subcommittee. To deal with our complaints that inspectors were passing pilots on types of planes the inspectors hadn't flown themselves, the FAA changed its requirements: as of June 1991, FAA pilots no longer had to be "type rated" on the aircraft used during flight checks.

In retrospect I wasn't too surprised at Broderick's testimony. Of course he would stand up for his agency even

if the only defense he could mount was over trivial issues.
But when he was finished, Oberstar took the microphone
and heaped praise on the FAA and Broderick. I felt my
stomach clench. Oberstar was almost fawning, compli-
menting Broderick's wit, intelligence and willingness to
testify. He said nothing about "getting to the bottom" of
any inspections failings. He didn't press Broderick to account for the shoddy inspections we'd discovered or the
discrepancies between the FAA's interpretation of inspections and ours. It was as if the briefing that I conducted
in his office had never happened.

Representative Oberstar and Broderick clearly knew
each other, liked and respected one another. Their relationship would prove to be a microcosm of the relationship
between the FAA and Congress. That day I began to understand that I was an outsider, trying to represent a constituency—the flying public—that had no real voice. It
certainly did not have a voice strong enough to compete
with the aviation industry and the FAA. Hearings, then,
were not like trials at all—there was no attempt to discover
new information or to rectify the problem. They were simply media events in which the participants presented what
they already knew and believed.

As a result of private meetings and public hearings, I
came to understand that there were two sides to Representative Oberstar. The reputation around Washington of
"Mr. Aviation," the keen, concerned expert, was won
through relentless hard work. But not the kind of work
everyone assumed—not the behind-the-scenes daily grind
of ensuring passenger safety. Instead, Oberstar worked
hard at cultivating an *image*—he issued press releases, was
always available for television interviews, called for public
hearings to "get to the bottom" of aviation controversies
and made sweeping promises. I reluctantly came to realize
that most of his energy went into those activities, performances keyed to maintaining the "Mr. Aviation" image.
Time and time again I would watch Oberstar on television
talking about aviation issues and using the royal "we"
("When we looked into this . . ." or "We found
that . . .") when I knew that in most cases his office had
not been involved in the investigation or audit he was

discussing. He'd had nothing to do with any of my office's investigations, but I often heard him talking about them as if they were his own. Did he believe that because he worked for government and I worked for government, we were on the same team and could therefore be referred to as one unit? Or that the Inspector General was simply an extension of Congress? Or had he asked one of his staff to call my office with a question, so therefore he was involved in our work?

It hardly mattered how Oberstar justified his proprietary demeanor. There wasn't much I could do about his grand-standing. Still, I would have been delighted to let him take credit for projects he had nothing to do with if only he had used his considerable power and influence to follow through with new safety regulations or laws. It was disap-pointing to discover that "Mr. Aviation" was nothing more than a part Oberstar played. But it was even more frustrating to watch him continually create the impression that safety was being addressed when, in fact, none of the hearings I attended resulted in any new bills or laws. Once the cameras were turned off and the hearings were over, "Mr. Aviation" apparently felt his job was done.

Though eventually I would testify before Congress doz-ens of times, the hearings almost never resulted in legisla-tion or any action that might impose financial or other burdens on big aviation business. Hearings are popular when intense public pressure and media attention are fo-cused on a tragedy; yet in nearly six years as Inspector General, I saw only one piece of proposed legislation re-sult. Only Senator John McCain of Arizona introduced a bill to prevent the diversion of money from the FAA air-port trust fund. Predictably, the bill died with the adjourn-ment of Congress.

Scores of members of Congress did nothing, took no action, did not follow up on hearings with bills. As soon as the hearings were over, their concern and their involve-ment evaporated. In fact, the media-driven hearings often reminded me of the old Judy Garland/Mickey Rooney movies. In those films, whenever the lead characters got into trouble, they'd gather together and exclaim: "Let's put on a show!'' Congress was the same—we'd all be called to their father's barn, but no action was ever taken. Their convictions fell with the curtain.

Even when laws were passed, the lawmakers could not be counted on to see that they were implemented. The 1990 Airport Safety Improvement Act—written, introduced and passed after the tragedy of the 1988 Pan Am flight 103 crash over Lockerbie, Scotland—called for the installation of approved bomb-detecting machines in airports by 1993. By the end of 1996, the machines had not been deployed because of the FAA's cumbersome, comical testing procedures. But the Pan Am flight 103 spotlight had long since moved away from Capitol Hill, making it pointless for any member of Congress to champion the 1990 Act until it became a headline issue again in the aftermath of the TWA flight 800 crash.

Like other industry groups, aviation has a powerful, diverse lobby base with deep pockets—staffed, funded and backed by groups like the Air Transport Association, the Regional Carriers Association, the Air Line Pilots Association, the Alaska Air Carriers, individual airlines, Boeing, McDonnell Douglas, Lockheed, Pratt & Whitney, and contractors like IBM, Wilcox Electronics and Loral. But it isn't only private industry that curries favor with politicians; the FAA does its own share of back-scratching, too. It may not have money to spread around, but it does have its fleet of planes, and it is not at all reluctant to chauffeur politicians around the country and fly members of Congress around on "fact-finding missions." Scheduling hearings in Alaska was another favorite tactic used by the FAA and by certain senators. Surely it was only coincidence if these hearings coincided with Senators Stevens's or Murkowski's salmon fishing tournaments. One of Hinson's trips to Alaska made news when he damaged the plane's landing gear as he overshot a runway that day. But never mind—he got a waiver from the FAA to keep flying.

Still, it is the aviation industry—represented by private businesses, trade groups and lobbyists—that gives millions of dollars to politicians every year. The Federal Election Commission reported that the transportation industry—a list made up of Northwest, Continental and United airlines,

Federal Express Corporation, Clipper Express and the Airline Brokers Co., Inc—gave the Democratic party
$1,348,008 between January 1995 and June 1996. A simi-
lar group made up of Federal Express, Northwest and UPS
contributed an overall $2 million to the Republican party.
These donations are called "soft money," because they
allow donors to contribute to political parties and circumvent the $1,000 limit on donations to individual politicians.
It isn't only money that influences politics and political
parties. Commercial airlines are economic powerhouses in
their communities, like USAir in North Carolina and Virginia, American Airlines in Texas, or ValuJet and Delta
in Georgia. They represent not only economic force and
commercial viability, but a strong connection to the rest
of the world. Politicians understand that if an airline leaves
a community, jobs and resources leave, too, but something
more is lost—the sense that the community is a vibrant
hub, a place worth staying in. Aviation is sexy, and that
is a powerful pull as well. Nobody's adrenaline flows
when the subject is washing machines, but flying excites
people. I had discovered early that members of Congress
were lined up behind commercial aviation, just as the FAA
was. Members who championed safety were the exception,
everyone else the rule. The issues did not break down
along party lines—if a politician had an airline or aircraft
manufacturer in his district or state, then it didn't matter
whether he was a Republican or a Democrat. He'd be
for airlines.

Individual politicians certainly get their share of money,
too. From January 1993 to March 1996, the air transport
industry Political Action Committees gave $919,833 to
Democrats and $1,120,749 to Republicans. Their favorite
senators were Larry Pressler, Chairman of the Senate Aviation Subcommittee ($64,040), Slade Gorton ($36,930 to
the man from Boeing's home state) and Kay Bailey Hutch-
inson ($25,500). Their favorite congressman, not surpris-
ingly, was James Oberstar ($40,250). In the 1994 election
cycle alone, he received a whopping $70,250 from air
transportation interests such as UPS, Federal Express,
Northwest Airlines, United Airlines, American Airlines,
Delta Airlines, Southern Air Transport, the Aircraft Own-

ers and Pilots Association, the American Association of
Airport Executives, and aviation contractors. Plus $45,000
from transportation unions.

Many trade groups do legwork for politicians and their
staff—compiling testimony and reports, packing hearing
rooms, hiring key Hill personnel as their lobbyists themselves. I cannot count the number of congressional staffers
I have worked with over the years who are now lobbyists.
But I remember only a few ever showing up to lobby for
safety, and they were not usually invited to testify. They
had to make their points in the hallway outside the hearing
room. Trade groups and individual lobbyists represent airlines and the aviation industry—not the concerns of
passengers.

A few weeks after my testimony at the 1992 inspections
hearings, reality hit. In spite of its assurances, the FAA
was not going to adopt our recommendations. No explanation, no description of how the agency had been forced to
reconsider its position, no apology for the about-face. The
FAA simply rejected many of our findings and refused to
implement most of our recommendations.

At this point, I realized that the FAA had cleverly ma-
neuvered me into telling Congress that even as we spoke,
action was being taken to remedy the inspections crisis.
Everything was fine, I essentially volunteered, because the
FAA and the Inspector General's office were in harmony,
and the recommended improvements were already being
put in place. It was clever; the FAA certainly played the
new Inspector General like a violin. I vowed that it would
never happen again.

I'd also learned an important lesson—the FAA's modus
operandi was crisis management. The agency saw no reason to change its bureaucratic culture, its devotion to promoting aviation and the practices that furthered that goal.
In time of crisis, like the revelation that airline inspections
were a mere shadow of what the rules called for, the
FAA resorted to media plays. It knew that news of shoddy
inspections would make headlines and top the TV news.
Its goal was to control what news got out and how the
public reacted. It did so with a variation of the mantra I

would hear often—"We have an audit problem, not a safety problem. Safety was not compromised." That meant the problem was not real, it was simply contrived by us because we didn't understand the business. By manipulating the way things look, the agency spins a situation until it is shaped in the most flattering way. It interprets numbers or facts in its favor. It tells the public what it wants the public to believe, then behaves as if that's the only way things can be. Thus relative truth becomes operative truth. These efforts are kept up for as long as a spotlight is on the issue, and just long enough to keep the public, Congress and the press happy or at bay. Once the media crisis has passed, the problem is gone, too, and the bureaucracy can plod along as usual.

Fortunately, I could choose and prioritize my own projects; under the rules of my presidential appointment, I didn't work for the FAA or even the Department of Transportation. My office was entirely independent; only the President could fire me, and only after showing cause. All right, so we were the first to tackle safety. So we hit the FAA wall. All that told me was that it was high time.

Yet in my first year on the job, I learned that the FAA assumed only an enemy would question, challenge or try to change its practices and policies. In truth, I measured my work against one yardstick: the safety and security of the flying public. Yet, at every turn, the FAA argued that I was ignoring a second, equally important consideration: the economic health of the aviation industry.

Soon, I found myself echoing the letter to the U.S. Attorney General: "The regulatees were regulating the regulators."

But that shouldn't have been surprising. A lot of safety mechanisms were overlooked at the FAA. Apparently, nobody at Headquarters ever double-checked on the FAA Examiners who decided whether a mechanic was qualified to work on planes. That is, until my office, astounded at the sloppy inspection of aircraft, decided to probe around in some of the FAA's other inspection activities. We knew that planes and pilots were poorly monitored, and we suspected that aircraft parts got scant attention. Would we

come full circle and find that the mechanics who installed
and repaired those parts and maintained the planes were
haphazardly selected? Perhaps the FAA believed that what
you don't know can't hurt you, but I didn't. I immediately
dispatched field officers to drop in on FAA Examiners and
watch how they did *their* jobs. One of the very first visits
convinced me I was right. Our field staff stood quietly to
one side while the FAA Examiner gave a test that was
supposed to include both a written and an oral exam, and
a practical project. In one case, the investigator watched
as a nervous mechanic waited for a question in the oral
exam. The mechanic needed to understand basic mathe-
matics to get his FAA certification.

"Cite the formula for the area of a rectangle," the Examiner said.

The applicant paused, then answered: "Area is equal to
one half the base times the height."

The Examiner looked at him. It was the wrong answer,
and both the Examiner and the Inspector General investigator knew that. "Okay," the Examiner said carefully.
"Draw a rectangle." The mechanic picked up a pencil—
and drew a parallelogram. The Examiner reached over,
took the pencil and drew a proper rectangle. He described
formulas for using the different sides of the rectangle,
pointing to each side. Opposite them, my agent made a
mental note: coaching the applicant. It would happen thirty
times during the test, even though only twenty-two subjects were covered.

The FAA Examiner went back to his original question.

"So," he said, pointing to the rectangle, "the area
equals base times height."

"Yes, that's it," the mechanic replied eagerly. He
passed.

In fact, thousands of mechanic candidates passed their
certification tests this way. The tests were given by nongovernment employees called Designated Mechanics Examiners. These guys are experienced plane mechanics
appointed by the FAA to test people who want to be certified aviation mechanics. Applicants can try for certification
for plane airframes, power plants, or both. In addition to
the written exam, there are supposed to be four oral ques-

tions and a hands-on project, so the applicants can inspect, troubleshoot, repair or overhaul a plane or plane components in front of an Examiner. The test is supposed to cover dozens of general aviation, airframe and power plant subjects. Our investigation was inspired, in part, by the remarkably high number that passed with no trouble.

When we looked closely at the track record of thirty-five Examiners, we were stunned to find that their testing methods were totally inconsistent, and rarely thorough, and that they frequently lowered test standards. They got away with it because the FAA didn't enforce the rules—partly because the FAA inspectors themselves often had no idea of what the test and equipment requirements were. In 1992, for example, 20,000 people were tested by nearly 700 Examiners—but the FAA scrutinized only 1,200 cases. In the end, it meant only one thing for safety: the FAA could not be sure that qualified applicants passed the test and were certified.

Glaring clues emerged from the nine FAA regions we looked at. They were in charge of supervising 150 Examiners every year. Yet for five years, from 1988, they found only twelve problems with five Examiners—and none were suspended or lost their jobs. Even more ominous, a computer tracked inspections of Examiners and test results, so we could immediately see that those same five Examiners had remarkable students—98.4 percent of the applicants passed. The FAA managers said they kept an eye on the adequacy of inspections by reviewing the pass/fail rate. But they couldn't prove it—there was no documentation that they had monitored things in that or any other way.

Warily, we audited the paperwork, then interviewed inspectors, FAA managers, Examiners and mechanic applicants. In the nine FAA regions, we watched while thirty-five Examiners gave forty-three oral and practical tests. Then we poked around in the tools, equipment and facilities of thirty-seven Examiners, and found that twenty-two of them could not give proper tests because they had bad equipment or were missing it altogether. Without the gear, an applicant couldn't even show he had basic mechanic skills. During the forty-three exams, the Examiners coached applicants, gave test questions in advance, helped

with the hands-on exercise, failed to ask questions in all
the subject areas, passed people who failed to get a minimum grade of 70, and didn't watch the applicants throughout the test. In fourteen cases, FAA inspectors were present. Once, two Examiners gave applicants the test questions in advance, let them study them before the exam, then let them take the test piecemeal over two weeks. The more we watched, the more the students' passing rate dropped. When we accompanied Examiners, the pass rate dropped to 58 percent. When we went with an FAA inspector in tow, the pass rate dropped again, to 40 percent. The results were even more disturbing when it became clear that the Examiners did not give the tests properly. My agents asked them to describe the minimum number of questions required for each subject and the minimum passing grade for each area. Eighty-five percent admitted they didn't know what they were required to ask. Many others couldn't have given the full test even if they had known. Examiners are supposed to have access to planes—a reciprocating and a turbine engine aircraft. Mechanics must demonstrate they can handle tools and parts, follow overhaul and maintenance procedures, inspect for safety and fill out the proper forms. Of thirty-seven Examiners we looked at, fifteen used planes at an approved aviation school. But another twenty-two didn't have the necessary facilities. They were unable to test one or more subjects, and they were limited in the practical tests they gave. One Examiner couldn't test ice and rain control systems, or hydraulic and pneumatic systems, because he just didn't have the equipment. He couldn't test for engine instrument systems, fire protection or engine exhaust. He had no access to aircraft. Yet he passed all 173 people he tested in 1992. We discovered another Examiner giving tests in his spare bedroom. He used books, small tools and equipment like metal tubing, hoses, gaskets, seals, a bit of wire and a voitohmmeter. He didn't have access to any planes, either, yet managed to pass all 126 of his applicants in 1992, too.

FAA inspectors had visited these guys—but found no problems. Could the applicants be blamed because most of the Examiners didn't have the tools, equipment or facilities to conduct the test?

While many of the problems were linked to poor management, there was also outright abuse. Whistle-blowers told us about an Examiner who offered a twenty-minute test for $600, and then gave it to dozens of applicants. Among his candidates were ten mechanics who had not trained for sufficient hours to qualify for the test—but he passed them and they got jobs. It was only after an anonymous complaint from the two airlines where they worked that the FAA decided to check out this corrupt Examiner. The man resigned at once. Eight of the ten mechanics in question also quit their jobs.

The FAA moved with uncharacteristic speed to toughen review of the people who certify mechanics. It agreed that its "surveillance of [Examiners] was not adequate," and promised to review its training programs, develop some Examiner inspection checklists, get regional officers to name an investigator in charge of Examiners' oversight, look into the twenty-two Examiners who abused their jobs and find the mechanics they had certified to see if those people were really qualified for work on planes. They all had to take the test over again.

When my staff moved on to FAA inspections of foreign-made aircraft parts, we had to suspend our investigation after the FAA admitted that the agency does not inspect foreign aircraft-parts manufacturers. At all. To be sure, the FAA completes an initial inspection of a parts manufacturer when the company first receives certification. The law calls for periodic surveillance. It doesn't happen. The FAA simply doesn't do it.

Aircraft parts are manufactured all over the world. Fifteen hundred parts manufacturers contribute to a Boeing 747. Factories churn out parts in Central and South America, Southeast Asia and Africa, producing everything from wing assemblies to avionics and lavatories. The business of parts manufacturing is so diversified that competitors even make parts for each other—McDonnell Douglas makes parts for Boeing; even Airbus makes some components for Boeing. The FAA argues that Boeing and other manufacturers certify every new airplane, meaning that

their inspectors check up on the parts producers more efficiently than the FAA can. But relying on Boeing to complete testing of parts is not fail-safe. In 1997, Boeing itself
was charged with using bogus parts—on government and
commercial aircraft. Furthermore, some foreign-made parts
go straight to the open market. So the final testing never
gets done.

This is especially dangerous because both the good and
the bad players in the aviation industry are keenly aware
that the FAA inspectors are paper tigers. The problem
reaches back for decades; the good guys have given up
expecting the FAA to do better, and the bad guys know
they can flaunt the law, confident they stand little chance
of being caught. This has been especially true since 1989,
when the FAA decided to spare the rod, moving away
from enforcement and penalties, declaring that it was better to work with the industry to solve safety problems
cooperatively. Besides, even when they were caught,
which was very rare, they were only assessed a small fine.

The approach to foreign parts suppliers is even more
hands-off. The FAA insisted that it had "reasonable assurances that supplier parts and services, both foreign and
domestic, are manufactured to an FAA-approved type design and are in safe operating condition." But what are
reasonable assurances? The FAA can't say. Manufacturers
must establish quality-control systems to get FAA certification in the first place, the FAA pointed out, and they
are "required to maintain the system" once they get their
permit. Somehow, the FAA reasons that all foreign manufacturers can be trusted to police themselves. It was
enough, the agency argued, to send inspectors to domestic manufacturers.

"FAA can accomplish foreign supplier surveillance
without regularly scheduled supplier audits by concentrating resources at the domestic manufacturer's facility," the
agency said. Forcing domestic parts makers to toe the line
could be done through "certificate management" of the
manufacturer's license, the FAA said in all seriousness.

Surely such threats just chill the blood of foreign
parts manufacturers.

CHAPTER FIVE

See No Evil: Bogus Parts

On a winter day a month into the Gulf War, a bomb exploded in a British Airways 747 at Kuwait International Airport, engulfing the plane in flames within minutes and spewing chunks of its engine and fuselage all over the tarmac. Lloyds of London insurance inspectors later declared that searing heat, shock waves and chemicals had ruined the plane's engine parts completely. The engine was unsalvageable and had to be destroyed. Workers from Aviation Salvage International gathered its bits and pieces from the airport grounds and put them into storage. The English company hired a local Kuwaiti businessman to keep an eye on the scrap.

The following November, a tip landed in FBI offices: suspicious engine parts were for sale at an Illinois company. Agents, armed with a search warrant, confiscated the parts and tracked the serial numbers—to the British Airways engine blown up in Kuwait. The Kuwaiti businessman had sold them to a Texas company, where a salesman told an undercover agent the parts had been blown up by a terrorist rocket attack in Kuwait. He said the parts were being sold "as is." But investigators discovered that the parts were sold with certificates guaranteeing they had not been subjected to severe heat, stress or fire.

Three troublesome threads combined to make this possible: scrap parts, bad brokers and a repair station willing to skirt the law. Suddenly, engine parts that had actually been blown up were circulating in the U.S., where unscrupulous dealers could sell them to airlines that farm out maintenance to unmonitored repair stations.

In my first months as Inspector General, I learned that my predecessors had made only occasional forays to review just how the FAA inspected parts manufacturers and parts suppliers. The FAA was satisfied with the procedures in place for monitoring parts makers and brokers. The system had been working for years, if not decades, without any critical flaws. But I couldn't help noticing the reports that crossed my desk: allegations about fraudulent aircraft parts were more numerous than ever, aging aircraft fleets still needed replacement parts that their manufacturers no longer made, more and more parts makers were foreign operations, the number of parts brokers and distributors was increasing every year and the price of parts was skyrocketing. Still, the FAA continued to assume that most parts were properly manufactured and safe. This last alarmed me: if the opportunity for making and selling counterfeit parts existed with little FAA oversight, then the chances of getting caught were slim. How could an unscrupulous manufacturer or broker pass up odds like that?

And how extensive was the potential problem of fraudulent parts? Was it a plague in the industry, or just a fraction of the parts out there? No one at the FAA or in my office could say. A computer search of newspaper and magazine articles revealed the bogus aviation parts problem had first been debated as far back as 1957.

But we did know there are over 4,900 FAA-certified aircraft repair stations in the world. If only 1 percent were criminal, that opened the door to hundreds of thousands of bogus parts. In 1991, the FAA got only a few hundred reports of bogus parts. Nevertheless, I knew each report could represent thousands of parts. The number of brokers, on the other hand, is unknown. The FAA says 2,000 to

5,000; some aviation industry estimates put the number at 20,000. Nobody knows, because brokers are unlicensed, unregistered, untrained—and ungoverned by the FAA. They are the broken link in the FAA's regulatory chain. We found that bad brokers would simply close up shop, move to another building or town and resume business under a new name. Eventually, the major airlines and their umbrella group, the Air Transport Association, wanted to see all brokers come under regulation. Yet time and again we would run into the same dead end at the FAA: the agency couldn't help us, since it had no authority over brokers and did not want it.

In the end, we would seize bad parts from almost every kind of aircraft: helicopter blades, brake components, engines, engine starters, fuel bladders, generators, bearings, speed drives, avionics, cockpit warning lights, landing gears, valves and switches, wheels, combustion liners, parts of helicopter tail rotors, windshields and entire wing and tail assemblies. We would confiscate parts made in basements, garages and weld shops, or from major U.S. manufacturers and from Germany, France, England, New Zealand, Canada, Japan, China, the Philippines, Taiwan or unknown countries of origin. They even showed up on the President's helicopters and in the oxygen and fire-extinguishing systems of Air Force One and Two.

Our five years of investigations took my agents all over the country and occasionally overseas, and filled our evidence rooms with crates of reworked scrap and other counterfeit parts. Yet the FAA would steadfastly shrug off what it called "suspected unapproved parts" as a paperwork problem. Some manufacturers made parts without the right FAA permits; others sold certified parts that were overruns and didn't have FAA approval. Unapproved parts could be those that were not manufactured or repaired under authorized procedures. One of the largest aviation manufacturers in the world is Pratt & Whitney, maker of one of the most popular jet engines. We would eventually track down a New York broker who had a local machine shop copy a Pratt & Whitney part. The broker had boxes and packaging printed with the Pratt & Whitney label, except that on some of the bogus boxes, the Pratt & Whitney eagle was flying into the ground. Those parts were new, but made with the wrong materials. The FAA said these were not safety issues. They were only unapproved parts. It was a label the FAA would come to rely on to blur the issue, allowing officials to talk about the investigation without appearing to endorse it or offend the repair stations, the parts manufacturers or the brokers. The FAA wouldn't even use the term "bogus parts." Administrator Hinson would tell Congress: ". . . unapproved parts may fit somebody's definition of bogus parts, but we only deal in 'approved' and 'unapproved.' "

"What we have in fact argued . . ." Anthony Broderick would tell *Air Transport World* in 1994, is "that there is no safety problem associated with undocumented parts; there is no safety problem associated with Part Manufacturer Approvals, and we've never had an accident from a counterfeit or fraudulently documented part."

The FAA would insist that bogus parts had never caused a plane to crash, and that there was no increase in the number of bogus parts, just more reports. But since there was no mandatory requirement that airlines or repair stations turn in fishy parts, how could the agency know?

On my desk lay a computer printout in a light blue folder that clearly indicated the NTSB did not agree. Page after dense page of the information described accidents all through the 1980s that the NTSB tied to counterfeit parts. There were fatal crashes.

". . . a bogus fuel filter was found . . ." in a Cessna that crash-landed in 1984. A "rusted, pitted and rough" fuel system line fitting described as a "bogus part" forced down an agricultural plane in 1985. In 1986, a Cessna lost engine power and flipped over short of a runway because a carburetor airbox had been "improperly repaired by re-drilling a hole in the control arm attachment point." The "total failure" of a "corroded" tail rotor driveshaft that "was not coated with aluminized lacquer as required" and whose "plugs were not installed at the correct distance from the end of the shaft" caused a pilot to lose control of his helicopter in 1986 and crash into a building. A Piper aircraft made an emergency landing after the cabin filled with smoke from a fire caused by a muffler whose "shroud was made of aluminum rather than stainless steel.'' A student pilot was killed in 1988 when the plane he was flying crash-landed after a ''bogus'' oil drain plug failed. Another helicopter crashed in 1989 when its main rotor stabilizer bar separated in flight because ''the tie rod nut was a bogus part and excessively worn.'' A Maule M-5 with ski landing gear crashed during takeoff in 1989 when the left ski broke ''due to being fabricated locally from the wrong steel . . .'' In 1990, a Pan Am Express flight crashed when its nose landing gear jammed ''due to the installation of a bogus part by unknown persons . . .'' In 1992, the pilot of an agricultural plane died when he crashed into a plowed field after his engine stalled and he lost control of his plane because of a ''bogus propeller pitch control cam.'' The NTSB said ''other incorrect or altered parts'' were also found in what was left of the plane's engine. That same year, another agricultural plane smashed into a telephone pole on landing after ''failure of the brake system due to installation of a bogus part.''

A bogus part was even found on a balloon in 1985— the NTSB blamed part of the problem on a ''bogus heater system.'' The pilot had to shut down three propane tanks by hand and landed by relighting a tank each time he wished to make a turn. When he touched down, the balloon blew over the flame, caught fire and was torched.

The pilots and passengers who were hurt or killed would surely argue—if they could—that bogus parts *had* been associated with these accidents. We would find that over a third of the bogus parts reported to us fell into categories that could have adversely affected safety—causing crashes that destroyed planes, injured passengers or took lives.

But the FAA would continue to argue that bogus parts had never caused a crash, largely because the agency changed its terminology. Disturbed by the NTSB reports, the FAA persuaded the board to delete the definition ''bogus'' from its database. All the ''bogus parts'' incidents became ''maintenance''-related problems instead. Moving the goal line like that also let the FAA argue, once again, that what we had was an auditing problem, not a safety problem.

*   *   *

Parts are another key area of the FAA's inspection authority. On a Boeing 737, the engine alone has thousands of different, individual parts. A Boeing 747 has six million, and the FAA says about twenty-six million parts are changed every year. Many are manufactured by subcontractors (some Boeing jets have over 1,500 parts suppliers), and a lot of those are offshore operations—parts suppliers who make wings, engines or windshields in Mexico, Brazil, Singapore, China or African countries. In theory, the FAA is responsible for certifying all these parts manufacturers, and then inspecting their blueprints, their factories, their assembly lines, their workers and, of course, the parts themselves, to guarantee that the machinery is all safe. In practice, the FAA argued it did not have the money to inspect foreign parts makers after they received their initial certification. Domestic parts suppliers, I would learn, were loosely surveyed. The FAA regularly closed cases of suspected unapproved parts without even investigating them if the hardware in question was a standard part, like a bolt. (Someone, somewhere, must once have thought bolts are critical to safety—the Fastner Quality Act sets standards for them.) Since the FAA had no authority over brokers, it often closed cases even when it had flagrantly bad parts in its possession if the alleged distributor was also a broker. When it did inspect parts bins, the agency was sometimes so unfamiliar with the equipment that the inspections were meaningless. And even when the FAA got reports of bogus parts, it had no system for preventing them from sliding into a black hole of neglect. That meant cases were rarely referred to us or the FBI for investigation.

But the extent of the bad-parts problem didn't surface until I met Harry Schaefer.

Schaefer was a supervisory investigator in the Inspector General's Atlanta office. A former Miami Metro-Dade cop, he had put together a case about a bogus parts broker that alarmed him so much he insisted on coming to Washington in early 1991 to see me. He knew that airplane flight is a feat of carefully calibrated engineering. The mechanical elements must operate together smoothly and reliably, and be made with the proper materials. Yet he

was also aware that much of the calibration relied on a
tangled web of repair contractors, maintenance subcontractors and parts brokers. Schaefer walked into my office
carrying a cardboard box of aircraft engine starters. Carefully laying them on the table, he gestured at me to look
them over. It was a bit like a shell game—I knew I was
supposed to guess where the phony was hiding. But I
couldn't tell the difference. My investigations and audits
chiefs looked the parts over and couldn't pick out the bad
ones. Victorious, Harry lifted the middle starter and asked
me to look again. It was a "strip and dip" part, he said.
Even though I turned the part over and peered at it in-
tensely, Schaefer had to point to the flaw. The starter's
side had literally blown out. The eruption had been welded
shut and then sprayed over until it was invisible. But the
weld, Schaefer said, was weak and badly finished. The
part was actually scrap.

This was not a case of improper documentation. The
real threat was from bad parts, not bad paperwork. These
starters were the proof I needed to see for myself—the
prosecutor in me clicked into gear: we needed to measure
the problem, develop cases and turn light fines into tough
criminal penalties.

Some of the most prevalent counterfeit parts were those
that had been sold as scrap (by the U.S. military, for example, one of the largest suppliers of scrap parts), bought by
a broker, rebuilt and then painted over to look like new.
Some were reworked scrap, some were car parts assembled
to look like plane parts. Once they were painted over, it
was impossible to tell whether they were new or counterfeit without tearing a part to pieces and destroying a several-
thousand-dollar investment.

Schaefer had confiscated parts from a guy named Ga-
briel Kish. Kish owned two airplane repair stations in
South Florida that were littered with butchered scrap parts.
Kish had FAA licenses and an FAA inspector had been
to his shop a couple of times. But one license had been
dropped off with no questions asked, and another Kish
himself had picked up at FAA offices. The inspector who
visited spent his time trying to date Kish's secretary. He
never saw the mangled aircraft parts.

"We had four different kinds of speed drives together," Kish later told Congress. "We were robbing parts from Peter to pay Paul, you know, switching parts. Parts were laid out in bags. It is much harder to trace a part like a starter or a constant speed driver, a generator, or a fuel control, because you could intermix all the parts. You could take one housing from one part and put it on another part and it is washed."

While this was going on all over the country, the FAA continued to insist that if we found uncertified parts, that didn't mean the mechanical pieces themselves were faulty or dangerous, it just meant that the paperwork was not up to par.

My office, the airlines and the FBI held a totally different view. Before he came to me, Harry Schaefer had tried to report a Miami manufacturer of bogus jet engine starters—several hundred of which had been confiscated—to the FAA. He knew many of the scrap starters had already been sold to airlines and probably installed on planes. But the FAA refused to order airlines to remove the parts from their shelves and check to make sure bad parts were not on their planes. At a meeting in my office after our investigation had begun, FAA officials insisted there was no epidemic of bogus parts. "We have to consider the economic impact to industry," they said, an explanation that echoed through my years as Inspector General. Schaefer felt, and I was beginning to agree, that the FAA seemed determined not to play second fiddle to the Inspector General. Its officials didn't want to find themselves in the position of having the Inspector General's office ahead of the agency on an investigation. They did not want us telling them what to do. Later, I would sense that a test of wills, even a battle of egos, surrounded the bogus parts investigation. I felt that most strongly when in May 1992, eighteen months after the initial report about the bad starters, the FAA finally ordered the airlines to pull the parts from their planes. It was almost as if they simply wanted to show the Inspector General's office they would take action on their schedule, not ours. Meanwhile, bogus parts proliferated.

Initially, the FAA dismissed the idea of a full-scale attack on bogus parts. They disagreed with our new assessment that the parts were a bigger problem than anyone knew. They were unimpressed with Schaefer's cases in Miami, and mocked him for pursuing them, saying that starters were not a critical part because they were used on the ground (I wondered about the pilots who had to restart shut down engines in flight). They refused to issue an "airworthiness directive," or recall order, for the starters. They defended the conventional wisdom—bogus parts were only a tiny percentage of the parts on the market and in planes. Agency officials insisted nothing we had shown them proved any different. We were asking them to invest money, time and manpower in investigations that simply were not warranted. We were operating outside our jurisdiction. Besides, planes weren't falling out of the sky.

I was concerned that the FAA's determination to protect parts manufacturers, aircraft companies and even airlines would destroy my office's investigations of bogus parts. I truly believed a line I had started using around the office— "if it's on a plane, it could be bogus." I didn't want such a critical safety issue to be dismissed because of the FAA's conflict of interest. Every year I had to appear before Congress and the Office of Management and Budget. During my first year on the job, I had simply presented my budget to these two authorities. I didn't feel I had enough experience—or enough confidence in my observations—to make recommendations for change to either of these groups. But by 1994 I felt differently. An important investigation might be at stake. It was critical for Congress to know that the Department of Transportation Inspector General believed there was a fundamental flaw in the FAA—its dual mandate to promote aviation and regulate safety. So when I sat down before the congressional budget committee, I urged the members to rewrite the Federal Aviation Act to remove the FAA's mandate to promote aviation. It was the first time I made such a suggestion. But it would not be the last.

Our investigation into bogus parts compelled the FAA to set up the first of two task forces on bogus parts. I was

cautiously optimistic that this might mean the agency was
going to join our probe, until an FAA official confided in
me that the real purpose of the task force was to take the
investigations away from us. I resisted and fortunately the
Assistant Secretary of Transportation for Management
agreed with my argument that the FAA was not competent
to take over our law enforcement powers. When that didn't
work, the FAA proposed that the Vice President's reinventing government project transfer jurisdiction for bogus
parts from the Inspector General to the FBI. Our difference
of opinion was irreconcilable. Not only would the FAA
often refuse to assist us in our investigations, it clearly
intended to actively try to thwart our efforts. Though we
had no additional funding, no extra staff and couldn't
change the law or get new regulations, we were determined to press ahead. But we could only get off-the-record
leads from FAA field staff who were clearly terrified of
filing official cases of bogus parts with headquarters. On
many of our investigations, the FAA waffled on declaring
whether a part was certified or not, leaving us with shaky
evidence. FAA officials complained repeatedly to the Secretary of Transportation that we were making the agency
look bad. They complained to Congress that we were
spending too much money, time and manpower on bogus
parts. It got to the point where we hoped officials at FAA
headquarters would not find out about specific cases we
were working on. With the help of the FBI and the airlines, we were gradually having an impact on our own. It
was better if the FAA headquarters stayed out of our way.

One afternoon in the Deputy Secretary's office, I made
a call to the chief of staff at the FAA. By that time,
officials at the agency had become so irrational about
bogus parts that she immediately began screaming at me.
Her shrieking was so loud that I placed the receiver on
the desk so others in the room could hear. Hysterical, she
accused me of destroying the FAA with a public relations
disaster over bogus parts that would scare people away
from flying. All because I had a vendetta against the
agency. Her words made it clear that the FAA was trying
to turn a disagreement with me over bogus parts into a
"personality conflict." That was a favorite tactic, used

frequently with their own inspectors. When inspectors got tough on airlines and the airlines complained, the FAA would cite "personality differences," and transfer the inspector.

If the initial meetings with FAA officials were supposed to intimidate me into backing off, they had the opposite effect. The FAA civil servants were already in over their heads. They clearly had no idea how to organize a criminal investigation or prepare for prosecution. They had no legal expertise in criminal law. Their experience in the past two decades had been limited to handing out fines. I, on the other hand, had handled scores of long-term projects like this. My staff was upset at the hostility and threats coming from FAA officials, but I knew what we would do.

"Don't worry," I said to Ray DeCarli and Harry Schaefer as we left a particularly acrimonious meeting at the agency. "We can work circles around the FAA."

If my staff was alarmed at the turn of events, I was not. I knew the Inspector General's office could do a better job than the FAA at enforcing the law on bogus parts. I could create a national prosecution program; I was thrilled at the prospect. I loved these kinds of investigations. Yet I also knew that if I had asked the FAA to step aside and let my office have this project, the agency would have taken on bogus parts itself. It was only because we initially insisted that they help us that they refused to do so, or even to admit there was such a thing as a bogus part.

The agency's hostility was an obstacle to overcome. There were other partners, and other outlets for information. If I had to embarrass the FAA publicly to force it to acknowledge bogus parts and respond to our evidence, then that was precisely what I would do.

Still, we couldn't get started without cases. We needed the evidence, and we were stymied by years of FAA indifference. The agency insisted that it relied on its own inspectors to detect bogus parts, and on tips from the industry. But only a paltry number of reports came in. The FAA argued that this was due to its vigorous enforcement of the law. The FAA would boast to Congress that its various inspection programs had eliminated the threat of bogus parts. What I knew about the caliber of those programs made me even more concerned.

Bogus parts were out there, in spite of the FAA's saying it had seen few, in spite of claims the problem was all a matter of paperwork. Quickly we discovered the secret—usually when airlines or repair shops found a bogus part, they pulled it out of stock or off the plane and returned it to the manufacturer or broker for a refund. They almost never reported it to the FAA, because that meant the parts would be confiscated as evidence and they couldn't get their money back. And the FAA had never encouraged them to do any different. So from the outset we had few cases and no good way to get reports and evidence of new ones. The only way to change that, we realized, was to educate the maintenance people about the importance of turning in bad parts. Before we could uncover the scope of criminal activity, we had to create a training program. Suddenly, we were not inspectors or investigators but educators. In 1992, we put together seminars for mechanics and quality-control personnel at airlines and repair stations, and for anyone else who would listen to us—the U.S. Customs Service, the FBI, foreign carriers and aviation quality-control organizations. We traveled around the country, setting up formal presentations, explaining what we knew about bogus parts. Schaefer again carried the ball. We carted boxes of sample bogus parts around with us, laid them out on tables and urged the maintenance people to take a good look. We needed them, we said, to hold on to any similar bogus parts they found. Call us, we pleaded, or call the FAA, but report the bogus parts and *hang on to the evidence.*

Almost immediately, reports of bogus parts skyrocketed. They came in because mechanics noticed their color was odd, or that metal edges were rough, or that boxes were improperly labeled. When FedEx mechanics ran across starters they thought were fakes, their quality-assurance department and Inspector General agents tore the $10,000 piece apart and found reworked scrap and car parts. When we made it clear we were building criminal cases that would put bad brokers in prison, FedEx managers saved the bills and letters sent to them as evidence of mail and wire fraud.

Suddenly it was abundantly clear that bogus parts were out there in great numbers. It was simply that no one had thought they were worth reporting. Samples streamed into our offices. There was no way to tell how many there might be, or what overall percentage of parts on airplanes, in parts bins and on the shelves at repair stations were bad parts. There was no way to know how many manufacturers or brokers were dealing in bogus parts. Was it 10 percent or 100 percent of the replacement parts on the market? One of the first steps had to be determining the scope of the problem. We crafted a series of audits and went to repair stations to count their stock. One of those was the FAA's own Logistics Center, where the agency kept the parts inventory for its own fleet. I felt considerable satisfaction at finding that 39 percent of the FAA's own spare parts were suspect. Inevitably, this finding outraged the FAA—they argued with us, insisting that our audit of random samples could not have been accurate, that what we had found was simply "suspected unapproved parts," not bogus parts. Indignant, they declared they would conduct their own survey of FAA bins—and promptly found more bogus parts than we had.

We lacked the authority to review the parts bins of private airlines like Delta or American. Our jurisdiction didn't exactly extend to parts bins in general. Besides, the airlines were cooperating and we suspected the root of the problem was elsewhere. But we were responsible for overseeing the FAA, and one of the FAA's duties was to insure the quality of the parts. So we had the authority to take a look at repair-station parts to determine whether the FAA was inspecting them and how well they did it. Repair stations are the independent airplane garages that subcontract with airlines to fix planes, and they buy a lot of parts. They are often at the low end of the maintenance scale; if an airline like Delta does not have its own facility in an area, it will farm out maintenance to a repair station. If a Delta jet flies to Hong Kong and needs a quick repair, it will be sent to a repair station. Repair station owners should fear bogus parts. But actually, the Repair Station

Owners Association was the most vocally opposed to our investigations. Its leaders seemed to want us to leave them alone and let the system work the way it always had—when the FAA left parts evaluation up to them. The FAA was insecure that its staff did not have the technical or engineering expertise to take a definitive stand on bogus parts. If a part had been examined at Boeing or an airline, then what could an FAA inspector hope to add?

Our studies of repair-station parts bins were mind-boggling: 43 percent of the parts bought from manufacturers were bogus; a shocking 95 percent were fraudulent when they came from parts brokers. With brokers, the repair stations had very little chance of buying genuine parts. *Again* the FAA argued that the parts we found were authentic, they were just missing their labels.

In spite of our findings—and in spite of having a staff of thousands compared with the 430 who worked for the Inspector General—the FAA never repeated our investigation to prove to themselves or the world that bogus parts were simply a matter of bad paperwork. They just insisted that our investigation was wrong.

But the tide had turned against the FAA. Once the parts began flooding in, the FBI joined our investigations. I had worked with FBI agents as a federal prosecutor, and knew they were especially well suited to this kind of detective work. We had the aviation expertise, but they had the manpower we lacked and the legal authority to go undercover, which we could not do without them. It was most interesting to me that, at the start of one large case, the FBI was reluctant to include the FAA. A confidential informant had insisted that the use of graphite spray to cover faulty parts was so widespread and so blatant that the FAA *had* to know about it. The FBI believed the FAA had chosen to ignore the problem. They did not want the FAA to know too much too soon. When we finally did tell the agency, the FAA's response was to threaten to release a statement declaring that the parts in question, jet engine turbine blades, were safe. These blades were used at TWA, and FAA Administrator Thomas Richards feared that proceeding with our case and seizing the blades would shut down the airline. Before any FAA announcement went out,

I rushed to the Secretary of Transportation. Any notion of such a statement had to be stopped. The FBI had a warrant to raid this parts manufacturer and seize hundreds of suspect blades. The U.S. Attorney's office was poised to subpoena all the major airlines and order them to check their inventories for blades or vanes bought or repaired through this company. The FAA knew this. It was outrageous that the FAA threatened to tell the world that these jet engine blades were safe, and the Secretary seemed to agree with me. But that wasn't the end for the FAA. When chemical tests detected graphite spray on the blades, the FAA's assistant chief counsel wrote a letter proclaiming that it was unconcerned about cracks in the blades.

"While certain defects may exceed permissible limits, the FAA cannot say at this time that they compromise safety of flight," the FAA attorney said. He also argued that the U.S. Attorney's office had to understand that the airlines were allowed to push parts standards to the limits. "Example: A blade, following a visual check, is found to be out of tolerance with specs for crack growth. An airline may, however, under existing performance and reliability procedures, be allowed, through its engineering departments in consultation with the FAA, to exceed original allowances or limitations."

Was he saying that no one should be prosecuted for selling faulty blades to airlines because the carriers were allowed to inspect the blades, decide they could stand the stress of flight, get a waiver for the blades from the FAA and then fly with the bad blades in place? Apparently so.

The ornate marble floor glinted, cold and elegant, down the hall and into the cavernous committee hearing room. Weary, I crossed the shiny, hard, imposing stone that was washed clean every day. Forget leaving a mark here. Had I tried already ten times? Or fifteen? Maybe this makes two dozen? Reluctance pulled on me like the heavy stack of documents in my briefcase. No comfort in the stiff chair aimed directly at the elevated platform for members of Congress. Many discussions, reports and days of testimony had evaporated into thin air in this room. The first time I had testified before Congress, I had felt honored to take

part in the legislative process. But since then I had been
alternately vilified and praised in rooms like these. I had
heard myself attacked for overstepping my boundaries and
inflicting burdens on the FAA or the aviation industry. I
had listened to compliments and congratulations for being
the only government representative willing to go out on a
limb for aviation safety. I had been told by congressional
staff that the only point of my testimony was so their
bosses could get on TV while they a) attacked me or b)
praised me. And I had seen more politicians than I care
to remember turn on a dime over an issue, depending on
whether their party was in power (and thus whether they
controlled the purse strings and the chairman's chair at
the hearings).

I made few friends in those chambers, and developed
little respect for most of the individuals I dealt with there.
Over the years, plenty of observers variously argued with
or supported my priorities as Inspector General, but none
ever accused me of abandoning my principles or changing
course in midstream. They said I was too prosecutorial.
They said I had an inappropriate interpretation of my mandate. But they never said I didn't believe in what I was
doing.

The bogus parts revelations were so critical that several
members of Congress clamored for hearings on the investigation. First, Representative Oberstar—in a repeat performance regarding our inspections investigation—asked for
a briefing of our findings. I had come to realize that in
spite of asking for briefings, Oberstar and his staff would
have their minds made up before we arrived and would
tell the FAA everything I said. I couldn't refuse, but I
went reluctantly, carrying charts, photographs and a few
bogus parts. This was March 1994, and it did not escape
my notice that in the three years my office had been investigating bogus parts, Oberstar had never expressed any
interest. Now that the media was very interested in our
findings, suddenly so was he. I watched as Oberstar, acting
appalled, examined some of the scrap parts and photos.
Shaking his head, he declared that his subcommittee had
to take up this matter. Mentally I reminded myself of
Oberstar's previous performance and later betrayal, yet it

was hard not to believe him as he stood in his office holding a counterfeit airplane part. How could he not see the seriousness of these investigations? The tangible evidence was in his hands! However, shortly after that meeting, Anthony Broderick called my office to complain that I had gone to see Oberstar. He was incensed that we had not invited along someone from the FAA so our offices could present a united front. I don't know if the FAA's anger had anything to do with it, but after that call, Oberstar lost interest in holding hearings on fraudulent parts. It would be another member of Congress, Senator William Cohen of Maine, who actually called the hearing.

That hearing was packed with reporters, representatives of the airline industry, aircraft, helicopter and parts manufacturing associations, and FBI agents, all ready to testify that bogus parts were a serious problem. Senator Cohen of Maine waved a plastic bag of bad blades just like those we'd confiscated before a Senate hearing on bogus parts. One of his staff had just bought the blades, he said. On a table in front of him and other members of Congress lay an array of our "props"—bogus spacers (the seals that keep oil in the engine from igniting), a counterfeit nose wheel, fake starters. Cohen was dismayed that many FAA employees he had invited to testify about finding bogus parts they could not report were afraid to come to Washington and speak out. But he did wave a signed letter from the Professional Airways Systems Specialists, the union representing 10,000 FAA engineers and electricians.

"Unfortunately, PASS strongly believes that aviation safety is seriously jeopardized by the FAA's continued failure to identify and to curtail the use of suspected unapproved parts (bogus parts) in our nation's aircraft," the PASS leaders wrote. "The production of unapproved parts is egregious and out of control. Eventually, PASS fears that bogus parts will have a direct adverse impact on operating safety and on the unsuspecting flying public."

The aviation industry left no doubt that in this case, it sided with the Inspector General. The Regional Airline Association, the Air Transport Association of America, the Aerospace Industries Association, the General Aviation Manufacturers Association, the Air Suppliers Association, and the Helicopter Association International all told Congress that something had to be done about bogus parts. And of course the FBI was not shy about it, either.

"The FBI currently has several major undercover investigations involving 'bogus' unapproved parts," Thomas Kubic, the FBI's chief of financial crimes section, told Congress in 1995. Bogus parts, he said, meant used parts that are offered as refurbished but to which nothing has been done, parts produced by machine shops that have no idea of the purpose or critical nature of the part, and scrap parts. "The FBI considers violations of law by persons selling defective or unapproved parts very seriously and accords these cases the highest priority."

But more telling than the FBI's position was the criticism of the aviation industry. Early in our investigation, the quality-assurance manager at Northwest Airlines wrote a stinging memo to the Air Transport Association.

"The subject/problem of bogus and unapproved parts in the Aviation Industry is real, perverse and it cannot be solved by any one industry segment," James Frisbee wrote. He warned that airlines like his were "very vulnerable to getting bogus or unapproved parts on our aircraft, in fact they were on our aircraft now."

Frisbee was equally blunt with Congress. At the same 1995 hearing, he blasted the ". . . lack of surveillance by the FAA over some twenty, thirty years . . .

"Rather than addressing the problem with an action that would solve it, the FAA has been a part of the problem," Frisbee charged. ". . . the FAA had to be dragged kicking and screaming to the point where they would admit a problem . . . existed."

Ironically, the only major agency not to testify that day was the NTSB. But there was a story in that morning's *Washington Post* that the NTSB had confirmed, once again, that bogus parts had never caused a plane crash. The NTSB was still playing along with the FAA's insistence that it not use the term "bogus parts" in its database.

Most of the hearing was detailed, respectful, important. Then Senator Carl Levin, a Democrat from Michigan with a large aviation industry back home, took the microphone. He didn't want to hear about crashes in which bogus parts had been a factor; he didn't want to dwell on the seized scrap parts arrayed in the hearing room; he wasn't eager to ask about the FBI's or the airlines' demand that something be done about bogus parts. Instead, Levin spent long, hostile minutes drilling me about my definition of "bogus," and how it differed from the term "suspected unapproved parts" favored by the FAA. For what seemed like an eternity we circled the subject, the Senator obsessed with splitting hairs over whether "bogus" meant "counterfeit" or simply "undocumented." It seemed to me that the reworked scrap metal on the table in front of him should amply have answered his questions. But I knew the point was not to establish whether bogus parts threatened people's lives. It was to attack the Inspector General on behalf of the FAA and the aviation interest groups back home and the companies that contributed to his war chest, like Northwest Airlines (even though Frisbee, one of its former managers, was concerned about bogus parts) and McDonnell Douglas.

With its own constituency so bitterly critical of it, the FAA could no longer deny that bogus parts were a problem. But as FAA staff began working with us officially, their "help" frequently amounted to writing letters to suspected bogus parts manufacturers and asking them to stop their unapproved business. Often this meant our leads went cold. Worse, evidence sometimes disappeared. At the FAA's own Oklahoma City facility, our investigators found suspicious brakes. The investigators told the FAA official in charge they would collect the brakes in the morning—but the next day the box of parts had disappeared. No one on the FAA staff could say what had happened to them. To this day the mystery has not been solved, nor is the FAA concerned that evidence disappeared into thin air at its guarded facility.

If FAA field staff wrote reports indicating they had found bogus parts, the rulings were often changed at FAA headquarters. When we insisted airlines and repair stations should be notified about bogus parts we had seized or received, the FAA consistently refused to issue warnings. To be sure, the FAA requested many meetings with my office—meetings that I later realized were nothing more

than a delay tactic. By the summer of 1992, the new FAA
Administrator, Thomas Richards (he'd replaced Barry Harris), was alarmed enough about our numerous bogus parts
cases and the black eyes we were giving the FAA to complain to the Secretary of Transportation.

"What does concern me deeply is the notion that may
have been conveyed that this problem is somehow new;
that it is rapidly growing; or that it presents a major present or future threat to aviation safety. None of these are
true," Richards wrote in a letter. "FAA inspectors have
been investigating instances of suspected unapproved parts
for decades. We are unaware of any evidence that shows
that instances of safety-related unapproved parts being sold
are substantially more prevalent now than a few years ago.
As I said, what is growing, and we are pleased to see, is
an interest in investigation of these cases for what some
of them merit—criminal prosecution."

Then he really came to the point. "Public statements
that give the impression that these are new issues, that
there is a growing safety problem, or that the public is
somehow threatened by a new breed of criminal activity,"
Richards wrote, "only serve to further depress an industry
which hardly needs that help."

Richards and I had clashed early over bogus parts. In
August 1992, the Secretary of Transportation and his senior staff asked to see the kinds of parts we were concerned about, and to hear what our investigation had
turned up so far. So we repeated Harry Schaefer's drama,
laying out fakes alongside genuine parts and asking Department of Transportation and FAA officials to pick the
real thing. We had bogus aircraft starters, flap indicators,
components for a Pratt & Whitney 727 engine, and parts
that were sold as aviation parts but that actually came
from a car. They were the same props we took to our
seminars around the country. I knew no one in the Secretary's office, or at the FAA, would be able to tell the good
from the bad. We had arrived early to lay out all this
machinery on tables in the Secretary's conference room
so that when the officials walked in, the first thing they
saw was tables full of aviation parts. Richards apparently
interpreted the display as a personal affront. He belliger-

ently explained that some so-called bogus parts were in fact used by the Air Force, and they were perfectly fine. Twenty minutes into our presentation, he got up pointedly and bolted from the room, his anger barely contained.

Later, his office said he had left because he had another meeting, but a member of his staff confided that he was overwhelmed—and insulted—by the boxload of bogus parts we brought with us. Two weeks later, the Secretary ordered a repeat performance. The room was jammed with FAA officials, including the Administrator, the Secretary's heads of budget and international affairs, and many Assistant Secretaries and the general counsel. That time, Richards stayed until the end.

Richards was a retired Air Force general, and not used to being questioned or defied. Like Admiral Busey, he liked a good dose of the chain of command and objected keenly to the idea of anyone telling him what to do. Every time I saw him, I couldn't help but remember a line in an old Bing Crosby song from the movie *White Christmas:* "What do you do with a general when he quits being a general?" In Richards's case, make him head of the FAA.

In the end, after three years of investigation and 160 convictions, there have been few substantial changes in the parts oversight at the FAA. It isn't against the law to make bogus aircraft parts; it is only illegal to falsely claim they are certified by the FAA. There was no criminal violation in selling faulty parts "as is" to airlines or repair stations. Since the Department of Transportation has no regulatory authority over parts brokers, we were hard pressed to charge the bad ones with a crime. The FAA refused to consider regulating parts brokers; the agency said new rules would not stop people who were already breaking existing laws. Our team wanted to charge them under a statute created for hijackers that declared it was illegal to endanger aviation, but the FAA fought us. In one case, it was reported that the FAA pressured the NTSB to alter a crash report so that a bogus part was blamed for being only one factor in the accident and not the direct cause of deaths. In another case, the FAA wrote a memo declaring that engine housing would contain any shrapnel created by fan blades disintegrating in flight—a tragic scenario that *does* happen; two were killed on a Delta flight in 1996. So in the end, taking a page from my experience as a federal prosecutor, we frequently charged the bogus parts dealers with wire and mail fraud—they had used telephone and postal services for felonious purposes: selling bogus parts. Though we got our convictions, I later read that Tony Broderick cited them as proof needed for a wholesale dismissal of our bogus parts investigation: "If you look at most of her convictions," Broderick told the industry newsletter, *Aviation Daily,* "it was from mail and wire fraud and had nothing to do with violations" of FAA regulations. Splitting hairs like that may absolve the FAA from failing to catch bogus parts, but it certainly does not send a safety message to parts manufacturers, brokers, repair stations and airlines.

The FAA did establish a "suspected unapproved parts" database, and sent out an announcement of the database and a warning about scrap parts. But it still refused to rule that bad parts had to be reported, even when the aviation industry clamored for mandatory reporting rules. The industry also asked the FAA to regulate brokers, and the agency refused to take that step, too. It would not require that old parts be destroyed so unscrupulous brokers could not recycle someone else's trash—partly because the Department of Defense balked at losing the money it earns from selling its scrap parts.

The FAA did announce an "enhanced compliance" rule—meaning a parts manufacturer who did not have approval for his parts could turn them in by a certain date and not face punishment. Anthony Broderick told Congress this was not an amnesty, since anyone illegally manufacturing parts could still be prosecuted if the information came to the FAA from a source other than the compliance program.

But in March 1995, Sarah MacLeod, the publisher of *The Hotline,* the newsletter from the Aeronautical Repair Station Association, cooed that Anthony Broderick "is due to be knighted for his PA (Parts Approval) Amnesty Program.

"He'll be one miracle shy of sainthood," MacLeod

gushed, praising the program for granting provisional parts manufacturing approvals. "Astride his white horse, Tony Broderick is leading the way."

In the midst of our investigations, Anthony Broderick stood up at a chicken-and-peas banquet held by the Aeronautical Repair Station Association and warned the audience about the Inspector General.

"In the past couple of years, the oversight equation has changed somewhat, as I am sure you have seen," Broderick began. "A relatively new participant in the oversight process—one whose participation has been greeted by us with mixed feelings—is the Office of the Inspector General of the Department of Transportation. The IG has two functions—oversight and criminal investigation. It is clear that you should carefully ascertain which of these functions is being exercised, should you come into contact with the IG auditors or investigators. The difference may be very important!" The remarks left no doubt where Broderick stood on bogus parts investigations.

"In doing this, she and her people are not making a statement that this is the number one safety problem in the industry," Broderick said. "Indeed, we know that is not true. But from all the activity in this area, the wide publicity that these investigations can generate, and the independence of the investigative element from the technical safety arm of the DOT, I am afraid that a large burden is being placed upon the industry."

Once again, the FAA was more concerned about the health of industry than the health of passengers.

But just when the Department of Transportation seemed completely unwilling to acknowledge the bogus parts problem, a letter arrived from the Coast Guard. Admiral J.W. Kime was a Coastie's Coastie, a commandant who often said the Coast Guard's only purpose was to save lives. We had not been able to afford an audit of their parts bins and had asked them to help us. They insisted on reviewing every single part, not just looking at a random sample as we had done at the FAA. They'd found bogus parts, but they were not defensive about them. Their swift response put an end to any controversy before it could even begin.

"Bogus parts are certainly a safety issue in the aviation community," the Admiral wrote. "Consequently, we undertook a coordinated program to identify and purge Bogus Parts that we were holding in our inventory and prevent their acquisition in the future. Initially we concentrated on flight critical parts, which could cause the loss of an aircraft if they failed in flight. Our efforts to date have resulted in over 1,200 parts purged from our inventory and we expect that number to grow as our inspection continues. We plan to enlarge the scope of our audit procedure to include all suspect parts."

I was thrilled with the Coast Guard's response (and not surprised at the number of bogus parts they found), but Kime was not finished. He had ordered a program to ensure that all flight critical parts would be bought, repaired or overhauled by certified suppliers. Those suppliers would be inspected, and a computer program would look for any pattern of bad parts. If the computer detected a surge in bad parts, then all the parts and facilities connected to that supplier would get an emergency inspection, he said.

A tangled knot of repair contractors, maintenance subcontractors and parts brokers complicates the FAA's already difficult job of monitoring aircraft repair and maintenance. The FAA's inspection infrastructure is set up and accustomed to dealing with major airlines. In recent years, however, there has been a surge in discount carriers and independent start-up commuter airlines. They buy old planes and patch them together with replacement parts. To keep costs low, these companies farm out maintenance and repair duties to dozens of contractors and repair stations. Lots of those, in turn, keep their costs down by buying parts from foreign manufacturers, dealing with discount brokers or opening shops overseas, where labor is cheap. ValuJet bought used planes and contracted with outside maintenance shops. So did Tower Air, and the new Pan Am. Thus a stickier web is spun for the FAA to sort out, something the agency does badly to begin with. Safety is not enhanced by the FAA's insistence that there is no epidemic of bogus parts. Harry Schaefer knew that, and for his role in exposing bogus parts, he later won the

Department of Transportation's highest honor, the Dwight
D. Eisenhower Award. He got $10,000, and a bronze bust
of Eisenhower, too.

Anthony Broderick was investigated by the FBI and the
Defense Criminal Investigation Service for obstruction of
justice and perjury in the jet engine fan blades case. He
was never indicted. Broderick now roves the world as a
consultant on U.S. aviation.

When I resigned, five years after starting the bogus parts
investigations and a year after the massive hearings in
Congress, the FAA had appointed an acting director for
its second "suspected unapproved parts" task force.
Throughout 1995 and 1996, we won convictions across
the country against brokers who had dealt in counterfeit
parts. But the FAA couldn't find anyone to accept the task
force job permanently. The acting head must have thought
he knew why. Shortly before I left the Inspector General's
office, he gave an interview and painstakingly explained to
the press and public: "There is no bogus parts problem."

But on May 3, 1997 even Boeing was charged by the
U.S. Department of Justice with using bogus parts on military helicopters. On October 29, 1997, a $10 billion civil
fraud suit was made public charging Boeing had encouraged inspectors to falsely certify parts as airworthy on the
747, 757, 767 and Air Force planes. Letters from within
the FAA surfaced after a December 1997 Silk Air crash
killing all aboard a new 737. The FAA had secretly chastised Boeing in 1993 for using bad parts on 737s from
1990 to 1992. Yet another whistleblower produced FAA
letters documenting unapproved parts problems on the 747
line in 1994.

CHAPTER SIX

Cash Cows: Where Your Airport Money Went

Tiny blue-gray numbers on a monitor flashed the boarding time for our TWA flight to Barcelona. I sighed; still several hours away. A long, uncomfortable trip loomed, and the delay in New York was not helping. My husband, Alex, and I were hungry, so we went in search of something to eat at Kennedy Airport. People charged around us, zigzagging through the terminal, pulling suitcases, pushing strollers and dragging children. Commotion drew me to the nearest cafeteria. People milled around the buffet while workers yelled in the kitchen. An exasperated manager announced a wildcat strike and then shouted at the crowd: "Help yourselves to whatever is left!"

Yogurt and battered fruit would have to do. We left money on the cash register and settled at a wobbly little square of Formica that passed for a table. Underfoot, napkins, straw wrappers and bits of food littered the floor. Overhead, a streetlight glinted crookedly through blinds that hung broken and uneven in a dirty picture window. A sudden movement caught my eye and I turned toward it just as Alex pivoted, too—and a rat scurried along the tile under our table.

As I watched the rat disappear, I thought about recent investigations my office had done—lax security at Kennedy Airport, bad engine blades on TWA planes. I took out a piece of paper, scribbled a quick will and mailed it to my sister.

Kennedy Airport—the flagship terminal for the United States. An Ellis Island for the end of the twentieth century. In my bag was a $600 ticket for the flight to Spain, and I shook my head at the coy little sum in the bottom right-hand corner—$6 for the international departure tax, plus a ticket tax, plus a passenger facility charge. Some facility. The place was revolting.

The law says the passenger tax cannot be more than $12. In fact, it doesn't need to be. So many people buy tickets every year that since the taxes were imposed—some as early as 1981—the airlines have collected about $10 billion from passengers in $6, $10 or $12 increments. The FAA gets about 70 percent of its budget from this fund. Until 1995, that is, when the tax expired while Congress fought for many months over that year's Appropriations Bill (it was restored in the second half of 1996; it expired again and was restored in 1997).

Large sums of the money are also used for grants to airports so they can make improvements. The airlines turn the tax over to the FAA, which then deposits the money in a trust fund. When an airport needs a new runway, it simply applies to the trust fund, gets a grant and starts building. This way, the fund distributes the burden of airport upkeep and modernization among the people who actually fly. There is no similar tax on railroads or ocean ports; this is special, just for air travel, and quid pro quo dictates that the money be used only for airport improvements. Airports can spend these funds on just about any infrastructure—the criteria are pretty lenient. New runways, taxiways, towers, terminals, passenger and baggage areas, or any measure that makes airports secure and safe. Even prettier, more comfortable passenger lounges. All an airport authority has to do is submit a grant request to the FAA. No priority system exists for projects. Money is awarded on a regional basis, and the doling out depends heavily on the judgment or whims or friendships of the regional administrators. Thus the awarding of money can become fraught with political intrigue. Members of Congress have been known to pressure the FAA. Some regional administrators are better at their jobs—or perhaps more susceptible to pressure—than others.

The fund is a good idea, but like many others in Washington, it has broken down at just about every level. The Airport and Airway Improvement Act of 1982 says that before an airport can get any money, it has to agree not to spend airport funds outside the airport, the airport system or other local facilities owned or operated by the airport. But some airports had signed contracts or other financial obligations that preceded 1982; the New York—New Jersey Port Authority had sold bonds backed by the fund, for example. So those airports were grandfathered into the law. Thus not all airports have the same rule. An even tougher dictate was included in the 1994 and 1995 appropriations legislation: no government legislation money would go to states or municipalities that diverted airport funds.

For much of 1996, it didn't matter. Renewal of the tax was hostage to Congress's fighting over the Appropriations Bill. The tax expired, and for most of 1996 none of the money was collected. The fund lost about $450 million to $500 million a month, going from $5.1 billion in 1995 to $2.4 billion in 1996. The money was eventually replaced by funds from the general revenue and the tax was reenacted in 1997, with a 7.5% ticket tax, plus a $3 segment fee imposed on each leg of the flight, international departure tax of $12, an international arrival tax of $12, and a passenger facility charge of $3 up to $12.

But the worst abuse may come from the FAA itself.

I never forgot that the $6 I had paid, and that many of those other people scurrying around me had paid, had not spared me from having to sit at Kennedy with rats, dirt, delays and fears.

"We're going to look at this fund," I announced after a congressional request echoed our concerns. "I want to know where the money is going."

We examined sixty-five airports—a tiny fraction of the five thousand in the country—run by forty-three different bodies. All of them took FAA funds, but more than half spent the money on projects outside the airport.

In every case in which money was spirited away, the airport authority was controlled by local city politicians. City officials appropriated passenger tax money to pay for projects off the airport property. If the airport had to answer to a political body—states, cities and other municipalities that appointed the airport board or managers—vast sums were siphoned away. Mayors and politicians used the FAA money as a source of revenue for projects for which they did not have money or want to raise their own taxes. Politicos dipped into air safety for a total of $170 million in diverted money.

In Westchester County, New York, the local airport had a budget surplus from 1990 to 1993, and $23.7 million of those funds were spent on nonairport projects.

In Hawaii in 1991, politicians allotted $64.4 million in airport trust funds to buy land next to the airport—for a dog track. The airport didn't need the land, and it wasn't used for the airport. But for months, the FAA, the airport and the city insisted that the land was originally required for the airport. We refused to accept this twisted explanation. Finally, the city agreed to give back the $64 million—in land. It would donate the unneeded land, instead of returning the cash. We fought this, too, and eventually the FAA conceded that the airport had no use for the land. Then the city folded. It said it would have to raise the payback money by selling bonds—though it just could not say whether enough bonds would sell, when the sale would begin or how long it would take.

Then there was Los Angeles. City politicians there diverted money for local police, expense account dinners, lobbying, contributions to city organizations, and to pay for a float each year in the Rose Bowl parade. A $6.4 million police substation was located on airport grounds, but 81 percent of its patrol calls were off the airport property and not airport-related. The city also kept $2.3 million in airport revenues from parking and traffic citations issued by airport police. The FAA, in 1995, agreed to try to figure out how much of the substation's activities were not airport-related and should not be paid by the airport.

In 1996, the agency still didn't know. For several years, Los Angeles has tried to justify taking airport money by arguing that it is only a fraction of what the airport owes the city on a debt that stretches back to the 1920s (a time when Orville Wright signed the nation's pilot licenses). It audited city and airport records, and found between $5 million and $30 million in airport debts to the city, which, with interest over the last seventy years, leaves the airport between $250 million and $350 million in the hole. However, the city didn't look for any debts it might owe the airport in return.

Even more twisted, in Los Angeles and Denver, the cities spent airport funds on trying to change the law banning the use of airport funds for city expenses. There is no ban on using airport revenue to pay for lobbyists working on airport issues. Airports cannot pay for unrelated promotion or marketing with the money. But they can use them for airport issues—even if that includes using airport funds to lobby officials to let the city divert airport money!

Yet where the airports were independent port authorities unbeholden to a mayor or a city council, there was no diversion of funds. In every case in which the port authority was independent, the funds stayed at the airport where they belonged. Twenty airports used their grant money only for improvements of the facilities.

Of course, the FAA is charged with monitoring how the grant money is used. But it never followed up after checks were handed out. There was no oversight of the program at all. The money was distributed when requested, and no FAA official ventured out to see how it was being spent. After our investigations began in 1992, the House of Representatives Appropriations Committee Subcommittee on Transportation grew irritated with the violations we found, and ordered the FAA to come up with stricter guidelines for the money and to get the diverted funds back. Congress was serious and set a 1994 deadline—but still the FAA took no action.

Finally, in 1996, with hearings in Congress looming, the FAA announced a proposal for compelling cities to pay back airport money they had used for other purposes. But the agency neglected to throw down the gauntlet—

there was no penalty for diverting the funds. Actually, it was an amnesty program. All the cities had to do was pay back the money, no questions asked. In the end, the burden was even less onerous—the proposal went out, all right, yet the rule was never enacted. The FAA never began checking on how money was spent, and the delinquent politicians who knew that my office had investigated the fund realized we could not keep up our audits forever. Both the House and the Senate eventually held hearings on the fund diversions. I knew nothing would come of the House hearings before the committee "Mr. Aviation" sat on. One congressman at the hearing even fumed and thundered that things were just fine until the IG started poking her nose in things. But I had hope in the Senate.

Arizona Senator John McCain asked my office to write legislation making it illegal to divert airport money. Ray DeCarli, Larry Weintrob, our staffs and I worked nonstop to produce the proposed legislation in two days. Our proposed law had some teeth. Airports had to hire outside independent auditors to certify there was no diversion. People who reported diversions would have whistleblower protection. If diversions were found and money recovered, the whistleblowers got a share of the cash—like a finder's fee. McCain introduced the bill the following week, but it died with the end of the 104th Congress. Inevitably, the dust eventually settled around the fund and the routine resumed—no one looks at how the money is spent, so the diversions probably persist. Hundreds or perhaps thousands of American airports continue to operate without modern radar, instrument landing systems, wind shear radar, proper security or clean terminals. But there is land for a nice dog track in Honolulu and several years' worth of beautiful Rose Bowl floats in Los Angeles to show for the fund.

CHAPTER SEVEN

Relative Truth:
CULT-ure at the FAA

In his management classes for FAA officials, Gregory May taught that there are four kinds of truth: Universal Truth, World Truth, Personal Truth and Belief. In his lectures, he fixated on truth as a matter of perspective, stressing that one person's truth may not be another's. This was Relative Truth.

Whether that meant there were really five kinds of truth, I'll never know. And exactly why May, a psychologist, was hired to redefine reality at the FAA, I will probably never understand. I tend to deal in tangible truths.

Like the fact that for eleven years, the FAA paid Gregory May and Associates a total of $1.6 million to run training seminars based on New Age lingo and the teachings of a middle-aged blond cult-like leader born in Roswell, New Mexico, who claims to have had an encounter with UFOs and says that a 35,000-year-old spirit named Ramtha channels its voice through her body to impart wisdom about the meaning of life. Media reports referred to the Ramtha group as a cult. Vanity Fair simply says "New Age fruit bat."

Or the truth recounted by FAA employees and trainers, who said that at these seminars, May and other trainers screamed they were "assholes, jerks and idiots" during classes; deprived them of sleep and food; forced them to discuss sexual habits, personal relationships, abuse or other trauma during group therapy sessions; and tied them together for days at a time and made them shower or go to the bathroom that way.

And the stranger-than-fiction truth that over 4,000 senior FAA managers volunteered for or were required to attend these courses and meekly endured the outrageous rituals because they were convinced May wielded such power with their bosses that he could make or break their careers.

Or the sad truth that everybody accepted this notion and nobody complained because for decades the FAA had crafted its own truths about many things, including its purpose and the importance of safety, and anyone who challenged those views was an enemy. Within the closed culture of the FAA, fear and intimidation dominated a top-down management style that expected workers to play along in order to get along. Change was not wanted, challenges were not welcome and neither were people who reported problems or abuses. Workers who exhibited such behavior were quickly broken down. The same people who called the FAA the Tombstone Agency sometimes also referred to it as the Stepford Wives Agency (Transportation Chief of Staff Ann Bormolini liked to use this term)— because everyone followed in lockstep with the party line. Employees were not encouraged to think for themselves.

Then there was the more craven truth that an initiate of May's got him hired at the agency, and then other cronies in the procurement department saw to it that his $1.6 million was paid in individual checks of $25,000 or less, so the more than 200 contracts would not have to be publicly offered for competitive bids and no one could determine a final figure of how much was paid to May.

And the truth that May was finally brought to justice not by degraded employees but because he defrauded FAA insurance carriers, falsifying medical records for FAA employees who filed claims saying the seminars they attended were really legitimate psychotherapy sessions.

Of course, it was also true that the FAA tried to block an Inspector General investigation into the May deal by retroactively approving the habit of breaking up the contracts to hide their real value. Our investigators struggled to collect evidence from some hysterical FAA managers convinced that we were on a witch hunt for anyone who had taken the cult-like training. In the midst of all this paranoia, I would realize it had been easier to get information out of Mob witnesses.

The truth about the Gregory May training was first visited upon me by a woman who worked in the Inspector General's office. She stopped by my office for a chat, and I was startled to learn that it was not about her job. Instead, she wanted to tell me about a training course. The seminar had compelled her to change her life—she had left her husband and gotten a divorce. It was, she said proudly, the best thing she had ever done. For several days, she said, she and a group of federal employees had contemplated their lives, talked about their innermost secrets, vented their feelings about their relationships, read books and taken long walks. It turned my life around, she said firmly.

Probably I just stared at her, feigning interest. I admit I have always disliked such seminars and management retreats. Usually they are artificial and a waste of time. Training courses that claim to promote personal empowerment so people can do their jobs better have always bugged me even more. I don't think I'd ever seen or heard of one that made a long-term tangible difference to job performance. Certainly people feel better for a while. But the euphoria is usually short-lived. I can safely say that a couple of weeks at a spa would make me do my job better, too. It is not something the government should pay for, however. Listening to my colleague gush about the group therapy sessions, role-playing games and meditation at her training course, I couldn't help but wonder: what did this training have to do with this office? And why should the taxpayer foot the bill?

More important, Inspector General funds were precious. I battled for our budget every year with Congress and the Department of Transportation. The FAA was constantly trying to have parts of my funding taken away to thwart our audits or punish us for our investigations. I didn't want any hard-won money spent on questionable "self-development" training courses. Besides, who would really miss a few obscure classes? I banned such training without hesitation.

Months later, it had become clear we were dealing with a much more insidious pattern than a few alternative theories offered in classes. The secret began unraveling with a hot-line tip: "There's a cult at work in the FAA." But the Administrator snubbed the complaint until the nuns went on television.

Experts who define what is or is not a cult often say leadership is the telling detail: must the guru come with the package, or is he willing to let his followers or organizations decide what they want for themselves? By that definition, the training regimen designed by Gregory May made him a guru and the seminars cultlike. But in 1984, May was hired for a much more mundane purpose: to conduct a three-day workshop on stress management at the FAA's Center for Management Development in Palm Coast, Florida. May expanded his repertoire until by 1990 he was conducting various seminars in "leadership" training, teaching such concepts as personal, interpersonal and organizational effectiveness, self-awareness and self-management skills. Eventually, 4,000 senior FAA executives went to May in pursuit of these traits, and many sent some of their employees, too. May traveled to FAA offices all over the country, and was hired by FAA managers to teach them "team building." His access and influence quickly became pervasive, and May cultivated contacts with senior recruiting and personnel officers. He boasted that his courses were required to get ahead in the agency.

"Within the context of the FAA I have . . . been in all regions," May crowed in 1990, "worked in every kind of facility up and down, worked with secretarial staff, worked with air traffic control, worked with [Flight Standards], worked with, you name it, security, legal, team building for the chief counsel, team building of all the director's management teams in separate regions. I spent a lot of time in headquarters, all in different capacities. So that pretty much, inside and out, upside and down, top side in the FAA, I don't think there's any group of people I haven't worked with at one point or other.''

The aura of power served to suppress criticism. Students believed May's courses were a rite of passage at the FAA. Any complaints, any balking, would mar a career. Employees heard that senior managers asked May to write evaluations of workers. Stories spread that May aimed harsh treatment at certain people because he had talked to their bosses about them before the training course started. They saw him wave a black book around in class and claim it was a list of every person who was going to be promoted to senior supervisor.

An FAA memo that circulated before a May workshop for couples told employees that ''obviously, it is not mandatory that you participate in this workshop, but the benefits you gain in a more fulfilling personal life will have a positive effect on your professional career.''

So the workers endured May's outrageous syllabus. A pervasive pattern of abuse spread throughout rank-and-file officials who hoped for promotion to senior positions. Even outside contractors endured degrading cult-like techniques they later called ''brainwashing'' and ''mind control.''

''Women would sit in the circle and say, 'I was raped,' or 'I was almost raped,' or 'I was molested as a child,' '' described FAA employee Suzanne Edwards. ''At the end of that, I was just devastated, I was devastated to hear these women crying, I was devastated to hear their pain.''

The workshop course descriptions were deliberately vague, so people rarely realized what they were getting themselves into. Helen Murphy knew only that she was asked to sign a ''Well-Being Agreement,'' essentially a waiver saying she would not hold her bosses responsible for anything that happened at the course. Murphy worked for the University Research Corporation, a contractor hired to teach FAA officials to manage and supervise other workers. After she signed, she was sent to a weeklong training course at a Florida beach house that May had rented with FAA money.

''I was tied to my boss, who happened to be a man,'' a shaken Murphy said later, on television and before Congress. "Partners of the same sex had to shower together and had to go to the bathroom together. I remember one of the gentlemen who had been tied up to another one coming back to the main group and saying he was embarrassed to have a bowel movement tied up to another man and in such close proximity, and Gregory tossed it off and said, 'Learn from it.'

"I felt a loss of dignity in myself and for that man and I got very angry," she continued. "What hits me . . . is the loss of control, complete loss of control. We were up till all hours of the night, we didn't know when we'd get sleep, we didn't know when we would eat, the food and diet were completely controlled, we were told when to run and when to stand. There was so much pressure in the training program—you went to late hours, sometimes one-thirty, two-thirty, three-thirty at night. You'd be exhausted, you'd be so emotionally drained, either from yourself or from other people going through stuff, that you would reveal things that you might not choose to reveal to anybody."

Another trainee, Carla Jones, felt equally demoralized: "He would tell us . . . and this went on for hours . . . stand up and everybody would stand up, sit down, stand up, sit down, sometimes do it faster and sometimes slower. And what he was looking for was any kind of impulse or movement, it appeared, that was different from complete obedience."

May's philosophies were rooted in the "human potential movement" of the 1970s, one that relied on repetitive training to win people over. But May himself attended the "Ramtha School of Enlightenment," a cult-like organization in Yelm, Washington, centered around J. Z. Knight, a woman who claimed to be the "channel" or voice for a 35,000-year-old spirit. From July 1988 to October 1990, May made fourteen corporate payments to Ramtha for a total of $21,770. Ramtha had predicted "end times" that include natural and economic disasters, and a plot between the U.S. government and aliens who raise humans to eat or enslave. Members were encouraged to store food, plant fruit trees, buy gold and move out of cities in preparation for a war between humans and the aliens.

The core of May's training principles seemed to depend on overwhelming students with emotional stress. Confrontation, exploitation and exposure were encouraged, if not required. As if that were not enough, another trainer was hired by the FAA to provide diversity training. She was paid $1.5 million to subject FAA employees to almost as degrading training. Her students were subjected to a series of cutely named games and exercises. In The Fishbowl, women sat inside a circle of men and discussed personal accounts of sexual discrimination and abuse. In The Speak Out, people of color confronted whites about racial discrimination. In The Dating Game, women pretended to come on to men using stereotypically male pickup lines and techniques. Other exercises in these "diversity" workshops involved writing vulgar or racist slurs on large pieces of butcher paper. Men wrote any terms they had ever used or heard used for women, female anatomy or sex. In another room, women did the same for men's terms, and the two groups compared notes. Then workshops of whites and minorities scribbled racist labels in the same way. Yet another trainer and May used The Walk, which began at eight o'clock at night. Participants had to take off all their clothes except their underwear, sit in a chair and discuss a personal issue. May's The Candle required students to squat and stare at lighted candles without moving for long periods of time.

Other management teachers compelled FAA managers to take similar courses. In the Five Element Training, the instructor had required students to hand over their clothing so she could sniff it and classify the students by their smell as either Water, Wood, Fire, Earth or Metal. Tax dollars went to pay this "teacher," too.

In The Gauntlet, the women formed a corridor through which the men had to pass. "A man walks into a room with women on each side of him," one student told investigators later. "The women act out the things that usually happen to women. They might make rude comments about your body, touch your back or rear, and generally make the men uncomfortable." He said women were encouraged to make comments like "Nice legs, nice ass, nice bulge, well hung and bet he's good in bed." The men were

touched all over their bodies, and several said they were
groped around the genitals during The Gauntlet. Then the
women rated the men with numbers printed on butcher
paper taped to the wall or an easel. In at least one workshop, names, ratings and drawings of erect penises were
displayed on an easel.

In total, the FAA spent millions of tax dollars for this
outrageous "training," tormenting, humiliating and in-
sulting government employees.

May's primary teaching technique was group therapy-
like sessions in which men and women sat in a "hot seat"
and revealed personal weaknesses or "psychological
glitches" in order to earn feedback from May and their
peers. May demanded that people talk about past sexual
harassment, rape or abuse. He wanted them to divulge
work and personal secrets. People cried, and got sad,
angry, guilty and resentful. They broke down in the sessions, and then were embarrassed at the way they had
exposed themselves. At least two were hospitalized for
stress after the training. Others were traumatized and emotionally drained and couldn't sleep. In the face of this
torment, May was frequently abusive.

"We'd be called asshole, jerk, idiot," said Ann Remorino, a former nun sent by a contractor to take the May
training.

Barry Harris didn't think I should investigate the contracts signed with Gregory May. Harris was already out
of the FAA when he called my office to make an appointment to see me, ostensibly about bogus parts. He arrived
and started to talk about parts, but quickly changed the
subject to the May case. The cult-like training had been
offered while he was Deputy Administrator and then Administrator. So he was concerned about our investigation.
Don't pursue the investigation, Harris warned, it will be
detrimental to women. Apparently May was something of
a Pied Piper with women, able to exert particular sway
over female FAA employees who were vulnerable or confused. Harris thought that fact should stop me from delving
into the FAA's involvement with May. I thought he was

patronizing the women—precisely the people who had complained about May.

But it seemed to me that he really wanted me to keep out of the FAA's internal culture. I think he was afraid the Inspector General's office would discover he had dismissed the early complaints about the cult seminars. The ten years of training courses were often described to me as part of the FAA's effort to change things after the air traffic controllers' strike, when the FAA had a reputation for being staid, behind the times, unable to adapt and respond to changes in society and in the workplace. Officials wanted to see the FAA become more dynamic and more diverse—the agency needed more women and more minorities among the people it hired and promoted.

Secretiveness appeared more the real issue to me. If FAA employees were willing and ready to rally around each other, to circle the wagons and take a vow of silence when their own sanity and dignity were at stake, then what would they do when confronted with criminal or civil investigations? The Gregory May scandal looked like a vivid illustration of my worst fears about the FAA—that the agency would do anything to protect its interests. That includes deceptively throwing away over a million dollars on a cult-like leader whose goal was to reprogram the way FAA employees defined truth and reality (the agency spent another $1.5 million on the diversity teacher).

In spite of Harris's admonishments, I couldn't ignore a letter he had received from Ann Remorino. She had first complained to Harris in July 1991. Her words were vivid: Remorino said the training was "very unconventional, intimidating, and to say the least, scary," and then described May "publicly humiliating faculty members, calling them reprehensible names," "tying faculty members up with rope for a 24 hour period," "telling faculty members not to tell their spouses or other non-participants of their experiences, in other words to lie about activities that took place."

The FAA had quickly dismissed Remorino as biased. Senior officials explained to Harris that she was just disgruntled—her husband had lost a contract to May. So for over a year, no one responded to Remorino's complaint.

Finally, satisfied that Remorino had been discredited, Harris wrote her in August 1992. Since Remorino took the May training as an employee of an FAA subcontractor, the FAA had nothing to do with the business deal between May and Remorino's bosses. In addition, "techniques complained of had never been used on FAA employees." A month later, Harris seemed to close the case by declaring: "I have been unable to find any evidence to suggest that the methodologies you criticize are or have ever been used with our employees."

However, Remorino's complaint appeared to break the taboo against speaking up. That summer, FAA managers began raising concerns about abuse at the training school. Two other students, Helen Murphy and Carla Jones, also protested. Both Remorino and Murphy were former nuns.

"We wrote to four administrators and a few assistant administrators," Murphy said later. "The only letters we ever got back officially from the FAA were to tell us they had looked into it and there was nothing to it. How could one person have so much influence? Who allowed this person to have this influence? Who in the FAA is responsible?"

Only after Remorino, Murphy and Jones called CNN the following February did the Secretary send Remorino's original letter of complaint to my office. By that time, even Representative James Oberstar, no fan of my investigations, had heard about the mess. Once again, he took to the airwaves.

"What was most bizarre was the course was being given for personal advancement within the FAA," Oberstar said on television, "and the perception was that if you didn't take this course and if you didn't have Mr. May's approval for having completed the course in good standing, you wouldn't advance. We found that there were large numbers of senior executive-level personnel in the FAA who had gone through this psychological combat training in a cult setting."

Oberstar had played no part in the investigation of May or the training courses. At the conclusion of the investigation, he offered no assistance in holding FAA officials accountable for procurement violations or for the tenor of the seminars. But the cult investigation generated a lot of media attention, and Oberstar apparently wanted a part of that.

To Joseph Bellino, an FAA union representative, the cult training destroyed lives. "People who had gone to work for years, never being late, never confronting their supervisor, never being argumentative, always being a team player," Bellino complained, "those people now had a hard time dealing with life because the FAA invaded their privacy, brainwashed them to certain beliefs, took all their weaknesses and exploited them and after a two- or three-day seminar said, well, hey, have a nice day, now go separate those airplanes."

We found considerable cause for our investigation. All the contracts awarded to May were noncompetitive. No evaluation was done of the training courses. Procurement rules were violated. Senior FAA officials influenced contractors like University Research Corporation to hire May, too. FAA managers with private business and social relationships with May got him FAA jobs. Many of those FAA officials had personal relationships with May, and some took free training from him.

Inspector General agents met sheer hysteria when our probe got under way. Stories that investigators harassed people, used heavy-handed "witch hunt" tactics and even caused one FAA employee to have a heart attack spread like wildfire through the ranks of people who had taken May's courses. People outside the agency reacted with paranoia when we tried to talk to them about May. Potential witnesses hired lawyers and threatened to sue us. The investigators received anonymous threats against me, forcing my husband and me to move to a new, more secure home. Our address was kept secret from even the department for over a year.

Even Ramtha, the 35,000-year-old spirit, apparently got spooked. He hired F. Lee Bailey to represent him. The blond, middle-aged cult leader who claimed to "channel" the Atlantis native got separate counsel. I still wonder how Ramtha paid Bailey and how they had privileged attorney-client conversations with the channeler around.

FAA employees who were questioned complained to the Vice President's commission on reinventing government, charging that the May investigation was nothing more than a vendetta against them for having suggested months before at the Vice President's town meeting that the Inspectors General offices be stripped of some of their power. The Vice President's office took this charge seriously, and asked the Secretary of Transportation's office whether it wanted me fired over this vendetta. Ann Bormolini advised me that Elaine Kamarck of Gore's office had called. The Secretary's office had to explain that the May investigation was part of a sweeping inquiry at the FAA, and not focused on only a handful of disgruntled individuals.

As a federal prosecutor, an Assistant Secretary of Labor and an Inspector General, I had never run into such intense levels of fear and resistance, nor such active efforts to thwart an investigation.

Nevertheless, we discovered that over nine years, the FAA authorized more than 200 small purchase orders for deals with May, each under the $25,000 cutoff for more stringent open bidding and competition. There was no central contract file, however. The purchase orders were scattered to the four winds all across the FAA's bureaucracy. Splitting up large contracts to slip them under the no-bid threshold is a clear violation of procurement rules. Neither could we find any record of training evaluations, or any documentation that might show the FAA had gotten some benefit from May's courses. No evaluations were ever done to measure whether the training helped FAA managers supervise their employees or had any beneficial impact on agency management. Also, we found that sixty-five FAA managers went to private workshops with May, some of which were held in their own homes. At a few of these, FAA managers served as May's "assistants" and were reimbursed for the several-hundred-dollar tuition paid by the FAA.

Procurement rules were violated, ethical boundaries were violated, employee privacy was violated. But those were FAA faults. May had done nothing illegal in setting up his cult-like courses at the FAA. We could not charge

him with a crime simply because he had sold the FAA
what I considered trash.

In April 1996, Gregory May was fined $5,000 and sent
to prison for six months for one count of mail fraud. His
crime: creating fake bills for psychotherapy for FAA employees who attended his "courses." They paid between
$550 and $1,250 for "courses" around the country. They
then submitted bills to the government's insurance company for eight one-hour sessions of "individual psychotherapy" in May's California office. The insurance
companies were charged for more than $33,000.

In the end, the FAA managers responsible for bringing
Gregory May into the agency and breaking up his contract
into $25,000 bits were only lightly disciplined. Two re-
ceived fourteen- and fifteen-day suspensions, two were allowed to take early retirement, one got a $25,000
"buyout" bonus, two received official reprimands and one
earned an official "admonishment." Two others who left
were later hired by the FAA as outside consultants.

In July 1997, out of the blue, I got a letter from the
State of California Board of Psychology. Bruce W. Ebert,
Ph.D., J.D., wanted me to know that he signed the revoca-
tion order on Dr. May's license in late 1996. He apologized, saying, "Unfortunately, we did not get to Dr. May
before he did a great deal of damage." The FAA never
apologized to the people it damaged.

In September, as I was preparing a lecture for my Government Ethics class, C-SPAN was providing the background noise. I was only half listening until the witnesses
at a congressional hearing related an all-too-familiar scenario. In their government agency, they were not to report
abuses, wrongdoers were protected, and the wagons circled
when trouble brewed. The agency was secretive and
abused or lied to the public. The agency had an internal
working version of the concept of relative truth. It was a
sadly familiar description, but the agency was not the
FAA. It was the IRS. The IRS too had received Gregory
May training. I couldn't help but echo the words of Dr.
Ebert: a great deal of damage. At least Dr. Ebert took
action.

CHAPTER EIGHT

The Second
Greatest Thrill

There is an old saying among pilots that flying is the second greatest thrill. Landing is the first.

As an eighteen-year-old student pilot at Ohio State University's Don Scott Field, I learned quickly that the mechanics of operating a plane are pretty straightforward. Once you master piloting, flying is a relaxing yet thrilling sport. The continuing challenge is to avoid hitting anything in the air—another aircraft, a building, a mountainside—and to get the plane up and down in one piece. Flying is often a solitary experience, but navigating the skies, landing safely and moving your plane around on the ground without a hitch are not. For those functions, every pilot has to rely on crucial partners in the airport control tower.

Yet for decades aviators in this country were forced to count on the most rudimentary help. The tower relied not on sophisticated electronic and computer equipment but on decades-old machinery and the eyes, ears, voices and judgments of people pulling a shift there. Every pilot had to assume those tower technicians were alert, accurate and fast—every day, for every flight. Certainly, for tens of thousands of planes of every shape, size and purpose, they were. But there have also been thousands that smashed into one another in midair, were pummeled into the ground by storms or ripped into each other on crowded runways when a forty-year-old radar monitor failed, or a controller peering through binoculars did not see two planes headed for each other in the air or on the ground, or an airport simply did not have any weather radar equipment.

In the late 1970s, the FAA decided it was time to yank traffic control into the high-tech age. It knew that such a leap would take years, require intricate planning and cost a fortune. But the FAA doesn't just promote the aviation business or protect passenger safety. It is charged with air traffic control—organizing the skies so planes don't crash into each other, ensuring that they can take off and land at airports without missing runways and guaranteeing that once on the tarmac, giant aircraft and little planes can taxi around the airport without fear of sideswiping or colliding into one another.

For decades, airports have separated air traffic by sticking to the military method set down during World War II—the low-tech, labor-intensive chore of literally watching airport territory. Air traffic controllers sit long hours at radar screens, straining to monitor the tiny blips that represent aircraft in the sky. Some controllers pass data about aircraft to one another on strips of paper. Other technicians stare out tower windows through binoculars to keep track of planes idling and cruising the taxiways. In all cases, safety relies on what these people see and can quickly bark into their radios to pilots.

By the 1980s, the FAA was forced to realize that these methods had become intolerably unsafe—the controllers in the tower simply could not keep up with the frantic pace of air traffic. In 1981 the agency announced a plan to overhaul the entire Air Traffic Control system. Four years later, nothing had been done. "The air traffic system is overloaded," declared Representative James Oberstar. It was the fall of 1985 when he demanded that the FAA begin dealing with the ATC dinosaur. But he would fail to hold the agency's feet to the fire, and his House Aviation Subcommittee would allow the FAA to waste hundreds of millions of dollars and more than a decade of time.

The agency embarked on a massive effort to design, buy and install a series of complex, computerized systems to replace the straining, watchful eyes and reflexes of the air traffic control workers. These were going to be cutting-edge, glittering new systems—the newest generation of whiz-bang electronics, avionics, software and hardware, many of them custom-designed to keep up-to-date with the needs and desires of American aviation. They would be the envy of the world, and make flying even more efficient, reliable and safe.

Thirteen years and nearly one billion dollars later, the FAA had to admit its ambitious program was an utter failure. In 1994, under Administrator Hinson, the program was canceled. In spite of the hundreds of millions of dollars spent and the manpower exerted, no new system had been produced, installed or was operating, and every attempt to see the program to its end only prolonged the disaster.

The beginning of the end had started a couple of years earlier. In 1992, a decade after the overhaul was launched, Congress got fed up. The General Accounting Office had looked into the modernization program, but increasingly frustrated senators and members of Congress asked my office to step in, too. After one meeting with FAA officials, my auditors returned in shock: the FAA's completely lost, they told me; the FAA is not in control of the contract, it could not answer any questions without the contractor, it does not know the cost, it does not have a delivery date, and the officials do not know what the system will ultimately be able to do. However, the FAA did know when it was going to test the system, my staff told me incredulously—*after* the FAA bought it!

Cash, checks, subsidies and contracts were doled out in a frenzy throughout the 1980s and into the 1990s, yet vast sums were entirely wasted. Shocking amounts were sucked into voids almost as soon as the money changed hands. After planning to spend $31 billion between 1982 and 2000 on air traffic control modernization, much of the custom-designed air traffic control system was scrapped after years of work but before even any significant hardware or software code was ever installed or switched on. A $305 million landing system that used microwaves to direct planes was rendered obsolete by satellite technology before it ever got off the drawing board. A multimillion-dollar ground radar system called A-MASS was nick-named "A Mess" because it was designed and implemented so poorly that most of the system is still not up and running. Three hundred and fifty million dollars in parts of a Doppler wind shear warning radar (promised after a horrible 1985 crash in Dallas) moldered away when truckloads of equipment went to dusty warehouses across the country instead of to the airports that needed it most.

No one argued with these projects. The money was there—taxpayers and passengers contributed it, Congress authorized it, the FAA spent it. The will to modernize existed. The need was crucial. But the FAA lacked the leadership to manage these enormous projects.

In 1994, the project was estimated to be $1.2 billion over budget. Already $244 million had been spent on equipment that was never delivered. In a letter written after an in-house review of the program, Administrator David Hinson said that "if this program is permitted to continue on its present course, costs could range from $6.5 to $7.3 billion and substantial additional delays could be incurred. This is unacceptable."

Hinson was the latest airline executive to head the FAA—unlike General Richards, Hinson had experience running a multimillion-dollar corporation. He was chairman of Midway Airlines when the carrier went bankrupt—and when it got in trouble for inflating passenger data given to the FAA and Northwest Airlines, a potential partner. Neither Midway nor Hinson was ever punished—after reviewing the data, the Office of Inspector General decided that Midway used faulty software to compile and analyze its own data on ticket sales, routes and profits. As a result, Midway overstated its revenues by 21 percent. The company was not deceptive, our review said, just dumb. Ironic, then, that Midway's leader, Hinson, was chosen to head the FAA.

Even with this questionable background, Hinson seemed to be a breath of fresh air when he joined the FAA in the summer of 1993. I was eager for a new administrator, someone who might have ideas and an action plan, someone who might provide strong backing and support. Hin-

son certainly seemed to be earnest about tackling some of
the FAA's more glaring problems. He immediately
grabbed the air traffic control modernization project by the
horns, announcing it was time to get this fiasco under
control. He was determined to make the FAA accountable,
to change operations, correct the inefficiencies, improve
safety standards. For someone from outside Washington,
Hinson seemed to be remarkably effective at making decisions and taking action within government bureaucracies.
In the beginning he saw what needed to be done—and
started doing it. Hinson slammed the brakes on the air
traffic control project with scathing condemnations of the
program. He told Congress that the plan had to be scaled
back considerably in parts and that there was no alternative
but to cancel certain wasteful segments. A debacle from
start to finish, the project had been damaged by some FAA
career employees who had no idea how to run a highly
technical, multibillion-dollar enterprise. For the most part,
they were civil servants who moved up through the FAA
ranks. They had no particular expertise in business or aviation. Few had MBAs. Few were procurement specialists
with experience in buying electronic systems that cost $3
billion to $5 billion. It's not unusual to find a human
resources clerk promoted into a job in the procurement
department, and then discover that once that person has
ordered a purchase, a different staffer in another department is charged with implementing the new program and
other staff members with maintaining it. The equipment
will arrive, leaving the staff in the other departments asking: now what do we do with it?

If proof was needed that management teams were woefully inexperienced at selecting and buying complicated
equipment, Hinson provided it when he replaced all the
senior managers responsible for the air traffic project.
Technical, engineering and computer experts at the agency
are poorly qualified to understand the systems they are
evaluating, and they are too easily intimidated by their
better-paid, better-educated counterparts in private industry. FAA administrators are overwhelmed by the demands
of controlling and tracking these projects once they are up
and running. None of the technical, management or field

administrators communicate clearly with one another, with
their own contractors or with each other's contractors.

In a 1991 report, the General Accounting Office didn't
mince words. The blue cover page bellowed: "Agency
Needs to Correct Widespread Deficiencies." The GAO
had looked at how the FAA manages its computers, databases and other information technology resources—and
concluded that it simply did not. At the time, the FAA
spent about $3 billion a year on about 200 computer and
communication systems, the GAO said, and "wide-ranging
and fundamental" problems managing those systems across
many programs meant the FAA just couldn't do its job
properly.

"Again and again, the same problems plague these systems," the GAO report warned. "Inadequate definition
requirements and considerations of alternatives, failure to
sufficiently test systems, ineffective management of computer capacity and unreliable data.

"As a result, systems are delivered late, they run millions of dollars over budget and they do not meet their
objectives."

In other words, billions of dollars are simply wasted.
Inevitably, without exception, the projects spin out of control. Deadlines are routinely missed, delays unavoidable,
budgets overrun, components rarely perfected, final products delivered with disappointing flaws, if at all.

The GAO put the blame squarely on FAA management's failure to come up with a good program to run
these information systems. Instead, the agency's haphazard
administration "has limited top management involvement,
does not have a complete strategic plan, and does not
ensure that sound practices are implemented."

At best, the FAA simply can't decide what it wants.
My office and the GAO repeatedly saw what frustrated
private contractors—the FAA would decide to spend
money and authorize projects before really figuring out
what it needed. The money and the authority to write the
checks existed—that was the easy part. But the technical
expertise and the administrative skill to define the project,
set a timetable and manage the process were sorely lacking. As the GAO so painfully pointed out, a $5 billion

project to replace the aging computers in the air traffic control system, which was called the Advanced Automation System, suffered more than a year's delay because the FAA hadn't told the contractor exactly what it wanted. The company had to stop work while the FAA decided. When the GAO looked more closely, it realized that the FAA had a preference for a particular system, even though an alternative would likely have met the agency's needs and saved it $500 million. But the FAA managers never fully analyzed or properly compared it to any other systems. While they delayed, another $400 million was spent on an interim program to keep the old computers working and increase their capacity until the new replacements arrived—and then *that* was delayed because the FAA's original requirements turned out to be imprecise.

Then the FAA planned to spend $1.5 billion on a project called CORN—Computer Resources Nucleus. The GAO took a look at CORN, decided it was so badly thought out—its design requirements dictated a system that didn't even satisfy the FAA's needs—that the GAO recommended that the FAA not be allowed to award a contract. The same thing happened when the FAA went hunting for a new computer system for its Airmen and Aircraft Registry. The agency looked at only a few systems in a way that the GAO said was "predisposed toward a specific type of optical disk technology that may not meet the agency's needs." The agency didn't even follow the basics that any first-year business school student would know— it hadn't figured out its own needs, the functional requirement of the equipment, whether any alternatives existed or what the costs and benefits would be.

The chaos is best illustrated just by looking at the agency's Keystone Kops attempt to use technology to improve navigation, landing and taxiing. The tale of the antiquated air traffic control system that routes thousands of planes through the skies every week may be the most tragic, outrageous example of how incompetence and bureaucratic bungling waste billions and cost lives.

In the fall of 1996, the American Automobile Association put out a scary report condemning the nation's air

traffic control system. Power failures at control towers
across the country routinely left air traffic controllers in
the dark.

That evening, Bryan Lehman, a young Kennedy International Airport controller, told a television reporter: "The
frequencies don't work. The sectors don't work. We're
using tape to keep the computers together. Problems like
that, that build to bigger problems that people don't see."
And a Cleveland controller told *Nightline*: "This [failure]
happens routinely, routinely."

Outsiders are forgiven for believing that air traffic control centers are like the most modern computer labs, with
skilled technicians arrayed before batteries of powerful,
complex computers, radar screens and monitoring equipment. I saw my first air traffic control center in 1974 when
instructors at Ohio State University loaded my class of
pilots on the school's vintage DC-3 "Gooneybird" and
flew us to tour the Indianapolis Air Traffic Control Center.
I was impressed to see the controllers at their glowing
screens watching the skies over the entire Midwest. Later,
while flying cross-country, I had to stop at little airports,
go into the tower and get my logbook signed by the manager (this gave the tower staff a chance to see that a
student pilot was not spooked or otherwise troubled by
solo flights). Beginning pilots find their way by picking
out landmarks on the ground. If you miss one or get lost,
you're in a heap of trouble. I flew with one eye out for
water towers, interstates and railroad tracks. From Columbus to Cleveland, Toledo or Cincinnati, the freeway was
a clear, straight ribbon to follow. We joked at school that
IFR—instrument flight rules—really meant "idiots following railroads." Visual flight rules, or VFR, require diligence, but free you of complicated electronic instruments.
You just hopscotch from the reservoir to the power plant
to the water tower. You have got to watch the ground all
the time—and know where your landmarks are from having studied the visual flight rules maps. The charts have
drawings of the landmarks on the ground, and obstacles
to avoid, like power lines. But in order to free pilots from
the vagaries of having to look for water towers and being
grounded by cloudy skies, you need technology. Blind fly-

ing—flying without reference to the ground or even being able to see where you are going—is using IFR, and you need Air Traffic Control to make it work.

Air Traffic Control is certainly better than looking for water towers, but in truth, the air traffic control setup is a dinosaur, a relic of the 1940s military. Radar beacons sweep the sky, sending readings to controllers sitting before vintage 1960s vacuum tube screens, watching tiny lines and blips appear, disappear and move around—just like a scene from a World War II movie. The controllers use what they see on the screens to manually pass responsibility for the planes back and forth between sectors. When TWA flight 800 crashed into the Atlantic off the coast of Long Island in July 1996, the air traffic controller at Kennedy Airport had just radioed his counterpart in Boston and verbally given the Boston controller responsibility for the doomed plane.

Still, computer systems are the backbone of the controller system, which handles over 200,000 flights a day in the U.S. Obviously, a cumbersome system that relies so completely on human performance is bound to be plagued with problems.

In 1986, an air traffic controller in Los Angeles was too busy to see the tiny blip of a Piper Archer on his screen as the little plane blundered into approach air space over Los Angeles International Airport. On that August day, an Aeromexico jet was at about 6,500 feet when the Piper Archer clipped its tail and sent both planes spiraling into a nearby neighborhood. Eighty-two people died, including fifteen people on the ground, and ten houses were destroyed as fire spread everywhere. The crash happened five years after President Ronald Reagan fired the striking controllers and the FAA announced it would replace them with a fully automated system.

But human error is a lesser threat to the air traffic control system than the decrepit condition of most of the ancient technology. Parts are hard to come by, replacements difficult to find, and skilled repair people fewer and fewer as the years go by. Like any aged mechanical device, the system needs frequent work. Towers all over the country suffer frequent power outages. Most are overloaded. The networks have long since maximized their capacity, leaving them unable to cope with the air traffic that crisscrosses their sector. The GAO report in 1991 pointed out that computer capacity shortages at many large airports made it impossible for controllers to ensure safety. In many towers, the GAO said, aircraft position and identification information disappeared from displays, data flickered on and off, and computer responses were delayed.

The Automobile Association of America cited New York, Chicago, and Dallas/Fort Worth as having the worst equipment failure records in the country in the fourteen months from July 1995 to August 1996. The FAA said its air traffic control computers failed thirty times in those fourteen months; the AAA said twenty-one of those thirty failures were in the three big cities. The breakdowns were dramatic—eight different computer failures in New York, including one that lasted almost six hours; seven failures in Chicago, and six in Fort Worth, including a fourteen-hour power failure there. Each failure caused a ripple effect of delayed aircraft all down the line. When the *new* tower opened at Washington National Airport in 1997, it suffered more failures than the old record holders—almost every day.

Though the FAA has been aware of this problem for years, it let the dilapidated system fester. Finally, after the devastating 1981 strike that prompted President Reagan to fire 11,000 controllers, the agency decided to replace the ancient system in one fell swoop. A new air traffic control network would be designed specifically for American aviation. It would reengineer air traffic control to replace outdated equipment, handle increased traffic more efficiently and enhance air traffic control through each phase of flight.

Air traffic is controlled through three types of facilities: airport towers and ground control systems monitor aircraft on the ground and in the vicinity of the airport. From there, terminal facilities sequence and separate aircraft from the point at which tower control ends to about twenty to thirty miles from the airport. After that, en route centers take over and control the aircraft until it enters terminal airspace at its destination. At en route centers controllers jot plane information down on strips of paper they pass back and forth.

The FAA intended to overhaul the system, building a custom computer network from the ground up and consolidating 230 terminal and en route centers into 23 facilities. It rejected the idea of buying, testing and gradually introducing new components to the system over time. It rejected buying off-the-shelf equipment. No, the agency wanted to create an entirely new system from scratch. The FAA knew it didn't have the scientists, the engineers, the computer programmers or even the aviation experts on staff to invent such an ambitious, complex system. But that didn't daunt the FAA. It simply did what all good government agencies do—it hired contractors: outside experts and manufacturers to build the thing. If nothing else, FAA officials knew they could award contracts, even if they did it poorly. That is, of course, how the Defense Department ended up with $600 toilet seats.

The system was designed to be phased in over a twenty-year period, in a building-block approach with five segments. It would replace aging and maintenance-intensive equipment with more reliable, computerized systems. Segments One and Two would replace equipment that helps controllers separate aircraft en route between airports. Electronic flight data would appear on high-resolution color displays, replacing strips of paper that controllers now pass back and forth to each other. The computers would be designed to process radar and limited flight data. Segment Three would replace equipment used to separate aircraft within twenty to thirty miles of airports. Segment Four would control aircraft on the ground and in the immediate vicinity of an airport. Finally, Five would combine equipment from Segments One, Two and Three into a single facility and provide new software that lets controllers choose more fuel-efficient routes for planes. At each controller's station, the result would look like a desk for a television fanatic—a huge main monitor sits in front of the controller, and on its top rests a smaller auxiliary screen. Beneath the main screen on the desk are two small display modules—in all, four different screens, operated with a keyboard, a mouse and a foot pedal. The whole thing was supposed to cost $2.5 billion, and be finished in 1996.

But that was only the beginning. It would be years before any work was done, but not before the price began to skyrocket and delays to set in. In 1988, when IBM signed on to write software for the main segment, the bill had jumped to $4.8 billion and the finish date was 1998. In 1993, the bill would be closer to $5.1 billion for a project completed in 2002. Later the same year, the FAA's own internal report said no, in fact, the bill would probably be between $6.5 billion and $7.3 billion—the agency still couldn't be sure.

Through all this, only the first segment, the least complex of all, has been partially completed. The FAA is still years away from fielding any major new equipment. Because of these delays, the FAA has had to come up with hundreds of millions of dollars to keep the antiquated systems at terminal and en route centers—the ones I saw in 1974 that should already have been phased out or replaced—running for even longer. This equipment was never expected to handle air traffic beyond the late 1980s. Now the FAA says it can last through 2000.

The technical challenge was immense—the project would require several million lines of software code, an extensive user-friendly design and unprecedented requirements for performance and reliability. Alas, the task proved more difficult than IBM or the FAA realized at first. The first casualty was the FAA's plan to consolidate its terminal and en route centers. Initially, the FAA wanted to replace all the fundamental hardware and software in every en route facility, terminal and airport tower under one large project that would be phased in over thirteen years. As a result, IBM and the FAA set schedules that proved unrealistic when IBM encountered technical difficulties. From the beginning, the software developers were overwhelmed, and the code they produced was inadequate. In 1994, the FAA's own internal review noted that IBM was adding, modifying or deleting elements in every line of code. Essentially, that meant IBM had to rewrite every single line of code at least once. On one project in 1993, the rewrite rate was 117 percent. In addition, the FAA also acknowledged that IBM had hundreds of requests to make changes in 655,000 lines of code in another part of the system. If that wasn't enough, IBM also had several thousand open "system error" files, with about two-thirds marked as having no known correction or solution.

Then, the system that was supposed to convert the flight strips from paper to digital turned out to be cumbersome and not user-friendly. So IBM had to go back to the drawing board and redesign that, too. The first plan failed to let a supervisor's workstation instantaneously display data from any controller's workstation. But one of the biggest problems occurred in creating software for individual controller workstations. The new stations had to be able to continue working independently in the event that the main network computer went down. And they did. The problem arose when the main computer was back on-line. Now the two systems had different flight data. Because of the two inconsistent databases, the main and workstation computers wouldn't work together anymore. IBM told the House Subcommittee on Aviation in 1993 that it didn't know how to solve this problem—but it was sure an answer would turn up.

These glitches meant that IBM and the FAA could not test the system. But that didn't stop the agency from scheduling acceptance of Segment Two for September 1994, to be followed by a year of operational testing at the FAA's test center, and then another year of field testing. Even the FAA, in an internal review, noted that the government would be "buying a system that might not meet its needs and might later be discovered to have deficiencies or defects." As the 1993 GAO report pointed out more succinctly: "What such testing will find is unknown." Basically, the FAA was buying a pig in a poke.

Segment Two was an unknown, in large part, because the FAA never really knew where IBM stood. The agency didn't watch IBM closely—it didn't assign enough staff or set any rules for assessing progress. Originally the FAA's software development branch had three people overseeing the massive IBM project. But they couldn't keep track of IBM. In 1992, a study done for the House Committee on Appropriations recommended the FAA have six or eight people in that department. The agency added only two. But no matter how many heads were put together, the FAA and IBM still had difficulty declaring where they were. They both said they were making good headway because they were working on the latest ''builds,'' the software increments. Except they neglected to mention in their reports that most of the software code for the middle builds (some of the most difficult functions) remained unwritten and untested. As late as March 1993, when the GAO asked the FAA for a progress report, it answered that ''this information was not yet available, but the agency was trying to develop such performance measures.'' On top of that, the FAA failed to set specific requirements for the second segment; for example, the agency did not nail down exactly what kind of formats it wanted for the new electronic flight strips or control screens. IBM tried to develop these systems with vague, continually changing guidelines from the FAA.

In fact, changing direction plagued the FAA. First, the agency decided not to consolidate all of its en route and terminal centers in case catastrophe struck one facility. Instead, it would keep 22 en route centers and 170 terminal facilities, and create 9 large terminal facilities. Not only did the agency decide not to consolidate its centers, but then it realized it really wanted to add even more advanced software, including programs that would allow controllers to choose more fuel-efficient routes. And this software should now be part of Segment One, not Segment Two. The airline industry was suffering financial difficulties, and the FAA tried to help by having the software installed sooner. Beyond that, the agency also changed the parameters for the tower segment, announcing it wanted to change the design and amount of equipment.

The problems continued to spiral out of control. IBM's contract required that it get 210 workstations running simultaneously, but as of February 1993, only 56 operated together for short periods.

We also learned that the FAA employee responsible for the IBM contract and millions of dollars of contract increases had a spouse who was buying IBM stock during the time the FAA employee was in charge of the IBM contract.

Perhaps most striking of all, even the FAA couldn't say specifically how all these costly new systems would enhance air traffic control. When the GAO asked for details, it took the agency six months to compile a reply. And then it just said the new system would "allow controllers to grant more use-preferred routes," without saying how many, and "increase system reliability," without saying by how much.

Other segments were plagued with problems, too. In one, the FAA had to find $16 million to fix a ground radar system that monitors planes on the ground in any weather. It seemed that the initial design caused some types of planes to appear as two or more craft on a controller's display screen when the radar was focused on specific parts of a runway. Then, thirty-six units of the Airport Surveillance Radar had to be put in storage because of problems with radiation and the failure of transmitter components. Costs for a voice switching-and-control system, the communication link for the Segment Two workstations, increased 400 percent between 1983 and 1993, and the project was delayed six years. Then there were troubles with Data Link, the system of ground-to-air communications between controllers and pilots. Too many misunderstandings occur when the two talk directly to each other, so Data Link is a digital communications system for air traffic and weather communications. The software includes Mode S, yet another radar system that has not been deployed. So the FAA in 1993 considered storing the Data Link processors until they can be used. But Data Link was also a critical communications program, making it a linchpin for several other projects. It had to come first. Without Data Link, those systems might have to be mothballed, too.

I was thrust into this mess in 1993. The Government Accounting Office had looked into the air traffic control project. Its findings, while harsh, were couched in gentle terms: "it needs improvement," the GAO said, but they're moving along. Finally, Senator Frank Lautenberg of New Jersey became suspicious that both the FAA and the Government Accounting Office were concealing the disastrous truth about the air traffic control program. He asked my office to step in.

Immediately we discovered a fatal defect. The Defense Contract Audit Agency, the office that evaluates how government money is being spent on outside contractors, could not convince the FAA to cooperate with its audits. The auditing agency is part of the Pentagon, but it monitors other departments' contracts to see if the government is getting what it pays for. It couldn't do its job without internal FAA documents and reports. But the FAA wouldn't turn those papers over. Unfortunately, that didn't stop the auditing agency from signing off on its reports anyway. This is the kind of thing that made me throw up my hands—piles of auditing agency reports on my desk, several years' worth of work at taxpayer expense, important studies whose findings we, the GAO and Congress needed to rely on, and they were meaningless because they were missing critical information due to the FAA's refusal to cooperate.

The final insult to the air traffic control project came when we discovered that IBM had billing discrepancies— millions of dollars worth. The giant computer company was padding its bills, inflating the expenses it asked the FAA to reimburse.

In the end, no new air traffic control system materialized. It never got off the drawing board. The software was never developed. The hardware was never perfected. After years of work, and a budget of billions of dollars, there was no prototype, nothing to test, no tires to kick—no system. Oh, many thousands of lines of custom software code had been written, virtually all useless before the computer bytes had time to settle. A few computer screens had been purchased, but they sat gathering dust in storage. No major hardware was ready to go.

During the same period of time, other countries in Europe and elsewhere needed new air traffic control systems. Their administrators looked over their crumbling systems, figured out what updates and upgrades they needed, and, in many cases, simply bought American equipment right off the shelf.

*   *   *

Once pilots and air traffic control technicians have ferried planes safely to the airspace over the airport where they are to land, controllers have to get them on the ground in one piece. Landing a plane is a tricky business—it is literally like flying through hoops. With instrument landing systems, the pilot relies on radio frequencies to guide him straight onto the runway. All airports send out a radio signal to provide horizontal guidance, a second "glide slope radio signal" that provides vertical guidance along the correct descent angle, and two radio marker beacons that give the pilot fixes along the approach to the runway. High-intensity lights and strobe lights help pilots visually locate the runway in bad weather. Now, imagine three hoops in the air on the approach to a runway. Each one gets smaller as you get closer to the runway. As you land, you want to fly your plane directly through these imaginary hoops. Radio signals tell you where to find the first hoop, which is pretty big, and when you pass through it, you move farther down the glide slope. Cockpit equipment picks up a radio beacon relayed from the ground, telling the pilot that he is on the slope. The next hoop is smaller, so your approach will be more precisely aimed at the end of the runway. When you pass through that second circle, equipment in the cockpit reassures you that you are still on the correct course. The third hoop is very small, and very close to the end of the runway. At that point there isn't much leeway—you have to glide through those narrow hoop coordinates perfectly because you are virtually on top of your touchdown point.

Even though this system has been in use for decades, it is imperfect. Pilots and the FAA have long wanted a more precise method of pinpointing coordinates for landing. In 1978, it looked like the agency had found one: the Microwave Landing System, which used microwave technology to guide planes to landing. The FAA decided it was technically superior to instrument landing systems because microwaves allowed airplanes to fly a variety of advanced procedures, like curved approaches, and let planes land and take off in bad weather. So the FAA decided to buy 1,280 MLSs for about $2.6 billion by the year 2008. It was a clever, efficient idea, but it soon had competition that should have killed MLS in germination: the Global Positioning System. As the GAO noted in 1992, the "FAA's decision to replace the ILS with MLS may be premature because satellite technology may provide the capabilities and benefits of MLS."

The Global Positioning System, masterminded by the military, used satellites to pinpoint a craft's location, and it made microwave devices obsolete, even pointless and silly. The GAO report noted that "satellite technology could allow the FAA to phase out older ground-based navigation equipment." Nevertheless, the FAA had already plowed ahead with plans for Microwave Landing Systems, awarding its first contract in 1984. But soon the Global Positioning System began to sweep the navigation world. By the early 1990s, anyone could buy hand-held, pocket-sized positioning devices for small boats or planes, or for just walking through the woods.

But the FAA was captivated with the beauty of the Microwave Landing System program. It replaced glide slopes and localizers with microwave signals beamed from the ground. These microwaves could tell a pilot his exact altitude, how many miles he was from the airport and what coordinates to follow all the way through his descent. The numbers were so precise a pilot could be ordered to steer left or right by degrees if necessary.

But microwaves are not worry-free—they are ground-based, and that meant that to install the devices the FAA had to obtain land and permits. People living around airports objected to the idea of giant microwaves bouncing around over their heads, and neighborhood opposition caused critical delays. But the FAA plugged away, announcing a worldwide Microwave Landing System in 1978, and winning funding from Congress every year from 1982 to 1994. It awarded the first contract for equipment in 1984, ignoring what should have been the loudest alarm bells—the airlines, usually so in synch with the FAA, were refusing to buy microwave equipment. Predictably, they balked at the cost—MLS did not offer a big enough improvement over existing systems to justify the expense.

But more important, the airlines had already turned their attention to satellite navigation.

A few carriers, like Northwest Airlines, had bought some microwave equipment. During a 1992 tour with Northwest mechanics of the huge hangar where their jets were stripped and overhauled, I heard the first griping about microwave landing equipment. They were putting it into the planes, the mechanics told me, shaking their heads, but they had no idea why. "It's never going to be used," one complained. "Everything is going to go global positioning."

I was surprised that the FAA was still keen on MLS because I knew how well my $900 hand-held Global Positioning System worked. It was no bigger than a couple of television remote controls, and with it my family could locate a little bitty buoy from the deck of our boat. GPS would give us a fix on our location relative to the buoy's location—so technically, we could locate a buoy on the other side of the world, or one ten feet away from us in a fog. Surely a pilot could use it to find the end of a runway. In fact, private pilots already were. Anyone could buy a system from Sporty's Pilot Shop, an Ohio store and mail-order catalog for general aviation equipment. Yet the FAA still wanted the airlines to buy microwave landing equipment.

Global positioning came from the stars—literally. I first heard of satellite-based navigation as a young prosecutor in Missouri. I was investigating interstate transportation of stolen vehicles—mostly big tractor-trailer rigs. One afternoon in 1985, I was on the road with an FBI agent named Emmet Trammel. Trammel could smell a stolen eighteen-wheeler as it drove by on the freeway. As we cruised toward Leavenworth Penitentiary to interview witnesses, Trammel rhapsodized about a hot new technology being used to track stolen vehicles—the Global Positioning System. Truck owners were installing receivers, and when the rigs were stolen, the system could track the vehicles right down to a specific parking slot at a truck stop anywhere in the country. Global positioning is based on the same kind of triangulation a navigator uses with a sexton. Cockpit equipment bounces a signal off the satellite, and the returning message gives the pilot his exact longitude, latitude and altitude. The satellite information is so precise that the Coast Guard uses it to place buoys. It also requires much less maintenance than ground machinery—and satellites don't have any complaining neighbors.

Eventually, the airlines dug in their heels and refused to buy microwave landing equipment in any big way. By 1989, even the FAA wanted to kill the microwave project. Few transmitters had been delivered. The whole thing was best forgotten. But not in Congress. Some of the major contractors were huge electronics manufacturers, and they had friends in Washington. They did not want to lose their contracts. Suddenly, Congress was pressing the FAA to evaluate nine new microwave systems. So the agency moved into Microwave Landing System Phase II. It would provide 786 microwave systems, it declared, and have them all in place and operating by 1996.

Yet by 1993, a GAO report noted that the FAA's budget for a Global Navigation Satellite System had gone from $18.7 million to an astronomical $97.7 million. The original $18 million was supposed to buy monitors so the GPS could supplement traditional en route navigation and nonprecision approaches. But the FAA had since grown wise—the $97 million would pay for a system for all civil aviation to use GPS exclusively for en route navigation, terminal nonprecision approaches and precision approaches. On another page the same report listed the MLS as twelve years behind schedule.

By 1996, when the agency's report on capital improvement projects came out, the Microwave Landing System was not mentioned at all. Neither was the $305 million it cost before it was finally killed.

Getting down safely is not always simply a matter of good navigating equipment. Planes often fly in weather that limits visibility and throws a wrench into the performance of the very best pilot or the most advanced plane. Mother Nature is a formidable opponent, and sometimes should not be challenged. Some weather must be avoided at all costs.

I learned this early, flying my Piper Cherokee over the

Ohio foothills. Even at eighteen, I strained the muscles in my arms so badly I felt the pain for days after struggling to steady my plane's yoke through rolling winds. On another day, a gusting crosswind tilted my tiny wings to the right so far, I thought I'd roll like a tumbleweed off the runway instead of landing. Luckily, the aberrant gust died as suddenly as it had come up, and my lightweight plane touched down safely. But neither of those experiences taught me what moving air can really do to a plane. That lesson came years later, on a 1985 flight from Kansas City to Dallas. The evening was calm, the plane full of bored business fliers. Over Texas we hit a sudden storm. The sky turned black and turbulent, but hardly anyone looked up from his or her report or magazine even as we prepared to land. A bit of bumping was not unusual. Then suddenly the pilot was speaking to us. Gone was his reassuring "cockpit" voice. Instead, he sounded shaky and hesitant.

"The Dallas–Fort Worth airport is temporarily closed," he croaked. "There's been an . . . uh . . . incident."

At first we diverted to Oklahoma City, but were rerouted back to Dallas when the airport reopened. As we circled in the twilight, I stared mesmerized at a blaze of flashing red, blue and white lights scattered all over the ground. I blinked, barely seeing a jet tail sticking out of the runway as if embedded there like a pin in a pincushion. In an eerie haze, I thought I saw thousands of emergency vehicles. Only my eyes seemed to be picking up information— my other senses were deadened. I couldn't breathe, I couldn't hear, I didn't move, I wasn't thinking. Nobody was. There wasn't a sound from the crowded cabin. My fellow passengers stared, stunned, frozen in time.

Our arrival gate was next door to the one the crashed plane was supposed to have used, and as I walked in a daze down my jetway I could hear people crying, screaming, wailing in agony. I emerged to see families still arriving at the airport, and watched them praying that the person they were expecting was not on board the plane that had been catapulted into the ground by a vicious weather condition called wind shear. I walked away quickly, unable to face the horror and hoping somehow to

flee the randomness of the tragedy. It could just as easily
have been my plane.

Wind shear rises in the snap of a finger. It happens
frequently in the South, where summer thunder and lightning storms can erupt, swirl violently and evaporate within
minutes. Storms build in circular patterns and create pockets of downdraft wind. A plane flying along on a head
wind can suddenly get sucked into a downdraft that ham-
mers it toward the ground. Planes rely on head wind to
give them airspeed—that's the rate at which air moves
over the wings. That air gives lift and stability to the
wings, and keeps the plane aloft. But those winds can shift
instantly, stripping a plane of buoyancy. A head wind can
suddenly become a gale from behind. If that happens as
the plane hits a downdraft, then in a nanosecond the airplane has no lift in its wings just as a giant celestial hand
is forcing the plane down. If the craft is already close to
the ground, there is almost no hope of recovery. The risk
is greatest for big, heavy airplanes: without airspeed, they
will stall, losing their lift and forward motion even though
they are still traveling at 150 or more miles an hour. A
small plane can stay in the sky even if airspeed is reduced
to less than fifty miles an hour. Faced with wind shear, a
pilot's only course of action is to open the throttle and
push for more power—just like flooring the gas in a car—
and fight through it. There's a delicate balance, however,
because as you pass through the wind shear, it can suddenly change direction.

No pilot in his right mind wants to face that situation.
And it's unnecessary; for the most part, such windstorms
blow over within minutes. Pilots on the ground with correct weather advisories and flexibility in air traffic control
sequencing can wait for storms to pass. Pilots know that
weather causes about 40 percent of aircraft accidents and
about 65 percent of air traffic delays over fifteen minutes.
But what about planes already in the sky, pilots and passengers unknowingly approaching a building storm?

Thankfully, technology can defuse the threat. Doppler
radar can predict and pinpoint these rapid, dramatic shifts
in wind by bouncing beacons off different air masses.
After the Dallas tragedy, the FAA decided such systems

should be installed at every major airport. To its credit, by 1992, the agency decided to spend $350 million on a radar system that can detect wind shear, microbursts of wind, gust fronts, wind shifts, and rain.

Today, most people think Doppler radar wind shear detection systems have been installed in every airport. In fact, only sixteen are installed and working. The other systems are either installed but haven't been switched on, are in the process of being installed or are gathering dust in storage. Seven of the remaining forty-seven scheduled for production haven't even been delivered yet. So only sixteen of forty-seven Doppler wind shear radar systems are of any use to pilots and passengers. In some places the delay again results from opposition in local communities where people are afraid of having radar radiation fill the air around their homes and businesses.

Yet in the years since the Dallas crash, other wind shear accidents have cost passenger lives. Two unsolved crashes in Pennsylvania and North Carolina have been tentatively attributed to wind shear that might have been avoided with Doppler radar. After a USAir flight crashed at Charlotte, North Carolina, in July 1994, the NTSB said the delay in installing the radar had cost the lives of thirty-seven persons. Charlotte was supposed to get the radar system in early 1993. As a southern airport, it was No. 5 on the FAA list. But the inevitable delays, red tape and land squabbles pushed Charlotte to No. 38, leaving the USAir pilots defenseless against the weather.

In spite of the drama inherent to air crashes, most accidents actually happen on the ground as aircraft taxi around the tarmac, power down the runway, take off or land. One of the worst aircraft crashes in history claimed 583 lives when two huge jets sideswiped one another at Tenerife, on the Canary Islands, Spain, in March 1977. Sadly, the two loaded Boeing 747s had been diverted there by a bomb scare at another airport. Bad luck brought them to Tenerife on a day when the airport was enveloped in thick fog. The pilots of the jets could not see each other through the dense vapors. Like many small and medium-sized airports, Tenerife had no ground radar. Once a plane lands, it leaves air radar beacons behind. Pilots would switch their radios to a ground control channel, and responsibility for their whereabouts on the tarmac would transfer to a different technician in the air control tower. That person would literally "keep an eye" on planes on the ground and steer them away from one another. But that foggy day, the tower couldn't see the tarmac at all. The pilot of one of the jets—KLM—thought he was released for take-off (but was not) and began barreling down a runway, building speed and power as it raced along. Suddenly the other 747 emerged from the thick fog. It had been directed to taxi on the runway, and hearing the KLM pilot radio he was taking off, the Pan Am pilot struggled to get his 747 off the runway and was lumbering across the runway directly in the path of the accelerating jet. The wing of the jet on the runway ripped into the fuselage of the crossing plane and tore the top off the cabin. Both planes came to crashing halts, but it was not the collision that killed most of the passengers. Fire erupted on both planes, and 583 people died of injuries, burns and smoke inhalation.

Five hundred and eighty-three people, more than in any other aviation disaster before or since.

Coincidentally, a planeload of journalists had also been grounded at Tenerife, and the photographers and camera crews swung immediately into action. Within hours, heart-stopping pictures of the two smashed planes reduced to fireballs were flashed around the world, along with horri-fying photos of passengers, bleeding and burned, strug-gling desperately to free themselves and their fellow passengers and flee the carnage.

What happened that day was not unique to a small, primitive airport on an out-of-the-way island. The same kinds of ground collisions happen at airports everywhere, even those with ground radar. In February 1991, an Air-West commuter plane was sent onto a Los Angeles runway where a USAir flight was already landing. The USAir 737 came down right on top of the commuter plane, killing thirty-four people. A year before, in January 1990, an East-ern Airlines 727 came down on an Atlanta runway hard on the tail of a Beechcraft King Air 100, a little six- to

eight-seat turbo prop plane. The 727 barreled right into
the Beechcraft, overrunning the plane and killing its pilot.

In 1991, a McDonnell Douglas 80 and a Boeing 737
collided on the ground at Newark Airport, the wing of one
plane embedded in the other's fuselage. Miraculously, no
one was killed. Passengers in Detroit in December 1990
were not so lucky when a Northwest Airlines DC-9 started
its takeoff roll and smashed into a Northwest 727. The
727's wing gouged the DC-9 just beneath a cockpit window, tearing a gash into the length of the DC-9's body
and ripping the engine off the plane. Fire exploded from
the gaping wound where the engine hung seconds before.
The 727 aborted its takeoff, and its panicked passengers
evacuated safely. But on the DC-9, three passengers were
killed when the 727 wing ripped into them in their seats.
Fire spread through the cabin like a flamethrower, forcing
four passengers to crawl to a tail exit door. A flight attendant reached for the emergency handle, only to have it
break off in her hand. All five were overcome by smoke
and flames, and they died right next to the escape hatch.
Eight people died on that DC-9, a plane that never even
left the ground.

The NTSB later blamed the accident on poor crew coor-
dination. It said air traffic control was shoddy because the
ground controller and the air controller failed to advise
each other of what they were doing with the two planes.
It also chastised the FAA for not correcting badly marked
runway surfaces, signs and lighting at the airport. Hundreds of collisions with potential for similar disaster and
loss of life happen every year. Since 1986, the FAA numbers have been startling: 325 collisions that year, 425 in
1987, 281 in 1990, 217 in 1992. A natural solution would
be a ground radar system, obviously. In the early 1980s,
about the same time it was gearing up to revolutionize air
traffic control, the FAA decided to create an automatic
ground monitoring system to replace the weary eyes of
ground controllers. In 1985, the agency announced it was
creating Airport Surface Detection Radar. The system
would work just like air control radar—beacons would fan
out over the ground and transmit plane positions to tower

radar screens. Norden Systems, a Connecticut company, won the first $30 million equipment contract.

But by 1991, the FAA had tested only a few antenna reflectors, installed a new antenna in Pittsburgh and delivered ground detection radar systems to its own training center in Oklahoma City and to the San Francisco airport. By that time, it was clear that the Airport Surface Detection Radar had serious flaws—chief among them, it neglected to alert ground controllers that an accident was about to happen. There was no automatic alarm system. So the FAA went back to the drawing board, announcing that it was going to replace the detection system with another project, this one called Airport Movement Safety System. The project quickly became known by its acronym, A-MASS, and was touted as the great fix. It would automate ground control so extensively that controllers would be alerted when planes came close enough to one another to be in danger of colliding. It was supposed to use existing airport surface radar to track targets, process information through safety logic, and generate sound and sight conflict alerts for the controllers.

At the start of the project in 1991, the FAA announced it would "buy 38 A-MASS systems for 35 sites." But by the end of 1995, there were still no A-MASS systems in place at all. That was partly because A-MASS relied on Data Link, another project that was delayed because it, in turn, relied on deployment of Segment Two, which was also delayed. Oh, the agency had "conducted A-MASS development" and "released an A-MASS solicitation for San Francisco," but that was it. By January 1996, the FAA was still "developing" A-MASS. In the meantime, the old ground control systems, ground radar without collision warning, continued to operate. True, the earlier system, the Airport Surface Detection Radar, had been installed in sixteen airports. The FAA hoped to improve it by adding A-MASS upgrades to it later. Thirteen more systems were scheduled to be installed in 1996, but, as usual, the FAA is woefully behind schedule and way over budget. It wasn't long before the A-MASS project picked up its less flattering moniker: A Mess.

*   *   *

After President Reagan fired 11,000 air traffic controllers in 1981, the FAA thought it would grab the chance to hire a better quality controller. After all, it was short thousands of controllers and had permission to replace them *all*.

So it spent $119 million to educate and recruit forty-one people.

In 1983, FAA planners sat down and created the Higher Education Program. For the next ten years it gave grants to university and college programs so they could create aviation schools and produce graduates with backgrounds in airway computer science, airway electronic systems, aircraft systems management and aviation maintenance management. It would produce air traffic control specialists, electronics technicians, general aviation maintenance inspectors and computer specialists. These people would make great controller candidates. Their names would go into an FAA hiring registry, and their college educations would reduce the FAA's cost of training new personnel.

The FAA dreamed of hiring 500 graduates a year, or 20 to 30 percent of its new hires. It estimated that 1,900 graduates would join the FAA from 1984 to 1988. But nearly ten years later, the FAA had hired fewer than 50 people from the program—while actively recruiting thousands the old-fashioned way, through the government's Office of Personnel Management—because the graduates of the Higher Education Program proved to be mostly useless to the FAA. The agency said their knowledge, skills and abilities just were not up to par.

In fact, FAA officials said the program's curriculum was of no benefit to their hiring efforts. The general aviation safety inspectors' curriculum didn't give students the number of flying hours to qualify as FAA candidates. Graduates couldn't get jobs as general aviation maintenance inspectors because they didn't get the supervisory experience required for that job. The FAA said the program's electronics instruction was too general, so no electronics technicians or computer specialists were hired.

By 1993, when my office looked at the education program, the situation was even less likely to change. FAA vacancies were hard to come by. Turnover was low, and over 80 percent of current controllers wouldn't be eligible for retirement until after the year 2000. To keep up with normal attrition the FAA hired about 150 controllers in 1993. But there was hardly any need for safety inspectors—the FAA already had more than its personnel regulations would allow—and there were no openings for computer science graduates. And if there were jobs, the FAA had a waiting list of 2,500 candidates who scored 95 or better on air traffic control tests.

Some of the $119 million provided schools with new buildings and other infrastructure, usually because a politician was savvy enough to earmark grants for his or her local institution. Florida Representative William Lehman, who headed the House Appropriations Subcommittee on Transportation, did so for Florida Memorial College in Miami, where money was used to build a $7.3 million aviation center. In 1993, the building had beat-up furniture used by classes in other programs, and an empty air traffic control tower. Aviation students still used it, however—they would climb to the top with hand-held radios to eavesdrop on transmission from a nearby FAA control tower.

In 1994, the FAA reluctantly agreed to kill the Higher Education Program—but not before it surfaced one more time as a subject of ridicule in the Clinton Administration's report on reinventing government. The $119 million might have been better spent at the Massachusetts Institute of Technology. For that money, the FAA could have hired the top forty-one graduates for salaries of about $3 million apiece. They probably would have accepted.

In 1981, the FAA knew the monumental strike was coming, and it was ready. The agency knew Reagan would fire illegal strikers. So when the controllers walked off the job, FAA management was poised to slip into their chairs. Military controllers stood at the ready. The FAA had contingency plans to increase the sequencing between planes and lighten the workload. The air traffic control system carried on with only a few delays. No accidents were caused by the strike. The FAA handled the crisis admirably.

In the aftermath, to reward the controllers who did not strike, and to attract new people to the job, Congress invented a fiction called "revitalization pay." Loyal controllers would get 5 percent of their annual salary as a bonus. Thirteen years later, when my office began an audit of controllers' benefits, I repeatedly asked: the strike has been over for more than a decade, the FAA has long since acknowledged that it has recovered from the strike and restaffed its entire controller corps—so why is the government still paying revitalization pay? But my question went unanswered. Congress eventually allowed the FAA to enact personnel reforms, and when the agency did that, it made revitalization pay a permanent feature. I lost that battle.

More than a decade after President Reagan fired 11,000 striking controllers, a new controllers' union had regained its power and status. But past experience left the FAA terrified of a work slowdown or a full-blown stoppage. As a result, the FAA treats controllers as a group of independent contractors, workers it is supposed to manage but cannot control. The FAA's intense fear of another strike and lack of conviction that the government would enforce the law against an illegal strike had led it to grant onerous collective bargaining agreements. These contracts vary from region to region and award benefits like excessive overtime pay, free flights, the freedom to refuse to relocate or the right to return to an old job after failing at a new one. Of the FAA's 50,000 employees about 23,000 are air traffic controllers who earn an average of $78,000 a year.

These controllers enjoy free air travel and free government-paid moves that are against the rules for other government employees. In addition, until 1996 the FAA could not require controllers to relocate, in spite of the fact that many towers had a shortage of controllers while other places were overstaffed. Now the FAA can move employees, but if a controller fails at a new job, the FAA is obliged to pay for his return to the old posting.

FAA perks first came to my attention as I was getting off a plane in Texas. Ahead of me, a man wearing an FAA identity tag waved to the pilot and said "Good-bye, Joe, see ya next week." Fleetingly I wondered why he flew every week. Later, a friend whose daughter was a USAir flight attendant told me her daughter had been forced to find free seats on a plane for an FAA employee and his entire family.

No one keeps track of who uses these free flights and why. No one keeps an eye on what the FAA employees do with the booklets of free airplane tickets they can help themselves to in the office. Every year the FAA requests a quarter of a million free tickets from airlines that willingly provide them. Officially, the freebies are used for inspections and "familiarization" flights—controllers have to know, the FAA insists, what it's like to sit in the cockpit of a 737 as it lands in Chicago, and how that experience differs from being in the cockpit of a DC-10 touching down in San Diego. This is required training, the FAA maintains, and every controller has to take these flights every year. FAA guidelines and union agreements allow these freebies—under union rules, each inspector is allowed eight domestic trips, and the inspectors can pick up a free-flight voucher at any time. But my office discovered that the system basically serves as a free transportation network. Once again, there is no FAA oversight of the program, no controls over how the tickets are used.

My office examined this "training" program and in 1996 revealed that only half of the FAA evaluators on staff ever took these "training" flights, but that the majority of those used the free tickets as a convenient transportation network. Sixty-two percent of FAA air traffic evaluators used their credentials to get free tickets for personal gain—to visit family, take weekend trips and vacations, reach military reserve duty stations, or commute to work or home—all flights that other workers have to pay for themselves. "In-flight evaluations" were done over and over on the same flight to the same destination, trips originated over weekends and holidays, the evaluator had family or friends at the destination point, the evaluation trip took place outside regular work schedules and no work was done in the destination city, and evaluators were frequently on leave or vacation while in the destination.

We found countless specific examples of abuse. An Atlanta evaluator used twenty-four tickets to visit family in

Tampa (eleven trips began on the last day of the week and ended on Sunday or Monday) and for a weeklong vacation in Denver. It became so excessive that the Tampa airport manager wanted to know why his people were getting so much attention! A Great Lakes Region evaluator used twenty tickets for weekend trips to Youngstown, Ohio, and two other tickets for a weekend trip to Orlando, Florida. He left on Friday, came back on Sunday and did no work while away. An FAA Headquarters evaluator used free tickets for a two-week holiday in London. A manager at the Air Traffic Control system Command Center used twenty tickets to fly to San Francisco for long weekends and holidays. Once he went to San Francisco for ten days—and the days between his evaluation flights were taken as leave. A Chicago evaluator used two tickets to fly to and from Munich, Germany, where he did no work but took seven days off. An Atlanta inspector used thirty-one of forty-one free tickets to fly to his military reserve duty stations. In Chicago, air traffic controllers took 134 trips to Las Vegas in a year. On some trips, groups would take different flights for free, and then spend the weekend in Vegas together. The Boston terminal racked up fifty in-flight evaluations from seventeen different evaluators between April and September of 1993. Twenty-one of those were done by the same guy, an evaluator who used to live in Boston and used his credentials to come back and visit friends.

Inspectors often rode in the plane cabin when they were supposed to be observing in the cockpit. Of 1,690 tickets, 26 percent were used for personal gain. But were the controllers in the wrong? No, because union agreements and FAA guidelines let the employees use these tickets. Yet our audit made it clear that training took a backseat to free transportation. My office demanded: restrict the use of free tickets to familiarization flights or kill the freebies altogether. Get the unions to drop this perk, and find out whether employees would owe the IRS any money for the value of the free tickets. The FAA was unapologetic: ethical abuses were outweighed by the training value, the agency said. It said that vacations at the destination were irrelevant as long as in-flight evaluations were completed.

When I asked that training trips not be allowed to coincide with vacation days, the FAA said that "the voluntary nature of the [program] permits the air traffic control specialist to choose when and on what days he/she will travel." When I insisted that all evaluators not be allowed to fly somewhere and then take several days off before flying back, the FAA said that "the agency does not impose time parameters for travel in an effort to ensure all employees are afforded an opportunity to take advantage of the training."

"Take advantage" is right. The FAA was not about to give up that perk. For its part, the controllers' union was outraged. It fought any attempt to restrict the free flights, arguing they were a critical training tool and an important method of maintaining good relations with customer airlines.

In the spring of 1996, Congress decided that one of the reasons the FAA was so poorly managed was because of crippling personnel and procurement rules. So Congress lifted the FAA's personnel rules. Once that was done, the FAA announced it would require controllers to relocate. But Congress did not lift the FAA's collective bargaining agreements with the union. Those arrangements differ from region to region around the country. Individual regional administrators cut their own deals. In Chicago and Denver, for example, any employee was entitled to a government-paid move. Another particularly onerous and wasteful example is overtime. If a controller is scheduled to work overtime, under union rules that person will get paid for the shift whether he or she works it or not. Simply being scheduled to work meets the requirement for getting paid. If the controller can find a colleague to take over the shift, then the controller will get out of working but will still get paid. Even more insidious, the colleague who agrees to fill in *also* gets paid!

In early 1996, the FAA decreed that controllers could get paid overtime only if they actually worked their shift. That way the agency would save enough money to pay controllers bonuses for being willing to relocate to under-staffed facilities. Some controllers took the sweetened pot and moved, but the union rattled its sabers. The collective bargaining agreement stipulates that controllers be paid for being *scheduled* to work overtime, the union complained. So the FAA suddenly found itself without any money put aside to pay the moving bonuses. It was stuck again, unable to shift its own workforce around as needed.

Once a controller was assigned to his tower of choice, even if that tower became overstaffed while a tower down the road suffered from a shortage, no one could force a controller to move. Understaffed towers meant the FAA had to assign workers to double shifts and pay overtime, or, as in many cases, simply get through the day shorthanded. The agency can't hire extra controllers to fill the gap because of limits on how many full-time employees it can have overall. If there are slots for 10,000 controllers only, then hiring 10,001 would put the agency over its congressionally mandated budget and personnel limits—even if the agency finds itself with an accounting surplus. The agency can hire controllers temporarily, or on a part-time basis, but that solution tends to be impractical because of the expensive, lengthy training in Oklahoma City that each controller must undergo.

At the same time, the FAA also allows controllers a perk called "return rights." Any controller who relocates has the right to move home at government expense. That certainly makes sense for controllers compelled to work temporarily overseas. But the FAA applied it to employees in the States, too, and, of course, abuses mounted. They weren't hard to find when, in 1995, we decided to see if the FAA had any way to ensure that paid moves were necessary. A spectacular new airport had opened in Denver (though it was cursed with technical problems) and a glittering new air traffic control center came on-line in Chicago. In both cities, air traffic controllers had to relocate to new workplaces. Across most of the country, the FAA rule was that if a controller's new workplace was thirty-five miles or more from his home, he was entitled to a government-paid move. But in Denver and Chicago there was no such minimum. Controllers' moving expenses were paid no matter where they moved. Some took appalling advantage—one controller moved a mile, another six-tenths of a mile, and a third had the audacity to charge

the government to move him one-tenth of a mile—literally
a couple of blocks to a new home. Others took advantage
of the loophole in minimum distances to move to new
homes that were actually *farther* away from the new job
center—one controller moved 1.3 miles distant and a
fourth moved 5.7 miles farther out. A Denver controller
sold his house, put his belongings in storage and gave his
new address as "unknown at this time." He was paid
$16,446 for that "move." In the end, the FAA spent $1.3
million on these bogus moves.

These moves were paid for because the FAA did not
include the thirty-five-mile minimum in its agreement with
the controllers' union in Chicago and Denver. In a 1991
survey, the FAA concluded that the thirty-five-mile limit
would stop only thirteen short-distance moves per year,
and save only $300,000. The agency didn't think that was
worth the aggravation to the controllers. But the FAA's
conclusion was erroneous: the thirty-five-mile limit would
actually have prevented many more than thirteen moves
in those cities. Without the deal between the union and
the FAA, almost none of the employees would have been
eligible for a paid move because the old and new facilities
were less than thirty-five miles apart.

For two years after the new Denver and Chicago facilities opened, hundreds of people had another two years to
decide if they wanted to move. So in the end, the FAA
may end up owing $57 million to employees moving
around the U.S. Our recommendation was simple: say no
to promises made to employees who don't qualify for paid
moves, open talks with the unions to set distance requirements and get back the money spent on bogus moves.
Also, cancel the "return rights" for FAA employees moving around the U.S. In this case, at least, the FAA
agreed—and in its own investigation found even more
workers in Denver who had gotten the government to pay
for their moves when it shouldn't have. It was trying to
get another $471,000 back from those people. At the same
time, the agency was hoping to get the unions back to the
negotiating table to set distance guidelines of fifty miles,
as established by the IRS. But the agency still refused to
outright cancel "return rights."

The law says that the FAA has to pay for return rights
from its budget first. So money that might be needed to
move a controller into a vacant job must first be spent on
sending someone else home. In 1994, for example, the
Southern Region air traffic division had twenty-nine vacancies—some of them unfilled for two years—and a shortage
of controllers. Yet the agency couldn't get anyone to move
there to take the jobs because it first had to come up with
money to send four controllers back to their original
homes. Thus critical, safety-related vacancies went
unfilled.

Had the agency eliminated ineligible relocations, it
could have saved $18.4 million. In 1996, the FAA bud-
geted $48.3 million for 1,206 moves. Once our investiga-
tion exposed the free-move abuses, the FAA announced it
was going to fix the thirty-five-mile rule. Everyone would
have to comply. But then the agency turned around and
sent letters to the air traffic controllers, explaining how
they could apply for waivers to dodge the new rule and
keep the money from their bogus moves.

The FAA did try to save money in other ways, however.
Like a lot of government agencies in the early 1990s, the
FAA offered early retirement packages to senior officials.
The offer was sweetened with a one-time lump payment
of $25,000. In return for the bonus money, senior officials
would take early retirement, their pensions and benefits
intact. Then the FAA could eliminate their positions and
save money over the long run. The strategy was called
a "buyout."

When my office did a routine review of the program in
the spring of 1996, we discovered that, unlike any other
agency, the FAA had its own unique way of encouraging
people to accept a buyout. We discovered that many FAA
employees had taken early retirement, only to return to
work the next day as hired independent consultants. In one
case, an FAA official took the buyout, pocketed the
$25,000 and retirement pay and then came to work the
next day in the same job, at the same desk, for more
money. Our report couldn't help but be highly critical of
this practice, especially when it hadn't occurred anywhere

else. As usual, the FAA was incensed and embarrassed by
our findings. The FAA leaked an early draft of our report
(which we sent to them for review and response) to Don
Phillips, an aviation reporter at the *Washington Post*. The
FAA knew no one in my office was allowed to comment
on a report in its draft form. But someone at the FAA
explained to Phillips—off the record, of course—all the
reasons that the Inspector General report on buyouts was
misleading, inconclusive and just plain wrong. I was
stunned to learn about this from Phillips, but when he
asked me to comment on the unfinished report and the
FAA's explanations, I began to realize how cleverly he
was being manipulated. The FAA knew perfectly well that
Phillips would get only their side of the story. I couldn't
quote from a draft report, cite its recommendations or fax
Phillips a copy of the findings. Those were our rules. The
FAA knew that even though I wouldn't be able to talk
about the report, a journalist like Phillips wouldn't be able
to resist printing what he had. So a skewed story about
the buyout investigation appeared in the paper. The FAA
seemed not to care about wasted money or violated ethics,
just its image.

That's when I came up with a new rule for the FAA:
''You leak, I speak.''

CHAPTER NINE

Who Watches the Manufacturers?

When I was in school at Harvard, it was against the rules for pupils to mark their own homework. The reason was obvious—the temptation to give yourself an A was too great. That rule makes sense to most people. Yet those same people would be stunned to learn that's exactly what happens at aircraft manufacturers like the Boeing Company, Lockheed and McDonnell Douglas. These corporations grant themselves federal certification of their own aircraft designs.

The temptation may be great to give a brand-new jet an A under normal circumstances. But what happens when a company is desperate to keep a multibillion-dollar project on schedule or is looking over its shoulders at its competitors? The story of the Boeing 777 should make most people question the value of the government oversight they are getting for the tax dollars they spend on the FAA.

The truth is, 95 percent of the tests required to certify the Boeing 777 as safe and sound were done by surrogates picked by the FAA from *among Boeing employees*. But the Boeing engineers didn't just sign off on FAA tests of the 777 and its systems—they wrote the questions, too. They set the standards for success or failure, then con-

ducted the tests and, finally, evaluated whether the plane
passed or not. Of course it did.

And that's not all. Even if the FAA had wanted to retrace
Boeing's steps, it couldn't have. FAA engineers, by their
own admission, can't compete with Boeing's cutting-edge
experts. The agency's employees don't understand much
of the technology inherent to twenty-first-century jets like
the 777. That's why Boeing surrogates had to do the tests
in the first place.

Surprisingly little has changed in aircraft technology
since the Jet Age began in the 1940s. Yet that enormous
leap from the piston engine to turbojet propulsion was
profound. Planes went from a top speed of about 300 miles
per hour to a subsonic 600 miles, then to supersonic, then
again to twice-the-speed-of-sound Mach 2 before the end
of the 1950s. Then, status quo—no comparable jump in
technology since.

Fighter pilots first used jets in World War II, but for
years after the war, the burgeoning commercial airlines
struggled to make faster piston planes that could fly longer
distances without a fuel stop. The McDonnell Douglas
DC-3, the 1940s airline workhorse, flew about 200 miles
per hour. In 1953, the company rolled out its DC-7, a
wonder that could fly 300 miles per hour and cover 3,000
miles at a leap. In the competition for the ultimate piston-
engine plane, the DC-7 duked it out with the Lockheed
Super-Constellation. In those days, the piston engine was
at its zenith. But airlines still wanted faster, bigger planes
that could carry more people and cargo. Competition was
intense. Across the sea, the British civil aviation industry
yearned for a chunk of the lucrative flying business, but
manufacturers there could not keep up with McDonnell
Douglas and Lockheed. Instead, they pinned their hopes
on an idea first proposed in 1927 by a Royal Air Force
cadet named Frank Whittle—jet propulsion. Throughout
the 1930s, Whittle and German and American scientists
had raced to develop the jet engine. By 1937, Whittle had
a working model—a mammoth turbojet engine so powerful that it seemed unlikely an airplane frame could withstand its force. After the war, researchers discovered that

jet engines could be installed in any size plane, and by the mid-1950s, Boeing was hard at work on designing the plane that would debut in 1958 as its 707. The 707 was expected to fly faster than any other plane, but nobody realized that it would also turn out to be cheap to run. When Pan Am put the 707 into service that October, it quickly became clear that it cost less to fly a 707 loaded with people and cargo than it would cost to fly the best piston-engine plane. And jets could fly farther with less maintenance. Soon commercial flight was a cheap, commonplace, efficient way to get around. Within a few years Boeing had a whole fleet—the 727 carried 100 passengers, like the best piston-engine planes. The 737, which carried about 150 people, became the workhorse of Boeing's fleet, while the 747, rolled out in 1970, carried 400 people and still had huge storage areas for luggage, mail and cargo.

In the 1970s, jet-plane speed reached Mach 3. With every engineering advance, the planes became more complex. The industry grew as design, materials, tooling, skills and manufacturing became increasingly sophisticated. Aircraft manufacturers like Boeing, which started building planes so it would have a fleet for its own mail run, began devoting more time, money and staff to research and development. Designing new planes became a huge part of the aviation industry. Because these planes performed so spectacularly, could fly thousands of miles without needing much maintenance and had such long working lives, soon fewer were needed. The aircraft companies went from rolling out massive numbers of planes to making a few, highly complex models. Because of this, fewer aircraft are actually built now than during World War II, in spite of fifty years of explosive growth in peacetime air travel.

For a manufacturer like Boeing, hanging on to the increasingly competitive airplane market as airlines struggle to keep costs down means new planes have to be cutting-edge. They have to fly faster, farther, with greater fuel efficiency, and offer all kinds of passenger comfort and cargo efficiency. For the Boeing Company at the end of the twentieth century, that means the twin-engine 777 jet.

Aircraft manufacture in the 1990s is more competitive than ever. For decades, the oversight of civil airplane de-

sign was a boring aspect of aviation that attracted little
attention, except for a brief flurry of interest when Jimmy
Stewart was a heroic civil aviation test engineer responsible for the airplane called The Reindeer in the movie
Highway in the Sky. The approval-and-certification process
plodded along according to dry, rigid regulations that interested few people beyond FAA officials and manufacturers.
Nothing about the process stirred up politicians, excited
economists, or jump-started lobbyists. Certification was little more than a necessary logistical detail that took care
of itself in its own due time. U.S. aircraft manufacturers
had virtually no foreign competition in the 1960s and early
1970s. No one else was horning in on their customers, so
there was little rush to approve planes or designs quickly
or speculatively.

But the market changed dramatically in the mid-1970s,
when a consortium of French, British and German aircraft
manufacturers got together and formed Airbus. Suddenly
Boeing and McDonnell Douglas found themselves facing
stiff, foreign government–subsidized competition. And
those governments were not above tying strings to their
national aviation industries. In some cases, airline landing
rights seemed to be contingent on buying Airbus planes.
Suddenly, American builders were under intense pressure
to beat Airbus. And just as suddenly, the FAA was no
longer a detached observer of plane designs. The agency
fell right in step with Boeing and McDonnell Douglas
(which merged in 1997) and others in their race to beat
the Europeans.

When Boeing engineers went to their drawing boards
in search of a product that would undercut Airbus sales,
the 777 was born. The plane is the first to be designed
entirely by computer modeling—5,000 engineers created
three-dimensional digital projections of the plane and its
four million parts, but no prototype was ever built. Rather
than making a faster plane, the designers concentrated on
creating a bigger, more comfortable aircraft. The 777 can
carry up to 550 people, has wider aisles (so passengers
can slip past the food trolley) and higher ceilings, and a
media center at each seat. A fuel-efficient, economical
plane, the 777 flies entirely "by wire." Essentially, the

aircraft is a computer with a plane built around it; pilots control the computer, and the computer flies the plane. Everything relies on software with thousands of lines of programming code. Conventional aircraft rely on hydraulic, mechanical and electrical systems—pilots control rudders, for example, with cables and pulleys. In the 777, software operates the rudders. One central computer and one central computer cable control the plane like the brain and spinal column.

Most aircraft manufacturers are building planes dominated by computers. Before the merger with Boeing, the McDonnell Douglas MD-11 was designed to use sophisticated software to continuously monitor and adjust the hydraulic, electrical and fuel systems without any action from the crew. These critical functions used to be handled by the flight engineer—but the new MD-11 needed two, not three, in the cockpit. (It was discontinued as a passenger plane after the merger.) The Boeing 747-400 uses an automated system to land during severe weather. The Airbus A320, with 150 computer systems, has "glass cockpit" technology, where cockpit gauges are replaced by computer systems that analyze flight data and display the results on video screens. NASA predicts that by 2005, commercial pilots will navigate using sensors and satellites, flying at three times the speed of current aircraft, rarely looking out the window but watching a video screen that displays an enhanced image of the skies around the plane. Other than the part about the speed, they are probably right.

It is absolutely critical for FAA inspectors to understand these complex systems in order to certify the safety of these new planes. However, the agency's involvement in the certification process has shrunk so dramatically that it threatens the FAA's ability even to understand these new devices. Fortunately, manufacturer expertise and commitment to safety have covered for the FAA.

But can software programs made up of millions of lines of code in several different computer languages ever be exhaustively tested? The flight control software in the Boeing 777 has 132,000 lines of code. All told, the 777 has over 4 million lines of code and 150 computers. Experts have been quoted as saying 20,000 lines of code is a program too complicated to test thoroughly. In addition, Boeing has been criticized for installing three identical primary flight computers in the 777. One team of programmers wrote one software program for all three systems. Critics contend that if a fault develops in the software, it will plague all three systems, perhaps even causing all three to collapse. Yet the plane has three flight computers precisely so there will be backup systems in case of a failure. Other manufacturers use this strategy to even better ends. Software on the Airbus flight computers was written by different teams of programmers. The programs use different computer languages and run out of sequence with one another. That way a failure of one is unlikely to infect the other two. Boeing defied these principles when it decided to use identical software on the 777. When the FAA asked Boeing to test its software, the aircraft manufacturer refused, arguing that the lines of code had already been tested and verified so extensively that any potential for error had been eliminated.

The FAA certified the 777 anyway. The agency admitted it allowed major changes to the plane's development plan so that it could stay on schedule for certification. But the FAA's national software expert admitted to the *Seattle Times*, "I'm in a very embarrassing situation. To say the software is safe, I cannot tell you that. I can tell you the software [development] has followed our procedures."

The importance of the 777 to Boeing cannot be overestimated. At its peak in 1989, Boeing employed more than 165,000 people. Then economic recession in the early 1990s drove the company into a tailspin; slashing its workforce left and right, the company pared down to 105,000 employees in 1995. That was the only way to survive the terrible year before, 1994, when the company sold only 120 planes. But Boeing's health improved in 1995 as orders surged to 346 planes, and stayed good through 1996. By the fall of that year, the company had orders for over 330 planes, many of them from airlines chomping at the bit to buy the new 777. Demand for that plane was so high, Boeing announced it would hire 13,200 new workers. The company was already having trouble keeping up with its production schedule—the 777 wing-tooling people were under great strain, for example. Then, at the end of the summer, United Airlines announced it wanted $2.5 billion in new planes from Boeing, including two 777s. The company rushed to up production of 777s from five a month to seven. Business was booming again at Boeing, the price of the company's stock jumped on Wall Street and stockbrokers began predicting even higher earnings estimates for the company.

Yet the FAA doesn't understand this plane. Its experts were left out of the crucial early-design stages because they didn't know what was going on at Boeing; the manufacturer was even able to change designs in midstream without the FAA immediately realizing what had happened. By 1993, the FAA had fallen so far behind in aircraft technology that over half the engineers with primary responsibility for the 777 had never participated in a major certification project.

It is the FAA's job to certify aircraft—to decide when a wholly new plane can roll out and fly, or when design modifications to an existing model are okay. The whole process typically takes five years. During that time, the manufacturer has to give the FAA detailed plans, drawings, test reports and analyses proving that the plane meets safety and design requirements. The manufacturer also has to produce a prototype of the plane and conduct ground and flight tests. FAA engineers and test pilots have to review this data and carry out tests and analyses. But the process isn't infallible. In 1979, a McDonnell Douglas DC-10, a plane that was also produced in a race to the market to beat the competition, crashed and killed 273 people; maintenance and design flaws were the cause. That was when the National Academy of Sciences took a look at FAA certification systems and said that while they were acceptable, they were in danger of falling behind in competence. In fact, the Academy found that engineers at the FAA were considerably less competent than their counterparts in industry. Many FAA engineers said inadequate training left them three to five years behind developments in their industry. In 1991, a study showed that the FAA certification staff had no comprehensive, up-to-date program that described training courses needed, related the courses to job performance, set a sequence for courses and made the courses available. At the FAA, only one course related to certification had been developed between 1982 and 1993.

Instead, to cope with the explosion in technology, the agency began to rely heavily on manufacturers like Boeing to help it evaluate all the bells and whistles associated with new planes—advanced avionics and electrical systems, computer software, flight loads and management, advanced composite materials, crash dynamics and metallurgy. This was well within the law—the FAA was allowed to choose "surrogate" inspectors from among Boeing employees. But it meant that, increasingly, manufacturers like Boeing were certifying their own planes. From 1980 to 1992, the agency increased its number of surrogates from 299 to 1,287—a whopping 330 percent. The agency now asks manufacturers to run 95 percent of certification activities—without defining how and where FAA staff should step in, without overseeing the surrogates or evaluating their performances. Rules established in 1967 say the FAA has to review only 5 percent of an experienced surrogate's work, and only 33 to 50 percent of a new guy's. (Naturally, the rules don't specify what areas should be reviewed, or the type of review to be done.) During the same years, the number of FAA staff engineers and test pilots dropped from 117 to 89. This hands-off approach not only means the FAA doesn't effectively oversee the certification process, it also means the agency has little firsthand contact with the newest technologies. The agency hasn't added engineering, computer and software experts to its staff—and its employees have had little training in the newest technologies. A GAO study found that between 1990 and 1992, only one of the twelve FAA engineers responsible for approving aircraft software went to a software-related training course. The FAA told the GAO it was setting up a new training program, but it didn't set any specific training requirements for staff in their area of expertise.

In real terms, for an aircraft like the Boeing 747-400, 95 percent of the certification steps have been handed over to the company. Surrogates approved the entire flight management system (it runs the navigational system and monitors the performance of other components) because the FAA staff "were not sufficiently familiar with the system to provide meaningful inputs to the testing requirements or to verify compliance with the regulatory standards," the GAO said. In other words, the FAA didn't know what it was doing, so it let Boeing manage the entire certification process. FAA personnel didn't understand ten other critical systems, either—including the aircraft braking system—so they gave those to the Boeing surrogates as well.

The FAA itself realized in 1989 that it simply couldn't delegate any more responsibility, even if it wanted to; any more surrogates and the FAA wouldn't be involved in the project at all. In 1993, a General Accounting Office report stated flatly that 95 percent was already too much. The FAA's increasing dependence on delegating "has weakened the safeguards . . . FAA is now delegating to [surrogates] critical decisions once reserved for itself." The agency even went so far as to ask surrogates to approve their own *test plans*—that is, the manufacturer's description of how it will prove that an aircraft design or system meets regulatory standards. That meant Boeing, for example, would set the scope and rigor of its own tests. The FAA was left with little input on how a design, component or system would be proved safe. If that were not enough, surrogates also took over "failure analyses"—the evaluations in which every aspect of design, structure, systems or components is assumed to malfunction or fail. On the 747-400, the FAA let Boeing engineers approve the failure analyses of ten major systems.

Looking at these figures, the GAO urged the FAA to get more involved in certifications. But the Department of Transportation balked. That would impose rigid requirements on the aviation industry, and put the government in the position of dictating to private companies the sequence of events and the participants involved in each step of a product's development. The government did not want to interfere that way.

In truth, safety may be more important to Boeing than to the FAA or any government agency. There's a reason for the old saw: if it ain't Boeing, I ain't going. Boeing would destroy its credibility with the traveling public and the airlines that bought its aircraft if it allowed poorly designed planes to leave its hangars: product liability lawyers would see a windfall. Business considerations aside, no one working at Boeing should allow corners cut if it means planes will crash. They fly, too. Aircraft manufacturers produce remarkably safe planes when they insist on rigorous quality control and incomparable expertise. They insist on redundancy, fail-safe and damage-tolerant designs. They could be excellent surrogates for less talented FAA officials.

But as manufacturers come under increasing competition for customers, the temptation to direct too much of the certification process is too great. Pinning such high hopes on the 777 meant that Boeing was determined nothing would interfere with the plane's production schedule or cost projections. The company planned a huge media event for the 777 rollout on the day it would get its FAA certificate. When it became clear that the jet would not be ready for certification by the chosen date, Boeing refused to postpone the party. Too much was riding on the timetable—the press, the aviation industry, Boeing's performance on the stock market, the perceived economy of its home base in the Pacific Northwest. Rather than reschedule, Boeing persuaded the FAA to take the highly unusual step of certifying the plane for zero passengers. Boeing could still roll out the plane and blow trumpets over the fact that it was certified to fly. But no passengers could board for the ride.

I couldn't ignore news reports of this unusual accreditation; it was astounding that a plane like the 777 had been certified this way. It was also unprecedented, leading me to believe that the manufacturer might have exerted undue pressure on the FAA. Could we count on aircraft manufacturers to continue policing themselves rigorously, or was the cutthroat marketplace creating dangerous conflicts of interest? I wanted to know more about the certification process. That meant starting an investigation of FAA practices.

Other certification "firsts" bothered me, too. The 777

was designed with early approval for flying-hour requirements. Those are the hours that a jet must spend in the
sky to earn the right to fly ocean routes that take it great
distances from the nearest airport. Usually it takes about
two years after a plane begins regular passenger flights to
accumulate that much time in the air. But Boeing wanted
the 777 to have its flying-hour requirements as soon as it
began passenger services. So the company put the plane
on a stringent program of takeoffs and landings, and flights
with only one engine operating (a jet must be able to fly
with only one engine for extended periods to prove it can
stay aloft if it loses one of its engines over the middle of
the ocean). The complication here was that, unlike the
747, the 777 has only two engines to begin with. The
company said its tests equaled five years' worth of single-
engine flying in a 767. In May 1995, the FAA granted the
777 another first: permission that allowed it to make extended trips over the ocean as soon as it was put into
service.

Boeing tried to control costs by limiting tests of the
777's components, too—including its thrust reverser. The
test should have been considered essential, since earlier
Boeing models had terrible problems with thrust reversers
that suddenly, mistakenly, activated during flight. Thrust
reversers, which are used to slow down or back up the
plane, are subject to tremendous stress, and fractures are
not uncommon. When the FAA certified the Boeing 767
in 1982, it asked the company to consider the possibility
of an in-flight thrust reverser deployment. In the end, the
agency left approval of the system to the Boeing surrogates. They submitted a statement saying that an in-flight
deployment had been considered and that, in their opinion,
the aircraft would operate safely. When the FAA reviewed
the Boeing paperwork, it didn't double-check this analysis
or the assumption. It simply accepted the statement, added
it to the paperwork and approved the plane's certification.
Less than a decade later, thrust reversers suddenly activated during flight on a Lauda Airlines 767 flight. Two
hundred and twenty-three people died. Boeing called it a
one-in-a-million tragedy, and blamed the fact that the

plane had no standard safety features, a problem its engineers immediately corrected.

Anthony Broderick, the FAA Associate Administrator for Regulation and Certification, told Congress that the thrust reverser problem might be caused by a series of electrical malfunctions, hydraulic contamination or a combination of the two. No one knew for sure. He also said the FAA had done tests of what happened when thrust reversers suddenly deployed during flight.

". . . it is not reasonable to expect even a highly skilled airline pilot to control an airplane under a thrust reverser deployment of the type that we think, from evidence we have seen so far, occurred in the Lauda accident. Within just a few seconds, the airplane would become uncontrollable.

"In other words, if it happens, we assume the airplane would be lost," he said. That meant, he added, that the FAA would require all new and existing airplane designs to be reviewed so that "it is not possible for an in-flight thrust reverser deployment to occur."

Even without these precedents, aircraft manufacturers are usually required to build prototype systems and actually run them through rigorous tests. But when the 777 was being designed, the FAA settled for computer modeling of the thrust reversers—because Boeing insisted that an in-air test would be *too dangerous*.

Rumors circulated that scientists at NASA, which studies civil aviation along with its space agency duties, had determined that the complex software required by the 777 would probably suffer over eighty glitches per system. The space agency should know what it's talking about—its craft, such as the space shuttle, rely on multiple lines of code. During the first years of its journey, the computer on the Galileo spacecraft switched itself into "safe mode" more than ten times. The shutdowns were relatively harmless—except that they cost NASA critical scientific data that it dearly wanted. But Galileo was otherwise okay, and parallel backup systems automatically kicked in to keep essential functions running. Scientists on Earth scrambled to fix the glitches so they wouldn't miss data as Galileo explored Jupiter and its moon. I've heard that a Mariner spacecraft failed for want of a comma in its software.

But there were no passengers on Galileo or Mariner. No lives were at stake. No people who assumed their safety had been thoroughly considered and accounted for. The complex, highly developed computer system inevitably had bugs. Scientists at NASA did not apologize for that or criticize themselves for some design fault; they knew better. Glitches are simply a fact of computer life, and the best insurance, plainly, is backup systems. Apparently Boeing did not agree, even though the 777 was to be the first entirely computer-controlled commercial airplane. There was no precedent for how such a plane would perform. NASA was cautious, skeptical. So how could FAA officials rest assured that Boeing was correct—that 777 software was glitch-free, entirely responsive and completely reliable?

NASA, for its part, refuses to make public the study that analyzed the 777 software system. "Boeing paid for it," a NASA spokesperson said, "so it's theirs. Besides, we assumed they fixed everything."

Apparently the FAA made the same assumptions.

In 1996, the media reported new worries stemming from the certification shortcuts. Experts were concerned about what would happen if a 777's engine lost a fan blade. Industrywide, this happens many, many times a year, and can cause fire, or death from flying shrapnel. On the 747, it can cause the plane to shake violently. Boeing and the FAA dismissed the concerns.

In the end, the Inspector General evaluation of the Boeing 777 certification process would be canceled by my successor. But a draft version of the report was prepared by my staff in June 1996. They concluded that the FAA inspectors could not have stopped the 777 rollout even if they had wanted to—because Secretary Peña, Administrator Hinson and Assistant Administrator Broderick all stepped in at critical junctures to keep the plane on its fast development track. In other words, they interfered with the certification process to keep Boeing's schedule.

Still, the shortcuts and pressures of production on the fast track would catch up with Boeing. On October 3,

1997, Boeing suspended its 747 and 737 production lines for a month. Besides fast-tracking the 777, Boeing had doubled production over the past eighteen months. Boeing was consuming parts and materials faster than they could get produced, at least legitimately, by thousands of sub-contractors all over the world. Boeing was having trouble hiring and training workers fast enough.

The FAA then stepped up inspections of Boeing because of assembly errors and systemic shortcomings. Boeing, even though swamped with over a thousand jet orders, was experiencing record losses. It was having to pay millions in late-delivery charges and it had to spend $700 million to fix problems on the 737; fixes which, after years of delay, the FAA had been forced to eventually demand. In October 1997, Boeing posted a third-quarter loss of $1.6 billion and another projected loss of $1 billion over the next five quarters.

Boeing had to discover what they taught us in college so many years ago: Don't rush through a test. You will probably miss something important.

On December 19, 1997, a new 737 crashed, killing all on board. On January 8, 1998, news reports said investigators believed fasteners were missing from the horizontal stabilizer at the tail—the bolts were feared to have been left off 185 Boeing 737s when they were built.

Also in 1997, one model of the 777 was decertified for extended over-water operations because of trouble with the engines. And a British software expert actually quantified the additional risk of relying on a single program instead of a triplex system to control a 777. The triplex system is twenty times more reliable.

CHAPTER TEN

TWA Flight 800

Running the Inspector General's office was a little like playing football at Ohio State—three yards and a cloud of dust. It was not a passing game. I fought battles one at a time, incrementally chalking up successes in major safety areas: airplane parts, airport security, maintenance, inspections, training. But I remained unable to break through the FAA's inertia and defensiveness to conquer the disorder at its core that allowed negligence and incompetence to dominate. I won skirmishes once I learned to sidestep the FAA, to join investigative forces with the FBI, U.S. Attorneys or the General Accounting Office, and to deliver my findings to certain members of Congress, the White House, the administration and the press. But I realized that my individual victories would never change the FAA. The agency could not be affected from within. Countless times over the years, I had watched in dismay as the FAA lumbered along, creating task forces and assigning studies, only to jump through hoops after an air tragedy and in the glare of television spotlights. I checked my anger and muttered instead about the Tombstone Agency. The FAA dealt with safety only in a crisis.

The tragic, troubled history of ValuJet had amply illustrated that sad lesson. ValuJet was the distilled essence of the corrosion from within at the FAA and the failings of the aviation industry. But Wall Street loved start-up airlines like ValuJet, and the FAA protected them as integral to a healthy aviation economy. It was the written policy of Secretary Peña and the Administration to protect start-ups, the low-cost carriers. Lobbyists ensured that regulations were friendly to them. In the end, it was inevitable that this house of cards would fall. Passengers paid with their lives. And just days after ValuJet fell from the sky, Secretary of Transportation Federico Peña appeared on national television to assure Americans that ValuJet and all airlines like it were safe. What was Peña talking about?

The ValuJet crash thrust before the public the fact that an inferior airline was allowed to continue flying because of economic pressure. Only public outrage forced Peña to finally acknowledge that Congress should eliminate the FAA's dual mandate to promote aviation.

After all, it wasn't the first time that hazardous materials had caused a terrible accident on a plane, nor the first time that a disaster might have been averted if the cargo hold had been properly equipped with smoke and fire warning systems. The FAA knew this; the airlines knew it; the NTSB, the Department of Transportation and its Inspector General all knew it. Perhaps the only ignorant players in the game were the passengers. Yet even after 110 of them died in the Everglades, Peña went on television to defend his agency and ValuJet. Still, Peña seemed to underestimate the significance of the mandate.

"This led to the unacceptable perception that the FAA had to make choices between ensuring safety and promoting the industry it regulates." That was it. He thought the problem was solved.

I was working at home on my computer when Peña took to the airwaves. As I heard his comments from the television across the room, my fingers froze over the keyboard. Was Peña ignorant of the true nature of the FAA? Or had the FAA spoon-fed him this line about the dual standard being no big deal? Whether he believed it himself or not, he and the FAA knew they could utter pablum about the FAA mandate and nobody would be the wiser. They counted on the public not knowing what the mandate really means to the FAA. Peña's recommendation to Congress, no doubt supported at the FAA, was to tweak the wording of the mandate, not to dig out the root of the problem. In truth, the mission is much more than just a few words in the act. It is threaded throughout the legislation, just the way the culture of promoting aviation is woven throughout the FAA, inherent in its practices, its policies, and the people who work there. Eliminating a few lines in the law won't change the agency's entrenched favoritism toward the aviation industry.

That culture propelled Peña to face the public after the ValuJet crash like a nervous cheerleader whose team was forty points down in the fourth quarter. His carefully crafted explanations that ValuJet was safe were meant to prevent the public from reacting with hysteria to the truth. But the Department of Transportation wanted to prevent hysteria not to safeguard the public, but to protect the moneymaking status quo of the airline industry, and especially the low-cost or start-up carriers. The ValuJet crisis trained a floodlight on one of the more striking FAA fallacies—that, once certified, an airline is always safe. That if an airline is not safe, it cannot fly. Those are simply myths. No one at the FAA or in the aviation industry wants to acknowledge that vast differences exist among airline maintenance facilities, the age and quality of aircraft, the caliber of spare-parts inventory and programs for screening bogus parts, the qualifications and experience of pilots and crew, and security practices. The public believes that caring professionals at the FAA regulate all of that through a finely honed, carefully orchestrated network of safety laws. The FAA does not want consumers to believe any differently. In reality, the FAA is at a loss to know how to deal with this new style of airline business, and with new threats to airplanes. The discount airlines that appeared and grew rapidly in the late 1980s and 1990s left the FAA stunned and blinking at a whirlwind of leased and used planes, contracted and subcontracted maintenance facilities, and inexperienced pilots and flight crews. But the FAA's inertia sent a message: what the public doesn't know can't hurt it. And the agency amply demonstrated that it wouldn't challenge that assumption until a major plane disaster claimed hundreds of lives.

And sometimes not even then.

*   *   *

In 1993, I learned that the FAA's abhorrence of action extended to airport security. As I discussed briefly in the introduction, plainclothes agents from my office sneaked into some of the nineteen busiest airports in the U.S. They wandered around in off-limits areas, seldom challenged by airport or airline employees. We saw other people milling about without proper identification, and they weren't stopped, either. Once my agents got into these supposedly secure areas, they walked around aircraft parking spaces, baggage processing centers, maintenance areas and ramp administrative offices. They got onto planes and into cargo holds. They wore no identification, dressed casually and didn't even pretend to belong there. They also carried guns, knives, fake bombs and a deactivated hand grenade through security screening points and x-ray machines. When we reported the lax state of airport security, our findings caused a stir in the media, on Capitol Hill, among the airlines and even at the Department of Transportation. The FAA noted that it ''concurred'' with virtually all of our recommendations to fix airport defenses. Unfortunately, agreement did not necessarily mean action.

So when I decided, in 1995, that we should repeat our security audit, I expected that most of the more obvious breaches would prove to be corrected. We decided to put particular emphasis on bomb detection this time, too. But I was bitterly disappointed: in 1995, my agents, together with FAA inspectors, carried fake bombs strapped to their bodies or in briefcases, marzipan candy or other substances arrayed on boards to look like plastic explosives, and guns and knives through metal detectors. They got in secure areas at the big international airports around the country.

They were not stopped 40 percent of the time.

Early in the summer of 1996, I gathered up the final report on airport security and made my way toward the FAA Administrator's office. I wasn't looking forward to this meeting. The FAA didn't like me, and had never liked my reports, and if I had somehow missed that message, a fresh signal had just been sent. Secretary Peña had been scheduled to come to this meeting; in fact, he had called it. But then his office must have discovered that the latest airport report was not substantially different from the 1993 study. So he bowed out of the briefing. The message seemed clear to me. The Secretary was seeking Washington's best protection—deniability. Peña didn't want to know about the security report. Since I insisted on discussing it, the Secretary had apparently decided not to hear me. Instead, he left it to the FAA Administrator.

Hinson's demeanor was familiar: he was his usual easygoing self. I fully expected the FAA staff and the Secretary's underlings not to like our findings, but I wasn't prepared for what emerged as the real point of our meeting: they wanted me to bury the report. The Olympic Games were opening in Atlanta that same month. I rustled the papers in front of me; the dismal truth was right there in black and white. I reminded the nonchalant FAA faces of the bomb-detection failure rates. At the nation's biggest, busiest airports. I spoke of my agents' success in getting past security almost half the time—at many of those same airports. Their expressions did not change. They chose to interpret our study their way: there was no real chance of a major attack, bombing or hijacking of an airline, airport or particular flight, they pointed out. The investigation might have miserable results, but "the threat is low," they kept repeating. Thousands of planes take off and land every day, yet people are in greater danger just driving their cars. What good would it do to upset the public and generate a lot of negative publicity right before the Olympics?

I couldn't say that an attack was imminent. Still, I knew that the number of attempted bombings had skyrocketed in recent years. And it made me nervous that no one could be sure an attack *wasn't* inevitable, and that I was one of the few people who knew that if a bomber made a move on an airport, he stood a pretty good chance of success. How could a few bureaucrats in a Washington office determine the odds? I thought of the World Trade Center, the trials in New York City of the terrorists responsible for that attack, the Oklahoma City bombing. In October 1995 and August 1996, supporters of the man on trial in New York for masterminding the World Trade Center bombing had threatened to attack a number of U.S. carriers. The

threats were taken seriously enough for the department to
quietly boost security in places like Kennedy Airport. In
1995, Secretary Peña had warned that American airports
"are not immune" to terrorist threats, and urged facilities
to buy bomb-detection equipment and hire a "competent,
highly motivated security workforce." Did the FAA think
that was enough to tighten the safety net around airports?
Apparently it was confident enough in the departmental
edict and scared enough about bad publicity from my office's report. It just couldn't stomach more public exposure
of how insecure U.S. airports really were.

The FAA did try to get airports to do a better job at
screening. In January 1996, it warned airline and airport
managers at major airports across the country that there
were serious problems not only with airline screening pro-
cesses, but with the airports' security procedures. I found
out later that they released to the airlines the very information they wanted me to withhold, and warned that it was
publicly available information—the failure rates at all the
category X, or large, international airports. Successful
checkpoint screening was "well below the national average," and bomb detection was poor. For example, O'Hare
was in sixteenth place among nineteen big international
airports. The FAA said its people watched 1,500 bags go
through checkpoints, and saw only one opened for closer
inspection.

"These kinds of results are disturbing in that it is hard
to believe that approximately 1,500 bags went through
without anything suspicious being observed, necessitating
a hand search," an FAA official wrote to O'Hare managers. "This leads me to believe that many screeners are
just going through the motions."

The official also complained that hardly any bags were
x-rayed, pointing out that "this is extremely unusual when
you consider that a good Explosive Detection System will
normally identify approximately 30 percent of baggage as
being suspect . . .

"If one of the issues aforementioned is found, it is
reason for concern and closer scrutiny," the FAA said.
"However, when all the reviews result in the aforemen-

tioned, the system is ineffective and needs to be addressed and corrected.''

Even though the FAA was urging airports and airlines to improve their security, it wanted me not only to ignore the alarms raised by my agents' experiences in airports, but to hide them from the public. No. I couldn't do it. It was too risky to hold the report back, not just so the FAA would not get a black eye, again. My staff had come up with vital information, and it wasn't up to me to decide the public couldn't handle it. I contended that the security report was so important that not only should it be released immediately, it should be delivered directly to the President.

But mine was the minority opinion in that office that day. The most the FAA officials and the Secretary's representative would agree to was to send a copy of the report to the National Security Adviser. The FAA, with the backing of the Secretary of Transportation, remained convinced it was best to withhold the report from the public indefinitely. Leaving the meeting, chilled, I wondered for the umpteenth time what good these investigations were doing when the department constantly whitewashed or downplayed them. And what about my professional responsibility, not to mention my personal obligation, to let people know what we'd found?

As I walked back to my office, I knew passengers were surging through Kennedy and the other airports in our report. What about their rights, their fates? Hadn't their taxpayer dollars paid for this investigation? Uneasy, I told my staff to prepare the report for my signature before the Fourth of July holiday. I would send it to the Secretary and to the Congress before the long weekend. I didn't want anyone to say I held the study back any longer than necessary. Even so, it never made it out of the department until after the political conventions, the Olympics and the TWA disaster. Right before the long weekend, the Department of Transportation insisted I hold on to the report; they were simultaneously requesting that the document be classified.

I knew I could no longer stay in my job. Once again, the FAA was manipulating a potential public relations crisis without a thought for the safety issues involved. The Secretary of Transportation's office was assisting the cover-up by insisting the report should be classified, even though the classifiers had already approved it for release. They didn't really care that the airport security report wouldn't qualify for classification; it would take weeks to figure that out, and by then the Olympics would be over, the goal accomplished, the crisis past.

I knew then that it was hopeless. Every major change I'd been able to force through had come without the help, understanding or assistance of the FAA and the Secretary or his staff. The FAA could not resolve its split personality. The airline industry was too powerful to thwart, the Department of Transportation was solidly behind it, Secretary Peña did not seem to comprehend the significance of many issues and was unwilling to act when necessary and the vast potential power of the average consumer was blocked because the truth about aviation safety was kept from the public. Even the grounding of ValuJet came as a result of pressure from the media and a White House embarrassed by its Secretary of Transportation and FAA Administrator.

The reluctance of the Secretary to take a stand on the airport security report struck me as glaring. Where was his grandstanding now? Why was he not eager to go on television and discuss this latest development in aviation?

If I expected change, I knew I had to devise yet another strategy to circumvent the FAA, to find a way to offer my concerns about safety and security directly to the public. I had to leave my job, the department and government altogether. I had to resign, even though it meant leaving the airport security report behind and unprotected. The Department of Transportation was adrift, blown wherever the winds of a media event or crisis carried it. The Secretary offered no leadership, no knowledge or understanding, no accountability. The Administrator of the FAA was a figurehead. Neither of them heeded NTSB recommendations; neither one followed through on the many reports detailing safety problems at the FAA. Looking around the table at the meeting on the security report, I'd felt painfully defeated for the first time. Nothing would change as

long as I sat in rooms like this. I couldn't continue working in a place where all we did was sit around, waiting
for people to die.

On July 3, I wrote my letter of resignation, but because
of the long holiday weekend, I could not find anyone at
the White House to take the letter until July 8. A week
later, the U.S. Senate Subcommittee on Aviation asked me
to explain why I left my job. I had asked that my appearance be limited because I was six months into a difficult
pregnancy. Nevertheless, the panel questioned me for
many more hours than I expected. They seemed most concerned that I intended to speak and write publicly on what
I knew about aviation safety. Transportation Secretary
Peña and Administrator Hinson were there, too, and they
seemed determined to distance themselves from any responsibility for the problems at the FAA that I complained
about. The Inspector General had never warned him about
ValuJet, Peña told the senators. He had no knowledge, he
insisted, of how deep the crisis ran at the discounter, and
he found it very troubling that I had implied that alarm
bells should have been ringing all over the Department of
Transportation for months.

It was this kind of revisionist pablum that had driven
me from my job. As soon as it was my turn again at the
microphone, I explained to the panel that months before,
the Secretary's own Chief of Staff, Ann Bormolini, had,
at the request of her close personal friend, a ValuJet lobbyist, asked me what I was doing snooping into ValuJet. I
told the senators that in response to this unusual request,
I'd written a stern memo outlining what the FAA and my
office were doing about ValuJet. Did Peña expect us to
believe that he had no idea what his Chief of Staff did
every day in the office suite they shared?

I was exhausted when I got home. I fell asleep early.
It was July 17.

"There's been another crash. It doesn't look good," I
heard my husband say through my fog of sleep. "A TWA
jet crashed into the ocean."

I got up and followed him to the television. TWA flight

800 had just plummeted into the Atlantic in a ball of flames off Long Island. Ugly orange flames dancing in the darkened sea on our television screen mesmerized my husband and me, just as millions of other people sat glued to the same pictures. The pattern of fire on the ocean traced a vicious outline of destruction that seemed to offer little hope for survivors. A familiar, wrenching dread tugged at me. Only too recently I'd stared blankly at the same TV, shocked and sickened by the ragged remains of the ValuJet plane that had smashed into the swampy Everglades. Struggling to absorb the unthinkable, I stared at another watery surface. Somewhere down below was the shattered cylindrical tomb of hundreds of innocent passengers. Echoes of ValuJet questions bounced around my head. Had the TWA jet crashed because an incompetent mechanic missed something? Because a bogus part sold to the airline by shady dealers had failed? Because the plane was so old it was falling apart but the airline had convinced the compliant authorities to extend its flying time? Or was the plane blown out of the sky because lax security had permitted a bomb to be hidden on the plane or slipped aboard as luggage or cargo?

That a bird might have flown into an engine or that lightning could have struck the plane never occurred to me. More likely that shoddy maintenance, an aging aircraft or lax security had led to the crash. The odds against a catastrophe like that were not a zillion to one. That's what the public believed. That's what the FAA told them, and what the airlines repeated constantly. But the failings in aviation maintenance systems that brought down the Valu-Jet plane hadn't been corrected, nor had loose security procedures at many airports been tightened. After my agents filed their reports on airline parts, maintenance, and airport security, none of us would fly certain airlines. We wouldn't let our families get on planes under certain conditions. We used what we knew to protect ourselves and our loved ones. The public hadn't been given the same advantage. The airlines didn't want the flying public making demands about security or parts integrity, and they didn't want reports of unsafe carriers to scare people away from air travel. And what the airlines wanted, the Federal

Aviation Administration wanted, too. Since protecting the public would often have required criticizing the aviation industry, over the decades the FAA learned to keep its opinions and its findings to itself.

For two weeks after TWA flight 800 blew up, I sat through interview after interview on television as the country tried to sort out what could have gone wrong with the flight. Yet it was difficult for me to reassure the public when I knew about the FAA's sloppy safety and security record. To be sure, many FAA field employees are hardworking civil servants, men and women who have devoted their careers to aviation. They fly all the time, and so do their families and friends. Many FAA inspectors helped my office with investigations, reports and testimony before Congress. Senior FAA officials tried to reach compromises with my office and with the NTSB. But most of the time we pursued opposite goals. The FAA wanted peace with the Inspector General and the NTSB, but it wanted harmony by convincing us to lay off, to leave its officials to do their jobs as they always had. Planes are not falling out of the sky, the FAA kept saying. Aircraft are not crashing. Stated over and over, this agency mantra was a blanket justification for business as usual.

But, in fact, planes were falling out of the sky.

In the end, the Olympics were overshadowed by the breathless, staccato voices of news anchors updating the body count from the explosion of TWA flight 800, and speculating on the chemical residue covering airplane parts pulled from the sea, the possibility of a mechanical failure, and mind-boggling theories of surface-to-air missiles. When the plane's black box was recovered, it held few clues because it was one of the older, less sophisticated recorders that the NTSB had for years wanted to see replaced. My office's knowledge that a bomb could easily be carried through an airport like Kennedy, into cargo areas and even onto a plane still had not been made public. It hadn't been released to the airlines or the airport administrators, either. The report was finally issued in September, after the Democratic National Convention was safely over. It barely caused a ripple. All the information about infiltration of airports with bombs was blacked out, as were the rates of failure to detect security threats at each airline. The FAA had the audacity to call these heavily censored pages a ''good-news report.'' It was not. But the agency's response showed that in spite of Peña's disavowal of the FAA mandate, business continued as usual. The entrenched culture of working hand in hand with the aviation industry endured. The same officials who carried out agency business before Peña's announcement continued in their jobs afterward, and would stay at their posts even if Congress did change the FAA statute.

In the year before TWA flight 800 crashed into the Atlantic Ocean, the FAA had cobbled together a group of aviation officials, each a manager from an airline, and anointed them the Airport Security Advisory Commission. Their job was to decide whether the Aviation Security Improvement Act of 1990 needed further strengthening. Never mind that many of the act's provisions—like bomb-screening machines—that were supposed to be in place by 1993 still had not been implemented. The commission was supposed to go ahead, anyway, and consider reports and studies about terrorists, plastic explosives, bomb-sniffing dogs and million-dollar machines that scan luggage. The members surely knew that in 1995, 165 people died because of domestic terrorism, yet 42,000 died in car crashes. They probably agreed with FAA logic that people shouldn't be scared away from flying and forced to rely on much more dangerous car travel. So they had to consider how much risk to tolerate, and how to achieve a balance between risk and cost. They were to assess how much security inconvenience American passengers might tolerate, how deeply security measures could invade privacy and personal freedom, and whether the cost-benefit ratio made heightened security worthwhile for airports and airlines. Yet they understood that much of their debate would be academic. The airlines had no intention of coughing up the money for a Sisyphean effort to make airports 100 percent secure. When—if—such a huge project would be launched, the government should pay for it, they contended. The advisory commission would be their vehicle for making sure the FAA understood this, and that it sympathized. FAA security experts reciprocated with analyses that clearly showed the amount of money spent guarding against bombs and hijackers far outstripped the value of a plane or two and even, somehow, the hundred or few hundred lives that might be lost in a bombing.

They knew this to be true (and the airlines agreed), even considering reports from the FBI Bomb Data Center that bombing attempts had skyrocketed from 803 in 1984 to 3,163 in 1994, and the findings of the Inspector General and the General Accounting Office that most big international airports in the U.S. were not only poorly secured, they were in fact sieves. Even the recent, vivid and devastating images of Pan Am flight 103, blown out of the sky over Lockerbie, Scotland, did not sway anyone. On the contrary, the Lockerbie trauma provided a good supporting argument for the commission. Pan Am flight 103 was rare, unusual, perhaps never to be repeated. Enhanced airport security was certain to be an even costlier ongoing burden. So—no contest.

As usual with government committees, it took the advisory commission months to get its act together. The members organized quietly, away from the public eye, attracting little attention, in no real hurry. Airports continued to operate; passengers continued to check baggage they vaguely believed would be sent down a conveyor belt to a secure cargo area where surely it would be screened. They queued up at airport metal detectors, certain that suspicious items would be flagged by contentious, well-trained security monitors. But when the advisory panel finally met, fate conspired against them. They gathered on July 17, 1996. That evening, TWA flight 800 blew up.

Within hours the White House stepped into the security fray and snatched the debate away from the sluggish influence of the Congress, the FAA and the airlines. Suddenly the advisory members had to scramble to catch a Vice President's commission with a forty-five-day turnaround. It was an election year, after all. Within weeks the commission announced a plan for bomb-detecting equipment, baggage matching and sophisticated computer profiling of passengers. But why did it take presidential pressure? The FAA always had the authority to order those measures.

The crisis was not entirely new to the FAA, however. In fact, the agency accepted these flare-ups as the inevitable cost of doing business. Time to pay the piper, or so the public thought. Most years, the FAA sailed along without serious sacrifices over new regulations either in money or in its relations with the aviation industry. But every now and then a tragedy happened that forced the FAA to abandon its loyalties and answer to public opinion—if only for a while.

In the fall of 1996, just weeks before the 104th Congress was due to adjourn for the election season and the winter holidays, the House and the Senate scrambled to pass a number of important pieces of legislation still on their tables. One of those was the FAA's budget reauthorization. Congress had to pass it, because otherwise the FAA would be out of money and out of business. Yet the horror of ValuJet flight 592 and TWA flight 800 was still very much on everyone's minds. All summer the pressure had been relentless from the National Transportation Safety Board, pilots' and flight attendants' union representatives, grieving relatives on television and me complaining about the FAA and safety. So tucked into the FAA budget bill was language rewriting the FAA's mandate. Section 401 was called "Elimination of Dual Mandate." The lawmakers inserted a first paragraph into the law that charged the FAA with "assigning, maintaining and enhancing safety and security as the highest priorities in air commerce." They changed "promoting, encouraging" the aviation industry to just plain "encouraging," and where the act had said the FAA should promote "air commerce," they inserted the words "safety of."

The FAA is now ordered to "encourage the safety of air commerce in addition to the development of civil aeronautics."

After I resigned, I tried to get one final piece of information out of the FAA that had been used for years to justify inaction: the monetary value of human life.

"I know very well what you mean," an FAA public affairs official said in response to a Freedom of Information Act request, "but I don't think you're going to get that from us.

"Do you expect anybody here to say what is the value we give to human life and then sign off on it and be left open to ridicule for the rest of our lives?" The question angered the official, and the Freedom of Information Act request was denied. The Death on the High Seas Act limits the liability of a manufacturer to the value of the lost wages of the passengers.

The truth is, no one needs government officials to put a dollar value on his or her life, or on the lives of loved ones. We consider ourselves priceless. So should the FAA.

CHAPTER ELEVEN

1997, 1998 . . .

The problem with the future of aviation is it's not what it used to be.

At a book signing in Ohio, I met a lady who was one of the first international aviation attorneys. Assigned by the U.S. government to a billet in Paris, she made her first flight overseas on a DC-4.

Then there were the Constellations. On one of her trips back to the States, she had to take a military transport. Seeing her disappointment at the plane, an officer sneered, "You were expecting a Connie?"

"You know," she said, "I was."

And then came the jets. Her first jet ride was in General DeGaulle's experimental jet, but the progression was rapid. Planes and technology were flying into the future at warp speed. And so on. Every time she went to the airport, she found a newer model. It seemed there were no limits.

"And now?" I asked her.

"Well, it's not like it used to be."

She experienced firsthand the development of commercial aviation—its dramatic development, the constant modernization, the rise of the jet age, and now its graying.

What's remarkable now is the public's acceptance, of twenty- and even thirty-year-old jets, and the matter-of-factness with which the FAA, Congress, and the media

have accepted our geriatric fleets. Hearing after congressional hearing, task force upon task force, newspapers,
magazines, and countless television specials have covered
the problems of our aviation system extensively and well,
but everybody seems to accept as unalterable fate flying
in second-, third-, fourth- or fifth-hand vehicles older than
many of the passengers.

As a kid I remember my dad being obsessed with getting a new Chevy every two or three years. Everybody
did. By the time I bought a car it was more like every
seven to ten years, as we lowered our expectations of
modernization. We waited for quantum leaps—front wheel
drive, anti-lock braking systems, five mile per hour bumpers (and then no five mile per hour bumpers), airbags, and
now airbag cutoff switches. Sometimes it was the government that ordered the change or forced the issue through
recalls. Sometimes it was technology. And sometimes it
was fiery crashes and big lawsuits.

Remember the Pinto? That case was not just about civil
damages; there was a *criminal trial* too. A quantum leap
of a different nature.

The richest guy in Pioneer, Ohio (well, second richest—
the richest won the Ohio lottery), figured out years ago
that Americans were going to start driving their vehicles
into the ground. He set up a chain of car parts shops to
cater to the rusting-of-America mindset. If we had had an
airport in Pioneer, Ohio, I suppose they might have carried
airplane parts too. Because the same thing happened in
aviation, and intentionally or not, it happened because of
deregulation.

As the one-year anniversary of the ValuJet tragedy approached, I found myself getting optimistic. Surely the
FAA would not let the tragic anniversary pass without enacting
the regulations to force safety changes that would have
saved the lives of the 110 people on ValuJet flight 592.
After all, the source of the fire and the need for the same
smoke- and fire-detection and -suppression systems required on wide-bodied planes were revealed within days of
the crash. The NTSB had been begging for them for years.

But the one-year anniversary came and went: no new

changes were ordered, and no carrier had installed the protective systems.

The final NTSB hearing was scheduled, and the families of the ValuJet victims asked if I would come and stand with them at their press conference after the hearing. They were demanding change. They were going to visit every senator and member of Congress on every aviation-related committee to try to get some action.

The NTSB hearing was horrible for the families. Nobody had done their job. Failsafe after failsafe had failed. Everybody asleep at the stick. Even NTSB board members said the disaster had been completely preventable. The NTSB found the FAA, Sabretech, and ValuJet to be at fault.

At the press conference, there were few dry eyes, and certainly not mine. How do you explain to people that their families are dead because the government, their government, failed. You really cannot. There is no excuse.

And so the burden to force safety changes all too often falls on families of victims and survivors of crashes rather than on quantum leaps of technology. Families have spoken out more forcefully than ever before. They have organized to demand the changes that eluded the system at the time their loved ones were lost. If they can help fix the system, then their loved ones did not die in vain.

But still the accidents continue. At the time we went to press with this edition, the big U.S. crash in 1997 occurred in Guam, but there were others—a cargo crash in Miami, crashes in China, Indonesia, Vietnam, South America, and en route to Singapore, myriad military crashes, and of course the hundreds of general aviation accidents barely even noted by most of America, unless it is a beloved American like John Denver at the stick. I no longer work for the Department of Transportation, but I know almost immediately when there has been another disaster even before I hear it on the news. The beeper starts buzzing, the message light flashing, and the fax spitting out the same message. There's been another crash. Can you help us understand why this keeps happening? And what can we do about it?

At least for the families of crash victims there is some improvement in how they are to be treated by the airlines, the government and others after crashes. A group of thoughtful, intelligent, and extremely knowledgeable families of crash victims helped to push through new federal legislation which for the first time gives families certain rights and protection and puts the Red Cross, not the airline that just killed their spouse, children, parents or siblings, in charge of coordinating matters concerning the families immediately after the crash. Airlines must now have a disaster plan in place to fly in this country.

Throughout the ValuJet hearings I often heard one voice, speaking very calmly, intelligently, reasonably and relentlessly through the process. I always put down what I was doing to listen to the families of victims when they spoke, and I could recognize many by face, but I could recognize this woman by voice.

One day, I heard that voice on my answering machine. I was coming in from another day of teaching government ethics and management at OSU and over the din of my three-year-old and my one-year-old, I heard that voice.

"I really respect what you are trying to do and I have some information you might be interested in and which might help you in your efforts."

By anybody's yardstick, Victoria Cummock is a most amazing person. Given what she and her family have been through, a less committed and less informed person might have given up or settled for excuses and face time. But she did not. She lost her husband on PanAm 103, a flight he was not scheduled to be on, but one he rushed to catch because it would get him home sooner. In the 103 aftermath, Victoria endured unbelievable indignities at the hands of the airline and the government agency that contributed to his death—the FAA. I knew her story well, her kids, her life. And I knew how hard she was working for aviation safety and security.

"Could we meet in Washington, D.C.?" I asked. I was going there to be with the ValuJet families after the NTSB hearing in August. So was she.

Victoria Cummock had sued the Vice President over airline safety, a not inconsequential effort, since most government officials, and especially the President and Vice President, are immune from suit for practically anything they do *in office*. But Victoria's suit was a little different.

She had been asked to be a member of the White House Commission on Aviation Safety and Security, which was headed by the Vice President, but she learned it was really a way for the government to *look like* it was doing something about aviation safety when in fact it was not. Cummock had a laundry list of the commission's failings. She had wasted her time and money and, worse, lent her name to a commission that was not on the up and up, she concluded.

She was sick of the FAA and the White House Commission on Aviation Safety comparing injuries and deaths of passengers in planes to those of people in cars.

For years I had heard the FAA excuse planeloads of dead people because the body count for cars was higher in overall numbers. I had found studies and statistics that pointed out that the plane was safer than the car if you compared them on a per mile basis. If you look at them on a per trip basis, the *car* is safer. It only makes sense. It can take thirty or fifty miles for a plane just to get up to cruising altitude, and most car accidents happen less than twenty-five miles from home. Nope, per mile is misleading, slanted, and inaccurate.

More interesting, most aviation accidents happen on takeoff or landing or right at the airport, including on the taxiway or runway. So the exposure is greater on takeoff and landing and is better measured on a per trip basis. One passenger advocate group argues that the best way to cut your risk of dying in a plane crash is to take nonstop rather than connecting flights; you cut your risk in half.

Some experts argue that the best assessment is to compare on an hours of exposure basis—hours stuffed in an airplane, no matter where it is, on the ground or cruising, versus hours stuffed in the car. In that comparison the risk is about the same.

Cummock even had to endure a presentation to the White House Commission by Boeing, which, straight-faced, compared death on a plane to death caused by household injuries (undoubtedly without consideration for the number of hours of exposure). Cummock was not convinced.

''We must compare injuries and deaths of passenger

aboard mass transportation. . . . Clearly flying is riskier
than traveling on a bus or a train. Last year hundreds of
people died aboard scheduled flights, a far cry from the
number of passenger deaths on board public buses or
trains,'' she wrote to the President, pleading that he get
control of the White House Commission.

Well put. Have you ever seen those little machines that
sell-on-the-spot life insurance polices at bus stations or on
train platforms?

In fact, the safest form of mass transportation in the
world is not the airplane, the bus, the car, or even American trains. It is the Japanese Shinkansen, or bullet train.
In all its years of operation, with almost half a million
passengers a day, it has never killed a passenger. According to the Japanese National Police, the Shinkansen
has never had a fatal accident. Just one person has been
killed on the bullet train—by another passenger, who went
crazy on drugs and murdered his seatmate. A few airlines,
like Southwest, can claim a comparable record of never
having killed a passenger, but very, very few.

Besides the crazy deflection of attention to household
injuries, Cummock was gravely concerned about the huge
holes in the commission's work as well as outright mis-
statements. Perhaps worst of all, the recommendations
lacked a timetable and a deadline and a way to make
someone in the government accountable for achievement
of the recommendations—exactly the two things the FAA
could be counted on never to do: meet a deadline and be
held accountable.

The commission language was terribly vague. It ''com-
mended the joint government-industry initiatives to equip
the cargo holds of all passenger aircraft with smoke detectors, and urges expeditious implementation of the rules
and other steps necessary to achieve the goal of both detection and suppression in cargo holds.'' Surely that recommendation did not send carriers to the bank to take out
cash to buy new equipment and new planes. In fact, in
news reports Boeing confirmed that while such equipment
is readily available, nobody ordered it.

The sad fact is there are about 2,900 airplanes without
smoke detectors (to warn the pilots there is a problem)

and fire suppression systems (to buy time) that regularly
fly passengers and hazardous materials and dangerous cargo in
the cargo hold, on the same plane. The cost of this equipment
is estimated to be about thirty cents a passenger. The FAA has
yet to enact regulations requiring the equipment. Over a year
and a half after the ValuJet disaster, only Delta had announced
it would start actual installation.

As for protective breathing equipment, which is already
on board planes to protect the crew (and by the way is on
Air Force One and Two to protect all the people on those
planes as well as on 60 percent of the Fortune 500 corporate jets and entertainers' jets), the commission made no
mention of it. Cummock and I and a host of other passengers already carry our own smoke hoods, because those
little oxygen masks that are supposed to fall from the
ceiling do nothing to protect passengers from smoke or
toxic fumes in the cabin. (Not to mention that you cannot
get up and run through fumes and smoke to exit the plane
if you are tied to the ceiling of the plane.) But we paid
over $100 each for our smoke hoods. To equip my family
of four I spent almost $500, plus more for practice models
and carrying cases. How much would it cost to equip
passenger planes with this equipment? About four cents a
ticketed passenger. Less than a bag of peanuts. Just about
every week you read in the news about a plane having to
make an emergency landing because of smoke or fumes
inside the plane, so we are not talking about a remote
possibility but a common occurrence.

So common that I once suggested at a Secretary's staff
meeting devoted to brainstorming new ideas for DOT to
get more in touch with its customers (I of course thought
our customers were the traveling public) that we create
mock-ups of an airplane emergency exit and let people try
to get one of these things open, so that if they ever had
to do it, they could. After all, during one recent crash,
passengers froze and couldn't open the window exit, and
a fight ensued to open the exit. No way, said the FAA.
We don't want to scare the public, and besides, we don't
really want people thinking they can open these things.
(On some flights, passengers had seen smoke and fire,
opened the doors, and got out, and the airline did not think

an emergency evacuation was necessary—the passengers could have waited to exit the regular doors. The emergency evacuation cost the airline money to have that plane out of service.)

At least the commission called for the FAA to eliminate the exemptions in the FAA regulations that condemn children under the age of two to a status lower than carry-on bags—no requirement to be secured in safety seats or even in seats at all. Did the FAA do it? Not a chance. On this one the people did it for themselves. The first edition of this book told parents about airline rule 190, which says you can bring on your safety seat, it is not to be counted as a carry-on bag, and you don't have to buy an extra ticket if there is space available. If there is an empty seat in that plane, you should demand your carry-on seat be in it as space available. Passengers did exactly that, and most major carriers adopted that policy officially in the summer of 1997, leaving the FAA in the dust. In 1998, the FAA finally said it would at least mandate that a safety seat did not count as a carry-on.

The commission did nothing about the FAA's selective application of the cost-benefit analysis that weighs the value of dead passengers against the cost of safety equipment to the airlines. For example, it could be mandated that the FAA require public hearings about the estimates or that the FAA reveal who or what did the analysis. (The FAA routinely accepts airline estimates and calculations that are based entirely on a guess—guessing about the possibility of an accident; there is nothing scientific about most of the guesswork; the key is in who the FAA hires to do the guessing.)

The commission failed to even mention waivers. I bet you think airlines have to comply with all the FAA safety regulations. Wrong again. Airlines routinely and frequently obtain waivers to safety and security rules, and no notice or knowledge is provided to the public or even the persons who board the plane. Why didn't the commission require airlines to post at eye level inside the cabin across from the door used by passengers to board every waiver the airline possesses that affects that plane?

I bet people have already forgotten that Pan Am claimed

it had a waiver from the FAA to skip hand-searching of unaccompanied bags on Pan Am planes in Europe, including PanAm 103. Why should citizens be duped into thinking federal safety regulations are complied with when they are not? How can the buyer beware when kept in the dark? I bet no passengers would have been on 103 if our government had revealed it had received threats which implicated that flight (after all, our government warned our embassy personnel but not the flying public) and there was a waiver so Pan Am did not have to search unaccompanied bags. The result: PanAm would have performed differently, and Lockerbie would be a town whose name was known only to those who live in it rather than by every American who has boarded a plane in the last ten years.

How about the cargo that sits under us like a powder keg? After the various aviation disasters of the last ten years linked to cargo, did our government order measures to protect us until cargo can be effectively screened? The commission did not call for such measures. Not surprisingly, neither did the FAA. Aside from PanAm 103, Valu-Jet, and several foreign crashes and fires, you might be interested to know that uninspected cargo jeopardizes passengers every day. For example, in 1997, one major jetliner full of passengers was carrying radioactive materials in the cargo. The containers broke, and the planeload of passengers was exposed to radiation. Most recently, in Miami, a courier checked in for an international flight with twenty-two suitcases. American Airlines accepted the cargo without inspecting and started loading it on the plane. One of the suitcases fell off the conveyor belt and the contents spilled. Pesticides. The fumes were so toxic that five people *on the plane* had to be taken to the hospital.

How easy is this to do? Several friends decided to make an overseas trip as couriers to find out. They showed up at the airport, baggage was loaded on the plane in their names, but they never saw it, did not pack it, and had no idea what was in it. All they had to do was sign a paper for the courier company, saying they would not carry hazardous materials. This is occurring every day on just about any plane going just about anywhere.

But that's minor compared to just plain old cargo or

mail. No passenger at all is connected with them. Just remember, many of the Unabomber's parcels were undoubtedly loaded on planes. The commission and the FAA did nothing to protect us from unknown cargo, yet there were dozens of hazardous materials violations on planes this year. The FAA even issued a warning about people packing fireworks, a common and deadly violation.

Most tragic and ironic among the commission's shortcomings was the failure to make significant improvement in aviation security. Most ironic because the commission was formed in the aftermath of TWA 800, when a bombing was among the possible explanations, and most tragic because so many have already died with the same rules already on the books which the commission now "proposes."

Most misleading was the commission's statements on bag-passenger matches. The commission stated it was requiring "implementation of a full bag-passenger match." But when you read further into the report, you find the rest of the story: "a full bag-passenger match . . . based on profiling . . . Bags of those selected either at random or through the use of automated profiling must either be screened or matched to a boarded passenger."

Such a security system would not have caught the suitcase containing the bomb that brought down PanAm 103 or similar terrorist bombings of foreign planes. Why? Because if you are checking the bags of those passengers identified through a profiling, you will never select for inspection an unaccompanied bag. The only way it would be caught is with a 100% bags-to-passenger match. Every bag must have an accompanying passenger. Otherwise our only chance lies in catching suicide bombers or dupes; terrorists will slip through.

How about the domestic system today and for the foreseeable future? The commission offers us little help. The airlines' policy is to send bags on the planes without a bag-to-passenger match. Even if a passenger misses a flight or connection and the airline knows it, it makes little or no effort to stop the bags.

I tested that one firsthand, albeit unwillingly. In September 1997, I had to fly from Edmonton, Alberta, Canada, to Columbus, Ohio. I was supposed to fly Northwest Air-

lines from Edmonton to Minneapolis and Minneapolis to
Columbus, but a one-hour weather shutdown in Minneapolis sent Northwest Airlines into meltdown. Our plane was
routed to Fargo to refuel and await a new landing time.
The trouble was, several other planes were rerouted to
Fargo, including some 747s. The 747s refueling ahead of
us sucked dry the fuel at the airport, so the fuel trucks
had to go off to the tank farm, and we spent the entire
day in the plane (we never went to a jetway, the doors
were never opened, so we could not deplane). Upon arrival
in Minneapolis that night, despite having spent $50 in
airplane telephone calls to get waitlisted on several flights, I
could not get on any Northwest plane to Columbus.

"Okay," I told the Northwest agents, "then give me
my bag back, and I will take United to Chicago and catch
the last night flight to Columbus from O'Hare." No such
luck was the reply. "Our policy is to put the bags on the
next plane to the bag's destination whether the passenger
gets on board or not." So much for a domestic bag match;
Northwest Airlines was the carrier that was supposedly
testing out such a system for the commission. By the way,
I did not get back to Columbus that night. My bag did.

The obvious problems the commission overlooked were
glaring. Nothing to mandate more and better background
checks. Even the person who sweeps the floor at the bank
gets one, but airline, airport, security, and maintenance
personnel do not. Does our government really intend to
say it is more important to protect money than lives? Apparently so.

How about the right of all citizens to have their griev-
ances redressed in court? Not when an airline is concerned.
Both the Warsaw Convention and the Death on the High
Seas Act give carriers liability loopholes big enough to
literally fly a 747 through it and crash. The Death on
the High Seas Act limits the liability of an air carrier
or manufacturer to actual wage earning, otherwise, about
$2,300. It was based on a 1920 treaty—before modern
commercial aviation was ever envisioned. Did the commission amend 49 United States Code Section 40120 to
change this inequity? No. TWA 800 passengers are having
to struggle in the courts hoping to get a chance to at least

review some of the evidence, and they are hardly alone. The passengers on the KAL 007 and the American Airlines flight that plowed into a Colombian mountain had to wage similar battles.

Meeting Victoria Cummock reminded me yet again of the staff meeting in the office of the Secretary of Transportation. That day, the group of families of crash victims was coming to the Department, and the Secretary and a group of the highest-ranking officials of the U.S. Department of Transportation were actually plotting and planning how they could get in, out of, and around the building without risk of meeting up with the victims' families.

Back then, I was astonished that such high-ranking government officials could be terrified of meeting a group of families. The extremes to which they would go to hide from Americans who certainly never volunteered for the moniker Victim's Families sickened me. Five minutes into the discussion with Victoria Cummock, I knew why. She and some other such persons had lived with the facts of aviation safety and security so long and had studied and researched the issues so thoroughly that some Johnny-come-lately political appointees, recently dropped into positions with oversight over aviation safety and security, were no match for their expertise. The officials ran to hide because they could not answer the questions and did not have the fortitude to even get in the arena to tackle the problem. Sound bites—"this airline is safe"—those were often the forte of the very leaders of government aviation safety. They knew they would be outgunned by a single mom from Florida.

The timing of several political contributions, it seemed, best explained what happened to the commission. Airlines gave $500,000 in political contributions after the President set up the commission and made Vice President Gore its chairman. Of course, the commission had to be finished with its work before the election. What Americans were demanding would cost the airlines billions, or so airlines said, so half a million was a bargain under anybody's cost-benefit analysis. On September 9, 1996, there was a press conference at which the White House promised the public sweeping changes in airport security. Total bag matches, foreign and domestic. Explosives-detection devices. Screening mail and cargo.

The airlines reacted. This was going to cost money, and they had no intention of paying. By September 19, 1996, the Vice President had sent a letter to the Air Transport Association promising the airlines that the White House Commission would not do anything that would cause the airlines to lose money.

How to get out of this one? Easy. TWA 800 will be found not to be caused by a terrorist act; the glare of the spotlight will be off the security issue, and we can forget about our promises.

Too close for coincidence, on September 19, 1996, the *Washington Post* and the *New York Times* ran front-page stories using the classic inside-the-Beltway trick. Leaks from unnamed sources in the NTSB assured the press that a malfunction, not bombing, was the cause of TWA 800. The FBI assisted on the next day, putting out a story about the plane having been used in bomb-dog training in St. Louis. Of course, later it would be revealed that the FBI could not say for sure it was in fact *that* plane, only that the TWA 800 plane had been through St. Louis on the day the training was done on *some* plane. No matter. The objective was achieved, and once again the government— and this time a White House commission—could backpedal on aviation safety.

The day after the Vice President promised to protect the airlines' bottom line rather than aviation safety and security, the rewards started arriving: $40,000 from TWA to the Democratic National Committee, $95,000 more from TWA, Northwest Airlines, United Airlines, and American Airlines. $250,000 more from American Airlines, and $100,000 more from United. Still another donation from Northwest brought the total to half a million bucks.

Victoria Cummock had called for the commission to change the way the government does cost-benefit analysis on airlines' safety and security issues, but this is not quite what she had in mind.

"There's more," she said. My head already hurt; how could things get worse for the traveling public? And I had publicly praised the President for forming the commission.

After Cummock had sued the Vice President for failing to follow the Administrative Procedures Act in the conduct and business of the commission, her attorney had requested the production of all the documents of the commission. The Federal Aviation Administration had put them in a room stuffed practically to the ceiling with documents, an old shyster lawyer trick to grind down the other side. They just assumed Cummock and counsel would give up. Instead, they read them—something the government apparently failed to do thoroughly—and there they found two smoking guns.

The first was an internal memorandum discussing what was to happen at the September 5, 1996 meeting of the commission. It was more concerned with how to manage the commissioners than with how to manage safety and security. It seems there had been a series of secret meetings to which only those persons who were on board with the predetermined recommendations were invited. The government members were all in cahoots and the recommendations already set. The government members could be easily managed, the memo concluded, "after some discussion and appreciation for the realities of implementation." But the memo's authors were worried about Ms. Cummock. They speculated she would resign if the commission was "another sell out to the airlines." The memo's author, one of the commission government functionaries who was controlling the operation, snidely wrote, "I sat next to her on the trip [on Air Force One] and tried to do a little DO [sic] like smoozing. My sense is that she can be kept in line if she believes progress is going to result from the effort." But if she believed the effort was one appeasing the airlines, "she could become a major problem."

Nonetheless, the report concluded, "We don't have the money, time or technology to examine every passenger, carry-on bag, or checked luggage, cargo and food cart going onto a U.S. plane. Without improved profiling the rest of the plan falls apart."

Finally, a last dismal conclusion, "All this will be of little value if the Airlines continue to take the lowest bidder, minimize standards and keep the passenger happy approach.''

''So what happened when they did the testing of the supposed new and improved passenger profiling system?'' I asked Cummock.

''Northwest was doing it. They basically booted up the system and it crashed in eight minutes, and that was that.''

So much for better profiling. I know what Northwest was doing in September, when my bag was on a plane to Columbus and I was heading to Chicago.

And the other smoking gun? ''There was another document buried in the mounds of paper. It was a letter addressed to Elaine Kamarck, at the White House Commission on Aviation Safety and Security, from some nuns. It said in sum, 'Hi, I'm Sister So-and-So and the Vice President suggested I write to Elaine Kamarck to set up some kind of a meeting or event to extend our support and ''gratitude'' to the Vice President.' ''

''This was in the *aviation* commission documents?'' I asked.

''Yes, specifically addressed to Kamarck at the aviation commission.''

Aviation, politics, money, the Vice President, and Kamarck. Where had I heard all that before? In 1993, when the Office of Inspector General was investigating the existence of the wacky training cult at the FAA, it had been Elaine Kamarck, I was advised by Ann Bormolini, Chief of Staff to Secretary Peña, who called over to the Department of Transportation and wanted to know if Secretary Peña wanted the Vice President to have the President fire me for harassing the FAA. What's more, it had been the Vice President's Reinvention Task Force that tried to strip my office of the power to investigate bogus parts, and two Reinvention Task Force officials and Gregory May, the wacky cult-like trainer at the FAA later convicted of insurance fraud as a result of our investigation, who had filed false complaints about me with the FBI to try to get me out of office, which of course, the FBI found to be meritless.

The tentacles of aviation money were extremely far-reaching, and the FAA was a convenient, if often hapless, vehicle. Money talks, and those who speak for the dead don't usually have it. Even more difficult, they are plucked from all walks of life without the skills to battle lobbyists, politicians, airlines, and big government.

I felt very tired that day. I was glad there were Victoria Cummocks in this world, with unlimited energy, patience, and focus.

"Thanks for filling me in. I guess I'd better stop speaking about my hopes for the commission."

Mostly I was sad. I felt I had lost my country, if only for a little while, that day. Even after the ValuJet tragedy, I had been able to say that the federal officials who were lying to and misleading the public were not representative of the government, not my government anyway, and surely not my country. Now the rot seemed even more pervasive and harder to stop.

Standing with the ValuJet families that day had been very hard. They were not statistics. They were like me and thrust into roles, which for some was a difficult, if not impossible, burden. The hardest part was meeting the relatives of the McNitt family of five that was lost on ValuJet. It had been their picture—the smiling family of proud parents and three little kids killed on Flight 592 after returning from a family vacation cruise—that I could not get out of my head in May 1996, and that led me to speak out about what the government knew about ValuJet. One of the family members pressed a copy of the picture into my hands. Another picture, a painting of the three little kids, two about the size of my three-year-old daughter, was also brought for me. "Keep these for us and for them," she said, "and thanks for all you've done."

I understood more about how aviation had changed then and the irony in the progress of aviation safety. Every major safety change was brought about on the backs of families like them. The last thing they ever would have wanted was the cause they were now compelled to champion. Yet I have met crash survivors and families of crash victims all over the country, now working for aviation safety and security, and to their credit, achieving the meager additional measures of safety they were able to squeeze out of the none too friendly closed club of the

aviation world. Yet it is they who are considered the opposition, annoyances, or people to be "handled" by the
FAA, the White House Commission, and even to a certain
extent by the National Transportation Safety Board.

The Korean Airline crash in Guam in the summer of
1997 only served as a reminder that the shortcomings in
our aviation safety oversight and equipment had not been
cured. A KAL 747 was landing in limited visibility with
a key part of the instrument landing system in Guam not
operational. Based on its fatal accident rate KAL was one
of the few carriers that earned a grade of less than A from
the Air Travelers Association in Washington. (It had a C
and with the most recent crash it should most likely have
got an F.)

KAL had some history, a lot of it bad. It had crashed
several times. It had an accident rate about ten times worse
than United Airlines, which also operates in the Far East.
It had doubled in size in less than ten years and was
planning to double again by 2005. It needed $10 billion
to do that. And it was diversified, or spread thin, depending on how you look at it, and also was engaged in
manufacturing planes, parts, and helicopters.

Some of its crashes were especially noteworthy. On July
27, 1989, KAL crashed in Libya while trying to land in the
fog with no instrument landing system. Conditions were so
bad even Aeroflot diverted. The two pilots went to prison.
On August 10, 1994, while trying to land in Cheju Island
in a typhoon, the pilots were actually fighting. And of
course there was KAL 007 on September 1, 1983.

Following some of the crashes, there were news reports
of bribery of the government to make sure the airline got
off easy, including the 007 shoot-down. It was reported
KAL had bribed the government to insure there would be
no trials and the Death on the High Seas Act would apply,
so there would be no trial and victims' recoveries would
be severely limited. Besides, there was always the Warsaw
treaty, which limits damages to $75,000. (Now for those
carriers that voluntarily waive the limit, it is about
$140,000.)

Under Warsaw limitations, victims' families can recover
no more than the limit, unless there is a finding of willful

misconduct. (This very ruling was made in late 1997 by a federal judge on the 1995 American Airlines crash in Colombia, permitting additional recovery. American Airlines did manage to prevail on the issue of being forced to turn over their internal safety data.) Warsaw protects the carrier, but not the manufacturer.

The Death on the High Seas Act, however, also protects the manufacturer. Recovery is limited to the economic damages—in other words, what you are worth as a wage-earner only. Not as a mom or a child or a spouse. You don't work, you aren't worth much. Passed to protect the widows and orphans of seamen after the *Titanic* sunk, it was never intended to cover 747s, but it does.

And after the crash of TWA 800, it was Boeing that went to court and said it was protected by the Death on the High Seas Act and the kids from Montoursville, Pennsylvania, were not worth anything.

Fortunately the families of the victims are again fighting. They have gotten a bill through the U.S. House of Representatives to remove Death on the High Seas as an aviation crash defense. The bill is pending in the U.S. Senate, where it has met with opposition from at least one senator from Washington state, home of Boeing.

I had tuned in to C-SPAN to watch some of the proceedings of the Task Force on Victims and Families. I thought it was a very important victory not only for the families but for all passengers. To me it was certainly a very serious undertaking.

This would also be the first public work of new FAA Administrator Garvey. I was taking a wait and see approach. After all, this Administrator had the best chance to make real changes. Coming in with a five-year term, a very important and needed change, a new Administrator would not have to be a "kidneystone" the rank and file could wait out until she passed on. And, though she was not a pilot, that could actually work out to be a plus. There would be no temptation to blow two or three days a week behind the controls of the state-of-the-art FAA executive jets instead of managing the place.

But there was also some bad news. Garvey was not unknown to the Office of Inspector General. We had found

lots of problems with the Federal Highway Administration
under Garvey's and the current Secretary of Transportation's management. One of the largest Federal Highway
projects in history was under way in Boston, Garvey's
pre-Beltway home. Nicknamed the Big Dig, the project
was approaching $10 billion. Garvey had been somehow
involved in the matter in Boston. When she came to the
Federal Highway Administration, we were first told she
was not recused from that project, then that she was recused, then finally that she was not. In fact, she was doing
a lot of the political heavy lifting, and there was a lot,
because the office of Inspector General did an investigation and found that the largest federal public works project
in history had no financing plan—those in charge of the
project did not know where all the money would come
from, but they were building anyway; costs and waste
were seriously out of control. So much for the track record
on managing large federal contracts, the hallmark of the
FAA. Not surprising, one of her first acts as FAA Administrator was to give Boston's Logan Airport, where she
used to work, a $2 million FAA grant.

Still, this appointment had to be an improvement. At
least there was potential.

The Victims and Families meeting had started, and Garvey began to address the group. People introduced themselves, and one very polite and reserved gentleman politely
noted it was nice to see Garvey again since their last
meeting in another city.

Oh my, Garvey cooed, and batted her eyes. Tell them
we were there on business. I wouldn't want anyone to get
the wrong impression.

This was most assuredly an inauspicious start. This poor
gentleman was terribly embarrassed, shifting in his seat.
A bit later she came back to hit on this poor guy again.

"I am disappointed you have not yet dated my daughter," Garvey scolded.

The poor gentleman was noticeably stunned and uncomfortable. It was pretty clear it had never occurred to him
to date the daughter either, but here he was on national
television in his Andy Warhol fifteen minutes and it was
not about aviation safety but dating. I couldn't help but

think that if a guy had done that, he'd have ended up as an example at the October hearings into sexual harassment at the FAA. I must say, the C-SPAN viewing population probably did increase.

In tribute to the families of victims and the crash survivors, many family members managed to push through tremendous and important changes that will help safeguard us all—not just the Family Assistance Act of 1996, but the additional recommendations and efforts that resulted after the act's passage. For example, the Foreign Family Assistance Act of 1997 requires foreign carriers also to file an emergency response plan, as U.S. carriers are required to do under the 1996 Act. There is also a permanent advisory board to follow up on the recommendations and implementation.

To date in 1997, the most insidious crash of the year was barely a three-day news story. Only the crew and one person on the ground were killed. When it occurred, Miami residents were still talking about the summer's astonishing flight of a cargo plane, an *old* plane, through the streets of Miami, below the level of many of the high rises. Astonished officer workers looked out their windows to see a large jet flying through the streets of Miami below them. Some folks estimated that the plane was about as high as a six-story building. Even more astonishing, the plane did not come back and land. It proceeded on to the JFK airport in crowded New York City, with wall-to-wall people and buildings, where it landed and took off again, before leaving U.S. airspace. The FAA never stopped it.

When Fine Air crashed, nobody knew much about the carrier. But they should have. Instead, a new name and a clean slate bought with a consent order from the FAA sent reporters and the public scrambling to research Fine Air. In one newsroom I overheard someone yell, ''Anyone know anything about Fine Air?''

''Nope,'' someone shot back.

In 1991 the U.S. Congress held hearings on the deplorable condition of some operators in Miami. Playing catch-up, the hearings were scheduled as a result of a five-part series in *Newsday* concerning foreign carrier operations endangering the citizens of Miami. But one of the big surprises of the hearings was the fact that one of the so-called foreign airlines under scrutiny at the hearings was not foreign at all. It was Agro Air, an operation out of Miami by Barry and Frank Fine.

Agro leased planes, or so it said, and maintained them in an FAA-approved repair station. Foreign entities were the "operators" rather than the Fines. The FAA started its investigation of Agro in 1988, but not too surprisingly, it was not until after the *Newsday* articles and before the congressional hearings that the FAA made a formal finding that Agro Air had violated FAA regulations by engaging in air transportation without the required authority. Following the usual modus operandi, the FAA allowed Agro Air to enter into a consent agreement by terminating its "leasing" business and paying a civil fine. The FAA in turn would agree to stop investigating the Fines' Agro Air, not an inconsequential promise. From January 19 to May 16, 1991, Agro had fourteen incidents at Miami International Airport, including hydraulic failures, lost, smoking and shut-down engines, vibration, and gear door problems. When questioned by members of Congress, the FAA reassured them there was just one major accident, but the flight crew lived. Of course, thirty-eight people were killed on the ground in Mexico City.

Like acquiring a new identity in the Federal Witness Protection Program, planes that used to belong to Frank and Barry Fine's Agro Air became the fleet of Fine Airlines (other than one new plane for "executive transportation"). Other carriers complained, to no avail. The consent agreement "appears to defang the [Department of Transportation's] Public Counsel —the staff that is supposed to protect the public interest. Public Counsel has agreed not to assert that the numerous violations committed by Fine Airlines' principals and related companies show lack of compliance . . . There will always be the cloud that [the consent order] presents a political fix."

None of the families of the thirty-eight dead in Mexico City testified; nor were they invited.

After the fiery crash in 1997 in Miami, the Fines voluntarily tendered their license temporarily. After all, the strategy had worked before, and soon they were right back in the air. But the problem wasn't solved, even though the FAA and Congress spelled it out in the *Congressional Record.* "Indeed if there was ever an accident waiting to happen, this is it," said Congressman Robert A. Borski, Chairman of the Subcomittee on Investigations and Oversight, Committee on Public Works and Transportation, on June 4, 1991. "It is even more regrettable that our transportation policy makers at the Federal Aviation Administration and the Department of Transportation have been unresponsive to those voicing concern. DOT officials dismiss the issue by implying that the legitimate domestic carriers, who are forced to compete against these renegade operators, are 'crybabies' who fear competition. This mindset is both disturbing and short-sighted.

"What determines the government's transportation policy? . . . Well, that depends on what floor of the DOT building you are on. The Coast Guard, Federal Highway Administration, and Federal Railroad Administration all require [that] . . . equipment meet U.S. standards."

"How can the government prevent an unsafe freighter from entering the Port of Miami, but do nothing to keep an unsafe airline from flying over schools, playgrounds, commercial and residential areas en route to Miami International Airport?"

In this dizzying game of congressional "Jeopardy!," of course, the question is the answer. *"Why is aviation the only mode of transportation in which there is a hands-off policy?"* Congress asked.

In that prophetic hearing in June 1991, they had the pieces of the puzzle, but instead of reaching conclusions and giving the FAA orders and deadlines, the committee put its findings in the form of a question, leaving the door open for the FAA to exit awaiting the second crash for their two-crash rule. (Which of course they got in 1997. Fine Air voluntarily suspended its operations on September 4, 1997. The FAA allowed it to resume flights on October 28, 1997.) For example, the committee mused about the fact that for pilots we have an age sixty retirement rule. We have an age sixty retirement rule because the FAA knows that at some point pilots "wear out," at least as far as the rigors of commercial flight is concerned, but it does not

know exactly at what age that happens, so they set age
sixty as the mandatory retirement age and require clear
and convincing evidence that it is safe to extend the flying
age of the pilots.

Then the committee questioned the FAA. What about
old planes as opposed to old pilots? In just five months,
didn't Agro Air have an excessive number of incidents?

The FAA responded, "For a modern aircraft it would
be excessive."

Since the FAA cannot determine when a pilot goes bad
from old age, it puts him out to pasture. But the FAA has
no such mandatory retirement policy for old planes. It has
no recent, comprehensive aging aircraft studies to tell them
at what age planes should be put out to pasture, so it lets
them fly until there is evidence to the contrary. Former
Boeing employees tell me Boeing doesn't even work on
its own planes after twenty years. Planes are built for a
twenty-year economic life. Yet what does the FAA do
when confronted with evidence that old planes have vastly
greater problems than new planes? Adjust the scale so the
FAA will tolerate excessive numbers of incidents on old
planes. Cargo or passenger, the attitude is the same.

What else was new in 1997? To answer that I had to
resort to a Freedom of Information Act request to the
FAA.

You see, the FAA promised that it would put safety
information on the Internet so that the public could pick
and choose among airlines and pick the safest. Unfortunately, however, when you get on line, all you find is raw
data, with no analysis whatsoever by our government-paid
rocket scientists. I thought that was indeed strange. After
all, in congressional reports, it is documented that one of
the key ways the FAA is supposed to determine the safety
and performance of airlines is by analyzing the accident
and incident rates.

When I was Inspector General, we investigated what
the FAA did with reports of problems by pilots, airlines,
mechanics, engineers, and others. I used to think the FAA
used all these reports to target and track, to make projections where there were problems and to avoid accidents
before they happen. Nope. What we discovered is that the

FAA did no such analysis, targeting, plotting trending lines. Nothing. We were so astonished that we actually wrote in our findings that the information went into a black hole. That was of course several years ago. Surely the FAA must have done something about this huge shortcoming and started using the data to try to stop crashes before they happen.

Things did not sound good when the new FAA Administrator spoke on October 28, 1997, at the Aero Club in Washington, D.C. "We learned that the analysis of routine flight data . . . provides significant data by identifying trends. These trends can point out potential problems and enable us to take steps **before** [emphasis in the original document] accidents happen. Let me repeat that—**before accidents happen** [emphasis in the original]."

And they say there is a shortage of rocket scientists at the FAA.

How about analyzing the data from accidents and incidents? How about figuring out who's got problems by looking at the accident/incident rates just as the FAA and the Office of Inspector General did in figuring out that ValuJet was headed for trouble before it crashed in May 1996?

What about the data that the FAA generated and used in their May 1996 report that warned that ValuJet had an accident/incident rate fourteen times worse than the major carriers and warned about ValuJet right on the cover of the report just one week before the crash? For that report the FAA compared carriers based on the rates of their accidents and incidents. Ah, I thought, problem solved. I will just file a Freedom of Information request for the following year's comparison.

I hand-carried my request to the FAA. I did not want it to get lost in the mail or overlooked. It was a pretty simple request. To make sure there would be no confusion or misunderstanding, I attached to my request copies of the very rate comparisons the FAA had generated and attached to their May 1996 report that wisely flagged ValuJet's existing dismal accident/incident rate and prophetically predicted ValuJet's problems. Just give me the same rates and data for 1997.

The FAA politely responded to me promptly. I know the gentleman who answered my letter. I had worked with him before. I liked him. I trusted him to tell me the truth. I have no doubt that he was telling me the truth again in his June 4, 1997 letter to me. It's just that I was astonished by the revelations.

"Dear Ms. Schiavo," Christopher Hart, the Assistant Administrator for System Safety of the FAA wrote.

This responds to your Freedom of Information Act request dated May 22, 1997, which was received in this office on this date. Your request sought accident, incident, pilot deviation, runway incursion and near midair collision event counts *and rates* [emphasis added] for individual airlines by year from 1991 through 1996. You attached certain documents prepared by the Federal Aviation Administration to support your assertion that the FAA has records of the information you are requesting.

So far, so good. Chris noted he was enclosing lots and lots of raw data. Hey, that's all on the Internet, too, he chastised me. Okay, okay, so I was testing them out to match it up with what's on the Internet for the public to get without having to file a Freedom of Information Act request.

A records search was conducted in FAA Headquarters offices to locate both the rate information and the runway incursion data that you requested. Other than the documents that you included with your request, no records were found of this information and data, and we are unaware of any other FAA offices likely to possess additional responsive records.

The nine charts attached to your request that are dated June 3, 1996 [the FAA updated the May 1996 charts to fix a few errors after the ValuJet crash], were all calculated on a one-time basis in response to a specific request by officials from the Department of Transportation's Office of Inspector General when you were Inspector General. While the FAA made no effort to prevent the public disclosure of the nine charts, the FAA would not have been required to calculate rates and prepare the charts in response to a request from the public. No records were found that update those rate charts for 1996. The other (undated) document attached to your request was calculated on a one-time basis for inclusion in a FAA report prepared in May 1996. No record was found, however, that updates that chart for 1996.

See no evil still.

The new FAA Administrator made it clear in her October 28, 1997 speech. "We plan to improve upon the relationship between the regulated and the regulator." Considering the U.S. Department of Justice, a U.S. federal judge, and a former Attorney General of the United States of America had already warned that the regulated were running the regulators, it was not readily apparent to me how they could get much closer.

But there was a plan—secret data analysis that the FAA would guarantee the public would never see. "More data is given to the FAA, but the agency agrees not to take punitive enforcement action." In return, the FAA would seek a new federal law prohibiting the release of any of this information to the public. Just the FAA and the airlines. Cozy. In the 1980s and 1990s we put hush kits on planes to keep tired iron flying past its useful life. Now we put hush kits on the government to keep it from revealing even the problems.

In 1997 we saw still more of the FAA hoping to wait out problems. An internal FAA memorandum was given to me by an FAA employee about the FAA's response strategy to this book. Just wait for the issues to blow over was the instruction. The media interest will soon die down and that will be that.

The FAA Public Affairs staff—bigger than poor old Chris Hart's aviation safety office—put out some spin press releases promising that the FAA would soon act on the ValuJet recommendations and the even older 737 recommendations, but it hadn't quite gotten it done yet. An official from the FAA's Civil Aviation Medical Institute appeared in *People* magazine in October 1997 to say that if you can hold your breath for thirty seconds, you can get out of a burning, smoke-filled, loaded-to-the-gills plane. (He forgot that the FAA regulations say evacuation takes ninety seconds, and in real life it has been documented in many cases to take much longer. Of course, all of this presumes the plane is on the ground and stopped when the smoke and fire appear, not airborne, which happens frequently.) I assume this piece of news was in lieu of smoke hoods and better fire suppression.

The 1998 budget of the FAA was increased to over $10 billion, but the increase was not tied to any deadlines for acting on the problems the additional money was supposed to fix.

"The replacement contract for the replacement contract for our antiquated air traffic control replacement system is way over budget and way behind schedule." That's what a concerned FAA employee wrote to tell me. "I thought you'd like to know," he said.

Well, I thought you'd like to know too.

In November 1997 the General Accounting Office issued an ominous warning. It said that the FAA's updating of the air traffic control system was an extremely high-risk project. Costs have now risen to $11 billion. It was $7.8 billion when I left the Department in 1996. The entire effort is threatened by the FAA's weaknesses, warned the GAO.

On November 24, 1997, even more bad news. Just as my former office had warned in 1991 and 1996, the GAO found that the FAA still routinely fails to determine whether maintenance violations uncovered by FAA inspectors are ever corrected.

On November 28, 1997, the Inspector General's office announced it had just completed another investigation looking at whether the FAA inspectors who check maintenance and electrical systems were qualified to do so. The investigation revealed many had taken no training courses before joining the FAA or since being hired. Even those who had taken training courses some time ago had received no updates to learn about changes in the systems.

U.S. Senator Ron Wyden may have said it best in November 1997, "[S]afety in the skies is directly related to quality aircraft maintenance on the ground," but the FAA "still doesn't get the message."

FLYING BLIND, FLYING SAFE

CHAPTER TWELVE

There's No Such Thing As "Safety" at the FAA

The FAA has no definition of safety—no official definition, that is. Safety is not defined in the Federal Aviation
Act of 1958. It is not specified in the FAA regulations. It
is not explained in the agency's guidelines. So FAA officials can't say what safety is, not technically, anyway.
And without a sanctioned definition of safety, there can
be no safety yardstick, no safety standard.

So the FAA cannot—will not—say what constitutes a
safety problem, when safety is compromised or what
makes aviation safe.

Thus aviation safety is subjective. Deciding that safety
is at risk, or should be improved, is an informal, fluid
quest, one that FAA officials determine on a case-by-case
basis. Yet when they consider safety, they do so through
a forty-year-old prism that skews their vision back to a
time when the government heavily regulated airline prices
and routes, when only a few brand-name carriers plied the
skies and when all airlines operated with the same procedures and rules. Then, a definition of safety was not important to the FAA because it had a more urgent, more vital
objective: to promote commercial aviation. So crucial was

this mandate to the framers of the Federal Aviation Act that in the law they spelled out exactly how the new agency should foster the aviation business. Safety, however lofty a goal, was first mentioned almost offhandedly in the act's fifth provision. It would be so for thirty-eight years.

The fact that the 104th Congress eliminated the FAA's mandate to promote aviation has not changed the long-standing tradition of loyalty to the aviation industry that prevails at the agency. I fear that the elimination of the mandate will make the public, the press and safety advocates complacent about the FAA's priorities. But today's FAA officials remain the philosophical descendants of the agency's framers: the business, military and government officials who had thrived under a "national industrial policy" of promoting aviation.

Still, today's aviation industry is nothing like the enterprise that existed when the FAA was founded. With deregulation in 1978, competition sliced through the industry like a razor, mercilessly driving historic airlines out of business, forcing others to revamp and enabling new carriers to dominate. The free-for-all that ensued affected airlines, aircraft builders, parts manufacturers, repair facilities—every facet of the industry mutated, expanded or adapted to exploit deregulation. But the FAA did not change in 1978. As a result, it couldn't keep up in the 1980s and has been unable to recover in the 1990s. And passengers have begun paying with their lives.

Now, on the cusp of the twenty-first century, the FAA, airlines and airplane manufacturers all make a similar prediction: more change is on the way. Demand for flights, already unprecedented, will continue to skyrocket over the next decade. Major carriers will add planes to their fleets and flights to their itineraries to meet the demand. Discounters, commuter airlines and air taxis will expand to offer competitive prices and secondary routes. Start-up airlines in all categories will continue to emerge and enlarge to exploit the market. Many of the smaller carriers will buy used planes, equipment and parts. Competition will encourage the practice of pushing pilots, mechanics and inspectors to get planes in and out of the gate in twenty-five minutes. Rivalry will spur cost-cutting habits like farming out maintenance and repairs to contractors. Taken together, this economic growth means the flying public can expect an increase in the number of accidents. More planes will crash, the experts warn, even if the safety rates remain the same. More planes taking to the sky will simply mean more accidents—one a week, some experts now say. The rate of accidents will not double but triple, said the FAA Administrator in a 1997 speech to industry insiders.

But the FAA won't tell you this. As a public safety agency, a regulatory body whose budget is paid by taxes and passenger ticket fees, the FAA is more secretive than the CIA. It won't release the charts and graphs it has prepared for internal use that lay out the projected increased crash rate. Although now it has decided to release raw data about accidents, incidents and maintenance shortcomings, it won't release accident and incident ratings. It won't reveal pilot performance records, or airport safety and security rates. It won't reveal airline safety records—even to announce which carriers score well. In the limited comparative safety information it does routinely release, it deletes the name of the airline and all identifying information. The FAA understands that knowledge is power, and that the aviation industry does not want the public in a position to make demands about safety. And what the aviation industry wants, the FAA wants, too.

It would be bad enough if the FAA only concealed safety ratings from the public. But it commits a greater sin when it goes out of its way to mislead the American public. The FAA betrays the people who fly. It told the passengers of ValuJet flight 592 that they were buying tickets for a safe airline when it had known better for months. It let passengers traveling through our major airports think they were safe from terrorist bombs when it had known otherwise for years.

The FAA zealously guards information, deliberately burying it in suppressed reports, not because of a vague threat to passengers but because of the very real threat to profits. Informing or angering passengers with safety details is just plain bad for business. Passengers with questions about safety might choose not to fly. They might demand safety improvements that cost money, put restrictions on how airlines can do business and subject large corporations to government regulation. The aviation industry wants nothing to do with any of that. Thus the FAA's two responsibilities are in direct conflict. It is impossible to guarantee the best and most innovative safety provisions while worrying about industry profit margins and cost ratios.

So the FAA addresses safety only when forced. Over the years, the agency has learned that when a plane goes down in flames and dozens or hundreds of lives are lost, what the public most wants is reassurance—reassurance that the accident was a fluke, that flying is statistically the safest way to travel and that someone is watching over aviation to guarantee it is safe. FAA officials and members of Congress automatically take to the airwaves, vying to outdo themselves with sound bites about oversight and safety. They know they have to keep it up only until the crisis fades—for the FAA's credo seems to be: once the media scrutiny passes, the safety problem will be gone, too.

Sometimes public grief and outrage are so great that people demand that a rule be passed, a procedure changed or some new equipment installed to ensure that such an accident never happens again. Reluctantly, the FAA will act, even though in the vast majority of cases the new rule, procedure or equipment is one the NTSB has already suggested and the FAA has already quietly rejected as too expensive to require of the airlines.

The same truth is apparent when safety concerns or lapses are brought to the FAA's attention—even behind closed doors. In six years as Inspector General of the Department of Transportation, I investigated with my staff and warned the FAA about dozens of safety issues, including dangerous flaws in its inspection programs, airplane parts supervision and airport security procedures. The fixes would have been simple had the FAA agreed with our conclusions. Change should have started at the top. The FAA needs a manager, someone who will liberate the agency from the military/aviation industry culture. The FAA needs a leader who is accountable to the public. The FAA

shouldn't have to sell itself to commercial aviation interests. The agency exists to ensure safety and regulate the
airlines, not to make life as comfortable and friendly as
possible for the carriers and their business partners. Even
though the words of the dual mandate have been eliminated, the change in spirit that is so drastically needed goes
well beyond rewriting the agency's guidelines. Workers at
the FAA will continue to follow the example set by their
own Administrator. As the structure stands today, it's impossible for the agency to change because employees are
rooted in its traditional policies and procedures. Improvements in safety standards are hostage to the intransigent
bureaucracy. Change has to be forced from the top down.
And the FAA has never had a leader with the strength,
determination, dedication and character to do that. No effective housecleaner has been able to sweep the FAA free
of its problems because the political leadership was
roundly, routinely scorned and ignored. And none of the
administrators themselves have been able to change that
attitude or policy. They knew when they took their jobs
that they wouldn't be staying long, and so did everybody else.

I had hoped this would change. Under new rules passed
in 1994, the new Administrator has a five-year term. She
will be less beholden to the tides of politics. What we
needed was someone with real management ability, a
proven track record, knowledge of aviation safety and the
independence to work for it. That's not what we got. Instead, the new Administrator pledged an even closer relationship between the airlines and the FAA.

Other glaring problems could be remedied, too, if the
FAA was willing to admit its deficiencies and set new
rules to enhance safety. One area I am still concerned
about is in aircraft inspections. A good inspector with
training and time can do a good job. And the FAA did
add over 1,000 inspectors between 1983 and 1992, and
continues to add several hundred more in 1997 and 1998.
But too often, training and time are luxuries. What the
FAA needs most is a structured system—a consistent, systematic approach rooted in minimum standards. Needed
for each inspection: a list of items that are critical and

must be reviewed; an insistence that all inspections be documented; a combination of scheduled and surprise inspections; realistic testing techniques; a grading scale that forces inspectors to assess whether or not standards are met; and a sole yardstick for measuring compliance—safety. Astonishingly, mandatory standards of these sorts are lacking, rejected by an agency that doesn't want to upset airlines, repair stations or manufacturers. Reporting violations also means paperwork, electronic or otherwise—and FAA officials have told me they have little desire to spend their days filling out government forms. Everyone is happier when the inspectors go easy on their clients.

For years I have argued that safety does not need an official definition, and it doesn't need a public relations burnish—it just requires common sense. But the FAA refused to state categorically that bogus engine parts were a safety problem because twin-engine aircraft are designed to fly even if an engine is disabled. Being forced to shut down an engine in flight was not a safety concern, the FAA insisted, because that contingency is accounted for. I could not understand this logic. A pilot myself, I know that losing an engine is a safety problem. All pilots consider losing an engine a safety problem. The airlines call it a safety problem and aircraft manufacturers look at it that way, too. Even engine makers like Pratt & Whitney warn that losing an engine in flight creates a safety problem. Yet the FAA would not budge. To the FAA losing an engine was not a safety problem. That attitude helps explain why the FAA itself was cited by the NTSB as a cause or contributing factor in 241 accidents with 970 fatalities from 1983 to 1995. Add to that the 1997 finding by the NTSB that the FAA was a cause of the ValuJet crash, and the FAA is now responsible for well over 1,000 deaths, and counting.

Real change will come only when consumers demand it. Perhaps no other industry touches people's lives in quite the same way as aviation. Virtually everyone flies at one time or another. Everyone has friends or loved ones who fly. Anyone who boards a plane places his or her destiny into the hands of airline security people, mechanics and pilots. Passengers can't kick the tires of an airplane. They can't see where they're going when they fly. If there's a problem, they can't jump up and take over. They have to rely on the airlines to get it all right, to get them to their destination safely.

Perhaps no aviation tragedy better illustrates the faults in the FAA than the crash of ValuJet flight 592 into the Florida Everglades. As with any preventable disaster, a random string of events culminated in the fire, crash, and 110 deaths. One scholar has likened airline security to a constantly shifting stack of Swiss cheese: the holes are gaps in the safety net, the solid layers are backup systems. Though the layers move, the holes are usually plugged by a solid layer below. Too much is still left to chance, however. Sometimes all the holes line up, and disaster slips through. The gaps in the safety net lined up like that for ValuJet on that fateful day in May. But the shuffling began long before.

Passengers need to know where those holes are, how they happen and what they can do to demand the gaps be plugged. They need to know they have choices that can help make a flight safe and comfortable, and ensure that they are getting the service they are paying for. They need to know that the FAA has information about airplanes, airlines and airports that can help them make those choices. That's what the rest of this book is designed to show you. And that's just what the FAA and the aviation industry fear most.

inevitably drop like a stone. But the truth is, if flown
correctly, that won't happen. The plane will because it

CHAPTER THIRTEEN

Airplanes

Airplanes want to fly. I first felt that at the age of nine,
when I took a plane ride with my family. Later, at Ohio
State University's flight school, I learned why. The secret
lies in the wing, and in the speed of air rushing over and
under it. Because the wing is curved on top and flat on
the bottom, the air has farther to travel when flowing over
the top than when flowing underneath. That small difference creates lift for a plane. Since the pressure is lower
above the wing than below it, the craft lifts up. With
enough forward power from the engines, you can't stop a
plane from flying unless it is overloaded. So when rolling
down the runway, a pilot must literally hold the plane on
the ground until he picks up enough airspeed for a safe
takeoff. Then he pulls back the yoke (the equivalent of a
car's steering wheel), and up he goes.

My first plane was a Beechcraft Musketeer. I loved it.
I still remember its tail number—N26OSU (for Ohio State
University). For a small plane, it had very long wings.
The instructors used to say, presumably in jest, that
nothing would knock it out of the sky. That is true about
all planes—they do not fall out of the sky unless something is wrong with the mechanics or with the pilot. In
the years since then, in conversations with nonpilot
friends, I have discovered that people believe that if
a plane's engine(s) quits in mid-flight, the plane will

inevitably drop like a stone. But the truth is, if flown correctly, that won't happen. The plane will become a glider, albeit a very heavy one. The pilot can glide back to the ground provided he keeps the plane's nose down to maintain airspeed. That brings me back to the wing. If the nose is angled up while the engines aren't working, a plane will lose lift because the air flowing *over* the wings slows down. The result: stalling, which means stalling of the air flowing over the wings, not stalling of the engines. Stalling can occur even with the engines running. That's when planes fall out of the sky. So the key is for the pilot to keep the plane's nose down and glide back to earth. Of course, finding a safe place to land is also critical—preferably one with no obstructions higher than the plane, such as mountains.

Over the years I also realized that most people do not understand what is normal for an airplane and what constitutes a problem. Many friends have told me they fear the wings can rip off in a storm. I am happy to reassure them that in the history of aviation there have been only a few cases of a commercial jet losing a "structural element" in flight. A handful of planes have lost wings or tail assemblies, but those were due to bad maintenance or construction—usually missing bolts. In three cases, planes lost tail sections, the first because ground crew failed to replace bolts, the other because maintenance people used substandard, or bogus, bolts, and the third because the manufacturer is believed to have left them off.

In truth, small signs of deterioration that if unchecked can grow into debilitating faults are a more likely occurrence on planes than catastrophic structural collapse. Small problems that grow into big ones can happen with aging aircraft, bad maintenance and design flaws. Worse yet, many small problems which by themselves would not bring down a plane can certainly cause an accident when added together. Accidents usually result when several things go wrong at once.

But often the catacylsmic chain reaction starts with one small problem that gets compounded. It takes 3 million bolts to put a plane in the sky. But just one nut can scatter that plane all over the ground.

AGING AIRCRAFT

Some of the greatest concerns about aircraft are related to aging. Like cars and other machinery, airplanes deteriorate over time simply from continuous operation, as well as from the environment in which they operate. The greatest wear and tear on an airplane comes from takeoff and landing. Each pressurization after the plane takes off expands the fuselage, like inflating a tire. Each depressurization upon landing has the reverse effect on the plane body. Over time, this can cause fatigue and cracking in the metal. Furthermore, during flight, the fuselage bends. Wings essentially "flap" during flight. In tests, wings are flexed as much as 150 degrees from their normal position. On small planes, that means about three to six feet. On a 747, that is twenty-nine feet. So a plane's life span is determined by the number of pressurizations and the hours of flight, in addition to normal wear and tear.

Aircraft have to be able to stand up to three tests: strength, stiffness and longevity. Strength means a plane's ability to carry a load without failure. Stiffness means the airframe's ability to keep its shape over time. And longevity means the airframe's ability to do its job over a specific time period without succumbing to flaws, cracks, corrosion or other damage. There's nothing particularly high-tech about these criteria—they were first established for World War I biplanes.

The typical "economic design life"—the aviation industry's jargon for how long a plane is designed to fly—is twenty years, or 60,000 "cycles" (more jargon, meaning each set of takeoffs and landings). Hundreds of the planes in American fleets are twenty years or more old, and still flying. Of approximately 4,000 jets at work in the U.S. in 1996, 1,000 are more than twenty years old and 500 others are more than twenty-five. This number is expected to continue growing as millions more people want to fly every year. With demand for flights and competitive pressures high and with the establishment of many new start-up carriers, more airlines keep their planes flying beyond their intended life span. When an airline buys planes, the new aircraft often become additions to a fleet instead of replacements, or are perhaps sold to a start-up.

PERCENT OF U.S. FLEET
TWENTY YEARS OR MORE IN AGE

1988	28%
1995	35%
2000	40% (projected)

These older planes suffer from stress fractures, wear and corrosion. Avionics and electronic systems are aged, as is the wiring, and the aircraft have greater need for repairs. Some have fewer safety features like flame-resistant upholstery and newer-generation black boxes. One of the most dramatic accidents in the 1980s happened when the top of an Aloha Airlines 737 was ripped off over the Pacific Ocean. The plane was nineteen years old, having been built in April 1969, but more important, it had flown over 89,000 cycles. A lot of that time was spent in flight in the corrosive environment of salt water. I saw for myself how salt water had eaten away at plane parts when I visited the U.S. Coast Guard's aircraft overhaul facility in Elizabeth City, North Carolina. Parts literally crumbled from prolonged exposure to sea air. As a result, the Coast Guard regularly strips down their planes to their shells and rebuilds them.

But salt water alone could not be blamed for what happened to Aloha. It was a geriatric jet, and its problems were known in the industry. Boeing had already begun manufacturing thicker panels of outer metal "skin" for old 737s, and installing thicker ones on its new 737s. This wasn't Boeing clairvoyance, but a result of a string of structural failures. An investigation revealed that weaknesses in outer skin panels caused a Far Eastern Air Transport plane crash in Taiwan that killed all 110 people on the flight. After that, the British Civil Aviation Authority ordered inspections of all 737s with more than 55,000 takeoffs and landings. It also directed that 737 exterior skin panels be replaced. Only then did Boeing recommend inspection of all older 737s and make available the thicker skin panels. Sadly, Aloha had ordered the replacement panels but had not installed them. The FAA had not required that the skin be inspected or replaced. Until April 28, 1988.

A crack in the Aloha fuselage turned into a hole in the craft, which caused a decompression explosion. At that moment the inflated tire that was the fuselage blew out. Eighteen feet of roof peeled off, and a flight attendant was sucked out of the plane. The NTSB later said the fuselage disintegrated after "disbonding of overlapping skin, metal fatigue and separation in the aircraft's skin and structure." In 1997, a new warning was issued to check for aging aircraft problems on the 737—cracks in the fuselage. Among the airlines with affected planes—Aloha again.

In the industry, it's called "tired iron." Airplanes and their parts simply wear out, just as they do in a Chevy. Perhaps Vernon Grose, a former NTSB member, said it best: "They do not last forever." Following the Aloha accident, aircraft manufacturers, the airlines and the government took a close look at aging aircraft. Within a week new recommendations were issued. They called for mandatory repairs or replacement of parts after an aircraft had flown a certain number of flights. For example, after 60,000 flights, a 727 would have to have major modifications, including reinforcement of its wing ribs, its horizontal stabilizer (the part on the top of the tail that looks like a small wing) and its window frames. Many other parts, especially bolts, rivets and fasteners, would have to be replaced altogether. The cost would amount to about $600,000 per Boeing aircraft. In September 1989, similar procedures were announced for McDonnell Douglas planes. The cost averaged about $269,000 per plane. Later, new rules were issued for the inspection, reinforcement or parts replacement of other planes—each set of regulations was specific to the planes manufactured by Lockheed, Airbus, British Aerospace and Fokker.

Congress introduced aging aircraft legislation on November 20, 1989, and later held hearings in 1989 and 1990. Soon thereafter, Congress passed the Aging Aircraft Safety Act of 1990. The new law required the retrofitting of old planes. Congress told the FAA to come up with rules for the airlines and aircraft makers. The agency responded with new regulations for major airlines and plane manufacturers, giving them from 1990 to 1994 to comply. As of 1997, however, the FAA still had no similar guidelines for commuter aircraft.

So how old is too old? For years, aircraft manufacturers, NASA, the military and various government agencies have tried to come up with a formula for predicting airplane "fatigue," or when a plane was becoming too geriatric to fly safely. Right after the Aloha Airlines accident, the FAA told Congress that "we are not smart enough to be able to pick the number of hours at which the airplane truly is . . . out of service or out of its useful life . . . the complexity of an aircraft, just the sheer number of parts, makes it not practical to pick such a number." (Yet it does so for pilots, who are as vastly different as airplanes. People, I guess, are expendable. Airplanes cost money.) Manufacturers originally intended a twenty-year economic life, but twenty years is quickly becoming the average age in U.S. fleets. Now manufacturers and the airlines refuse to say when old is *too* old, instead emphasizing that the life of a plane can be extended for many years through systematic, periodic repairs and retrofitting.

The FAA says it studies computer analyses of load distributions on planes, and trains its inspectors to look more carefully at older craft. This is in addition to the five inspections, called A Check, B Check and so on, that each plane must undergo at specific points in its life:

AIRCRAFT INSPECTIONS

INSPECTION TYPE		CHECKPOINTS
Overnight	Ad-hoc repairs	Varies; whatever is necessary
A	Primary exam	Fuselage exterior, power plant, subsystems
B	Intermediate inspection	Panels, cowlings, oil filters and airframe
C	Detailed inspection	Engine and components, flight controls, major internal mechanisms
D	Major reconditioning or heavy structural inspection	Cabin interior removed, flight controls examined, fuel system checked

Some people claim planes can fly virtually forever if they have a complete retrofitting at the end of their conventional life. For an airline, such a huge project is still usually cheaper than buying a new plane. For example, Northwest Airlines is retrofitting old DC-9s for a cost of about $3 to $6 million per plane. Three million of that must be spent on the plane's "hush kit," the equipment that enables the plane to fly more quietly to comply with noise reduction standards. A brand-new Airbus, which Northwest is also acquiring to replace some of its aged fleet, costs $50 million. Obviously new planes cost much more than retrofitting old ones. The very first 747, built in 1969, was almost twenty years old when retrofitted in 1988 at a cost of $21 million. At that time, a new 747 cost $150 million.

A retrofit involves rebuilding the entire plane—a new inner and outer skin, a strengthened frame, new engines, new avionics, reinforced cargo holds, new floors. Seats, carpets, lavatories and galleys are torn out and replaced. The only part of the plane left generally untouched is the wings, because those would have been overhauled right down to their bolts during a late-life maintenance inspection. In some cases, whole sections of a plane may be cut off and replaced. Boeing developed a retrofit plan for the B727-200 that involved redesigning the tail, replacing the three engines with a two-engine configuration and redesigning the cockpit so only a crew of two would be needed. Even so, an airline would still be left with a twenty-year-old plane, one that had been subjected to tens of thousands of takeoffs and landings. Such a plane could easily have unknown hazards—the kinds of problems that do not surface until a plane is long past its original intended life span. Since so many planes over twenty years old are still flying, passengers should know which airlines have them in their fleets.

AGE OF DOMESTIC AIRLINE FLEETS

AIRLINE	AIRCRAFT	NUMBER	AVERAGE AGE
Air South	Boeing 737	7	21.3
	Total Fleet	**7**	**21.3**
Alaska	Boeing 737	32	6.8
	MD-80	46	6.9
	Total Fleet	**78**	**6.86**
Aloha	Boeing 737	22	11.7
	Total Fleet	**22**	**11.7**
America West	Airbus 320	23	5.1
	Boeing 737	61	11.6
	Boeing 757	14	9.7
	Total Fleet	**98**	**9.8**
American	Airbus 300	35	6.9
	Boeing 727	81	19.3
	Boeing 757	90	4.4
	Boeing 767	71	7.5
	DC-10	19	19.7
	Fokker 100	75	3.6
	MD-11	16	4.0
	MD-80	260	8.3
	Total Fleet	**647**	**8.7**
Carnival*	Airbus 300	8	14.9
	Boeing 727	6	17.8
	Boeing 737	9	10.2
	Total Fleet	**23**	**13.8**
Continental	Boeing 727	42	19.1
	Boeing 737	132	11.2
	Boeing 747	2	24.0
	Boeing 757	17	1.5
	DC-9	31	24.4
	DC-10	21	20.7
	MD-80	67	11.5
	Total Fleet	**312**	**13.8**

*Purchased by Pan Am in late 1997, discontinued flying Airbus models.

AIRLINE	AIRCRAFT	NUMBER	AVERAGE AGE
Delta	Boeing 727	129	19.4
	Boeing 737	67	11.4
	Boeing 757	86	7.5
	Boeing 767	61	7.5
	Lockheed L-1011	55	17.6
	MD-11	11	3.7
	MD-80	120	6.0
	MD-90	15	0.7
	Total Fleet	**544**	**11.2**
Eastwind	Boeing 737	2	26.0
	Total Fleet	**2**	**26.0**
Frontier	Boeing 737	7	22.6
	Total Fleet	**7**	**22.6**
Hawaiian	DC-9	13	18.9
	DC-10	8	23.6
	Total Fleet	**21**	**20.7**
Midway	Airbus 320	1	4.0
	Fokker 100	12	3.5
	Total Fleet	**13**	**3.54**
Midwest Express	DC-9	20	25.2
	MD-80	2	7.0
	Total Fleet	**22**	**23.6**
Northwest	Airbus 320	50	4.5
	Boeing 727	45	17.0
	Boeing 747	33	14.6
	Boeing 757	48	6.8
	DC-9	185	25.8
	DC-10	33	22.3
	MD-80	8	14.0
	Total Fleet	**402**	**18.5**
Pan Am*	Airbus 300	3	13.7
	Total Fleet	**3**	**13.7**

*Acquired Carnival Airlines in 1997 and discontinued Airbus.

AIRLINE	AIRCRAFT	NUMBER	AVERAGE AGE
Reno	MD-80	26	5.8
	MD-90	2	0.5
	Total Fleet	**28**	**5.4**
Rich	DC-8	4	27.5
International	Lockheed L-1011	12	21.1
	Total Fleet	**16**	**22.7**
Southwest	Boeing 737	242	7.6
	Total Fleet	**242**	**7.6**
Tower Air	Boeing 747	18	22.7
	Total Fleet	**18**	**22.7**

(Tower includes two freighter-passenger combination planes)

AIRLINE	AIRCRAFT	NUMBER	AVERAGE AGE
TWA	Boeing 727	40	22.0
	Boeing 747	12	25.6
	Boeing 757	3	0.3
	Boeing 767	15	11.6
	DC-9	58	25.0
	Lockheed L-1011	14	22.0
	MD-80	50	9.2
	Total Fleet	**192**	**18.6**
United	Airbus 320	36	1.7
	Boeing 727	75	17.4
	Boeing 737	226	11.6
	Boeing 747	52	13.3
	Boeing 757	92	4.5
	Boeing 767	42	8.4
	Boeing 777	16	0.9
	DC-10	35	19.7
	Total Fleet	**574**	**10.7**
USAir	Boeing 737	203	10.0
	Boeing 757	34	5.8
	Boeing 767	12	6.9
	DC-9	63	21.7
	Fokker 28	14	11.3
	Fokker 100	40	5.5

AIRLINE	AIRCRAFT	NUMBER	AVERAGE AGE
USAir (*cont.*)	MD-80	31	14.3
	Total Fleet	**397**	**11.3**
USAir Shuttle	Boeing 727	13	25.2
	Total Fleet	**13**	**25.2**
ValuJet (as of April 1996)*	DC-9	47	26.6
	MD-80	4	13.5
	Total Fleet	**51**	**25.6**
Western Pacific	Boeing 737	13	10.2
	Total Fleet	**13**	**10.2**
World	DC-10	4	17.5
	MD-11	7	2.4
	Total Fleet	**11**	**7.9**

(Chart does not include planes on order for delivery after December 31, 1996, or with no delivery date, or planes stored or leased to another airline.)

Many European, Russian, South American and North American manufacturers build aircraft that operate all over the world, including in the U.S. Some of those planes are decades old. Since there are thousands of airlines worldwide, it is impossible to list the type and age of craft in every airline's fleet. But here are some of the biggest:

AGE OF MAJOR FOREIGN FLEETS

AIRLINE	AIRCRAFT	NUMBER	AVERAGE AGE
Aereomexico	Boeing 757	6	2.3
	Boeing 767	2	4.0
	DC-9	18	20.6
	MD-80	25	8.6
	Total Fleet	**51**	**11.9**

---

*Acquired AirTran in 1997 and took its name.

AIRLINE	AIRCRAFT	NUMBER	AVERAGE AGE
Air Canada	Airbus 320	34	4.9
	Airbus 340	4	0.5
	Boeing 747	9	15.9
	Boeing 767	29	9.2
	Canadian Regional Jet	24	1.0
	DC-9	35	27.0
	Lockheed L-1011	4	22.8
	Total Fleet	**139**	**11.8**
Air France	Airbus 300	12	18.7
	Airbus 310	10	9.2
	Airbus 320	26	6.3
	Airbus 340	13	2.4
	Boeing 737	43	8.2
	Boeing 747	35	12.7
	Boeing 767	7	4.7
	Concorde	6	19.7
	Total Fleet	**152**	**9.6**
Alitalia	Airbus 300	14	16.3
	Airbus 321	17	1.1
	Boeing 747	8	14.8
	Boeing 767	5	1.2
	DC-9	13	26.5
	MD-11	8	3.6
	MD-80	90	6.7
	Total Fleet	**155**	**8.7**
British Airways	Airbus 320	10	7.2
	Boeing 737	29	6.2
	Boeing 747	65	11.6
	Boeing 757	42	9.6
	Boeing 767	23	4.6
	Boeing 777	6	0.8
	Concorde	7	19.1
	DC-10	7	17.1
	Total Fleet	**189**	**9.4**
Cathay Pacific	Airbus 330	10	1.2

AIRLINE	AIRCRAFT	NUMBER	AVERAGE AGE
Cathay Pacific (*cont.*)	Airbus 340	4	0.25
	Boeing 747	32	7.8
	Boeing 777	4	0.5
	Lockheed L-1011	7	22.9
	Total Fleet	**57**	**7.5**
El Al	Boeing 747	10	15.6
	Boeing 757	7	4.9
	Boeing 767	4	12.5
	Total Fleet	**21**	**11.4**
Japan Airlines (JAL)	Boeing 737	4	0.75
	Boeing 747	72	10.7
	Boeing 767	21	7.1
	Boeing 777	3	0.5
	DC-10	13	16.8
	MD-11	9	1.8
	Total Fleet	**122**	**9.5**
Royal Dutch Airlines (KLM)	Boeing 737	31	6.7
	Boeing 747	30	9.8
	Boeing 767	8	0.4
	Fokker 100	6	7.5
	MD-11	9	1.8
	Total Fleet	**84**	**6.7**
Korean Air (KAL)	Airbus 300	33	9.5
	Boeing 727	3	18.0
	Boeing 747	30	7.8
	DC-10	3	21.7
	Fokker 100	12	2.8
	MD-11	3	4.7
	MD-80	14	5.0
	Total Fleet	**98**	**8.0**
Lufthansa	Airbus 300	12	7.0
	Airbus 310	12	6.6
	Airbus 319	6	0.3
	Airbus 320	33	5.4

AIRLINE	AIRCRAFT	NUMBER	AVERAGE AGE
Lufthansa (*cont.*)	Airbus 321	15	1.5
	Airbus 340	15	2.5
	Boeing 737	95	6.9
	Boeing 747	26	8.2
	Total Fleet	**214**	**5.9**
Mexicana	Airbus 320	12	4.3
	Boeing 727	23	16.1
	Fokker 100	10	4.2
	Total Fleet	**45**	**10.7**
Qantas	Airbus 300	4	14.3
	Boeing 737	38	6.1
	Boeing 747	31	8.8
	Boeing 767	24	6.6
	Total Fleet	**97**	**7.4**
SAS	Fokker-28/ 1000	3	14.0
	Fokker 4000	16	15.8
	Boeing 767	15	6.4
	DC-9	28	21.8
	MD-80	71	7.4
	MD-90	6	0.25
	Total Fleet	**139**	**11.0**
Singapore Airlines	Airbus 310	23	6.6
	Airbus 340	6	0.5
	Boeing 747	45	5.5
	Total Fleet	**74**	**5.5**
Transbrasil	Boeing 737	11	7.0
	Boeing 767	11	8.7
	Total Fleet	**22**	**7.9**
Varig Brasil	Boeing 737	42	12.1
	Boeing 747	5	9.2
	Boeing 767	10	7.9
	DC-10	8	18.6
	MD-11	6	4.0
	Total Fleet	**71**	**11.4**

AIRLINE	AIRCRAFT	NUMBER	AVERAGE AGE
Virgin Atlantic	Airbus 320	1	3.0
	Airbus 340	5	2.2
	Boeing 747	9	16.0
	Total Fleet	**15**	**10.5**

It is also useful for passengers to be familiar with the age of some of the most common airplanes flown outside the U.S. The following chart will give you an idea how old your plane might be.

AGE OF AIRCRAFT IN FLIGHT TODAY

PLANE	FIRST FLOWN	BUILT BY
Aerospatiate/British		France, United
Aerospace Concorde	1969	Kingdom
Airbus		
A-300	1972	Germany, France,
A-310	1982	United Kingdom,
A-320	1987	Spain
A-330	1992	
A-340	1991	
Airtech-235	1983	Indonesia, Spain
Antonov		
An-24/26/32	1960/70/77	Russia
An-28	1969	
An-38	1994	
Avions de Transport		
ATR 42	1984	
ATR 72	1985	France, Italy
Avro RJ/British		
Aerospace 146	1981	United Kingdom
Beechcraft 1900C	1982	U.S.A.
Boeing		
707	1954	U.S.A.
727	1963	
737	1967	
747	1969	

PLANE	FIRST FLOWN	BUILT BY
757	1982	
767	1981	
777	1994	
British Aerospace One-Eleven	1963	United Kingdom
Canadian Challenger/ Regional Jet	1978	Canada
de Havilland		
DHC 6 Twin Otter	1965	Canada
DHC 7 Dash 7	1975	
DHC 8 Dash 8	1983	
Dornier 228	1981	Germany
Dornier 328	1991	
Embraer 110 Bandeirante	1968	Brazil
Embraer 120 Brasilia	1983	
Embraer 145	1995	
Fairchild Metro	1969	U.S.A.
Fokker 27	1955	Netherlands
Fokker 28	1967	
Fokker 50	1985	
Fokker 70	1993	
Fokker 100	1986	
Ilyushin 62	1963	Russia
Ilyushin 86	1976	
Ilyushin 96	1988	
Ilyushin 114	1990	
Jetstream 31	1967	United Kingdom
Jetstream 41	1991	
Lockheed L-1011 Tristar	1970	U.S.A.
McDonnell Douglas		
DC-8	1958	U.S.A.
DC-9	1965	
DC-10	1970	
MD-11	1990	
MD-80	1979	
MD-90	1993	

PLANE	FIRST FLOWN	BUILT BY
Saab 340	1983	Sweden
Saab 2000	1992	
Shorts 330	1974	United Kingdom
Shorts 360	1981	
Tupolev 134	1962	Russia
Tupolev 154	1968	
Tupolev 204	1989	
Vickers Viscount	1948	United Kingdom
Yakovtev 40	1966	Russia
Yakovtev 42	1975	
Xian Y-7	1984	China

AVIATION'S SENIOR CITIZENS

You know the old joke about getting rid of your used car. It may be broken-down and rusted, but just try to sell it to someone else and it becomes "good as new." Well, it's the same with airplanes, except it is the FAA that says "It's as good as new."

Not exactly. Some planes are just plain old. Many of them are worth avoiding if alternatives are available.

Airlines can substitute one plane for another right up to departure time, so if the airline you choose owns a lot of old planes, you stand a greater chance of being on one. A last-minute switch can thwart all your advance planning. Often it comes down to what is in an airline's fleet—an airline cannot substitute a thirty-year-old L-1011 for a new 747 if it does not own any. If you are booked on the airline's only new plane and its others are twenty-five years old, do not expect a new plane if there is a change of equipment.

Here are some of the prevalent geriatric jets in passenger service:

DC-9, Series 10, 20, 30, 40, 50. All of these are aging aircraft, having been built in the 1960s and 1970s. There are many, many in service, and many being retrofitted to serve well into the next century. You cannot avoid them all, so stick with the reputable carriers that are retrofitting their DC-9s to meet or exceed current standards, such as Northwest. But now there is a new concern. It seems that in trying to make an old plane new, you cannot necessarily make it "as good as new," because the retrofit itself can cause problems. In 1997, it was discovered that the hush kit—the equipment that makes old engines quiet enough to comply with today's noise abatement laws—doesn't quite fit right. Some experts warn that the problems could even cause the plane to crash. USAir, Northwest, AirTran (née ValuJet), and TWA fly a lot of DC-9s. Let's watch this one very closely.

DC-10, Series 10, 30, 40. This plane had trouble a few years ago when it was discovered that a flawed design for metal welds in its engine caused an engine to fall off in mid-flight. The NTSB found the bad welds in more than 200 DC-10 engines. The manufacturer fixed the flaw. DC-10s are no longer built, and the ones still in service are very old. Some DC-10-10s and DC-10-30s are among the oldest planes still flying at twenty-five to thirty years old. Avoid them.

DC-8. First flown in 1958, the DC-8 pioneered the Jet Age, along with the Boeing 707 (in 1954). Still flying at thirty-plus years, it is used mostly by charter and cargo carriers. You are unlikely to be on this one, and should not be.

707. This wonderful plane ushered in the Jet Age in 1954. Most recently it was in the news for its inglorious uses in its golden years—in 1996 one crashed in South America while hauling a load of fish to Miami. I recently happened upon one of these in foreign charter passenger service, but now it is used mostly for hauling cargo.

727, Series 100, 200. Built for over thirty years (ending in 1984), this plane can be very old. I liked the 727. But it's long in the tooth and needs to be flown by a reputable airline with good maintenance and quality control, and with completed aging aircraft overhauls. Aim for the very well-maintained fleets with major carriers.

737, Series 100, 200. The most widely used jet in the U.S., the plane is alleged to have difficulty with its rudder design, resulting in two accidents that to date the NTSB believes were caused by a jamming of the rudder. The mysterious flaw may have also caused hundreds of mishaps, including eleven crashes overseas. Yet the FAA persists in denying that the test conditions in which the rudders failed could happen in real life. Throughout 1994 and 1995 the NTSB, the FAA and Boeing debated what changes should be made to the 737 rudder control mechanism. The FAA did not believe the 737 was unsafe. Boeing insisted there were no flaws in its design. Finally, the White House stepped in and on January 15, 1997, announced more remedial measures would be ordered. Unfortunately, the NTSB says the measures do not go far enough.

Later in 1997, things looked even worse for old 737s. In October, the FAA ordered inspections and modifications on older planes because of cracks in the fuselage (''skin panel lap joints''), which could ''cause a rapid decompression.'' What the FAA forgot to put in its public statement is that a ''rapid decompression'' can lead to ''a catastrophic loss of the plane''—a crash. Which airlines have this ''tired iron''? AirTran Airways (yes, the new ValuJet), Aloha Airlines (which gave us the dramatic event of a plane opening like a sardine can in flight), Aviateca, Sierra Pacific, Vanguard, and—shame on you—Southwest Airlines. Thus, my recommendation on this plane will have to remain almost the same as before the 1997 announcement. Avoid the older 737s for good, premanently, and avoid all but reputable carriers' 737s until the fixes are made, as careful checks and preventive maintenance of the rudder control mechanisms are thought to reduce the chance of a rudder problem. Unfortunately, nobody yet knows when these fixes will be made, because the FAA has not yet established a deadline. The FAA says the airlines will have three years from the date of the final airworthiness directive. There is no final airworthiness

directive to date. The cost to the entire worldwide fleet is
$126 million. In the US alone last year, there were 600
million passengers. Guess what, folks, that's twenty cents
a passenger (if we paid for the whole world's repair) to
avoid the deadly safety problem that has already killed
two planeloads of US passengers and caused hundreds of
other deaths worldwide. I'd gladly pay the share of the
entire city of Columbus. Where is the FAA cost-benefit
analysis on this one? Southwest Airlines, months ahead of
the government directive, announced it would make
changes immediately, and seek further remedies, such as
additional training and procedures for its pilots—a good
thing, too, since it flies only 737s. As for other airlines
with 737s (see the charts on pages 247–250), you will
have to specifically inquire or watch the news to learn
when the changes are made or "tired iron" is retired.
Remember, however, that not all 737s are old. The 737-
300, -400 and -500 series are now in production. The 600,
700 and 800 series will be in production through 2015.

747, Series 100, 200. As crash statistics go, the 747 has
a split personality. The older models have a worse crash
record than the industry average. The newer model 747-
400 has a much better crash record than the industry average. Even before the TWA flight 800 crash, I avoided
aging 747s, especially in foreign fleets. Remember, too,
the 747 is still in production and will be in production for
some time to come, so unlike the 727 example, not all
747s are old. Some are brand new. The 747 is very reliable
and a workhorse of international fleets. I especially like the
newest model, 747-400, easily distinguished by its wingtip
winglets. But the NTSB found something is terribly wrong
with certain older models of the 747. Something caused
the center fuel tank to explode. New 747s have insulation
between heat sources and the fuel tank: a modification the
manufacturer made before the TWA 800 crash. Did they
recognize the plane's vulnerability? It sure looks like it to
me. Airlines will need to monitor the temperature in the
fuel tanks, avoid flying with empty tanks, put an inert gas
in the tanks to displace the dangerous explosive fumes,
fill the tanks with fuel that has been cooled, and use less

explosive jet fuel, as does the military. The military has been "inerting" the tank and using less explosive fuel for years. Even before the TWA flight 800 crash, older Boeing 747s had to be inspected for cracks in the center fuel tank wall and for problems with some electrical switches that can cause fires. (Remember, too, a fuel pump is still missing at the crash site. It is possible the pump was a factor, and may even have been malfunctioning or bogus.) The explosion might also have been sparked by bad wire—wire which the military scrapped years ago, and made sure was not on Air Force One and Two.

Lockheed L-1011. About twenty-five to thirty years old, this plane is being phased out of major passenger airline service. Look for them to disappear. With the DC-10, their past troubles made a lot of people wary of flying them. The only major U.S. airlines still flying the L-1011 are Delta and TWA. Rich International, which had a record of installing bogus parts, also flies this plane. It's time for the L-1011 to be phased out of passenger service.

Concorde. This supersonic marvel will soon celebrate its thirtieth birthday, and it is showing its age. In 1994, British Airways announced it was repairing hairline cracks found inside the wings of seven Concordes, and in 1996 a protocol was announced to "drill out" cracks to stop them from spreading, pending further repairs. The sleek craft, of which eighteen were built, is no longer made. The airlines that fly the Concorde, British Airways and Air France, must keep the original craft in the air. Thirteen are still in service, and they are expected to be used until 2010. Don't bet on it.

After two decades of flight, manufacturers, airlines and economists say a plane's maintenance costs go up and it is not economically feasible to keep flying aged aircraft. At that point, airlines get rid of them. Where do some of these old planes go? To start-up and low-cost carriers. I am going to stay off old planes belonging to start-ups or any airline short on cash that also farms out maintenance to the lowest bidder. It's easy to see that repairs and retro-fits will get the short end of the stick.

Some major carriers say refurbishing twenty-year-old planes renders the aircraft as good as new. I'm not convinced. Because of aviation business trends and policies in the U.S., we may be fast approaching a time when the foreign carriers will be preferable to many U.S. carriers because the U.S. will be flying increasingly older equipment. The chart on pages 250–254 shows that many foreign carriers already have fleets more youthful than most U.S. carriers.

Remember, however, that aging aircraft in foreign countries are not required to meet U.S. standards. Thus you may find yourself booked on an aging aircraft that has not had a recommended aging-aircraft check or repair. This is a dangerous proposition.

Some American carriers are upgrading their fleets with the newest planes. We can only hope the turnaround in airlines' fortunes spells a turnaround in aircraft replacement. But if it remains our fate as Americans to be stuck on aging aircraft, stick with the major carriers. Boeing was the first manufacturer to establish aging-aircraft protocol. In 1989, Boeing had manufacturing quality control problems. The FAA fined the company $125,000, which seems like a pittance when one airplane can sell for $150 million. At the time, however, it was the largest fine the FAA had ever imposed on Boeing. Boeing claims to have fixed the problems, and frankly, the company is certainly well ahead of the government in its ability to spot problems and do trend analysis. Besides, the FAA would never know anyway, since self-inspection is the predominant method of policing in the industry. These factors, plus Boeing's years of experience and its fear of getting sued over any potential downfall, gave Boeing an advantage—until 1997.

In 1997, Boeing had quality control problems seemingly everywhere. It shut down two lines, and the FAA increased surveillance. Boeing is under tremendous financial pressure, too, and has reached a point where it has farmed out so much of its manufacturing of parts and components that it has difficulty controlling its supplies and suppliers. Given the undercurrent of problems, the stand-down and reevaluation was actually good news. The Silk Air crash of a new 737 revealed even more allegations of poor quality control and rushed assembly. The FAA issued, on January 8, 1998, an air worthiness directive to inspect all 737s delivered after September 20, 1995.

The bottom line on aging aircraft is this: avoid airplanes over twenty years old. Select those airlines that retire aging aircraft and periodically update their fleets with new planes. While U.S. carriers have aging-aircraft programs to detect and correct problems associated with aging aircraft, foreign carriers may not. So it's most important to avoid foreign carriers' aging aircraft, especially those from countries that don't pass the FAA safety review, as listed in the chart on pages 306–308. Until the retrofit is complete on the 737s, stick with 737s in reputable newer U.S. fleets that are moving immediately to make repairs, such as Southwest. Until the crash of TWA flight 800 is finally resolved, I am going to avoid older 747s. It can't be mere coincidence that TWA is getting rid of its fleet of old 747s and replacing them with newer 767s and 757s.

ROUTES TO SAFETY

Another safety consideration, as far as airplanes are concerned, is how to get out quickly in the event of an emergency. Exit doors and windows are the only way, but they are not always accessible; sometimes they are far from passengers' seats, or blocked by smoke or debris after a crash or onboard fire. Sometimes the emergency slide is broken—in fact, the Boeing 747, the DC-10 and the Lockheed 1011 are allowed to fly with one malfunctioning evacuation slide. This FAA rule dates to the days when the slides were new technology and had kinks that needed working out. In 1976, the FAA issued a temporary ruling: those three planes could fly with one out-of-order slide. The original ruling was specifically limited to those three planes. Then in 1978, the FAA included the Airbus 300 in the exemption. But by the 1980s, the airline industry was clamoring for more waivers—and the FAA caved. It expanded the rule to include the Boeing 767, the new 777

and the Airbus 300-600. All of those planes are allowed
to fly with one emergency slide in useless condition. The
question is, which one is it? You won't know until you
board and see the yellow tape on the exit closest to *your*
assigned seat.

Of course, perhaps we should be grateful to have the
emergency exits we do, even if sometimes they do not
work. If the Aviation Rule Making Advisory Committee,
the industry's mouthpiece in the FAA, has its way, the
rule that says there should be an emergency exit every
sixty feet along the fuselage will be eliminated. For
years the flight attendants' union has opposed efforts by
Boeing to eliminate a pair of exits along the fuselage
of the 747. That way the airlines would be able to fit
in a few more rows of seats. Pilot unions also object to
the idea. So far, it has not gone beyond the talking
stage. But the rule-making committee is top-heavy with
industry representatives, who have a lot more money
and manpower than pilot and flight attendant unions and
safety groups.

The industry also wants to change the amount of space
people must squeeze through to escape a plane. On February 1, 1991, a 737 burned after a runway collision with a
Skywest Metroliner. The space between the rows of seats
at the emergency exit was just six inches. Passengers could
not get through the space quickly. A passenger at one
emergency door froze, and the other passengers fought
over the exit. A flight attendant tried to get to the mid-
fuselage exit to coordinate the evacuation but never made
it. Twenty-one people died of smoke inhalation because
of the bottleneck in the narrow passageway to the exit.
Eleven victims were lined up within feet of the wing exits.
Smoke had filled the cabin in just forty-five seconds.

After that tragedy, congressional hearings prompted the
FAA to require that the space between exit seat rows be
twenty inches. Tests had shown that with twenty inches,
there was a 14 percent increase in the number of passengers who could get out quickly. But that was still too
much for the airlines. They balked at twenty inches—that
meant they would have to push other rows closer together
(making passengers complain about leg room) or lose rows

of seats altogether. Even though the FAA's own cost-benefit analysis said the twenty-inch rule was good for business, the airlines fought it until they won a waiver allowing them to set exit seat rows thirteen inches apart. The airlines said thirteen inches was the same as twenty when it came to emergency evacuations.

Other than those with broken emergency slides, some planes in particular concern flight attendants and others involved in passenger safety. Here is a look at some aircraft with emergency exit problems:

757-200: Six Exit Scenarios. This plane is flown by eight major domestic carriers. It has six different exit configurations—meaning different 757s have emergency doors in varying seat rows, and in varying locations and numbers along the fuselage. Thus, just knowing you are flying on a 757 will not help you when requesting seat assignments. You will need to know the configuration of each airline, as with these eight carriers:

CARRIER	DOOR EXITS	DOOR EXITS WITH SEATS	WINDOW EXITS
America West	6	1 (2R)	0
American	6	2 (2R, 2L)	4
Continental	6	0	4
Delta	6	0	4
Northwest	8	1 (2R)	0
TWA	8	1 (2R)	0
United	6	1 (2R)	4
USAir	8	1 (2R)	0

R = right; L = left.

Fokker 100 and 28. Neither has a rear emergency exit. The operators of these Dutch planes got a waiver from the FAA, making these among the only planes that lack a rear exit door. There are ninety seats for passengers in the F-100 coach cabin and sixty-five in the F-28. There are also two emergency exits in the front of the plane and four window exits in the mid-coach cabin. In an emergency, dozens of passengers have to reach the middle of the plane to escape, a feat that might be impossible in case of a fire at the front of the plane. Flight attendants for airlines which fly the F-100 (American Airlines, USAir and Midway) have complained about the danger of not having a rear exit.

Canadair Jet. A fifty-seat plane with no rear exit door.

Lockheed L-1011. Some models have no exit doors in the coach section for twenty rows with five seats across in the middle. The coach section can seat about 200 passengers. So those passengers must go all the way forward or all the way to the rear to evacuate the plane. There are no exits over wings. The plane has only six exits, as opposed to eight in most planes. Delta Airlines and TWA fly several L-1011s.

The only way to help yourself is to ask your airline agent when getting your seat assignment where the exit rows are, and book your seat accordingly. You can also check in the front of the Official Airline Guide, or ask your travel agent to do so. In that book you will find diagrams of the major airlines' seat configurations.

Experience has also shown that more people escape planes when a flight attendant is present at an emergency exit to give loud, strong commands. But flight attendants spend most of their time in the front or back of a plane, and when accidents happen they may not be near the mid-cabin side exits. Some safety advocates have suggested that flight-attendant jump seats should be placed at those mid-cabin exits.

WHICH WAY?

Okay, so you're in a smoke-filled plane; luckily the pilot got it safely to the ground and ordered an evacuation. Do you head forward or back? Did you remember the seat count—how many rows forward or back to the nearest exit? The FAA finally even put on their safety Internet site what the first edition of this book suggested—count the rows to the nearest exits when you get on board. But is everyone going to know to do that and head to the nearest exit? What if you know the nearest exit is two rows back and others are heading six rows forward? Here again, the carriers could incur a simple, one-time, two-cents-per-seat cost to make you a whole lot safer—put a small notice on the back of the seat in front of you that tells you where the nearest exits are.

PLANES WITH A PAST

Just mention the names of certain aircraft and some people get nervous. This was true of the DC-10 and the L-1011 in the 1980s. Here are the planes on my nervous-flier list:

ATR. Certain models were notorious for becoming suddenly difficult to control in extremely cold temperatures. Pilots have complained about problems with de-icing the plane's wings. The de-icing boot—a rubber sleeve on the wings that is designed to expand and crack accumulated ice—is not long enough to cover the entire length of the wing. Improvements (making the boot longer) have been required. *Presumably,* that fixed the problem. Personally, I am going to give ATR operators ample time to test their repairs. Think of ATR as fair-weather flying.

Embraer 120. Known as the Brasilia, this Brazilian-made plane has had its share of troubles: five fatal crashes in the U.S. since 1990, and at least two more crashes of foreign carriers. Only about 300 were built, most of which went to North America. U.S. carriers are the largest users of these planes. Severe weather, icing, controller and possibly pilot error appear to have caused January 1997's crash in Detroit. The sad fact is that these smaller propeller-driven planes cannot operate as well as big jets in bad weather conditions. Nor can they fly at altitudes as high as the larger jets. That limits their options to fly over storms or climb out of icing conditions. In addition, the Embraer's de-icing equipment is different. It relies on pneumatic boots to expand and break the ice, as opposed to the heated surfaces of the big jets. Unrelated to the 1997 crash, Embraer was already subject to some Airworthiness Directives (ADs) requiring remedial measures for other parts of the plane. I stopped flying in this plane after the second crash, and I am going to give the authorities and Embraer ample time to resolve the cause of this crash and fix the problems before I fly them again. Again, better for fair-weather flying.

All Russian Planes. These craft are notorious for poor maintenance and parts. The FAA has yet to approve safety and maintenance standards for many former Soviet countries, including Russia, even though Aeroflot Russian International Airlines flies to Kennedy International Airport in New York, Dulles in Washington, D.C., Miami, O'Hare in Chicago, and Sea-Tac in Seattle. The breakup of the Soviet Union has made Russian planes even more dangerous because parts are harder to get or not available at all, and there are few experienced maintenance crews to work on the planes outside the old Soviet Union. Even airlines in Russia and the former Baltic republics are jettisoning their Russian-made craft. I spent two weeks in the former Soviet Union and was appalled at its civil aviation. Maintenance was not the only problem. Planes simply did not have the most obvious safety features we take for granted in the U.S. Overhead cargo bins were open shelves; planes were overloaded; cargo, passengers and even animals were piled in the aisles and bathrooms. The tray table was a piece of sheet metal reminiscent of a guillotine. (On the ground, passengers fared no better, having to push their bags through the x-ray scanner with their hands, thus getting a body x-ray gratis in the process.) Aeroflot also flies Airbus (A310) and Boeing (767) jets. If you must fly Aeroflot or another Russian carrier, make sure you are not booked on a Russian-made plane. Good reason for this caution was illustrated in the winter of 1996 when a Boeing 747 collided with an Ilyushin jet over India. The Russian plane had no collision avoidance equipment (the kind required on all planes that serve the U.S.) because it simply can't be installed on that particular craft. So avoid Russian-made planes.

AIRPLANE WATCH LIST

Recent accidents involving the following planes have made me uneasy. Here's why:

Boeing 737. As discussed previously, the older models had problems with the rudder, one brand new one with the stabilizer. Many passengers have already turned tail and run. It is hard to avoid the 737, if not impossible. Stick with reputable carriers—your best bet for good maintenance.

Boeing 757. There is nothing to suggest there is an inherent problem with this plane, yet two of these planes in foreign fleets had fatal crashes in 1996 after cockpit instruments failed. Why? Maintenance mistakes. Subsequent investigations revealed that outlets on wingtips, Pitot tubes or static ports, which must be open to give the pilot accurate instrument readings, were blocked during maintenance in foreign countries in one case covered with masking tape. Boeing says it is now going to make covers with bright orange streamers to warn mechanics to remove them before flight. These kinds of covers are already available for a few bucks for general aviation pilots. If it's that easy to make these deadly mistakes twice, can we rely on foreign mechanics to use the streamers? (A third fatal 757 crash, that of American Airlines in December 1995 in Colombia, was not related to maintenance. It occurred because the pilot made a mistake entering directional information into the plane's flight computer and the airport was missing guidance equipment as a result of local drug wars.) The problem has been limited to foreign maintenance, so there is no cause for alarm, only cause to watch out that there are no more such crashes related to this type

of maintenance error. U.S. carriers have not experienced
such problems.

Boeing 747. As I mentioned earlier in this chapter, I am
skipping the older 747s. Aim for the 747-400.

Canadair Regional Jets. These small jets, CRJs, used in
the U.S. on many routes which would otherwise be flown
by commuter service propeller planes, were temporarily
grounded in 1997 for cracks in the fuselage. SkyWest Airlines found a fourteen-inch crack in the fuselage and upon
further inspection found seven of its ten planes had similar
problems. Delta Connection also found seven of its ten
CRJs had problems with cracks. The manufacturer said
the problem was a repair problem, not a safety problem.
Look folks, a repair problem *is* a safety problem.

Bottom Line:

The man credited by many with being the father of airline
deregulation is reported to have said, "I really don't know
one plane from the other. To me they are just marginal
costs with wings." With that, our fate as passengers was
sealed for the next two decades. The airlines and the FAA
expect you to accept whatever aircraft the airlines send to
the gate, no matter how old, no matter its track record, no
matter that the NTSB has recommended repairs, no matter
that the FAA has given the airlines until well into the next
century to complete the fixes. There is a lot more to a
plane than marginal costs, but if that is how they want to
play the game, you can do it too. You should select those
carriers and those flights which use the aircraft you want,
not just the cheapest thing flying. What do you suppose
is the marginal cost for *empty* old planes? You will actually be helping the airlines by forcing them to upgrade
their fleets and modernize their equipment, which in the
long run will enable them to better compete with the more
youthful fleets of many foreign carriers. You can be a
policymaker as well as a passenger.

U.S. and Foreign Airlines 271

missing parts. A mechanic will have already completed a walk around. The pilot will then review the plane logs

CHAPTER FOURTEEN

U.S. and Foreign Airlines

Your airline has to do a lot. When done well, by experienced people, under perfect conditions, flying looks easy, effortless. But behind the scenes, operations are rather complex.

WHAT AIRLINES DO WHILE YOU ARE SITTING IN YOUR SEAT

The process from boarding the plane through takeoff is fairly routine no matter which airline you fly. Some perform better than others. Here is a brief look at what happens from the time you get on the plane until you get off at your destination:

• Commercial airline pilots are required to walk around a plane before its first flight of the day. The pilot will literally walk the tarmac under and around a parked plane, looking up at the craft for signs of trouble. Obviously, the pilot cannot see the top of the plane from this point, or any internal faults. But he can spot fluid leaks, cracks or missing parts. A mechanic will have already completed a walk-around. The pilot will then review the plane's logs and pertinent data for the flight.

• The plane is loaded with passengers and baggage as allowed by the plane's weight limits. Overloaded planes are not usually a factor in U.S. commercial airline accidents or crashes. Most weight-related problems happen to cargo and charter planes—if a group rents a plane for a fishing trip and wants to stow too much gear aboard, for example. Most travelers on commercial jets become aware of weight limits only when they and their bags part company. Sometimes when bags are "lost," it is really because the airline took luggage off a plane that was overloaded and sent it on another plane, particularly when bad weather has shut down service for a day or two and must-go cargo flies first.

• The pilot and first officer go through checklists and examine all the major equipment. They discuss which routes and procedures they will use, and also alternative plans they may use should that become necessary.

• The pilot receives permission from ground controllers to back away, or "push back," from the departure gate. At very large airports he might get permission from the ramp controller and then get directions from the ground controller. He also receives takeoff traffic sequence instructions, and finds his place in the takeoff line. In some airports, small trucks hook a tow bar to the plane's front wheel. In other places, the pilot revs the engine and pushes back with the thrust reverser. The method depends on local airport rules and the amount of room the pilot has to maneuver at his gate. (In October 1996, a group of passengers in Europe made news during an airport strike by getting off the plane and pushing it back from the gate themselves.)

• When the pilot nears the start of the runway, he stops in the run-up area or holding bay and goes through another short checklist. He reviews engine performance, position of the flaps, altimeters and other control settings before being cleared to taxi into takeoff position.

• The flaps, or movable panels on the trailing edge (back) of the wings that help to provide lift, are extended. Flaps on both the right and left wings should be in matching positions. The flaps should not be confused with the ailerons farther out on the wings. The ailerons are used for steering left or right and therefore do not match (like turning a rowboat by putting one oar in the water while the other is elevated). There are also slats on the leading edge (front) of the wing.

• If it is winter, before getting in line to take off, the plane may undergo de-icing to clear accumulated ice or snow on the wings. This de-icing may occur at the gate, where the plane is sprayed from a truck. In newer airports, the plane will taxi to a de-icing area where a ''cherry-picker'' style of machine does the job. Passengers can often see ice on the wings that pilots cannot see from the cockpit, so take a look.

• The pilot will tell the flight attendants to prepare for takeoff and ''cross check,'' meaning that the attendant will check the emergency exit at her assigned position. The attendant will arm the emergency exit, then check the one across the aisle on the other side of the plane. Hence the term ''cross check.''

• The local controller then gives the pilot runway clearance for takeoff. The local controller also gives the pilot another briefing on weather, wind, visibility and local conditions. This is when the pilot may find out that he is caught in ''flow control.'' That means he'll be denied permission to take off until there is a time for the plane to land at its destination, or until there is sufficient airspace to merge into air traffic. The controller will also make sure to properly sequence the plane so that a small, light plane is not too close to a big, heavy jet. Following too closely behind a big plane can cause a small craft to be sucked into the jet's wake vortex. Wake vortex is like two horizontal tornadoes flowing from the jet's wing tips. No small plane wants to be caught in this "wing-tip tornado."

• The pilot powers up the engines and allows the plane to move forward. He speeds down the runway until he reaches the critical minimum airspeed necessary for "rotation," or pulling back on the yoke and allowing the nose to head up into the air. That speed is called V-R. If a takeoff has to be aborted, the pilot must decide to do so before the plane attains a certain airspeed. That airspeed is called V-1. Once there, the pilot cannot be sure he can safely stop the plane. Each of these speeds is different depending on the plane, the runway length, weather conditions and elevation. The pilot has the information necessary to make these calculations.

• Once aloft, the flaps are retracted, sometimes with grinding, whining and thuds. The wing ailerons and tail stabilizer operate to keep the plane level, and with the rudder, turn it to the left or right. On small planes, the entire tail moves like a fish when the pilot pulls on the yoke. But on big jets, only the movable rudder and stabilizer surfaces in the tail fluctuate to direct the craft.

• The plane will be assigned a flight level or altitude. On any plane serving the U.S., a collision-avoidance system will help the plane "see and be seen" and avoid other planes. The plane will automatically take evasive measures if it senses other craft are on a collision course, or might be close enough for a "near miss."

• After takeoff, the pilot is in contact with the departure controller until leaving the airport's controlled airspace, or positive control area. That's a large section of air often described as being shaped like an upside-down wedding cake. Larger airports have this controlled airspace. So complicated is the configuration of some controlled airspace that plastic models of it are sold for pilots to study.

• Once out of the airport's positive control area, the pilot is handed off to en route controllers. Located at twenty-four en route centers across the country, these controllers direct all the airline traffic around the country through the use of their radar screens, computers and radio contact. Only controllers at airports can look out windows and see planes.

• In preparation for landing, the flaps again extend, with a repeat of the disquieting sound effects. (The big-jet pilots are lucky; on many small planes, you pull a big lever and extend the flaps with pure brute force.) The pilot is given a landing position and instructions from Air Traffic Control. Again, the controllers should ensure the plane does not get too close to the one preceding it so it does not get caught in the wake vortex of that plane.

• As the plane touches down on the runway, the pilot deploys the thrust reversers, which are actually plates that drop down behind the engine so that air coming out of the engine is forced forward. The engines do not actually reverse. In fact, they keep running just as they have throughout the flight. At the same time, panels on the wings called "spoilers" pop up to interrupt the flow of the air over the wing and slow the plane. Once the plane slows to a safe speed, the pilot applies the brakes. If used alone, the brakes would cause the plane to "skid" (even though big planes have the equivalent of anti-skid brakes), stop too abruptly, or risk blowing out the tires. Sometimes pilots have to tap the brakes sooner, and passengers can feel the brakes grab and the plane jolt. This happens if the pilot needs to slow down more quickly than usual, perhaps because he needs to get off the runway in a hurry.

How well these procedures and a whole host of behind-the-scenes operations are done depends to a large extent on the airline, not on the U.S. government.

WHAT YOU DO NOT KNOW ABOUT AIRLINE SAFETY

There are two very important principles you need to know about airlines and safety.

First, all airlines are *not* created equal. The FAA requires the companies to meet minimum safety standards—but much of the safety diligence beyond that is left to the airlines themselves. The FAA now seems to understand that fact particularly well with carriers like ValuJet. When the discounter was allowed to resume flying in the fall of 1996, FAA Director of Aircraft Certification (whose department decides whether a plane is certified to fly) Thomas McSweeny was quick to point out that the agency was responsible for only the basic evaluation of the airline. Everything else was up to ValuJet, he said. This statement was a dramatic change in the FAA party line, and much more accurate than previous FAA statements.

Second, the airlines themselves control airline safety. Because the FAA encourages the airlines to police, evaluate, report and improve themselves, and because when it does inspect an airline it usually announces its intention, the FAA has little firsthand knowledge of precisely what goes on in any particular airline—until there is a disaster.

None of this should have been news to authorities. Yet I was quite disappointed in 1996 when members of Congress appeared stunned to hear me voice these facts. After all, over a decade ago, the aviation writer and airline pilot John Nance had written a book about such problems, particularly as they related to deregulation. The Congressional Office of Technology Assessment found many similar problems with FAA oversight in 1988 and reported so to both the House and the Senate. In fact, the Office's report is still for sale today at the Government Printing Office. A glance at the summary reveals the predicament:

> Pivotal members of this safety network, the airlines each follow individual corporate philosophies, but each have one common characteristic—during the past decade each has changed operating practices to control costs, eliminating some of the layers of the old safety system and replacing them with alternatives that must still be evaluated. While "safety comes first" is the instant response of airlines executives when asked the basis for management decisions, this universal answer masks wide variances in airline corporate cultures and operating procedures. Safety

first means one set of corporate guidelines to the airline
that already owns adequate landing slots at a crowded airport and has ample financial reserves to purchase additional slots. It means something else entirely to a
financially strapped airline that must choose between discretionary maintenance of its aircraft and purchase of additional airport slots, because it cannot afford both. These
alternatives illustrate that each airline uses different parameters to make the choices necessary to satisfy customers
with reliable, low-fare service and still make a profit in a
fiercely competitive industry.

For years before the ValuJet crash, the FAA insisted
that all airlines were equally safe. Immediately after the
crash, the agency rushed to the public with the same reassurance. "When we say an airline is safe to fly, it is safe
to fly. There is no gray area," said FAA Administrator
David Hinson. Now, after the humiliating revelations of
that tragedy, all the FAA says is that airlines flying today
meet the agency's minimum safety standards. It will not
rank airlines, or assess how much an airline exceeds the
minimum. That is left for the public to ponder. In 1997,
though, while appearing with me on *Meet the Press,* even
Congressman Oberstar admitted that safety is largely up
to the airline.

But how safe are the airlines? Is one major crash per year
nothing to get excited about? Are three too many to tolerate?
How about two? Would you be surprised to learn that there
have been dozens of accidents and incidents that you have
never read about? Precisely which airlines do a better job of
protecting your safety is not just a secret the FAA keeps
from the public. Even the agency does not know.

The FAA's own ninety-day safety review of ValuJet
over the summer of 1996 pointed out the discrepancies in
safety, maintenance and supervision among major carriers,
discount airlines and start-up organizations. (The report
was published just as ValuJet resumed flying.) The FAA
does compile this safety data about all air carriers, as well
as thousands of private planes and rotorcraft like helicopters. But it does not analyze its own information. Instead

it keeps the statistics within the agency, making them extremely difficult for anyone to obtain—including journalists, members of Congress, government officials or the public. The FAA intends to keep it that way. In 1996, the FAA proposed a safety data collection system called GAIN—Global Analysis and Information Network. It suggested that GAIN would be a nongovernment clearinghouse for aviation safety statistics. It sounded like a great idea—the collecting, analyzing and distributing of safety data would surely create another layer of checks and balances for the airlines. But the fine print of the proposal told a different story: the FAA recommended that the owners of the network would be insurers, manufacturers, airlines and airports. The reason: *to prevent public disclosure of sensitive information.* The flying consumer—the person with the greatest interest in knowing the safety rates of airlines—would be deliberately excluded. I objected to this plan. GAIN is still in its formative stages and in 1997 the FAA announced it will seek a new federal law to keep the data secret from the public.

After my article in *Newsweek* discussing the great holes in the safety net and stating that some airlines are safer than others, and following my testimony before Congress about the shortcomings in airline safety, the FAA said it might consider a safety ranking for the public. But it never compiled one. I thought a 1996 special report in *U.S. News and World Report* said it best: "How can fliers find out which carriers are safest? They can't. Mr. and Mrs. Average Citizen would have to be both dogged and patient to pry a carrier's 'accidents per mission miles flown' statistics out of the Federal Aviation Administration, and the figures aren't very useful anyway. Accidents alone don't paint a meaningful picture of an airline's safety. . . ." An expert quoted in a 1996 article in *The Wall Street Journal* noted that "indeed, the FAA has frequently come under criticism for failing to disclose even routine safety data. News organizations often have to file Freedom of Information Act requests to get any of these records, and the agency typically doesn't compile national statistics. This week, an FAA representative referred a reporter to three different federal agencies to answer a question on an airline's safety record." Imagine the average traveler trying to make those phone calls.

The FAA and the airline industry do not like the idea of publicly available safety statistics. The events of 1996 and 1997 forced the FAA to answer questions from politicians and the press about making public a safety ranking of airlines. In a test of the FAA's new openness, I had a friend file several Freedom of Information Act (FOIA) requests for airlines' accident rates. He received a computer disk full of data, but all identifying information, like the names of the airlines, the locations of the accidents, the experience and qualifications of the pilots and even the dates of the accidents, had been deleted. Also cut were the numbers of killed or injured. It was impossible to tell which airlines had what accidents. Yet another FAA database had last been updated in 1983. With great effort and expenditure of time, you can match the accidents with the NTSB database. But much crucial data, such as the number of an airline's annual takeoffs and landings, were still missing. That had to be obtained from a different agency, the Bureau of Transportation Statistics.

By the end of 1997, after pressure from Congress, the media and the public, the FAA posted "safety information" on its Internet site. But it is only raw data. Some of the so-called "new" information was sleight of hand, since the FAA gave the public nothing that was actually new. The information was already available at the NTSB Internet site. The FAA did make good on its promise, however, that anyone browsing its Internet site would be unable to make heads or tails of the data. The agency said it would not organize the data or rank the accidents and incidents. Why? Because the airlines objected. Worse, the FAA confirmed in a 1997 letter to me that the rating of airlines that it did in 1996 before and after the ValuJet crash was an aberration, done only because of probing by the Inspector General's office. The FAA advised it will not do it again.

Just as they balked in the 1980s at publication of their on-time arrival and departure records, the airline industry objects to safety ratings. They say the same airline can look unsafe by one set of statistics and perfectly safe by another, and publication of safety rates would make airlines reluctant to share information. Finally, opponents say the airlines would just start competing to have the better record—and they should not be competing over safety.

But why not? Perhaps that is precisely what they *should* be doing. As much as the airline industry railed against publication of their on-time rates, they now work hard to keep them reliable so they can boast about them in advertisements. Perhaps the same would someday be true of safety rates.

The public cannot get the figures from the airlines. They are impossible to obtain, since the airlines are not government entities and are not subject to FOIA requests. Even parties to lawsuits have a hard time getting the information. The families of passengers killed in 1994 in a USAir crash near Charlotte, North Carolina, had to go to the Supreme Court to force the airline to turn over safety records from the accident. The families of the victims of the American Airlines crash in Cali, Colombia, were not so lucky. In 1997, American Airlines beat the families in federal court and got to keep secret its safety information. There is no law against dissemination of these statistics. And there is no good reason why the taxpayers who support the FAA and are the consumers who buy airline tickets should be denied the data necessary to make informed choices about flying.

Since you can't rely on the government or the airlines, I got the data for you.

ACCIDENT/INCIDENT RATES

Here are the FAA's own internal rates of the major carriers for the first five years of the 1990s. They are divided into accidents (causing death, serious injury or significant aircraft damage) and incidents (less severe mishaps), near misses in the air, and pilot deviations (any action that prevents a pilot from reaching his destination, including "turn-backs" due to mechanical problems). I found pilot deviations and near-mid-air collisions to be almost as telling as accident and incident rates. If all airlines were created equal, these rates should be roughly the same. They are not.

These rates reflect the number of safety problems *for every 100,000 takeoffs* from 1991 to 1995 (the number of annual takeoffs for each carrier is in parentheses beneath its name).

MAJOR PASSENGER CARRIERS

CARRIER	ACCIDENT AND INCIDENT RATES	NEAR MISSES IN THE AIR	PILOT DEVIATIONS
America West (997,347)	3.9	1.8	0.9
American (4,425,578)	5.9	1.1	3.8
Continental (2,452,472)	6.8	0.8	3.4
Delta (4,865,814)	6.3	0.9	2.5
Northwest (2,727,858)	5.5	1.0	1.8
Southwest (2,606,206)	1.5	0.9	1.3
TWA (1,353,526)	5.4	0.5	2.4
United (3,672,909)	4.7	1.4	2.5
USAir (4,418,100)	4.6	0.6	2.4

Near-midair collisions are not as rare as passengers may think. In 1995, the FAA recorded 216 near-midair collisions. In 1996, there were 201. In the first five months of 1997, there were 98.

Pilots are forced to abandon their flight plans for a variety of reasons—weather, mechanical failure, sickness of a passenger. Though FAA rates do not specify the cause, the agency recorded 1,039 deviations in 1995, 1,323 in 1996, and 561 in the first five months of 1997. All carriers experience deviations due to weather and medical emergencies. Some carriers have many more mechanical problems and deviations than others, and this does have safety implications. Near-midair collisions are certainly often not the carrier's fault. Pilots must follow instructions from Air Traffic Control. Thus, you would expect all carriers' rates to be the same. They are not. That is one of the reasons the FAA collects the data—it has safety implications.

Accident/incident rates among major carriers, #1 being the best:

1. Southwest
2. America West
3. USAir
4. United
5. TWA
6. Northwest
7. American
8. Delta
9. Continental

Pilot deviations among major carriers, #1 being the best:

1. America West
2. Southwest
3. Northwest
4. USAir
5. TWA
6. United
7. Delta
8. Continental
9. American

Near-midair collisions, #1 being the best:

1. TWA
2. USAir
3. Continental
4. Southwest
5. Delta
6. Northwest
7. American
8. United
9. America West

I put the most stock in the Accident/Incident rates. The other two are important, and accidents as collected by the NTSB, as opposed to incidents reported to the FAA, are more reliable. Curiously, in the most recent data, there was a dramatic drop in some carriers' reporting of incidents— undoubtedly not because the carriers got a lot better but because they curtailed their reporting.

Using only the most current accident and incident data, from January 1995 to June 1997, the safety lineup looks like this:

Accidents per 100,000 flights, from safest to least safe:

1. Southwest .14
2. America West .20
3. United .31
4. USAir .36
5. American Airlines .39
6. Northwest Airlines .40
7. Continental .41
8. TWA .43
9. Delta .44

Just about any way you figure it, Delta and Continental come out at the bottom.

WHAT'S IN A NAME?

Or rather, what isn't? As it turns out, some names mislead, and others cover up past woes. Many accidents occur on carriers that passengers believe are part of the major airlines listed above. But in fact, they are often a commuter, smaller or even foreign airline with a code-sharing agreement with the major carrier. As commuter airlines began flying routes served by major airlines or carved out routes in places that had no air service, more partnerships developed between the two. In the process, the distinction between commuters and major carriers blurred. (Changes in the regulations in 1995, many of which did not take effect until 1997 or thereafter, made many "commuters" become majors—at least where their operating rules are concerned. Since everyone still refers to them as commuters, so will I.) Commuters usually paint their planes with the same colors and logo lettering as the major airline, and often call themselves something reminiscent of the larger carrier—United Express, Delta Connection, American Eagle or Northwest Airlink. Often the two are integrated under the major carrier's name in the Official Airline Guide's (OAG) schedule listings. But a commuter airline's operating practices and legal safety standards can be very different from the major carriers it is affiliated with—a distinction of which most passengers are unaware. Passengers are routinely referred to commuter carriers when they want to reach a small or isolated airport. They do not know that the major partner has no say in the commuter airline's operations, maintenance or safety practices. In some arrangements, the commuter airlines only pay a fee to paint their planes in the familiar colors and use the name of a major carrier. Some operators may serve several majors, under different names.

Furthermore, just because the same name is used does not mean it is the same airline. The new Pan Am, launched in the fall of 1996, is a start-up that has no connection to the old, once venerable airline—other than having bought the name and famous blue globe logo at a bankruptcy auction. The name cost $1.2 million, but it could be price-less. Passengers who might be wary about flying an unknown start-up may be more inclined to board Pan Am just because of the familiar name.

On the other hand, perhaps the name will make people think twice. Passengers might very well remember that the previous Pan Am was found by a jury to have exhibited gross negligence in the safety and security of passengers on Pan Am 103. Pan Am also claimed to employ bomb-sniffing dogs, but the animals turned out to be ordinary German shepherds leased from a local kennel. Passengers might also remember that the old Pan Am had an executive named Martin Shugrue, Jr. He became CEO of the new Pan Am (and now he's been replaced by the Carnival Airlines chief). Travelers might also remember that the old Pan Am left thousands of passengers stranded around the globe just before Christmas 1991. The airline filed for bankruptcy, abruptly shut down and made no effort to help customers holding tickets—even those caught between connecting flights. Essentially, it milked its last round of passengers to help fill the bankruptcy coffers. There is almost no chance a passenger will get a ticket refund once a carrier declares bankruptcy.

Passengers might also be interested in knowing that the new Pan Am leased planes that came from the old Eastern Airlines inventory, planes Eastern flew when it was convicted of falsifying its maintenance records. Shugrue certainly knows this because he agreed to the guilty plea and the fine when he was the trustee during Eastern's bankruptcy proceedings.

Thus the name on the plane may not tell you everything you need to know about the carrier you'll be flying. Here are some familiar carriers and the independent code-sharers that fly under their banner:

America West/America West Express
    Desert Sun Airlines
    Mesa Airlines
    Mountain West
American/American Eagle
    Flagship Airlines
    Simmons
    Wings West

Continental/Continental Express
Delta/Delta Connection
    Atlantic Southeast
    Business Express
    Comair
    SkyWest
Northwest/Northwest Airlink
    Express Airlines
    Mesaba
TWA/Trans World Express
    Trans States Airlines
United/United Express
    Air Wisconsin
    Atlantic Coast Airlines
    Great Lakes Airlines
    Mountain West
    UFS
    Westair Commuter
USAir/USAir Express
    Air Midwest
    Allegheny Commuter
    CC Air
    Chautauqua
    Commutair
    Florida Gulf
    Liberty Express
    Paradise Island Airlines
    Piedmont
    PSA Airlines

NATIONALS, REGIONALS, COMMUTERS AND CHARTERS

One of the main indications that all airlines are not
equal is that they have vastly different accident, incident
and other safety rates. For example, commuter carriers
have twice as many accidents as the major carriers, in part
because before 1997, commuter planes with ten to thirty
passenger seats were not subject to the same safety regulations as the major carriers. Planes that carry fewer than

ten passengers still have less stringent standards. But beginning in 1997, ten- to thirty-seat aircraft had to meet the same safety tests as larger jets flown by major carriers.

Between the commuters and the majors there are several types of airlines. They are categorized by the size of their annual operating revenues and not by the number of seats on their planes. On average, the major carriers statistically have better safety rates than the other types of carriers. Non-major carriers have all kinds of planes—from small propeller planes to jets, from ten-seaters to 747s. They also have widely divergent safety rates—from zero accidents to statistical rates of 100 or more accidents and incidents per 100,000 takeoffs.

Use the information on pages 287–289 and 292–293 to decide for yourself whether you want to fly a carrier with, on average, a poorer safety record than that of the major airlines. Sometimes you have no choice. More people are flying national and regional carriers, often because they are the only ones serving small airports. Commuter airlines evolved from air taxi services—small outfits that offered planes-for-hire to people flying to remote areas not served by larger carriers. When they became popular, the routes could support regularly scheduled flights, and the air taxi company became a commuter airline. (The category was established only in 1969, when the Civil Aeronautics Board said a commuter airline is an air taxi operation that has at least five round-trip flights a week between two or more points, and publishes its flight schedules. In 1972, the Board said that included planes with up to twenty seats, and in 1978, it upped the number to sixty seats.) In 1980, 1,339 planes flew commuter routes and carried 15 million passengers. By 1993, those numbers had surged to 2,208 planes ferrying 52 million people. Seventy percent of communities in the U.S. rely on commuter airlines for their regular flight service. Although many commuters have added bigger planes to their fleets, the majority still fly ten- to twenty-seat aircraft.

More lenient safety standards give operators of smaller planes different pilot training criteria, flight-time limits, operational control and maintenance guidelines. In real life, that means many commuter pilots have reported flying while exhausted, working long shifts or working until late at night when they had an early-morning shift the next day, and getting inadequate rest. (Though the NTSB says there have been no crashes due to pilot fatigue alone, it does warn that fatigue has contributed to crashes, and reports that in 1993, there were 100 fatigue-related mishaps.) These pilots have complained about training sessions being held at the end of a long workday, and having to be responsible for single-handedly checking the weather, calculating fuel loads and figuring aircraft weight and balance before every flight. For many of the aircraft they fly, there are no simulators on which to train in hazardous maneuvers, wind shear recovery and low-altitude stalling. Under the less stringent FAA rules for small commuters, there are no requirements for such simulators.

It was only in February 1995 that the FAA announced that cargo and passenger planes with between ten and thirty passenger seats could not fly without traffic alert and collision avoidance systems. It also said no transport plane could fly without airborne weather radar, and decreed that turbine-powered planes built after 1991 had to have an airborne wind shear warning and flight guidance system, and an airborne wind shear detection and avoidance system, or a combination of the two. Planes built before 1991 would have to be retrofitted at least with wind shear warning systems, the FAA said. This was good news because passengers on commuters would now have standards comparable to those of the major carriers to protect them, such as in equipment, flight crew restrictions and other safety measures. But existing carriers were given a number of years to comply, so they are not equal yet.

As with the major airlines, one method of judging other airlines' safety standards is to take a look at their safety records. *Again, the statistics are per 100,000 takeoffs* (with the airlines' average number of takeoffs for the years 1991–1995 in parentheses beneath the name except where a later start date is noted). Note that in the case of carriers with a small number of flights per year, suffering only one or two accidents per year will yield a high rate.

NATIONAL AND REGIONAL PASSENGER CARRIERS
(INCLUDING SELECTED CHARTERS)

CARRIER	ACCIDENT AND INCIDENT RATES 1991–1995	PILOT DEVIATIONS 1991–1995	NEAR MISSES IN THE AIR 1992–1995
Air South ('94: 25,581)	2.25	2.25	0
Air Transport International ('94: 28,596)	9.46	3.40	0
Air Wisconsin (320,394)	6.40	1.90	0.25
AirTran Airways* ('94: 4,183)	0	0	14.25
Alaska (619,449)	4.30	1.25	2.66
Aloha (379,285)	1.55	0.77	0.35
AmerTrans Air (146,725)	10.60	2.62	0
Arrow Air (38,767)	15.71	0	0
Atlantic Southeast ('93: 516,227)	0.81	0	0.15
Business Express ('93: 468,857)	2.47	1.09	0.42
Carnival Airlines** (62,386)	9.32	1.93	1.64

---

*AirTran merged with ValuJet in 1997.

**Carnival became part of PanAm in 1997.

CARRIER	ACCIDENT AND INCIDENT RATES 1991–1995	PILOT DEVIATIONS 1991–1995	NEAR MISSES IN THE AIR 1992–1995
Continental Express ('95: 206,473)	1.45	0	0
Evergreen (50,593)	7.48	0	0
Executive Airlines (242,375)	2.71	0	0
Express One (64,938)	25.11	0	0
Frontier ('95: 19,952)	13.78	0	0
Hawaiian Airlines (301,369)	4.62	1.83	0
Horizon (977,009)	0.96	1.03	0
Kiwi ('92: 43,464)	3.03	1.88	0
Mesa ('95: 212,002)	.45	0	0
Miami Air (13,468)	109.37	5.56	0
Midway ('94: 33,171)	4.12	0	0
Midwest Express (133,310)	2.88	2.83	1.12
Reeve (17,206)	21.85	0	7.48
Reno ('92: 124,278)	3.80	1.09	1.09
Rich International (10,856)	52.90	0	0

CARRIER	ACCIDENT AND INCIDENT RATES 1991–1995	PILOT DEVIATIONS 1991–1995	NEAR MISSES IN THE AIR 1992–1995
Ryan International ('92: 31,543)	47.59	5.64	0
Sierra Pacific ('92: 12,196)	34.55	5.06	0
Simmons ('92: 691,288)	4.06	0.13	0.47
Spirit Airlines ('92: 16,421)	6.92	3.46	0
Sun Country (64,390)	7.58	0	2.12
Sun Jet International ('95: 4,441)	45.03	22.51	0
Tower Air (19,321)	48.87	0	6.81
Trans States Airlines (524,327)	2.22	0	0.26
UFS ('94: 46,732)	8.61	0	0
USAir Shuttle (and Trump prev.) (111,678)	6.20	2.67	0
ValuJet* ('93: 98,815)	7.14	3.92	0
Viscount ('94: 9,983)	7.93	0	0
World Airways (11,288)	5.52	0	0

---

*ValuJet became AirTran in 1997.

THE DARLINGS OF DEREG

The Airline Deregulation Act of 1978 spawned the Marshall's or Filene's Basement of the airline world—low-budget, discount start-ups. Deregulation made greater competition possible through the flexibility of airfares. Suddenly, start-up airlines bloomed to offer travelers cheap alternatives to the major carriers. Some fly the oldest fleets in the country. In the long run, it is deregulation which may put U.S. carriers behind many foreign carriers where age and modernization of equipment (like safety features) are concerned. Start-ups were made possible by the deregulation policies of the Carter Administration, were left unsupervised by the Reagan and Bush Administrations and are actively protected and promoted by the Clinton Administration. In one of its annual reports, the FAA actually said it believed it should try to emulate ValuJet. And Secretary of Transportation Federico Peña stated: ". . . we will do whatever we can to make sure fledgling carriers have a fair shot." With that, the stage was set for disaster.

The FAA says that about seven new start-up airlines are certified to fly every year. But of the more than 250 new airlines created since deregulation, only America West and Midwest Express have survived from 1978. That fact alone indicates grave weaknesses in start-up operations. A 1996 Government Accounting Office report said that between 1990 and 1994, 79 airlines had been in business less than five years. GAO found that the start-ups had more accidents and needed more inspections than established airlines. But the FAA couldn't tell the GAO why that was so.

Instead, the agency said it was "unaware of these trends and had not done an analysis similar to ours for new airlines, nor were they aware of any other studies addressing this issue," the GAO wrote. With few exceptions, start-ups by definition are more likely to have an aging aircraft problem because they buy used equipment—and those planes tend to be older than the aircraft in a major carrier's fleet. Sometimes they are the planes that a major carrier has replaced because they are too old. To make matters worse, these planes may have been "horse-traded" more than once. Consider the history of one Boeing 727-200, serial number 20438. It was delivered new in 1970 to Pacific Southwest Airlines. USAir then took over Pacific Southwest and sold the plane to Eastern Airlines. After Eastern sold the Eastern Shuttle, the plane became part of the Trump Shuttle. Then a New York consortium bought Trump, and the plane was passed on to the USAir Shuttle (but not home to USAir, because that is a different company), where at age twenty-seven, it flew until 1997 as tail number N912TS. After this plane's history was detailed in the first edition of this book, the plane was removed from the USAir fleet.

Used planes may have belonged to carriers in countries with questionable safety practices, such as Turkey. Bogus parts were often installed on planes in these foreign ports, becoming undetectable unless the plane or part was disassembled. Some start-ups buy entire fleets of used planes—and then hire subcontractors to do the maintenance. Even older planes, or crashed planes, are cannibalized to provide parts to the aged aircraft market. So the start-ups find themselves owning old planes and having no real participation in their upkeep and repair, particularly in quality-control oversight. In addition, it is precisely this mishmash of planes and maintenance facilities that the FAA finds exceedingly difficult to inspect.

Even the FAA admits this is a problem.

"Air carriers using a variety of aircraft types, or a mix of models of the same type, have a far more complex operation than those using a single fleet make and model," the FAA reported in September 1996. Many fly a variety of planes because "it may be cheaper to acquire whatever aircraft are currently 'available.' In some instances, these aircraft are available because they are models that were turned back into the marketplace due to new purchases and trade-ins by larger air carriers."

In spite of reports like this, the FAA remains mired in pre-deregulation inspection and oversight methods. Airlines that have been grounded by the FAA did business right under the FAA's nose. ValuJet flew old, used planes that underwent unapproved repairs in Turkey. The new Pan Am leased used planes that had belonged to maintenance-falsifying Eastern Airlines. Rich International installed bogus parts. Checkered pasts like these can be—and have been—hidden time bombs for a plane's new operator. In addition, start-ups generally pay their pilots less than the majors do, so they often hire less experienced fliers. An inexperienced pilot can inflict a lot of wear and tear on a plane with "hard landings" or other mistakes.

A government study shows that from January 1990 through December 1994, airlines that had offered scheduled service for less than five years had, on average, higher accident/incident rates. The rates held true in ValuJet's case. Many other start-ups didn't stay in business long enough to be evaluated. There are many reasons for this increased accident/incident rate—older equipment, farmed-out maintenance and corporate philosophy.

"Every other start-up wants to be another United or Delta or American. . . . We just want to get rich," said Lawrence Priddy, ValuJet's CEO. Personally, I want to fly the carrier that emulates United, Delta or American. No one should ever fly an airline whose executives just want to get rich.

As with the major airlines, one method of judging start-up carrier safety standards is to take a look at their safety records. Here are the numbers as computed by the FAA. Again, *the statistics are per 100,000 takeoffs* from 1991 to 1995 and the number in parentheses is the number of flights made by the carrier during those years. Remember that in the case of carriers with a small number of flights per year, suffering only one or two accidents per year will yield a high rate.

SELECTED LOW-COST CARRIERS*

CARRIER	ACCIDENT AND INCIDENT RATES	NEAR MISSES IN THE AIR	PILOT DEVIATIONS
Air South (25,581)	3.9	0	3.9
AmeriJet (39,850)	5.0	0	5.0

*As computed by the FAA.

CARRIER	ACCIDENT AND INCIDENT RATES	NEAR MISSES IN THE AIR	PILOT DEVIATIONS
AmerTrans Air (142,057)	11.3	0	0.7
Carnival Airlines (61,258)	9.8	1.8	1.6
Frontier (19,954)	10.0	0	0
Morris (71,795)	4.2	0	5.6
Reno (123,651)	4.9	1.6	1.6
Southwest (2,606,206)	1.5	0.9	1.3
Spirit Airlines (16,596)	12.1	0	6.0
Tower Air (19,217)	46.8	5.7	0
ValuJet (98,815)	8.1	0	8.1
Vanguard (10,877)	N/A	0	9.2
Western Pacific (8,638)	N/A	0	0

THE CAUSES OF CRASHES

In the ten years between 1985 and 1995, half of all accidents happened during approach and landing. Forty percent of those occurred when a perfectly normal plane suddenly crashed into a mountain or the ground. In all those cases, the pilot and crew did not realize they were about to crash. These accidents killed more than half the people who died in plane crashes. Figuring out why so many planes crash into terrain without the crew knowing danger was imminent would go a long way toward minimizing fatal accidents.

This is where pilot training and discipline and an airline's corporate philosophy make an enormous difference.

Here are the causes of airline crashes from 1991 to 1995:

CAUSE OF AIRLINE ACCIDENTS

CAUSE	FREQUENCY
Midair	1
Fire	1
Wind shear	2
Ice, snow	3
Out of fuel	3
Runway	4
Landing	7
Loss of control in flight	16
Flying into terrain	17
Other	5

The difference between major carriers, commuter airlines, air taxis and other planes can be seen most vividly in the FAA's accident rates *per 100,000 hours of operation* for each. The actual number of accidents is in parentheses.

	1992	1993	1994
Large Air Carrier	.14 (18)	.18 (23)	.17 (23)
Commuter	1.05 (23)	.66 (16)	.43 (10)
Air Taxi	3.78 (76)	3.33 (70)	4.25 (85)
General Aviation	8.89 (2,114)	9.21 (2,069)	9.66 (2,029)

	1995	1996	1997 (Jan–May)
Large Air Carrier	.27 (36)	.28 (38)	(20)
Commuter	.43 (11)	.48 (12)	(9)
Air Taxi	3.75 (75)	2.97 (87)	(24)
General Aviation	10.41 (2,082)	8.11 (1908)	(632)

Other than in commuter operations, which still have almost double the accident rate of the large air carriers, the accident rates are definitely *not* improving.

THE WORST CRASHES IN THE WORLD
AND IN THE U.S.

People always ask about the worst crashes in history, who crashed and why. Sadly, four of the worst accidents happened in 1996.

The worst crashes in the world include:

1. Pan Am and KLM Boeing 747s collided in dense fog and burst into fire on the runway at Tenerife in the Canary Islands, Spain. Some of the passengers survived, but 583 people died, giving this accident the terrible distinction of having the highest death toll in any aviation disaster. These flights were not even bound for Tenerife—they were directed there because of a terrorist airport bombing at their intended destination. March 27, 1977.

2. A Japan Airlines Boeing 747 crashed into a mountain in Japan after a mechanical failure. Four lived; 520 died. The worst death toll of any single-aircraft accident. Boeing accepted responsibility for a bad repair. August 12, 1985.

3. A Russian Antonov-32 flown by a Zairean airline crashed into a city market in Kinshasa. The total death toll is not known, but 350 are believed to have died. January 8, 1996.

4. A Saudi Arabian Boeing 747 and a Kazak Airlines Ilyushin 76 collided in midair over Charkhi Dadri, India. All 349 on board the two planes were killed. November 12, 1996.

5. The first crash of a jumbo jet, 346 people died when a Turkish Airlines DC-10 crashed north of Paris after takeoff. The plane was loaded to capacity because of a strike at British Airways. The loss of a door brought down the plane. March 3, 1974.

6. An Air India Boeing 747 exploded off the Irish coast. A terrorist bomb was suspected as the cause of the crash. It killed 329. Lax security in screening bags and allowing bags to be checked and loaded without a matching passenger on board were believed responsible. June 23, 1985.

7. A Saudi Arabian Airlines L-1011 burned during an emergency landing in Riyadh, killing 301 people, including 15 infants. There were warnings of smoke in the cargo compartment. There was confusion in the cockpit. Instead of stopping immediately after landing and evacuating, the cockpit crew taxied and delayed evacuation by five minutes and fifty-five seconds. August 19, 1980.

8. The U.S. Navy cruiser *Vincennes* mistakenly shot down an Iran Air Airbus over the sea off coastal Iran, killing 290 people. July 3, 1988.

9. A terrorist bomb exploded on Pan Am flight 103 over Lockerbie, Scotland. All 259 people on the Boeing 747 and 11 on the ground were killed. December 21, 1988.

10. The Soviet Union shot down Korean Airlines flight 007 (a Boeing 747) when it strayed into Soviet airspace. All 269 passengers and crew died. September 1, 1983.

The worst accidents in the U.S. include:

1. An engine fell off an American Airlines DC-10 on takeoff from Chicago's O'Hare Airport and pilots lost

cockpit controls. All 271 on board were killed, as were two people on the ground. May 25, 1979.

2. TWA flight 800 (a Boeing 747) blew up over the Atlantic Ocean just off Long Island, killing all 230 passengers. July 17, 1996.

3. A Korean Airlines 747 flew into the ground while attempting to land in bad weather in Guam without a key part of the instrument landing system. All 227 on board were killed. August 6, 1997.

4. A Northwest Airlines DC-9's engine caught fire as the plane took off from Detroit. Only a four-year-old girl survived because her mother unfastened her own seat belt and used her body to shield the child; 156 other passengers were killed. The crew skipped a before-takeoff check of the flaps and slats and the plane lost lift and stalled on takeoff. August 16, 1987.

5. A Pan Am 727 crashed on takeoff from New Orleans, killing 154 people. Wind shear was to blame. July 9, 1982.

6. A Pacific Southwest 727 and a Cessna 172 collided over San Diego, killing 135 passengers on the jet, two people in the Cessna and seven people on the ground. September 25, 1978.

7. A United Airlines DC-8 and a TWA Lockheed Super Constellation collided in a snowstorm over New York. The United jet crashed in Brooklyn, killing all 84 aboard and eight people on the ground. The TWA plane crashed into the water just off Staten Island, killing its 43 passengers and crew, bringing the death toll to 135. December 16, 1960.

8. A Delta Airlines L-1011 smashed into the ground in Dallas after being caught in severe wind shear; 133 people died. August 2, 1985.

9. A USAir Boeing 737 crashed while preparing to land near Pittsburgh, killing 132 passengers and crew. A malfunction of the rudder seems to have been the cause. September 8, 1994.

10. A United Airlines DC-7 and a TWA Super Constellation collided in the air over the Grand Canyon, killing 128 people from both planes. In then-uncontrolled airspace clouds obscured the pilots' vision. June 30, 1956.

11. An Eastern Airlines L-1011 crashed while landing in New York in a storm; 115 people died. Wind shear was to blame. June 24, 1975.

12. A ValuJet DC-9 crashed into the Everglades after its cargo hold caught fire and smoke filled the aircraft; 110 people on board died. May 11, 1996.

AIRLINES THAT HAVE BEEN GROUNDED, HIT WITH ENFORCEMENT ACTIONS, AND OTHER RED FLAGS

Ours is a nation that likes to believe in the possibility of rehabilitation, the return of the prodigal son, seeing the light and changing your ways. After all, at various times in the last decade, American, Delta and USAir all had their troubles. For three years I refused to fly USAir because it had such a number of crashes. Thus, despite the FAA's permitting the following airlines to fly, I say we need to watch them closely to make sure they are not safety violation junkies. Perhaps it is the old prosecutor in me, having put away a few repeat offenders in my time.

Alaska — The FAA proposed a $810,000 penalty against Alaska Airlines for improperly modifying the main landing gear of a Boeing 737 and flying it that way on 9,000 passenger-carrying flights. Come on, Alaska, we have enough problems already with the 737s, and the FAA is known to be a cream puff on waivers and approvals.

Couldn't you at least get FAA approval? Alaskans should not have to settle for the "bush pilot syndrome."

AirTran (including ValuJet)— They're now joined with ValuJet and have proudly announced, "It's Something Else!" The question is "What?" If you are not convinced by now, then perhaps nothing will keep you away from ValuJet in sheep's clothing. I developed a special aviation rule because of ValuJet—never fly an airline that paints cartoons on its planes and keeps handy a ready supply of duct tape.

Even ValuJet's president, chairman and two other executives sold millions of dollars of stock in late 1996. They called it "diversification." I called it cashing out before you lost your shirt.

If ever there was reason for the First Amendment to the Constitution (freedom of the press), the sorry tale of Air-Tran/ValuJet and the FAA is it. On January 11, 1998, the *Cleveland Plain Dealer* (Beth Marchak reporting) said it had learned that while giving the old ValuJet cartoon planes a new paint job—in a red, teal and white-wash scheme—they found the rudders (necessary to steer the plane) were installed wrong. They also reported that the FAA found serious safety violations, falsified documents, improper maintenance, faulty repairs, and failures to supervise contractors—more serious safety-related violations than the February 14, 1996 report that recommended grounding the airline. Did the FAA tell you, the traveling public? Not hardly; they had no comment. It's "something else," alright, but not an airline you should be on.

Arrow Air — A cargo-hauler and charter fined $1.5 million for thousands of airworthiness violations. Grounded from March to June 1995, but then allowed to resume flying, it is remembered for a crash in Gander, Newfoundland, on December 12, 1985, which killed 248 members of the U.S. armed forces and 8 crew.

AvAtlantic — The charter airline that flew for Bob Dole's campaign, was previously grounded for safety violations, was grounded again in March 1997. AvAtlantic signed a

consent order with the FAA to let it resume limited flights
even though its "certificate remains suspended."

Delta — Something is going on at Delta. The folks at
Delta and the FAA don't seem to be able to put their
fingers on it. After this book first came out, I got the most
mail and some pretty interesting information on Delta.
However, all you have to do is read the NTSB accident
reports, note other FAA enforcement action in 1997, and
take several Delta flights, like the one I took from Detroit
to Atlanta on July 17, 1997. The plane was in terrible
shape. Several overhead bins were taped shut with duct
tape. The plane—outside and in—was worn and shabby.
It smelled of old curry. The guy next to me sat down,
leaned on the arm rest, and it fell to the floor. A flight
attendant came by and said, "Oh, that again," and shoved
it back up. We were delayed so long in departing that the
pilot announced that because of the delay he was going
to show an in-flight movie, but, he added, "It never happened, because I am not going to report it, because then
we have to pay for showing it." But the pilot added an
apology to the passengers sitting in the two rows along
the windows on either side of the plane. The speaker system was out in all of those seats, and Delta was waiting
to mend it until the plane went in for its next scheduled
maintenance. My next Delta flight on Delta "lite" was on
an almost thirty-year-old 737, which I most assuredly
wished not to be on. Delta was my first commercial flight
in 1971 and Delta is probably still flying that plane. Delta
is at the bottom of almost everybody's list of major carriers these days. Again in 1997 Delta had uncontained engine failures—that means the engine explodes and pieces
fly through the airplane. And it was hit with an FAA
enforcement order for making 69 flights with a closet door
that would not open—Delta had sealed it shut because the
door wouldn't stay closed. Inside the closet was emergency equipment and fire extinguishers! What's going on?

Great American Airways — What can be so great about an
airline that falsifies training, flight and duty time and load
records and documents? Target Airways of Reno flies as

Great American Airways and the FAA revoked its certificate—that is of course supposed to mean grounded. This carrier certainly missed the target and is a great one to avoid.

Great Lakes Aviation — Either the FAA just got around to the Gs on their list of inspections, or "Great" is a moniker best avoided by air carriers. Under a code-sharing arrangement, Great Lakes Aviation operates flights for United and Midway as United Express and Midway Express. As United Express, it crashed in Quincy, Illinois. Great Lakes "voluntarily suspended their operations" after the FAA found they flew unairworthy planes. Unairworthy planes, especially commuters, is enough for me to say this is another great airline to avoid.

Kiwi — Strangled by bankruptcy, Kiwi got an infusion of funds in December 1996. Although it slashed its flight schedules, it still did not make it. Be wary of operations on such a short shoestring. As the name suggests, this bird is flightless.

Markair — Maintenance violations caused the FAA to shut down this airline in August 1995.

Mesa — Mesa had twenty incidents and one accident in just three years. Even its pilots complained about their working conditions to Congress. The FAA decided to get tough in 1996—but that lasted only a few weeks. After a September 25 consent order, in which Mesa agreed to pay a $500,000 fine, the airline was allowed to operate its 142 planes on 2,000 daily flights. In November 1997 they were caught again—flying a plane with loose bolts on 75 passenger flights, no less—and fined. I will take the bus or the train, drive or walk before I'd fly Mesa right now. So should you.

Pan Am — Be wary of this "reborn" airline. It is Pan Am in name only, launched with used planes from Eastern and led by an executive of the former Pan Am who was also a trustee of Eastern. Let them work out their start-up missteps first. In 1997, it also is alleged to have been the target of domestic sabotage and acquired Carnival, a carrier with an accident rate that earned it comparisons with ValuJet. Steer clear.

Rich International — This charter airline admitted it stocked bogus parts in its maintenance bays. The FAA levied a $2.6 million fine and grounded Rich. There is no guarantee, however, that every bad part was pulled from every plane. Since I believe bogus parts are ticking time bombs, Rich International is another maverick airline to avoid.

Skyway Airlines —In November 1997, the former head of this airline's maintenance operation was sent to prison for using bogus parts, lying to FAA inspectors, and submitting fake warranty claims to cover it up. Other employees were also charged. When the events occurred, Skyway contracted with Mesa under a code share. Now the airline says it has new ownership and new management, but does it have new parts and new planes?

Tower Airlines — This airline has an accident/incident rate six times WORSE than ValuJet, as well as the highest near-miss rate in the FAA study of low-cost carriers.

ValuJet/AirTran — See AirTran.

VIP Air Charter — In March 1997, the FAA issued an emergency order revoking the air carrier certificate of VIP for falsifying pilot training records, using unqualified pilots, operating unairworthy and unauthorized aircraft, and a host of other violations. Falsifying records can be a federal criminal offense. When I was Inspector General, we prosecuted people for such things; even put some in jail. Don't you be an inmate on a VIP Air Charter.

World Airways — Hit with a whopping $610,000 fine in 1997 for security violations—the details of which the FAA says it cannot discuss for security reasons. Find another way to see the world. This was a consent order and "settlement." If this was the settlement, can you imagine how bad things are at World?

WHO HAS BEEN TAKEN OFF
THE RED FLAG LIST SINCE 1997?

One airline was "reformed"—or at least released from probation.

America West — It was really tough to put America West on probation in 1997. After all, I live in Columbus, and if you want a nonstop jet, America West is about it. But problems are problems, and an FAA enforcement action for superficial attention to safety is a very serious matter.

Since then America West has turned in a good, solid performance, with no further enforcement action. On the routes it flies, its equipment is often newer, and it uses jet service, which always gets my vote, especially in bad weather. On the flights I took to look at America West, the equipment was newer or overhauled, unlike its route competitors, and it was running a tight ship. OK, America West, I'm back on board. Please keep it up.

PILOT SALARIES AND EXPERIENCE

"There is not a gun big enough to make us give a higher base pay and higher bonuses," ValuJet President Lewis Jordan once told the *Wall Street Journal*. In fact, ValuJet pilots were among some of the lowest paid—and they got their checks only if they completed their flights. Any "pilot deviation"—meaning the pilot could not reach his destination for any reason—would leave a flier short at the end of the month. So the pilots were under immense pressure to get their planes off the ground and moving, even if it might mean rushing through maintenance or flying in bad weather.

Obviously, this "gotta get there to get paid" policy can endanger safety. It certainly did at ValuJet in February 1996. As a blizzard struck Dulles International Airport near Washington, D.C., every major airline declined to take off. But the ValuJet pilot decided to go for it. Only the ValuJet plane took off in the blizzard, and after it was gone, the airport closed.

Pilots and crews can get sloppy for other reasons as well. Airlines allow them to live anywhere they want. Their residence city doesn't have to be where they are based for work. If a pilot who lives in Miami is based in Washington, D.C., then all of his flights will originate in Washington. That means pilots and crews often juggle their schedules to win consecutive days off and bunched flying days. These schedules can lead to long stretches of fatiguing work. My office once received an anonymous letter from a pilot complaining about the consequences of this habit. "I'm tired," the pilot wrote, "of flying across the Atlantic solo, in a two-man cockpit with a copilot who is asleep."

These days, pilots may not get the kind of training they used to receive, either. Because of computerization, pilots may not be honing their "old-fashioned" flying skills. Most of their training is on simulators, leaving very little in-the-air flight training. Even when pilots are at work, computers perform many of their traditional tasks. The pilot behind the controls of the New York City to Washington, D.C., shuttle will actually land the plane himself. The pilot of a Boeing 767, an MD-90 or an Airbus 340 will spend most of his time watching the computer fly the plane. He inputs data into a flight computer to set coordinates. He pushes buttons instead of a throttle. The 737-400 does not even have what we think of as a throttle. Some of the newest generation aircraft (747-400, A-330 and 340) can fly twelve to fifteen hours nonstop. Some carry two crews who spell each other so they do not exceed their duty time. On long flights where there is very little for a pilot to do, it's not hard to imagine boredom and complacency setting in. Pilots themselves are concerned about this possibility.

The bottom line on pilot experience is this: pilots with commuters, air taxis and charters make less money and generally have less experience. A thumbnail rule is the bigger the plane, the higher paid and more experienced the captain.

FOREIGN COUNTRIES WITH POOR SAFETY OVERSIGHT

Foreign airlines are under no obligation to meet the FAA's safety standards. Even though I have been very critical of the FAA's oversight, and although I still believe it needs tremendous improvement, in most cases it exceeds the oversight in other countries. However, if foreign carriers want to land their planes in the U.S., they are supposed to pass our muster. The FAA says each airline must meet or be on its way toward meeting safety minimums established by the International Civil Aviation Organization (ICAO). The ICAO is part of the United Nations. Headquartered in Montreal, its member countries, including the U.S., establish safety standards and rules to govern their carriers. But ICAO has no staff to evaluate, monitor and enforce a country's compliance. Worse yet, the ICAO refuses to reveal any statistics about international airlines' safety records. So we come back to the FAA. And the FAA has not gotten around to inspecting all of the civil aviation systems of 103 nations that are home to 340 airlines flying regularly into the U.S. As of January 10, 1998, the FAA had checked out 79 of those countries. It had failed airlines from 14 countries at the time of this writing, but still had 24 foreign nations to inspect.

The FAA states that the assessments are not an indication of whether individual carriers are safe or unsafe. The agency says it is determining whether or not foreign countries even have a civil aviation authority and the extent to which those authorities ensure that operational and safety procedures are maintained by their air carriers. The countries are assessed for their adherence to ICAO's standards, not U.S. standards. By agreement with those countries whose airlines want to fly to the U.S., the FAA is supposedly given the information it needs to make these assessments. Of course, matters of state and diplomacy have been known to affect the FAA's rating of a foreign country, and it is most ironic that except for two countries, all those that fail do not have any airlines. My strong recommendation therefore is to avoid not only those countries which fail, but also those which receive a conditional rating. The FAA explains its ratings as follows:

- **Category I, Does Comply with ICAO Standards:** A civil aviation authority has been assessed by FAA inspectors and has been found to license and oversee air carriers in accordance with ICAO aviation safety standards.

- **Category II, Conditional:** A civil aviation authority in which FAA inspectors found areas that did not meet ICAO aviation safety standards and the FAA is negotiating actively with the authority to implement corrective measures. During these negotiations, limited operations by the foreign air carriers to the U.S. are permitted under heightened FAA operations inspections and surveillance.
- **Category III, Does Not Comply with ICAO Standards:** A civil aviation authority has been found not to meet ICAO standards for aviation oversight. Unacceptable ratings apply if the civil aviation authority has not developed or implemented laws or regulations in accordance with ICAO standards; if it lacks the technical expertise or resources to license or oversee civil aviation; if it lacks the flight operations capability to certify, oversee and enforce air carrier operations requirements; if it lacks the aircraft maintenance capability to certify, oversee and enforce air carrier maintenance requirements; or if it lacks appropriately trained inspector personnel required by ICAO standards. Operations to the U.S. by a carrier from a country that has received a Category III rating are not permitted unless the country arranges to have its flights conducted by a duly authorized and properly supervised air carrier appropriately certified from a country meeting international aviation safety standards.

The ratings are as follows:

INTERNATIONAL AVIATION SAFETY
ASSESSMENT PROGRAM (IASA)

COUNTRY	CATEGORY	COUNTRY	CATEGORY
Argentina	1	Belize	3
Aruba	1	(no current operators)	
Australia	1	Bermuda	1
Bahamas	1	Bolivia	2
Bangladesh	1	Brazil	1

COUNTRY	CATEGORY	COUNTRY	CATEGORY
Brunei Darussalam	1	Marshall Islands	1
Bulgaria	1	Malaysia	1
Canada	1	Malta	3
Cayman Islands	1	Mexico	1
Chile	1	Morocco	1
Colombia	2	Nauru	1
Costa Rica	1	Netherlands	1
Cote D'Ivoire	2	Netherlands Antilles:	
Czech Republic	1	Curacau, St. Martin,	
Dominican Republic	3	Bonaire, Saba,	
(no current operators)		St. Eustatius	1
Ecuador	2	New Zealand	1
Egypt	1	Nicaragua	3
El Salvador	1	(no current operators)	
France	1	Oman	1
Fiji	1	Organization of Eastern	
Federal Republic of		Caribbean States	
Yugoslavia		(OECS) covers:	
(Serbia and		Anguilla, Antigua &	
Montenegro)	1	Barbuda, Dominica,	
Gambia	3	Grenada, Montserrat,	
(no current operators)		St. Lucia, St. Vincent	
Germany	1	and The Grenadines,	
Ghana	1	St. Kitts and Nevis	2
Guatemala	2	Pakistan	2
Guyana	1	Panama	1
Haiti	3	Paraguay	3
Honduras	3	(no current operators)	
(no current operators)		Peru	1
Hong Kong	1	Philippines	1
Hungary	1	Poland	1
India	1	Romania	1
Indonesia	1	Saudi Arabia	1
Israel	1	Singapore	1
Jamaica	1	South Africa	1
Jordan	1	South Korea	1
Kiribati	3	Suriname	3
(no current operators)		Swaziland	3
Kuwait	2	(no current operators)	

COUNTRY	CATEGORY	COUNTRY	CATEGORY
Taiwan	1	Uzbekistan	1
Thailand	1	Venezuela	2
Trinidad & Tobago	1	Western Samoa	1
Turkey	1	Zaire	3
Turks & Caicos	2	(no current operators)	
Ukraine	1	Zimbabwe	3
United Kingdom	1	(no current operators)	
Uruguay	3		
(no current operators)			

(Updated as of January 10, 1998.)

CODE SHARING WITH CONDITIONAL
OR UNRATED COUNTRIES

It may prove difficult for passengers to decipher whether an airline (including some U.S. carriers) books them on a "conditional" or "does not comply" foreign carrier. Several American carriers are signing code-sharing agreements with foreign airlines whose safety records are unnerving. Taiwan's China Airlines has had 5.2 fatal accidents for every one million flights, and 323 people have died on China Airlines planes from 1989 to 1996. In the fall of 1996, American Airlines put the finishing touches on a code-sharing agreement with China Airlines that would make the two appear as one to travel agents and passengers. The agreement lets China Airlines carry American Airlines passengers between California and Taiwan. Continental Airlines signed a similar agreement with China Airlines early in 1996. United had a similar agreement with Thai Airways, when Thailand's aviation system was rated conditional. It also code shares with Lufthansa, Air Canada, Scandinavian, Air Wisconsin, and Great Lakes, which was recently grounded. There are now hundreds of code shares, and more every week. American Airlines has code shares with TAM, British Midland and South African; Delta shares with KAL, China Southern, and Varig; all of these are on my international warning list.

Passengers may not know they are being transferred to a foreign airline—and if they do, they probably will not know about the airline's safety lapses. The FAA will not offer much assistance in this area, and the airlines often tell passengers about switches only in the fine print. Even then, they never mention that the home country of the partner airline fails FAA safety tests. You must ask when you make your reservation.

RANKING THE INTERNATIONAL CARRIERS

How do we compare with the rest of the world's carriers? Unfortunately we cannot use the same yardstick we used to rank the U.S. carriers on accidents and incidents, because the rest of the world does not use our reporting or inspection system. The most objective ranking is by comparing the rates of fatal accidents, and of course adding a commonsense overlay for certain areas of the world. For example, aside from the table on pages 306–308, which show which countries meet or fail ICAO standards, at least one high-ranking FAA official has a separate list, maintaining that about ten countries may actually exceed our oversight, those being Canada, Australia and several western European countries. Thus, you probably would not be surprised to learn that the data reveals that the major Canadian airlines have not suffered a fatal accident in ten years, nor have airlines in Australia and New Zealand. Thus, the data actually backs up Dustin Hoffman's character's insistence in the movie *Rain Man* that they fly to Las Vegas by way of Australia so he can take Quantas.

Still, the data for some carriers gives an overly optimistic picture, showing good track records because they have not suffered a fatal crash, even though the safety conditions in that country are certainly not comparable to U.S. passengers' standards, and the training, government oversight, and corporate or national philosophy do not bode well for aviation safety.

The Air Travelers Association came up with an Airline Safety Report Card, which ranked all major international carriers on their rate of fatal crashes over the past ten years. Their list (integrated with the FAA's list of countries that fail to meet ICAO standards), and my warnings on which countries and carriers to avoid, yield the following warning list of international airlines:

Canada — No fatal accidents by major carriers in ten years.

Caribbean — No fatal crashes by major carriers in ten years, but BWIA International Airways hails from Trinidad and Tobago, which was only ranked conditional in ICAO standards until 1998.

Central America — Flying Central American carriers is by almost any ranking system among the riskiest in the world. Avoid these carriers and try to find major western carriers instead. Those with failing records, at least as far as a fatal accident rate, are Aviateca from Guatemala and COPA from Panama.

South America — Statistically, on average, it is best to avoid South American carriers, but after flying in South America for several years, I have come to believe that carriers in South America range from the sublime to the ridiculous.

Avoid all carriers from Bolivia, Colombia and Venezuela because those countries are only ranked conditional, and Peru, because it was ranked conditional until 1997. That includes ACES (Colombia), Aero Peru, Aeropublica (Colombia), AeroSur (Bolivia), Americana de Aviacion (Peru), Aserca (Venezuela), AVENSA (Venezuela), Avianca (Colombia), Faucett (Peru), Intercontinental Colombia, LAV (Venezuela), Lloyd Aereo Boliviano, SAM Colombia, SATENA (Colombia), SAM (Colombia), Servivensa (Venezuela), and VIASA (Venezuela).

Carriers to avoid because of a poor fatal accident rate: Aero Peru, Austral (Argentina, and suffering another fatal crash in 1997), Avianca (Colombia), Faucett (Peru), Intercontinental Colombia, LAN Chile, SAM Colombia, and TAM (Brazil), which had an attempted on-board suicide bombing in 1997.

While not an "avoid," Varig was certainly not at the bottom, but was also not at the top—just make sure you put it on your avoid list if it has another fatal accident.

Western Europe — Only five carriers failed to earn top marks in the statistically acceptable category—Air France, British Midland, Lauda, Martinair Holland, and THY Turkish Airlines. Of those, only Martinair Holland flunked.

Unfortunately Western Europe may be about to repeat our history by throwing caution and each country's safety enforcement to the winds under the new European Union. Right now, with several European carriers with accident rates equal to the U.S. carriers yet sporting much more youthful fleets, and U.S. carriers expecting to have about 40 percent of their fleet over twenty years old by 2000, European carriers would stand to reap a bounty of U.S. passengers searching for carriers with planes less than twenty years old. With the prediciton of a major airliner crash a week in about ten years, safety will be a very hot commodity after the turn of the century. If the U.S. is in short supply, passengers will turn to Europe, unless Europe blows it in its own deregulation debacle, and unless the FAA finally mandates some sundown provisions for the "tired iron" in U.S. fleets and puts planes out to pasture just like it does pilots.

Eastern Europe — Avoid carriers from countries from the former Soviet Union. First of all, the old Aeroflot had perhaps the worst accident rate in the world. The new one isn't so hot either. It earns an F from the Air Travelers Association because of its fatal accident rate. Another F goes to Tarom of Romania. Sheer numbers don't tell the whole story. Let me relate my personal experience flying on the old Aeroflot. Passengers would wait hours, and in some cases days, for the flight. We had to push our carry-on bags through the X-ray machines with our own hands (getting a gratuitous full-body X-ray in the process). Once on board, the Soviet-made planes' seats were so close together that getting out was an impossibility. If the passenger ahead of you reclined at all, the seat was literally in your face. The tray table was a piece of sheet metal, and on one of my flights the latch did not work, so it was reminiscent of a guillotine positioned at my throat. I tied it up with a ribbon I had with me. When I tried to use the forward restroom on one flight, the flight attendant blocked my path, repeating *Nyet*. Pretending not to understand, I pushed my way past her to find both pilots out of the cockpit, sitting on the floor, playing chess and drinking vodka. There was no water in the bathroom, but pools of liquid on the floor. In the rear of the plane on one flight, live animals (at least in crates) and other baggage were piled in the aisles. The overhead bin was nothing more than a shelf. The one emergency exit in the rear mysteriously had emergency evacuation instructions in Russian and in English. It said, "The crew goes first."

Did all this change overnight because the Soviet Union broke up? Hardly. Simply adding some western planes and having the FAA come over and hang out for a couple of weeks (including one fellow who was shown the door after ValuJet) will not erase decades of putting the passengers' safety and lives last. Besides, Russia has not yet been given a passing grade under ICAO standards. Also, remember that the new Aeroflot gained international fame by suffering a fatal crash because the pilot allowed his sixteen-year-old son in the cockpit to fly the plane, which he did, into the ground.

Africa — Again, one of the most dangerous places on earth on average, at least for air safety, is Africa. So many carriers fail in the fatal crash statistics and so many countries fail to meet the ICAO standards or just have not been reviewed that in the aviation world, the African continent is the most dangerous place on earth.

Carriers that fail because of their fatal accident rate are ADC Airlines (Nigeria), Air Mauritanie (Mauritania), Ethiopian Airlines, Libyan Arab Airlines, Nigeria Airways, and Okada Air (Nigeria).

In the category of most dangerous place on earth for aviation, Nigeria would appear to be a frontrunner, not to mention the fact that the one place on earth which consistently fails the U.S. State Department rankings as a security sinkhole is Nigeria. Little wonder, then, that they hire former high-ranking NTSB and other government officials to "advise" them how to escape their notorious distinctions.

South African Airways also does not get top ratings because of one fatal accident in ten years.

Middle East — All carriers get passing grades under the fatal air crash rankings (including Saudi Arabian Airlines with one crash), except for Iran Air, which also suffered one fatal crash but is one fourth the size of Saudi.

Indian subcontinent — Air India gets an F for four fatal crashes in ten years. Pakistan International Airways earns a C for one crash, and Pakistan is only rated as conditional, anyway.

Australia, New Zealand, and South Pacific — Ten years after Dustin Hoffman started us all looking for Quantas in the Official Airline Guide, the record still holds. Australia, New Zealand, Fiji and Papua New Guinea also all hold #1 or pass ratings on ICAO standards. Safety sells— they're on my vacation wish list.

Southern Asia — Until 1997, Indonesia, Thailand and the Philippines were all only rated conditional. Not surprising, then, that the airlines that fail are Garuda Indonesia (also with another crash in 1997), Merpati Nusantara Airlines (Indonesia), Philippine Airlines, and Thai International (with a C).

Not rated and therefore to be avoided is Vietnam. Vietnam Airlines also suffered a fatal crash in 1997.

Singapore Airlines, which consistently wins consumer satisfaction surveys, has had no fatal accidents in ten years.

Northern Asia — First of all, we need to break Japanese carriers out of the pack. I spent three months in Japan studying their transportation systems, and odd as it may sound to us westerners, individual—not just corporate— honor is at stake for any failing or disaster. In any system, accountability makes a difference. Aviation is very tidy in Japan, and operations are precise. They have few planes other than commecial jetliners cluttering their skies and runways. Domestic fares are outrageous, so carriers can afford new planes and still compete in the international markets. Japanese carriers were careful about my infant (suggesting I keep her infant life vest at my seat so I could get it on baby quickly if needed—unlike the U.S. carriers, who treated me like I was pulling off a Brinks heist when I asked to keep the infant life vest with me during a six-hour over-water flight, insisting they would remember to bring it to me in an emergency in a fully loaded 747) and providing a crib that affixed to the bulkhead, with safety fasteners to keep the baby from getting out. Air Nippon, All Nippon Airways, Japan Airlines, Japan Air System, Japan Asia Airways, and Japan TransOcean Air have had no fatal accidents in the last ten years.

Now as concerns the rest of the Northern Asia pack— beware. Both major Korean carriers have had fatal accidents and their share of rumor, scandal and problems recently. Asiana fails with a C and Korean Airlines with an F and four fatal crashes in ten years, including the 1997 crash in Guam.

Taiwan was in 1997 upgraded from a conditional to a pass, but Taiwan's China Airlines does not pass.

The Peoples' Republic (PRC) or Mainland China has a number of carriers with F ratings—China Eastern Airlines, China Northern Airlines, China Northwest Airlines, China Southern Airlines, and Xiamen Airlines. Of course, another problem with the PRC is the airport system. Many airports are lacking in instrumentation and equipment that we would consider basic or absolute necessities. Many western carriers can take you to various cities in China; use them.

On the other hand, Hong Kong's Cathay Pacific and Dragonair have had no fatal accidents in the past ten years.

With approximately 260 airlines operating over 20,000 or more flights each—and some, of course, operating millions—around the globe, it is impossible to discuss each one here. For information on individual carriers or updates after 1997, the Air Travelers Association can be contacted at www.1800airsafe.com or 1-800-247-7233. For updates after 1977 to the assessment of countries' meeting of ICAO standards, the FAA can be contacted at http://www.faa.gov/avr/iasaxls or 1-800-322-7873.

GENERAL PRECAUTIONS FOR INTERNATIONAL FLYING

Aviation safety advances arise from many circumstances, not the least of which is the legal system in which the carrier operates and the protections the laws of the land give to its citizens or those harmed or wronged by its nation's carriers or manufacturers. Individual rights and the value the legal system places on the heads of each of its citizens are important, too. Even with all our safety shortcomings, the U.S. system gives passengers a far greater measure of protection and right to redress wrongs than most other countries. Thus, part of the consideration in deciding how to travel is in deciding what your protections are if something goes wrong. Here is how to quadruple your rights as an international traveler:

1. Fly on a U.S. carrier—as long as its record is good. If disaster does strike, our courts have shown a willingness to reject unfairly applied treaties and laws and reach decisions that offer a greater measure of fairness and equity.
2. Originate your travel in the United States if possible. You have a better shot at U.S. courts' jurisdiction. After crashes in some other countries, you hear of bribes and graft to pay off judges and influence the outcome in legal systems. At least in the U.S., airlines seem to limit their influence-peddling to Congress and the FAA.
3. Even if you are not flying on U.S. carriers, purchase your ticket in the U.S. or from a U.S. agent or carrier.
4. Charge your ticket to a U.S. credit card. The Federal Truth in Lending Act may be your only protection if you are holding a ticket when your carrier goes bankrupt, and that they do. In the past, folks holding unused tickets charged to their credit cards did not have to pay for the ticket. If you paid by cash or check, you were out of luck. You became a "creditor." You most likely got nothing.

SECURITY

Hijackings, once the stuff of action-adventure movies, are extremely rare in the U.S.—in fact, FAA records show zero hijackings of American carriers since 1993. Foreign carriers are not so secure; the FAA reports twelve hijackings of foreign airliners in 1993 and 1994, four in 1995 and a dozen or so in 1996. Many have been political dissidents commandeering a plane in search of asylum. Their actions are nevertheless dangerous to the pilots, crews and passengers. In November 1996, several hijackers seized an Air Ethiopia jet and demanded to be flown to Australia. The pilot argued that the plane did not have enough fuel to travel that far. He was right, and the plane crashed into the ocean, killing 125 passengers.

American carriers fare less well when it comes to bomb threats. The FBI and the FAA report those assaults increased dramatically in the 1990s, both in the U.S. and abroad.

BOMB THREATS AGAINST AIRCRAFT (U.S. AND FOREIGN) WORLDWIDE

1992	1993	1994	1995	1996
215	248	218	327	419

BOMB THREATS AGAINST U.S. AIRPORTS

1992	1993	1994	1995	1996
188	304	250	346	284

Just in the first half of 1997, there were seventy domestic sabotage attempts on U.S. carriers.

KEEP AN EYE ON AIRLINE FINANCIAL HEALTH. THE FAA DOES.

The FAA told Congress in 1989 that it uses "the financial, let's say, performance of a company as one of the indicators in determining how much oversight we should provide an airline and, as a standard measure, when we see financial difficulties, difficulty in payment, difficulty in payroll, the threat of bankruptcy, we always increase surveillance of that airline."

Yet the FAA also said it had never established a link between an airline's "profitability or stock price or anything like that and the airline's compliance with maintenance requirements."

Consider Eastern Airlines and its slide into bankruptcy. Since 1985, Eastern had been in a desperate bid to save itself by slashing spending and costs. One area that it cut dramatically was maintenance—except that Eastern did not want anyone to know. It doctored its maintenance records to hide the fact that some inspections and repairs were never done or were only partially completed. Such measures did not help its plight in the long run; competition, low numbers of passengers and high fuel prices still drove the airline out of business. At the same time, Eastern earned a spot in the history books for falsifying its maintenance records. Martin Shugrue, Jr., trustee on behalf of the bankrupt Eastern, agreed the company would plead guilty to conspiring to prevent the FAA from determining if Eastern employees and managers were falsifying maintenance records. A court fined the company $2.5 million. The fine might have been as high as $26.5 million if Eastern had been convicted of all of the original fifty-three counts charged against it. In addition to the company, ten Eastern managers were indicted.

The FAA didn't uncover these crimes; it took a U.S. Department of Justice investigation. Only then did the FAA levy an $839,000 *civil* penalty, and reassured the public that Eastern maintenance compared favorably with that of other airlines.

Poor financial conditions (or banking the money instead of spending it on safety) can also force an airline to put off buying new planes, to hire cheaper, more inexperienced pilots, to grant maintenance a low priority and to develop a culture attuned to making money rather than ensuring safety. All those conditions happened at ValuJet. A similar scenario occurred at USAir between 1990 and 1994. The airline had five accidents in five years, and great financial trouble. Pilots complained of reporting malfunctions on planes several times before the problems were corrected. The FAA put USAir under special watch, and my office began digging into its troubled history. USAir acted to save itself and started a special program to improve safety. There has been no sixth fatal accident in the years since.

In November 1996, USAir paid $450,000 to settle eighty-four cases of alleged maintenance, security and operations violations. Rather than pursue the charges, the FAA let USAir pay the relatively low settlement because it said the violations did not indicate an inherent safety problem at USAir. But remember—the charges came after that string of accidents at USAir in the years preceding, and after a series of years of negative cash flow.

Passengers can watch for these developments, as they are often reported by the media. The press reported in the fall of 1996 that the IRS had ruled that an airline could not take an immediate deduction for the cost of a heavy-engine inspection. The IRS said the inspection was a capital investment, not a business expense. That meant the airline could only depreciate the cost over a period of years. The airline industry immediately cried foul, saying it could lose up to a billion dollars if the rule was applied to all airlines. The question for passengers is: does this new expense mean airlines will ask the FAA to delay those heavy-engine inspections? Watch for announcements of the answer.

The first indication that an airline is troubled may appear when a carrier begins to eliminate destinations from its routes, or sell its "slots" at those airports. Eastern and others like it resorted to "playing the slots" to try to save themselves—it sold off parts of its operation, including the New York to Washington shuttle, to finance what was left.

Generally, there are three kinds of financial states among airlines. Stable carriers are essentially healthy in spite of several years of industrywide losses. Carriers like United may have downsized and cut costs, but have remained healthy enough to make capital improvements and reinvest profits in the business. Receivership carriers like TWA have fought their way back from bankruptcy (in TWA's case, twice). Underfinanced start-ups have emerged, expanded and expired rapidly, like People Express, Air Atlanta, Muse Air, Air Florida, MGM Grand Air, Kiwi, Frontier and Presidential Air.

But then we come to ValuJet. ValuJet had cash reserves—$250 million by some counts—when it was shut down. It just did not spend its money on needed maintenance. That's why it is unwise to rely exclusively on "profitability" as an indicator of safety.

TRENDS

I have examined the predominant safety indicators used by the FAA, the industry, passenger associations, Wall Street investors (where safety plays almost no role), and the media. Everyone is looking for the magic bullet—the bellwether indicator of an airline's safety. What do the FAA statistics show for 1996–7? We have an increase of operational errors and increased pilot deviations. So what do we do with all this information? Simple: we apply the same principle I used when warning about USAir in the early 1990s and ValuJet in February 1996—common sense. Ask yourself: What is really going on? What do I really know about a carrier? What am I willing to do about it—will I refuse to fly a marginal carrier even if it might cost more to fly with another company? I know I would. But it takes more than a couple of people to force change.

So here is the bottom line:

1. Stay off all carriers that the FAA has grounded or seriously reprimanded in recent years, as listed in this chapter. Watch the media for new ones.

2. Do not rely on rating lists based on self-reported main-

tenance problems or FAA inspections. The worst airlines may have no reports—they are simply not
catching, fixing and reporting their problems, and neither is the FAA.

3. Avoid start-up carriers in their second and third years
of operation: on average they have double the incident
rates of the established majors. For new large airlines
it's even worse.

4. Stay off all foreign carriers from the lists of countries
that fail the FAA checks or are awarded only ''conditional'' approval.

5. Although the FAA has not completed a review of
Russia or the People's Republic of China, stay off all
Russian-built planes and avoid People's Republic of
China airlines even if the FAA grants them No. 1
ratings. Only by constantly questioning and inspecting
can we know the current state of an airline's safety.
But U.S. authorities have a very difficult time getting
any accurate reading on the number of accidents, incidents and maintenance records on these planes and
among these countries' airlines. A look at the numbers
of crashes of these airlines (which no one really believes to be the total) is enough to keep me off, even
if Aeroflot is now flying Boeing and Airbus aircraft.

6. While Eastern Europe (Russia and the former Soviet
republics) and Asia/Pacific (China and others) are bad,
with roughly five times our U.S. accident rates, Africa
and Latin America are much worse, eight times worse
than the U.S. rate. The U.S. is far from being as safe
as it should be, and it is not as safe as we pay for,
but the U.S. is still twice as safe as Western Europe
and much safer than the rest of the world. Select major
U.S. carriers or major Western European carriers, no
matter where in the world you are going.

7. Buy your ticket in the U.S., even if you have to go

on a foreign carrier, start your travel in the U.S., and put it on your charge card. By doing so, you will have quadrupled your rights as a passenger. Stricter liability laws apply. You have a better nexus for a U.S. trial if something goes wrong. The U.S. is about to abolish the Death on the High Seas defense for carriers and manufacturers. Some U.S. (and Western European) carriers have adopted higher Warsaw treaty recovery limits—about double (they went from $75,000 to $140,000). U.S. courts have abrogated Warsaw limits 0for gross or willful negligence. If a carrier goes bankrupt, you don't have to pay for those flights you did not get if you charge the ticket to your credit card. (Take it from someone who was a Braniff "creditor" twice, an Eastern "creditor," and a Pan Am "creditor.")

8. Avoid commuter airlines and propeller/turboprop planes. Think of them as fair-weather flying. Smaller prop planes just cannot take bad weather as well as the big jets. The de-icing equipment is different, and they are more limited in certain altitudes and cannot escape some weather systems. Additionally, lighter planes (prop or smaller jets) are more vulnerable to wake turbulence left behind by the bigger jets.

9. Avoid air taxi, air charter, and on-demand air service (planes and pilots for hire).

10. Watch what is going on. You may be surprised to learn that after analyzing the accidents over the last year, I have grown concerned about what is going on at American and Delta Airlines. These two carriers dominate the U.S. domestic aviation business. They crisscross this country and fly numerous international flights. Their success comes in part from the image they have of being safe, competent organizations. But in fact, each has experienced mechanical problems and pilot errors that should not be happening. If these two carriers do not make im-

provements, I am afraid it may only be a matter of time before another accident or an incident like one of the dozens that happened last year turns into a major tragedy.

Take a look at American Airlines' record from November 1995 to December 1996. (I have also included here the incidents at American Eagle. As I've already discussed, American Eagle is operated independently of American though owned by the same parent company. Since you may be routed onto one of their planes when you fly American, the safety record of this commuter carrier is important to know when you are considering whether to fly American.) That year:

- An MD-83 flew 309 feet below minimum altitude for landing at Hartford in November 1995, sheared trees and had both engines stall before landing safely.
- A Boeing 757 crashed into a mountain on a clear December night in Colombia. A pilot's mistake cost 160 people their lives.
- An uncontained engine failure left an Airbus 300 with a foot-wide hole, dents and nicks in its tail in January 1996.
- Landing gear collapsed on an American Eagle ATR in April.
- The tail of an MD-82 struck the ground while landing in wind shear in June.
- Another uncontained engine failure during a July American Eagle Saab aircraft flight.
- An elevator trim cable failed in-flight on an American Eagle Short airplane in July.
- A pilot was reported incoherent at the controls of an Airbus 300 in July.
- An MD-11 suddenly changed altitude in July, even though the pilot had not ordered any such action.
- A shipment of chemicals spilled in the cargo compartment of a Boeing 757 in August.
- With the nose landing gear stuck in the "up" position, an MD-80 landed in October.

- When the right engine of an MD-80 caught fire in November 1996, takeoff was aborted.
- An uncontained engine failure left an eight-by-three-inch hole in the engine case of a DC-9 in November 1996.
- The FAA, the pilot's union and the airline itself are investigating American's training and operations.

Here's what happened in 1997:

February—The tail of an Airbus 300 hit the runway in a very hard landing in Antigua.

March—A DC-9 slid off the runway in Cleveland and the landing gear collapsed. There was snow on the runway, so it does not appear to be the pilot's fault.

April—An engine exploded resulting in a tailpipe fire on a MD-82 over Tucson, Arizona. Several houses under the aircraft's flight track were damaged from falling hot engine parts.

June—A DC-10 had a contained engine failure on its takeoff roll at San Juan, Puerto Rico.

October—American accepted twenty-two suitcases from a courier at Miami, without checking the contents. While loading the suitcases in the cargo hold, one fell off the conveyor belt onto the tarmac and five people who had already boarded the plane went to the hospital. The suitcases contained potent pesticides, which also did a pretty good job of getting rid of passengers. The FBI ordered the FAA out of the case, which is a good move in a serious criminal investigation. Remember the Eastern Airlines investigation, wherein the FAA tried to thwart the criminal investigation and leaked grand jury information to the airline. (Here's another good reason to get a good smoke hood—fumes from the cargo!)

Other than the pesticide incident, that was not a bad year for America's largest carrier.

Over at Delta, from December 1995 to December 1996, look what has happened:

- A wing struck a runway on landing in December 1995, due to pilot miscalculation.

- An uncontained engine failure on a Boeing 727 was discovered when Air Traffic Control tower personnel saw smoke coming from the plane in January 1996. The explosion blew a hole in the engine housing and dented and nicked the plane's tail.
- Another uncontained engine failure blew parts through the #1 and #2 engines of a Boeing 727 in January.
- After a pilot failed to maintain his airspeed, he brought his MD-88 in for a "hard landing" in February that seriously damaged the plane.
- A Boeing 757 hit another carrier's plane while departing a ramp area in February even though the pilot was told to stop.
- An auxiliary power unit caught fire on a Boeing 767 in February.
- A third uncontained engine failure made an MD-80 vibrate so violently in April, the flight had to be diverted.
- A fourth uncontained engine failure sent a fan blade spiraling through the engine housing of an MD-88 in June when the 767 engine caught fire during the climb after takeoff.
- An uncontained engine failure, discovered by Air Traffic Control tower personnel who saw smoke and fire, blew an eight-inch hole in the engine case of a Boeing 767 in the third such incident in June.
- An uncontained engine failure killed two people and injured three others when a fan disk separated from the engine and pierced the fuselage of an MD-88 in July.
- Engine debris from another engine failure fell off a Boeing 727 and onto a house and car when turbine blades failed in August.
- Landing gear was sheared off when an MD-88 landed short of a runway in August. The plane skidded, spun around, and was seriously damaged.
- Tail controls failed on an MD-11 in November.
- An MD-88 ran off a runway in snow in November.
- January 28, 1997, an engine exploded on a Boeing 727, leaving two basketball-sized holes in the fuselage.
- On January 31, 1997, an uncontrolled engine failure

occurred during a 757 climb-out at Atlanta. Pieces blew out of the engine housing.

- The aft cargo door of a 727 opened during a passenger flight from Atlanta to South Carolina on February 13, 1997.
- March 27, 1997: a twenty-foot section of the right wing—the flap—fell off a 767 near Dallas/Fort Worth Airport.
- March 27, 1997: an L-1011 ran over a ground crew member at JFK airport.
- An elevator connecting with the galley of an L-1011 dropped with a flight attendant inside on June 26, 1997.
- A 727 was substantially damaged when the landing gear collapsed at Albuquerque on July 6, 1997. Four passengers were injured.
- On August 7, 1997, there was a wheel and brake fire after the pilot had to abort an L-1011 takeoff. After the pilots got the plane stopped, they heard people in the cabin yelling *Fire!* and started evacuation of the plane. The 2R and 4R doors did not work. The 4L door could not be used because of the proximity of the smoke and fire. So everyone was rushing toward the 1L door. But there was a pileup at the foot of the slide. So the pilot ordered passengers to slow down their evacuation—if you can imagine that. The passengers did not and proceeded to get out as fast as they could. Everybody got out.

These incidents and accidents tell me that something is going wrong in some areas at these two airlines, allowing the kind of sloppy maintenance or lax oversight that leads to accidents that both airlines are entirely capable of preventing. I still fly American, but it is trends like these we need to watch. If either airline suffers a fatal accident in 1998 like the one that killed a mother and her son when the fan blade sliced into the cabin, then I will stay off the carrier until it completes at least a year without a fatal accident.

Look also at the Delta 1997 accidents and incidents— mostly L-1011s and 727s—old planes.

Airline safety is not static. The good can go bad, and the bad can get better. You have to watch the aviation industry constantly—just as the FAA should. Ask yourself: Are they in it "just to get rich," or are they really trying to build a safe, reputable airline that will grow in a measured way and prosper as customers know and trust its service? With common sense you can rank the safety of airlines almost as well as the FAA can—maybe better.

CHAPTER FIFTEEN

Airports

One of the most breathtaking views I ever saw was of an airport during my first night flight in 1974. My instructor knew what awaited me, because we departed Don Scott Field in Columbus without looking back. I didn't know that Don Scott Field turns its lights off at night. It may be a university airport, but Don Scott Field is no slouch—it is fully instrumented and lit. But when the students go home for the day, the airport managers shut off the outside lights to save money. After my practice flight that night, as we headed home, I peered through the dark sky and wondered: where are the runways? The taxiways? All I could see was the airport's beacon—but at least that meant I was in the right place. Then my instructor told me to click my radio microphone three times, in a pilot's version of Dorothy's tapping her ruby-red slippers together. I did as he said, and instantly all the airport lights came on in a dazzling display. I've never forgotten that blaze of lights, even though it was more than twenty years ago. It was like a candle in the window—albeit one heck of a big candle.

Airports are like that—landfall. Almost home. The third part of the aviation safety triad, after aircraft and airlines, is airports. There are over 5,000 public airports in the United States, most too small to serve anything on a regular basis except for small private planes. Hundreds of them are large local airports (352 have FAA control towers), but only nineteen are the airports where jets of all sizes put down in a variety of terrains and continually changing weather conditions. These bustling facilities are called "Category X" airports. The rate of traffic through an airport, the geography around the airport, the airport's facilities, the airport's configuration, and the climate and weather at the time of operation each have a lot to do with how safely pilots can maneuver, take off and land. Fortunately, technology exists to help pilots overcome or avoid many potential impediments to a smooth departure or arrival. Unfortunately, at many airports some of the best safety systems sit locked in storage sheds. Other airports do not have the equipment at all because they cannot afford it (in many cases because both federal and local government authorities misused the money that was supposed to buy these systems).

The United States is one of the most technologically advanced countries in the world. There is no reason that our airports should go without Doppler wind shear radar or ground-collision avoidance systems. Yet many do. The public hears about the invention of these high-tech marvels and assumes if they exist, they must be in use. The truth is more dispiriting. Though Congress appropriated money for A-MASS (the ground radar called the Airport Movement Safety System) to prevent collisions on taxiways, for Doppler wind shear systems for dozens of airports, and for Microwave Landing Systems (MLS), few were actually put to work. In 1996, only one A-MASS and just sixteen wind shear detectors were in place. In both cases, additional systems sat gathering dust in storage, hostage to local political or ecological disputes, tangles of bureaucratic red tape, or budget woes. MLS was dumped entirely after the FAA spent $305.9 million of your tax dollars to develop it. To this day, new Instrument Landing Systems sit in warehouses.

Passengers need to know which airports have these systems, and which are making do with outdated technology. You need this information to make safe flying decisions even though you often have very little choice in airports. But with this information, you can demand that airport and municipal authorities install the most advanced equipment, and stop spending the money on boondoggles and politics.

The following is a list of the equipment available at the nineteen Category X airports, plus a few others I thought should be included. It demonstrates that some of the largest, busiest airports in the U.S. do not have modern equipment to help pilots cope with weather and navigation—in many cases, equipment that was ordered years ago, designed, paid for and then stuck in storage. A glaring example of this is the terminal Doppler wind shear detection radar. Not all of the Category X airports have this critical equipment. And almost none of the non–Category X airports have it.

AIRPORT EQUIPMENT

AIRPORT	WEATHER AIDS	NAVIGATION AIDS	HAZARD WARNINGS
Anchorage Intl.	TWEB	ILS on 2 runways, MLS on 1	Birds
Atlanta Hartsfield Intl.	ASOS, LLWAS, TDWR	ILS on all runways	Birds
Baltimore Washington Intl. (BWI)	ASOS, LLWAS	ILS on 6 runways	
Boston-Logan Intl.	ASOS, LLWAS, TDWR	ILS on 5 runways	
Charlotte-Douglas Intl.	LLWAS, TDWR	ILS on 5 runways	Birds
Chicago Midway	LAWRS	ILS on 3 runways MLS on 1 runway	Birds
Chicago O'Hare Intl.	ASOS, LLWAS	ILS on 12 runways	Birds

AIRPORT	WEATHER AIDS	NAVIGATION AIDS	HAZARD WARNINGS
Cleveland Hopkins Intl.	ASOS, LLWAS	ILS on 3 runways	Birds, deer
Dallas-Fort Worth Intl.	ASOS, LLWAS, TDWR	ILS on 12 runways	
Denver Intl.	ASOS, LLWAS, TDWR	ILS on all runways	
Detroit Metro-Wayne Co.	LLAWS	ILS on 6 runways	
Houston Intercontinental	ASOS, LLWAS, TDWR	ILS on 6 runways	Birds
Honolulu Intl.	LLWAS	ILS on 2 runways	
JFK Intl., NY	ASOS, LLWAS	ILS on 7 runways, MLS on 1	Birds
Kansas City Intl.	ASOS, LLWAS, TDWR	ILS on 5 runways	Birds
LaGuardia, NY	ASOS, LLWAS	ILS on all runways	Birds, wind shear
Las Vegas McCarran Intl.	ASOS, LLWAS	ILS on 2 runways	
Los Angeles Intl.	LLWAS	ILS on all runways	Birds
Memphis Intl.	LLWAS, TDWR	ILS on all runways	Birds
Miami Intl.	ASOS, LLWAS, TDWR	ILS on all runways	
Minneapolis-St. Paul Intl.	ASOS, LLWAS	ILS on all runways	Birds
Newark Intl.	LLWAS	ILS on 4 runways	Birds

AIRPORT	WEATHER AIDS	NAVIGATION AIDS	HAZARD WARNINGS
New Orleans Intl.	ASOS, LLWAS, TDWR	ILS on 3 runways	Birds
Orlando Intl.	TDWR, ASOS, LLWAS	ILS on 4 runways	Birds, deer
Philadelphia Intl.	ASOS, LLWAS	ILS on 5 runways	Birds, deer
Phoenix Sky Harbor Intl.	ASOS, LLWAS	ILS on 2 runways	
Pittsburgh Intl.	ASOS, LLWAS	ILS on 5 runways	Deer
St. Louis Lambert Intl.	ASOS, LAWRS, LLWAS, TDWR	ILS on 5 runways	
Salt Lake City Intl.	LLWAS	ILS on 6 runways	
San Diego Lindbergh Field	ASOS	ILS on all runways	
San Francisco Intl.	AWOS, LLWAS	ILS on 3 runways	Birds
Seattle-Tacoma Intl.	LLWAS, TDWR	ILS on 3 runways	Birds
Tampa Intl.	ASOS, LLWAS, TDWR	ILS on 3 runways	Birds
Washington/ Dulles Intl.	ASOS, LLWAS	ILS on 5 runways	Birds, deer
Washington National	LLWAS, TDWR	ILS on 1 runway	Birds, high-density traffic warning

(As of December 1996)

TERMINOLOGY

ASOS (AUTOMATED SURFACE OBSERVATION SYSTEM).
This is the U.S.'s primary ground observation system. It
provides up-to-the-minute assessments of visibility, precip-
itation, temperature and freezing rain. It does not sense
and report tornadoes, thunderstorms, hail, ice crystals, drizzle or freezing drizzle, or clouds above 12,000 feet. So
ASOS must be augmented by other systems.

AWOS (AUTOMATED WEATHER OBSERVING SYSTEM).
This system offers the information that ASOS misses. It
is increasingly being installed at airports.

LLWAS (LOW LEVEL WIND SHEAR ALERT SYSTEM). This
system gauges wind speed to predict wind shear.

**LAWRS (LIMITED AVIATION WEATHER REPORTING STA-
TION).** This system reports cloud heights, weather obstructions to vision, temperature and altitude.

TDWR (TERMINAL DOPPLER WEATHER RADAR). The
most recent system for detecting wind shear, this technology is much more accurate than LLWAS. Though it was
promised in 1985 after a violent crash at the Dallas-Fort
Worth airport, only 16 units are in use.

TWEB (TRANSCRIBED WEATHER BROADCAST). A continuous recording of meteorological and aeronautical information that is broadcast to pilots. In some locations the
number is listed in the phone book under the FAA's Flight
Service Station.

ILS (INSTRUMENT LANDING SYSTEM). A radio aid to navigation that helps pilots land their planes.

MLS (MICROWAVE LANDING SYSTEM). Congress ended
this program before it was fully implemented. MLS was

supposed to be more accurate than ILS, but the Global Positioning System (see page 158) made MLS obsolete before it was even deployed.

AIRPORTS PILOTS DO NOT LIKE

Some airports are particularly dangerous, and pilots do not like them. In the United States, those are Logan in Boston, Washington National, San Diego, Los Angeles, San Francisco, Cleveland, Detroit, LaGuardia, Juneau and Sun Valley in Idaho. Washington National, LaGuardia, Detroit, Cleveland, San Diego are all hampered by intersecting runways and/or taxiways, are hemmed in by city neighborhoods and have small, aged facilities that cannot keep up with passenger demands. You can almost see into the windows of nearby office buildings while landing at San Diego and Washington National. Air traffic is dense at Washington National, where flight paths zigzag through restricted airspace. Short runways intersect one another and only one runway has an overrun area and it is limited. Noise abatement procedures are stringent. New York's La-Guardia is another high density airport with two short intersecting runways and almost no overrun area. Three runways end at the edge of a bay, and the other ends at a highway. Complaints about Boston's Logan center on airport management, poor snow removal and the occasional use of salt on the runways and taxiways, which is not allowed. Pilots also complain about troubling landing rules and unnecessary hazards at the ends of runways (light piers and a huge wood and steel blast fence). Most upsetting to pilots is that there is plenty of money to make improvements, but it goes to fund other city functions. Detroit's Metro, which has had more than its share of accidents, has been cited for confusing, spaghetti runways and taxiways and poor markings. Confusion reigns at Cleveland's Hopkins, where construction has left pilots stopping to ask for directions—construction that is expected to go on for years. Los Angeles is very congested, and San Francisco has seemingly wingtip-to-wingtip parallel runways and bad fog and visibility, a complaint often lodged against Seattle's Sea-Tac. Sun Valley is just a thriller. A plane comes into Sun Valley over the mountains and then drops sharply to land. On takeoff, passengers and crew alike hold their breath for a few seconds until the plane clears mountains looming dead ahead. Juneau is surrounded by glaciers and mountain peaks, and is plagued with ice, fog and severe wind shear.

For sheer thrills internationally, fly into Hong Kong's Kai Tak International Airport. Thankfully, Hong Kong is building a new airport on land reclaimed from the sea farther from the city. At Kai Tak, planes coming into Hong Kong weave precariously among the skyscrapers. The office towers and apartment buildings loom over the runways, and if that's not enough, jagged mountains hem the city, too. The only place to ditch a plane is in the water. You wouldn't want to wander off course while approaching La Paz, Bolivia, either. That city is surrounded by the Andes Mountains. Some are capped with glacial ice. One has an Eastern Airlines jet embedded in its side. The crashed plane has never been removed because the terrain is too high and too rugged to cross. The plane is a grim reminder of what can go wrong while landing in La Paz. Yet Quito, Ecuador, is even more spectacular. That city's airport requires that a pilot skip over mountains and then drop in to land. Bogotá, Colombia, is also nestled in the mountains.

In any country plagued by terrorists or war, airports can be compromised. The airports in Colombia, Peru, Bosnia, Afghanistan and many African countries are a concern for this reason. In 1996, there were seventeen fatal carrier crashes in Africa. My husband was on two near-disastrous flights in Africa, once when they landed with one engine on fire and another when the plane was hit with surface-to-air weapons. The State Department and the FAA have hot-line numbers that passengers can call for the list of countries officially decreed to be unsafe. But those hot lines do not offer any advice or warnings about more fluid situations at foreign airports—like when instrument landing equipment was destroyed by fighting factions during the war in Bosnia, or when similar equipment was destroyed by drug lords fighting a different kind of war in

Cali, Colombia. Once again, use common sense and avoid war zones: military actions, civil wars or drug wars—they all pose dangers to civil aviation.

WIND SHEAR AND AIRPORTS

Wind shear is a deadly phenomenon. It is also a mystery—no one really understands how it affects plane performance. Following a horrific crash at the Dallas-Fort Worth airport in 1985, the FAA promised to install wind shear detection equipment called terminal Doppler radar at all major airports. To date—more than a decade later—only sixteen systems are in place.

Conventional wisdom used to say that wind shear posed the greatest danger to southern airports in the summer. In recent years, however, wind shear accidents have occurred all over the country, in all seasons. Theories about how best to handle wind shear come and go. Among the most recent were the ideas that wind shear is harder on large planes than on small ones, or that a twin-engine craft could cope better than a triple-engine plane, or that wind shear was more dangerous on takeoff than on landing. It's unclear whether these are the definitive answers to wind shear questions. But passengers have no control over any of these factors, except to stay off all planes when the weatherman says conditions are ripe for wind shear—and that means heavy thunderstorms. I don't fly in hurricanes, tornadoes or snowstorms, either. (As much as that sounds ridiculously obvious, you'd be surprised how often people are unaware that a severe storm is brewing and an airline decides to fly anyway without warning passengers.) There are logistical reasons for waiting out bad weather, too. After trying to beat a storm by diverting to different cities a few times and ending up stranded only halfway to my destination, I realized that in the long run it's more efficient to wait out a storm than to race it.

How do you avoid bad weather in the first place? Use common sense again. Do you want to change planes in the winter at Denver, where the old airport was closed for a couple of weeks each year and the new, supposedly weather-immune airport has already closed in October 1997? Or do you want to opt for a switch at usually snow-less Dallas/Fort Worth? The same can be said for changing planes in winter in Chicago, Minneapolis, Detroit or Cleveland.

Even in obviously bad weather conditions, you cannot rely only on an airline. In July 1996, just as a hurricane was slamming into New York, I boarded a train for Manhattan—I assumed the airport would be closed. The winds were so strong, the train rocked; the rain so intense, it leaked into the compartment in several places. Yet just as the train approached New York City, I looked out my window to see a commercial jet pass overhead, its wings buffeted wildly by the storm. I was astounded. Luckily, the plane landed safely. But why had the airline even risked it?

In July 1997, I had the misfortune to be in Pensacola during Hurricane Danny. All airlines canceled all flights except one—Continental. I did not take it.

AIRPORT SECURITY

Sadly, in the 1990s, the terrorism that has plagued Europe and the Middle East for decades arrived in the U.S. This grim reality most dramatically hit Americans with the 1988 bombing of Pan Am flight 103 over Lockerbie, Scotland. Later, bombs went off at the World Trade Center in New York City and the Oklahoma City federal building. In this atmosphere, it became even more critical that airports and aircraft, the high-profile targets-of-choice for terrorists, had thorough, efficient and proactive security systems and procedures. As discussed earlier, in 1993 and 1995, the Office of Inspector General and the Federal Aviation Administration took a close look at airport security around the country. All airports are equipped with metal detectors to stop gun-toting or knife-wielding passengers. But in many places, the operators behind the x-ray machines and other security personnel proved inept at their jobs. Often they were hired with no background checks, and started work with minimal training. In Washington,

D.C., officials tried background checks—but only if an applicant had a year's gap in his employment history, and only for certain offenses, such as rape. A record of theft did not count. Even after the Pan Am flight 103 bombing, the FAA did nothing to force airports and airlines to improve security. As late as November 1996, the NBC television show *Dateline* sent reporters to Kennedy International Airport in New York to pose as job seekers. The reporters were hired on the spot with no background checks. After *Dateline* revealed what had happened, the FAA announced they had made such subterfuge illegal—why censure your own people when you can focus on the misdeeds of a television crew instead?

The FAA's scramble to force smarter hiring policies hasn't helped other critical aspects of aviation security. As of 1998, U.S. airlines were not required by any law to x-ray passenger baggage. The 1990 Aviation Security Improvement Act called for automatic screening, but many airports and airlines balked at the extra costs involved. Most do not scan luggage, and when they do, it is a random activity. Many commuter airlines do not have x-ray equipment at all, even for passengers who are checking luggage through to an international flight. Uninspected bags can be transferred to a plane bound for Europe that is carrying passengers whose bags may have been screened in a random test—and who certainly think that the entire cargo loaded onto their plane has been examined. Think again.

Before the 1990 Act, teams of bomb-sniffing dogs were thought to be one answer to security. But the dogs got lost in the shuffle: the aviation industry decided it did not want to spend money to buy, train and keep the animals if sensitive, million-dollar bomb-detecting machines were just around the corner. Of course, the machines never made it to the vast majority of airports—and the dogs didn't, either. Pan Am once claimed to have teams of bomb-sniffing dogs, but those turned out to be regular pooches recruited from a dog kennel. The FAA has no bomb-dog program—all it has is a fund that doles out money to local authorities whose canine police units are interested in bomb training for their dogs. It was those units that were reported to have contaminated every plane in America by training their animals with the kind of plastic-explosives residue found on TWA flight 800.

Regardless of the eventual ruling on the cause as mechanical, the TWA flight 800 crash galvanized politicians and aviation industry leaders to call for improved security equipment and passenger-screening methods at U.S. airports. While those ideas were good, it may be years before they become standard operating procedure. Some of the best bomb-screening machines cost $1 million apiece. Just three are in place in the U.S.—two in Atlanta and one in San Francisco—even though Congress ordered the FAA to get them up and running years ago and the White House Commission echoed that plea.

In the meantime, all the metal detectors and bomb detectors in the world are useless if a criminal can simply circumvent the screening point and get directly into the "sterile areas" where security is supposedly enforced in airports. My employees tested this. In a 1993 investigation, they slipped through 75 percent of the time. In 1996, plainclothes inspectors got through 40 percent of the time. Undoubtedly there was improvement, but it offered small comfort. Passengers are relying on airports and airlines to protect them with the kinds of methods that my agents easily thwarted. By the way, even though the FAA tried to keep this kind of information from the public when my office was releasing its security report in January 1996, the FAA sent this information to airlines across the country and admitted that it was available to the public and subject to the Freedom of Information Act.

Right now, the nineteen major airports in the U.S. are using *metal* detectors to catch *explosives*. They're not very good at it:

BOMB DETECTION RATE USING NEW
MODULAR BOMB SAMPLES—1995

AIRPORT	RATES (%)
San Juan, Puerto Rico	100
Honolulu	64
Orlando	60
Dulles (Washington, D.C.)	56
Kennedy (New York)	56
Dallas-Fort Worth	53
National (Washington, D.C.)	46
St. Louis	46
Denver	45
Baltimore-Washington	42
Houston	32
San Francisco	30
Atlanta	28
Boston	23
Detroit	23
O'Hare (Chicago)	22
Miami	15
Seattle-Tacoma	12
Los Angeles	10

Fortunately, when metal detectors are used to find metal—guns, knives, grenades, bombs with metal—they do much better.

AIRPORT DETECTION RATE OF USUAL TEST ITEMS

AIRPORT	RATES (%) 1994	RATES (%) 1995
Houston	100	95
San Juan, Puerto Rico	100	91
Honolulu	98	100
Kennedy (New York)	98	97
Orlando	98	97
Dulles (Washington, D.C.)	97	96

AIRPORT	RATES (%) 1994	RATES (%) 1995
Seattle-Tacoma	97	95
National (Washington, D.C.)	95	98
Dallas-Fort Worth	95	95
Los Angeles	94	94
St. Louis	94	93
Detroit	93	77
San Francisco	93	97
Boston	92	93
Miami	92	90
Baltimore-Washington	92	86
Denver	90	91
O'Hare (Chicago)	88	88
Atlanta	86	81

PROFILING

Profiling has been much discussed in the decade since Pan Am flight 103. Profiling—the art of evaluating a passenger as a security threat based on his appearance, actions, language or personal history—is a substitute for a 100 percent passenger and bag check. Were an airline to screen all passengers and their bags with reliable metal-weapons *and* explosives detectors, profiling would be nearly superfluous. But since this is impossible—the equipment does not yet exist and the time required for 100 percent screening horrifies the airlines—profiling was instituted to help the airlines figure out whose bags to check.

In some countries, airlines carry out 100 percent bag matching. When people are boarding a domestic Alitalia flight in Italy, luggage is lined up on the tarmac, and as passengers walk to the plane, they stop and identify their bags for handlers, who then load the luggage on the plane. The system is not very elaborate, but it works. It doesn't identify passengers duped into carrying explosives, or suicide bombers, however.

Since the U.S. passenger load is so great (and we don't

want passengers running around the tarmac) we had to come up with other systems, and since the U.S. airlines have complained that a 100 percent bag screen and match is impossible, we have profiling to tell us which few bags should be checked. But this procedure is weak. Would a terrorist really answer "yes" when asked if someone else packed his bag or asked him to carry something on board?

In this country, our courts also have something to say about profiling. In other countries race, nationality, color of skin, sex, religious affiliation or even the possession of facial hair may peg a person as suspect. Here, profiling on many such characteristics is not allowed—the Constitution and the courts protect Americans against this kind of stereotyping. The success of profiling with limited parameters is unproven. So profiling will never be the answer in this country.

In 1997, the White House Aviation Commission envisioned a computer profiling system that would use information fed into the computer to tell the airline which bags to check. That system crashed just minutes into its first test run. They are going to try again in 1998.

It's probably only a matter of time before the security practices used on international flights originating in the U.S. are adopted on domestic flights as well. I hope it does not come about because of a senseless and horrible act of domestic terrorism, but with seventy attempts on domestic U.S. aviation in the first half of 1997, the future does not look good. Eventually we will have more or 100 percent screening of checked luggage, closer examination of carry-on bags, increased questioning of passengers before they board a plane and limits on cargo on passenger flights. Polls have shown that travelers would gladly pay a $10-per-ticket surcharge for security.

TOWER POWER

Included under "airports" in the flying-safe triad is air traffic control—or perhaps, to be more correct, I should say equipment failures and power outages in air traffic control towers. What does an equipment failure mean in real terms? For example, when the Aurora, Illinois, air traffic control center failed at 8:05 A.M. on May 17, 1995, it was controlling 450 aircraft. These problems are not the fault of air traffic controllers, who are as concerned as the rest of us about safety. The FAA leadership failed to provide necessary modern and reliable equipment. Decades-old equipment cannot withstand the rigors of controlling air traffic, and the FAA squandered hundreds of millions (perhaps billions if all botched projects were tallied) on a mismanaged project to overhaul the system. Yet even though there is nothing travelers can do about this situation, it worries people, and they always want to know which airports have the worst records of air traffic control equipment failure. In 1996, the American Automobile Association provided some answers with a study of power and equipment failures at Category X airports across the country:

AIRPORT	FAILURE	LENGTH	DATE
John F. Kennedy, New York	Power	36 minutes	April 1995
	Communications	2.5 hours	May 1995
	Power	5 hours, 49 minutes	May 1995
	Computer	48 minutes	Nov. 1995
	Computer	74 minutes	Dec. 1995
	Computer	37 minutes	May 1996
	Computer	2 hours, 17 minutes	July 1996
	Computer	1 hour, 8 minutes	Aug. 1996
O'Hare, Chicago	Computer	1 hour, 5 minutes	May 1995
	Computer	44 minutes	July 1995
	Computer	25 minutes	July 1995
	Computer	122 hours, 22 minutes	July 1995

AIRPORT	FAILURE	LENGTH	DATE
	Computer	2 hours, 8 minutes	Sept. 1995
	Computer	13 minutes	Nov. 1995
	Computer	46 minutes	Nov. 1995
Dallas/Fort Worth	Computer	31 minutes	July 1995
	Power	14 hours, 35 minutes	Oct. 1995
	Computer	11 hours, 5 minutes	Dec. 1995
	Computer	2 hours, 29 minutes	Jan. 1996
	Computer	3 hours, 49 minutes	March 1996
	Computer	2 hours, 17 minutes	April 1996
Oakland	Power	34 minutes	Aug. 1995
	Computer	42 minutes	Nov. 1995
National, Washington, D.C.	Computer	49 hours, 59 minutes	June 1996
Kansas City	Computer	6 hours, 23 minutes	Sept. 1995
	Computer	7 hours, 20 minutes	Oct. 1995
Seattle-Tacoma	Computer	2 hours, 2 minutes	Jan. 1996
Logan, Boston	Power	2 hours, 26 minutes	April 1996
	Communications	1 hour, 44 minutes	April 1996
Jacksonville	Computer	1 hour, 12 minutes	July 1996
Los Angeles			

The air traffic control equipment outages listed here are only a sampling of the crisis. Even though the FAA says we can expect a new air traffic control system by the next century, computers are only a part of the problem. Power systems are as varied as the airports they serve. The FAA is working toward standardization, but the fix will take years. Meanwhile, we need to look beyond mere standardization in planning the airports of the twenty-first century: they will need to be constructed to accommodate the best in high-tech security, instead of security being cobbled together with room dividers and folding tables. All airport functions will have to be considered during development and construction, from passenger terminal, cargo and maintenance, to food service and access roads.

We need long, wide, parallel runways so takeoffs and landings can operate in different lanes. We need high-speed runway exits and taxiways—much like freeway exit ramps—so planes can exit while still moving quickly.

The FAA needs to be forceful in prohibiting obstructions near airports. When the federal government spends your money to build newer, safer airports further from the city, the older airport it replaces must close.

We need to have the wind shear radar and other bad-weather equipment we were promised. Airport managers should be better trained to evaluate weather conditions and forecasting so airports will close in very bad weather. The most effective de-icing methods and fluids should be used, further decreasing the danger of takeoff and landing in freezing temperatures.

Finally, our ticket taxes, passenger facility charges and federal tax dollars channeled to the FAA should be spent to enhance safety—starting with the new Air Traffic Control and other navigational facilities we have long been promised—not wasted on trade missions, political functions, works of art or parade floats, unless perhaps it is a float informing people about new air safety measures installed at the airport.

CHAPTER SIXTEEN

Straighten Up and Fly Right

In its glossy little blue-and-white brochure *Fly Rights,* the FAA tells travelers how airfares are set, how to make reservations and get tickets, whether smoking is permitted on planes and to watch out for travel scams. It does not say much about safety.

"Air travel is so safe you'll probably never have to use any of the advice we're about to give you," the brochure says, and then proceeds to tell passengers to test their seat belts, be careful about what they put in overhead bins and listen closely to the flight attendant's safety briefing.

But passengers need to know a great deal more to fly safe. Avoiding crashes is only a small part of flying smart. Much of what makes a flight safe and comfortable is within passengers' control. After all, statistically speaking 50 percent of passengers survive a plane crash, and what you do may influence your fate. The flying public deserves to know what safety equipment you should demand during a flight, and what you have to bring for yourselves. You need to know your rights in case flights are canceled or equipment is switched, or if you want to get off a plane. You also need to know what to do if something is amiss on a plane and how to bring it to light.

Many of the following suggestions are not merely theo-

retical—most come from my own experiences flying for
business, with my family and children, in all kinds of
weather and on all sizes of aircraft.

BEST SEATS IN THE HOUSE

The first insight into flying that virtually every passenger wants is how to choose the safest seat on an airplane.
Conventional wisdom advises that survivability is greatest
in the back of a plane, convincing most passengers that a
seat nearest the tail is the safest. But that may be because
when people think of crashes, they picture a nosedive that
leaves a plane with a smashed-in hull, a torn-away fuselage or blown-apart wings or engines. Most people believe
the front of a plane (or a train or bus, for that matter) is
damaged more often than the rear. That thought prevailed
until an engine on a Delta plane exploded, killing a mother
and her son seated in the very back of the plane. Shortly
afterward, a grim cartoon appeared in a newspaper. It
showed a plane sitting on its nose and the pilot announcing, "Ladies and gentlemen, some of you will have to sit
in the rear of the plane." When I saw it, I remembered a
similar cartoon from a decade earlier, after a crash in
which the only survivors were seated in the tail section.
It depicted a plane sitting on its tail and a pilot announcing, "Ladies and gentlemen, some of you will have to sit
in the front." In truth, there is no statistically "safest"
place to sit during a plane crash. But there are seats that
increase your chances of surviving the aftermath of a
crash.

Most accidents happen on takeoff or landing, are nonfa-
tal and involve overshooting a runway, aborting a takeoff,
failed landing gear or running off the runway. The plane
slides, spins and gets banged up. It comes to a full stop
and people slide down the chutes. They get cuts, bruises
or sprained ankles, and hobble away. But if a fire erupts,
the outcome can be very different. Most people who die
in plane accidents die from smoke inhalation and fumes.
Smoke can overcome and kill a person in minutes, even
on an immobile plane on the ground. That means the safest

place to sit is an aisle seat near an exit, so that if you have to, you can get out *fast*.

Of course, the FAA, aircraft designers and the airlines intend that everyone will get out of a damaged plane quickly and efficiently. The FAA says that all planes must be designed so that a full load of passengers can evacuate within ninety seconds. Aircraft manufacturers and the airlines stage mock evacuations to test escape procedures and train crews. Though they may use some aviation employees in these tests, regulations mandate they at least try to make them realistic. But the regulations expressly specify that persons in normal health be used. At least 30 percent must be females, 5 percent over age sixty, not more than 10 percent must be children under twelve, and three life-sized dolls must be carried by three passengers to simulate live infants under two years of age. Some of the mock passengers have been through "evacuations" many times, but the test must also include some people who have never done it before. The test directors must throw items around the cabin—one half of the average amount of cabin debris such as carry-ons, blankets and other articles must be tossed in the aisles and around emergency exits. Lastly, they do not tell the "passengers" which exits will open smoothly.

But no mock emergency can reproduce the danger, terror and panic a huge group might feel during a life-threatening accident. A real evacuation can easily be complicated by screaming children, slow or elderly people and even drug- or alcohol-impaired passengers.

In many crashes investigated by the NTSB, evacuations were sadly hampered when people stopped to collect their carry-ons or simply froze in the face of danger. Grown men have fought at emergency exits, and children have been separated from their parents. The aviation industry adopted new policies about emergency-row seating after the USAir jet runway collision and fire in Los Angeles, in which a passenger seated adjacent to the emergency door was immobilized with fear while others fought over the exit. Twenty-one passengers died of smoke inhalation when a bottleneck formed. Now airlines advise anyone sitting next to an emergency exit that he or she must have the strength and presence of mind to operate the door in case of an emergency. Anyone who does not want that responsibility can move to another seat. Anyone who is disabled or traveling with children will be asked to sit elsewhere.

➤ *Together, all of this means that the best seat is the one with the fewest people and potential obstacles as possible between you and an exit door. In most large, commercial aircraft, that generally means a seat somewhere in the middle of the plane. The aisle is probably better, because if there is a fire, one side may be blocked by flames.*

Most planes have four exits over the wings, two exits in the front near the cockpit and one in the tail of the plane. There are some exceptions, as discussed in chapter twelve. The Lockheed L-1011 has mid-fuselage exits, but because the plane is so huge, there are twenty rows, ten seats across, between the first and second sets of exits. In a crisis on a fully loaded plane, a lot of people need to file down two aisles toward those exits. The Fokker 100 and 28 have no rear exits at all, a feature of the planes about which flight attendants complain. Furthermore, a plane can be configured in many different ways, depending on the airline, such as the 757. Many aircraft have eight or ten exit doors, others have only six.

➤ *Generally, the best way to plan a safe flight is to ask for a seat near the exit when you make reservations. But bear in mind, every airline has the right to change the plane you are flying on at any time. A seat you have carefully booked in an exit row may turn into a seat several rows from a door because you are ultimately flying on a different plane. In addition, seat configurations change all the time—airlines add or subtract seats and rows of seats from planes, so exit rows are not always the same. Ask the agent where the exit rows are on your plane when getting your seat assignment and in the event of a last-minute equipment change. Get an aisle seat near the greatest concentration of exits. Before takeoff, count the rows to the nearest exit, both ahead of you and behind you. Use a Post-it Note. Pay attention to the oxygen mask demonstration and carry your own smoke hood. Read the emergency card to familiarize yourself with the exit doors and windows, and with how to open them. Do this before every take-off, without exception.*

FLYING WITH CHILDREN

The airline industry allows children aged two and under to fly for free on domestic flights as passengers on an adult's lap. At the same time, the agency recommends that children who weigh less than forty pounds (certainly all infants and virtually all toddlers) should be strapped into child safety seats. But there is no rule that says they have to be, and no airline gives safety seats to passengers with children. On the contrary, many airlines make it difficult for concerned parents to bring their own car safety seats onto a plane. This is particularly true on quick turnaround airlines like Southwest, which once forbade me to carry on a car safety seat, unless I bought another ticket. Thus the youngest, most vulnerable passengers often end up flying with only an adult's grip to secure them and no safety equipment of their own in case of an accident.

The FAA's own glossy brochure *Fly Smart, An Air Traveler's Guide* says that "of all the safety features aboard the aircraft, one of the most important is right at your fingertips . . . YOUR SEAT BELT." The pamphlet says 300 people were seriously injured in turbulence accidents over ten years because they did not have their seat belts fastened.

"To prevent turbulence-related injuries, Fly Smart travelers should always keep their seat belt fastened at all times," a bright-eyed cartoon plane warns in the pamphlet. Yet the FAA has no rules about strapping in babies and toddlers.

In case of an accident, children are grossly unprotected. Child safety advocate Stewart Miller has waged a twenty-five-year battle with the FAA over seat restraints for babies and children. He has argued that since every state requires child safety seats for automobiles, since car rental agencies provide them for customers, and since the FAA requires airlines to have seat belts for adults, it is ludicrous that thousands of infants and small children fly every day as mere ''lap'' passengers. Miller has charged the FAA and the airlines with discriminating against children when it comes to safety. Thanks to his efforts, all car safety seats approved by the National Highway Transportation Safety Administration can be used on planes.

Miller says no agency or organization keeps track of how many children are injured on planes every year because they are not strapped into their own seats—in part because for years the airlines and the FAA didn't even keep records of how many lap children were flying. No studies have been done to prove that placing lap children on the floor of a plane in case of an emergency is safe, either, Miller says. In years of studying the subject, Miller has not found any substantiation for the FAA's claim that if families are forced to pay, even in part, for a ticket for a small child, 20 percent will drive their cars instead, thus exposing themselves to greater danger on the highways. But children flying as lap passengers are definitely at risk. Two small ''lap'' children flew without safety seats on the United Airlines jet that crashed in Sioux City, Iowa, in 1989. Following the flight attendant's emergency instructions, the children's mothers put them on the floor and held them down firmly as everyone braced for the crash. But their frightened grip was not enough. On impact, both children were ripped from their mothers' grasps. One was killed. The other child was found, alive, in an overhead luggage bin fifteen rows behind his mother. In the crash of USAir flight 1016 in 1994, a lap baby was ripped from her mother's arms and hurled five rows. She died of massive head injuries. There is no evidence indicating that placing a child or a baby on the floor is safe.

In 1996, when a mother and her son were killed by the debris from an exploding Delta engine, seated near them was an infant in a car seat. The car seat was also battered with flying metal, but the infant was protected by the sides of the seat.

Your plane does not have to crash to expose your baby to grave danger. Though the FAA doesn't keep track of how many lap babies have been injured because they were not restrained, there are plenty of examples of anecdotal evidence and media reports that indicate there are dozens every year. The examples include lap children ripped from their parents' arms in turbulence. For example, on September 8, 1996, a Lufthansa flight traveling over Texas hit clear air turbulence. The pilot knew it was coming and told passengers to put on their seat belts and brace for a rocky ride. Still, four people had to be hospitalized with injuries. Three of the four were lap babies ripped from their parents' arms during the bumpy flight. In early December 1996, an American Airlines jet flew through turbulence so severe that several passengers were injured and had to be hospitalized—including a three-month-old lap baby.

In the summer of 1996, the House Aviation Subcommittee held hearings on child safety seats—but these were not the first discussions on Capitol Hill. Earlier hearings took place in 1990. An FAA spokesperson is reported to have stated, "There haven't been enough infants killed on airlines to justify changing [the law]." The FAA told Congress that it opposes requiring child safety seats because too many paying passengers would be discouraged from flying if they had to buy an additional ticket for a small child.

"Twenty percent of families would choose other modes of transportation," said Margaret Gilligan, Acting Deputy Associate Administrator for Regulation and Certification. Those families whose infants and toddlers now fly free would be forced to drive their cars, thus exposing themselves to the higher likelihood of a car crash, the FAA reasoned. But the FAA refuses to reveal how it knows this—a request for the data to support these claims was refused. The flight attendants' union says the FAA is relying on a study by Apogee Research, dated June 4, 1990, prepared at the request of the FAA. But flight attendants, the people who have to bandage and console injured babies and children, commissioned their own study, and it refutes the FAA claim and the Apogee findings. The flight atten-

dants' union study found no valid evidence to support the
FAA claim that if infant seats were required, parents
would forgo flying and drive.

The flight attendants' union is right. Already the majority of adults fly on discounted tickets. Most airlines offer
even deeper discounts for children, and most also have
kids-fly-free promotions. Major carriers have made it a
rule, stating that children aged two to eleven receive a
discount and pay what an adult would on a supersaver
fare. Cite Airline Rule 50 when asking. None of these
airlines charge full price for an infant under two. No airline would risk the revenue possible from one or two paying adults and often an older sibling. Still, the FAA balks
at requiring child safety seats. In contrast, when by 1996
several children had been killed by automobile air bags,
the NTSB and automakers acted swiftly. Some vehicles
are now sold with an air bag cutoff switch. Automakers
are also developing bags with less explosive force and a
smart air bag to judge the size of the person it protects.

Yet when larger numbers of children are killed or injured due to a policy directly under the FAA's control, all
the agency does is claim there are not enough fatalities to
justify imposing new rules on the airlines.

➤ *If you can't afford a separate ticket for a child, at least
push the issue and take along a safety seat. There may
be an unsold spot on the plane you can use. Most major
carriers specifically allow you to bring your safety seat
on board, and this is not contingent on buying an extra
ticket even though they say "if space is available."
Cite Airline Rule 190.*

➤ *All adults flying with children under two should bring
a car safety seat onto a flight as carry-on luggage.
There is no law prohibiting this practice, and, contrary
to what some airlines claim, no FAA regulation that
says only aircraft-approved safety seats can be used on
planes. One FAA regulation says that seats have to
have a label stating they are approved for aircraft use.
But almost all car seats manufactured since 1985 are
also approved for planes, and no airline checks. Even*

if there are unoccupied seats on a plane, some flight attendants, citing airline policy, will not allow parents to put their child and safety seat in the empty seat. USAir insisted on following this policy with me. Southwest tried but, when I resisted, relented. Don't give up. In 1997, several carriers joined together to announce they had finally adopted the policy of allowing you to bring your kid's safety seat on board without buying an additional ticket for the baby if there was an empty seat available. Others, like Southwest, while not officially joining in the announcement, have that policy. Ask.

➤ *What's more, there's another loophole. Money talks. If the child's parent, guardian, or attendant pays for the seat, then the parent, guardian, or attendant cannot be prohibited from putting the child in the seat paid for— though still may not use a booster or harness that ties the child to the seat (14 CFR 121.311 (C)(2)).*

➤ *Some airlines will try to keep a center seat open for people flying with small children, especially on an international flight. After all, on an international flight, you have to pay 10 percent of the cost of your ticket to bring aboard a lap baby. You should demand some courtesies for your money—certainly more than warming a jar of baby food.*

➤ *Parents should have a car safety seat handy so the child can be strapped in, rear facing forward, just like when they ride in a car. A car safety seat will be necessary anyway to reach the airport, and then again when you get off the plane at your destination. Rather than checking the safety seat, take it on the plane. Car safety seats do not count as one of your bags, carry-on or checked (Airline Rule 190). If you are from another country and bring a child safety seat from your nation, our law says we must recognize your country's safety regulation and if your seat is OK in your country, it is OK in ours. No airline checks.*

LIFE VESTS

Every plane that flies over water is stocked with life vests, and among them there should be enough infant life vests for all babies on board. Life vests are a problem, however, even for adults. There are at least five varieties of adult vests, and they are often hard to put on. The children's and infants' vests are even more difficult. The adult-sized vests under each seat are too big for babies (passengers should always check under the seat to make sure their life vest is really there). But babies' vests are not distributed to passengers. Instead, if there is an emergency, flight attendants are supposed to hand out infant life vests. As much as I admire and respect flight attendants, I would rather not rely on them to remember in the midst of a crisis that there might be one or two babies on board who need special gear. That is why, when I fly on a long trip over water with my young children, I always ask the flight attendant to let me keep the baby life vest at my seat until we land. Flight attendants have frequently balked at this request (often telling me they would get in trouble), but there is no regulation against a parent taking responsibility for the infant life vest.

Since babies can die very quickly of hypothermia in cold water, a tiny flotation tent that envelops the child and keeps his body above the water's surface is also worth considering if you often fly on small planes or non-major carriers over water. The airlines do not provide this kind of equipment, which is bulky and expensive. Like car safety seats, this has to be bought by parents themselves. Such tents are available from outlets like Sporty's Pilot Shop in Batavia, Ohio, or Boats U.S.

CHILDREN FLYING ALONE

No one knows how many small children fly alone every day, but aviation experts estimate it may be as many as 20,000 to 40,000, or one to two children on just about every flight, and that number is increasing. Some airlines estimate that half of these children are flying back and forth between divorced parents. Most airlines allow children to fly alone from the age of five. They restrict youngsters to nonstop or direct (which may make a stop en route) flights until the age of eight.

From the age of eight, children are allowed to make connecting flights. Some airlines have special waiting rooms where children pass the time during layovers, but these do not exist at most airports. A service fee applies to connecting flights and, on many carriers, unaccompanied children are not accepted on the last connecting flight of the day (Rule 50). From the age of twelve, kids are no longer considered unaccompanied minors and can fly however they or their parents choose. Common sense dictates some extra safety precautions.

➤ *Never book a child on the last connecting flight at night. If stranded, the child would have to go to a hotel. Anecdotes abound, such as one in which a child was stranded late at night on Christmas Eve. An airline employee took the child to his own home for Christmas, and shared presents from under his tree. Reality may be a little bleaker. Northwest Airlines will book a child in a hotel room and have an employee stand guard outside the door. But Southwest Airlines might put your child on a bus. Before booking your unaccompanied child on an airline, ask the carrier what will happen if your child's flight is diverted or a connecting flight is missed. Go over the plan with your child.*

➤ *Explain what a plane flight is like to the child, so he or she will know what to expect and who to turn to with questions.*

➤ *Pack toys and books for a child to play with on-board, and send along special snacks. Include essential items such as a toothbrush and any medicines needed, in case of delay.*

➤ *Make sure the child can take care of his own personal hygiene. Because of claimed liability issues, airline employees cannot assist with such matters. For example,*

USAir employees are not allowed to accompany the
child into the bathroom.

➤ Get to the airport with enough time to fill out a Travel
Card, which asks for names, addresses and phone numbers of people sending and picking up the child, flight
details and any medical information. Give a copy to
the child, in case the airline loses its copy. Include with
the Travel Card what you have confirmed will be done
in the event of a diverted or missed flight. Never send
your child on any airline that will turn your child over
to the child welfare authorities or the police. From my
days as a prosecutor, I can tell you that is no place
for a child.

➤ Do not leave the airport before the child's flight de-
parts—even if the plane has left the gate. If the plane
is delayed or taken out of service and the passengers
told to disembark, someone should be there to take care
of the child.

➤ Make sure the person picking up the child at her destination is there early. Do not rely on the kindness of
strangers. There have been at least three reported cases
of young girls being molested by male passengers during flights. One molester was a rabbi's assistant who
had just given a speech on morality. On two of the
flights, other passengers came to the girls' aid and
helped them report the abuse. Sadly, on the third flight,
when the little girl loudly protested the fondling, other
passengers told her to be quiet. When she got off the
plane, the molester even had the audacity to take her
parent to task for letting the child fly alone.

FLYING WITH DISABILITIES

The 1986 Air Carrier Access Act changed air travel for
people with disabilities. Before that law, airlines could
reject wheelchair-bound travelers and put all kinds of re-

strictions on flight for disabled people. Not only did the act outlaw discrimination against passengers on the basis of disability alone, it also forbade airlines from limiting the number of disabled people per flight or denying flights to people with disabilities that might annoy other passengers or create extra work for the crew.

The law has some exceptions. Airlines are not required to let anyone fly who would endanger the health of other passengers, and they can turn away a disabled person if the only seat available is in an emergency-exit row. Commuter aircraft with fewer than thirty seats and no special equipment for disabled passengers may also decline to accept handicapped travelers.

Airlines are slowly adapting planes to accommodate disabled passengers. Accessible bathrooms are required by law, but the airlines do not have to rush out and install them in older planes. The new bathrooms can wait until the plane undergoes a major overhaul.

Carriers have the right to insist that a disabled person travel with a companion so there will be someone to help in case of an emergency evacuation. The companion could even be an off-duty flight attendant. But whoever it is, the airline cannot charge that person for his or her seat. If the airline insists on a companion but there is no seat for him, the airline can refuse to board the disabled person. In that case, the carrier must reimburse the disabled passenger.

Airlines cannot demand a medical certificate from a disabled person unless he or she is traveling with a stretcher, an incubator or oxygen, or has a communicable disease or other condition that makes the airline believe the passenger may not be able to complete the flight.

Special equipment—like a wheelchair—does not count as carry-on baggage. It also takes priority in storage closets or bins over bags brought on board by other passengers. A wheelchair or other equipment checked into the cargo hold is supposed to be the first thing unloaded.

And when a disabled person is transferring from one flight or airline to another, the crew from the plane he arrived on is responsible for helping him make his connection.

Airlines must allow guide dogs and other assisting animals to travel in the cabin with their masters as long as they do not block the aisle. They cannot charge a service (cleaning) fee for them.

➤ *In preparing for an airplane trip, disabled passengers should ask about configurations on the designated plane that might limit access (like emergency-exit rows), seats that have removable armrests, storage space for a wheelchair, braces or other equipment, bathroom access and, if relevant, onboard wheelchairs for getting around on the plane. If you have a battery-powered wheelchair with a spillable battery, arrange to have it stored in hazardous-materials packaging. With enough notice, airlines can provide oxygen, incubators, electricity for a respirator or space for a stretcher. Be sure to ask if there is a charge for these extra services. Ask about gate access at airports—whether there is a level ramp or a lift.*

SMOKE HOODS

In Hong Kong and Korea, even the most ordinary hotels offer their guests smoke hoods in each room. The plastic hoods slip over the head, fasten around the neck or have a mouthpiece and have an air filter that protects against smoke and fumes. In most designs, the filter purifies air through a three-stage process: the first absorbs drops of potentially noxious moisture, the second removes tiny particles produced by smoke and ashes that can build up in the lungs, and the third traps gases like carbon monoxide. The hoods also protect the eyes and skin. In case of a fire, guests are supposed to slip on the smoke hoods and evacuate the building.

Airplanes offer passengers oxygen through the small temporary masks that drop out of the bulkhead above each seat in case of emergency. These masks are intended to supplement air in a plane cabin should pressure drop suddenly. They work only so long as the tube is attached to the ceiling of the plane, and it mixes cabin air. A passenger who needs to get up and run through a wall of smoke cannot take that oxygen mask with him. Here's what the FAA says to do if your plane fills with smoke. Got to the bathroom and get wet towels or handkerchiefs to cover your nose and mouth, and move away from the smoke and fire. Sort of makes you wonder whether anyone at the FAA actually flies, doesn't it? Consumer groups have long encouraged the airlines to provide smoke hoods for each flying passenger, and prodded the FAA to require them. The agency and the airlines resist the idea, arguing that smoke hoods are unnecessary, and worse, only slow down passenger evacuation. Once again, however, cost seems to be the real obstacle for the industry. A Department of Transportation study found no indication that pulling out and putting on a smoke hood slowed people down as they fled a plane.

➤ *Do not rely on the FAA or the airlines. The best solution is to buy and carry your own smoke hood. I have owned one for each member of my family since 1994. Mine are about the size of the a soda-pop can, others are about the size of a child's shoe box, which means it definitely takes up room in your carry-on, especially for a family of four. The most sophisticated models cost $100 or more, so outfitting an entire family can also be expensive. But the gear can be carried on a plane over and over until needed—and many companies will replace the smoke hood for free if it has to be used. Do not put your smoke hood in the overhead bin. Keep it with you at your seat, easily accessible. Tape a small flashlight to it, too.*

Many manufacturers sell smoke hoods to the public to keep at home or in high-rise offices, or to take on the road. They can be found in travel and safety stores, and in travel and safety equipment mail-order catalogs. Some are small canister models that look like a soda can projecting from a plastic rain bonnet, others look like the headgear on a haz-mat suit. You must buy smoke hoods that protect against carbon monoxide. They cost $100 or more. You must not open it until you need to use it. You can buy a practice hood for about $15 to familiarize yourself with the gear.

SECURITY

In the immediate aftermath of the TWA flight 800 crash, as politicians, the media and the public worried that a terrorist bomb had brought down the plane, the aviation industry scrambled to put new security measures into place. Yet the public still does not realize how little security is routinely practiced for each flight.

It is generally a myth that everything that goes onto a plane first passes through a security check. Passengers, cargo, mail, hazardous material and carry-on bags are rarely screened, and then only for metal detection. Cargo—like the turtles and theatrical glitter on TWA flight 800—gets only spotty screening. Mail is not scanned at all. Witness the rash of letter bombs from overseas in January 1997 and the passengers radiated and overcome by pesticide fumes on passenger planes in 1997. Packages are not routinely x-rayed, and the airlines often do not subject them to pressurization tests (in which packages are subjected to air pressure levels found in flight to see if a pressure-sensitive detonator explodes). Packages are sporadically delayed, but there is no routine security system for inspecting the countless boxes and bundles that are loaded onto planes every day. Suitcases and other baggage on domestic flights are not screened, and some of those bags are transferred to international flight connections without being x-rayed, either.

➤ *Passengers should be on the lookout for anything suspicious—like a traveler who boards a plane and then gets off the aircraft. After the crash of TWA flight 800, a passenger on another flight did just that, and many of the passengers on the same plane followed his lead. Report to airport security all unattended bags, suspicious persons and baggage screeners not paying attention to their screens.*

➤ *Complain about airlines with shoddy security. Report them to the FAA and to your member of Congress. Better yet, call the media—they might report the incident. When you read about an airline with a pattern of shoddy security, stay off that airline. Security is an airline's responsibility. Remember that the old Pan Am was caught passing off untrained dogs from the kennel as bomb-sniffing experts. And don't forget American Airlines in 1997 letting a courier on board with twenty-two suitcases of pesticides. People try to pack fireworks so often that the FAA put out a press release for July 4, 1997, warning folks not to do it.*

EQUIPMENT AND CARRIER CHANGES AND CODE SHARES

Many airlines have business partnerships with other carriers that enable them to sell tickets to destinations they do not serve. This practice is called ''code sharing.'' Thus if you book a flight with a U.S. carrier to a South American city, you may find yourself on a Peruvian airline before you finally get there. You definitely don't want that to happen.

Contrary to popular belief, there are not a lot of so-called airline passenger rights actually contained in federal law, but code sharing happens to be regulated. The law says it is deceptive and illegal for two airlines to pass themselves off as one in order to sell a ticket *unless* the air carriers give reasonable and timely notice of the code sharing arrangement (14 Code of Federal Regulations Section 399.88). That means air carriers must identify each flight in which the airline code is different from the code of the carrier actually providing the service in written or electronic schedule information provided to the public, the Official Airline Guide, and in computer reservation systems. The airline must also tell the traveler orally if the passenger buys the ticket directly from the airline, and it must publish frequent, periodic notice in advertisements. But in real life, passengers do not subscribe to the OAG, travel agents or the airline representative may forget to warn you about the change in carrier or gloss over it in official sounding language (or you may not be paying attention), or you may overlook the notice in the advertising: that very tiny type at the bottom of the advertisement that starts off talking about having to stay over Saturday night.

So what do you do? *You ask*—each time, every time there is a change of planes involved, because on your ticket this information only appears in code that most people do not know how to read. Putting the code sharing disclosure on the ticket is not required by the law.

Airlines are also often forced to change equipment because of mechanical or scheduling problems. There are regulations governing some equipment changes—for example, the rules say if one plane is substituted for another, the substitute plane must be a similar aircraft. In other words, passengers cannot be forced to switch from a jet to a turbo prop. FAA regulations say that an airline must offer a passenger "comparable transportation" or owe him a full refund. But comparable transportation can be on virtually any other airline. Thus, if your flight is canceled, your airline is free to book you on the airline of its choice and on entirely different aircraft.

The airline can even offer you any form of transportation, including a bus ticket. You can refuse such noncomparable transportation, and if you do, the airline will owe you a 200 percent refund on the price of your ticket. The same is true if your carrier tries to rebook you on an airline that has different standards, like an air taxi or a commuter carrier.

➤ *Your best defense is to ask your agent or your carrier when booking whether or not there is any code share, and whether your service is on your selected airline all the way to your destination. Take the name of the employee who answers your question. If your ticket becomes subject to a dispute, the airline will ask who gave you your information. Be prepared.*

GETTING OFF THE PLANE

In practice, a passenger has been able to board, but then get off a plane up until the door is closed and the plane pushes away from the gate. Once the door is closed, how-ever, the passenger's ability to demand to get off disap-pears. Sometimes, when faced with a mechanical problem, an airline will close the plane's door and remove the jet-way so it can fix the plane without losing any passengers. Airlines will deny it, but I have been stuck on planes in just that situation.

➤ *If you are not certain you want to take a flight, or if you see something on the airplane that makes you uncomfortable, you need to decide right away whether you want to get off the plane. You must act on your decision before the main cabin door is closed. You can-not wait until the plane is moving away from the termi-nal building or taxiing toward the runway—at that point, it's the pilot's decision.*

If a passenger becomes sick, suffers a heart attack or goes into labor on a flight, it is entirely up to the discretion of the pilot whether or not to divert the aircraft and land at the nearest airport. In November 1994, a baby was named after Dulles Airport outside Washington, D.C., when his mother gave birth on a TWA flight that made an emergency landing there. In more tragic cases, widows sued Lufthansa and Continental Airlines in 1996 after their spouses suffered in-air heart attacks and the pilots chose not to divert to the nearest airports.

➤ *However desperate the passenger, no one has the right to override a pilot's decision not to make an emergency landing. The safe operation of the plane is up to the pilot's and the airline's discretion. If you are in a late-term pregnancy or have a tenuous medical condition, consider carefully whether you should fly at all. Consult your doctor and carry your necessary medicines or emergency supplies.*

MEDICAL EQUIPMENT

All planes are equipped with basic first-aid kits, but other than a stethoscope and sphygmomanometer, they have no medical equipment. The kits contain bandages, tourniquets, antiseptic, tape, dextrose, epinephrine and nitroglycerin. But there is no guarantee a doctor, nurse or other health-care worker will be aboard. Flight attendants and crew cannot perform medical functions. New FAA regulations may soon require that planes carry a heart defibrillator. Quantas has carried defibrillators on its flights since 1991 and reports it has saved five lives. And British Airways planes carry equipment that monitors a sick passenger's condition and electronically transmits the information to a medical facility.

➤ *If you are very ill, consider a private air ambulance. You can also buy air ambulance insurance, to pay for such a plane if you should need it. If you have a chronic serious condition, check into buying such coverage.*

SPEAK UP

Before some of the most tragic, dramatic accidents in recent history, passengers aboard the planes saw something amiss but did not speak up. People sitting in the back of an Air Florida jet noticed snow piled on its wings just before it took off and crashed in the icy Potomac River in 1982. They did not alert the pilot.

Two passengers boarding an Aloha Airlines jet in 1988 saw cracks in the plane's skin near the main cabin door. They did not say anything, and a few hours later, the top of the plane ripped off and the jet landed with the passenger cabin exposed.

Flight attendants and passengers on a British Midlands Boeing 737 saw a fire in the left engine during a 1989 flight. When the pilot came on the intercom and announced there was trouble with the right engine, no one corrected him. He shut down the working engine on the right—and the plane crashed.

Also in 1989, flight attendants saw snow and ice on the wings of an Air Ontario F-28. Assuming the pilot knew what he was doing, they didn't alert him. The plane crashed, killing twenty-seven.

Passengers on USAir flight 405 saw ice on the wings before the March 22, 1992, takeoff. They did not speak up, figuring the pilots had seen the same icing. *The New York Times* reported that one passenger said, "If we take off like this, we're all dead," while another said, "We're on the plane to hell." A third kissed his wife and said, "We're going to die." The plane crashed, killing twenty-seven.

In all five of these accidents, people died.

In 1993, I sat on board an idling USAir plane, watching other aircraft taxi over to a de-icing station. When I asked the flight attendant to tell the captain there was ice buildup on our wings, too, she refused. I had to produce my Inspector General business card to get the flight attendant to act. The captain walked back through the passenger cabin to look out the window and check the wings. He ordered the plane out of the runway lineup and went back to de-ice. Then we took off safely.

▶ *If you see odd mechanical activity, parts missing from a plane, cracks or faults in a plane's body, or leaks of oil or hydraulic fluid, do not assume that mechanics or flight crew are aware of everything or can see everything you can. Speak up—you paid for a safe plane. Do not be intimidated if flight attendants tell you to mind your own business. If speaking to a flight attendant does not satisfy concerns, then if possible draw your complaint to the cockpit crew's attention directly.*

▶ *Trouble is not always confined to the plane, either. In 1990, passengers flying from Fargo, North Dakota, to Minneapolis, Minnesota, reported a Northwest Airlines flight crew drinking alcohol in an airport lounge—for eight continuous hours. The crew members were tested and found to be beyond the legal limit for doing their jobs. They were prosecuted.*

▶ *Always speak up if you see snow or ice on the wings before takeoff. The threat is real and enough planes have crashed because of ice and snow buildup that good pilots will be thankful, not scornful, that you spoke up.*

CHAPTER SEVENTEEN

Flying Healthy

Safe flying is not restricted to the mechanics of a plane or its emergency equipment. Virtually everyone has boarded an aircraft feeling fine, only to get off at the other end with a stuffy nose, a headache and the first twinges of a cold. Germs circulating through recycled cabin air are only the most obvious health concern aboard a plane. You should also be aware of the quality of food and water supplied in countries where unfriendly microbes are common, whether pesticides are used on aircraft, and what to do about sick or drunk fellow passengers.

CABIN AIR

The air in a plane is not fresh: it is a mixture of outside air (pressurized so you can actually breathe) and recycled cabin air. But there is no regulation governing the ratio of the two. To keep costs down, airlines usually bring in very little outside air; some use none at all. The cockpit is continuously filled with clean outside air to keep the pilots healthy and alert. People riding in the plane breathe air that is recirculated—along with whatever germs may come from sick passengers. Airlines set their own standards for cabin air, deciding for themselves how much outside air to mix with the recycled. There are no regulations speci-

fying how much clean air should be brought into a plane—
not even for long intercontinental flights.

The air filters on planes are touted by the airlines as stopping microbes and bacteria from floating through the plane,
but they cannot catch viruses like those responsible for the
common cold or the flu. And most cannot catch the extremely small bacteria that cause tuberculosis. In 1994, a
woman infected with tuberculosis flew on four planes between Chicago and Honolulu, exposing almost a thousand
passengers to her illness. A week after the flight, she died of
complications in a Hawaii hospital. The Centers for Disease
Control in Atlanta tracked down the passengers who flew
with her and discovered that fourteen had contracted tuberculosis. Though the Centers said the risk of getting tuberculosis on a plane was small—an infected person would have
to cough and sneeze continuously for hours in the close
proximity of others who must inhale the bacteria-filled mist
(like on a plane flight)—it also asked TB carriers not to
make long commercial flights.

Airlines are essentially allowed to set their own air-quality standards. Most opt for the minimum necessary—the
amount of fresh air required to pressurize the cabin. Pump-
ing in more fresh air is more expensive for the carrier's operation. The FAA does not calculate how much it would cost
the airlines to boost their air-quality standards, and the private carriers won't disclose their price estimates. Whatever
the explanation, the result is that a lot less fresh air circulates
in an airplane than in a typical office building. Health standards mandate that most office buildings pump twenty cubic
feet per minute of fresh air into rooms and hallways. Most
airlines cycle five to seven cubic feet per minute into airplanes. That amount is less than half of what a typical building gets, and that is for people who are trapped in a small
space for hours at a time.

In June 1996, as she introduced a bill that would require
airlines to provide twenty cubic feet of fresh air per minute, California Senator Dianne Feinstein pointed out that
"prison inmates get more fresh air than many airline passengers." Unfortunately, her legislation did not pass.

The Association of Flight Attendants has been fighting
for years for an FAA standard on cabin air quality. The

Association wants planes to get as much fresh air as office buildings, restaurants, movie theaters—and prisons. It says its members report greater rates of common colds, the flu and other sicknesses from passengers carrying the germs. The flight attendants get caught in a vicious circle—since they are allowed only a limited number of sick days, many report to work with colds picked up on previous flights. They bring the virus onto their next plane, spreading germs in recycled air to even more people. But do not blame the poor flight attendants. The only people I have ever seen coughing and sneezing on passengers are other passengers.

The Air Transport Association insists that no link has ever been proved between cabin air quality and flight attendant sicknesses. Try telling that to anyone who has ever caught a cold on a plane or the fourteen people with TB.

Some of the newest planes use the same air filters that the Centers for Disease Control recommends for hospitals. Reportedly, they can trap tuberculosis bacteria. And the FAA has ruled that all *new* types of aircraft must provide ten cubic feet of fresh air per minute—but only new types approved after the Boeing 777. Entirely new types of planes are a rare event; most new planes are variations of existing models. The new regulation does not apply to any of those. The 777 is the newest. But ten cubic feet is still only half of what is usually required in an ordinary office building.

➤ *There is little you can do about cabin air quality. Since proximity is required for the transmission of tuberculosis and certainly aids the spread of colds and the flu, if the passenger seated next to you starts coughing and wheezing, get up and change seats if you can.*

➤ *Ear, nose and throat doctors suggest getting saline nasal spray to keep nasal passages moist during the flight. Drying and cracking make it easier for germs and viruses to infect a person. An alternative is an atomizer with water or a small aerosol bottle of water, which I have seen in some airport shops. Others recommend drinking lots of fluids.*

➤ *Consumers and the flying public should demand laws
that set better standards for the outside-air/recircu-
lated-air mix and guarantee that the amount of fresh
air will be calibrated to the length of a flight. The
airlines won't do it themselves, and they don't tell the
public what their varying air quality rates are.*

PESTICIDES

Passengers with concerns about pesticides should be
aware that several countries require airlines to spray plane
interiors with chemicals to kill insects. In each of these
places, local laws require flight attendants to spray insecti-
cides *inside the cabin with the passengers on board* upon
landing. Their laws apply to all carriers, including major
U.S. airlines that would never otherwise douse their customers with chemicals. I have seen flight attendants vigor-
ously blanket an entire cabin with pesticides, and others
who more kindly, if sheepishly, spritzed a bit of Black
Knight here and there on the floor of the cabin.

Some airlines also spray their planes inside and out before
flying—even if they are leaving a country that requires pesticide spraying. Often they use pesticides that are not approved
in the U.S. Many of these chemicals linger for weeks. Flight
attendants have reported feeling sick after working on planes
that were proactively sprayed with pesticides.

The countries which as of January 15, 1997 require the
incoming passengers to be sprayed include Grenada, Kiri-
bati, Madagascar and Trinidad and Tobago. The following
countries require the plane to be treated, but let the passengers off first: Australia, Barbados, Fiji, Jamaica, New
Zealand and Panama.

➤ *Ask the carrier beforehand if you are going to be
sprayed. There are two ways to help protect yourself.
After you are airborne, inform the attendants that you
are allergic to bug spray and ask them not to spray on
or near you. Do this especially if you are traveling with
small children or someone with breathing problems. Al-
ternatively, get a letter from a doctor if you (and your*

*children) are allergic to bug spray that says you should
be allowed off the plane before spraying. You should
present this to the flight crew in advance of the flight.*

PETS

Most major carriers allow a cat, dog, bird or other small
pet to travel with you as long as the animal fits in an under-
the-seat pet carrier. In addition, seeing-eye dogs travel without a cage. There are no regulations against carrying animals
in the cabin of a plane, and no requirement that other passengers be warned in advance of the flight. Conversely, you
have no ''right'' to carry a pet on board, and the animal must
remain in its cage throughout the flight.

➤ *Passengers with allergies or other reasons to object to
sitting near an animal must explain their concerns before the plane leaves the gate. People with severe allergies should ask a gate agent if there is a pet anywhere
on board, because the air carrying cat dander and dog
hair will be recirculated throughout the flight.*

Large pets must ride in the cargo hold. Owners should
be aware that pets have died from dehydration and suffoca-
tion after being neglected in a cargo container or lost
among baggage for extended periods of time.

➤ *Airlines can require a veterinarian's letter stating that
your pet is healthy and has had its shots. They can also
charge a fee (currently about $50) and require advance
reservations (Airline Rule 190).*

➤ *If your flight is delayed, be aware that your pet will be
in the cargo hold for extra hours with no food or water.
If the weather is hot, this can be a lethal combination.
There is no air-conditioning if a plane sits on the tarmac without its systems running. Place a bowl of ice
in the cage so the animal can lick it and get water.*

➤ *Realize that if some cargo doesn't make a flight, your pet may be among what is left behind.*

➤ *Consider that if your flight includes a change of planes, your pet might sit at length on a luggage cart on the tarmac in extreme heat or cold. Airlines can refuse to transport pets in cases of extreme weather.*

➤ *Make sure the cage is secure, because scared or frantic pets have gotten loose on the tarmac and been killed in traffic.*

➤ *The best advice is to leave your pet at home or in a kennel.*

DON'T DRINK THE WATER

Fresh fruit or vegetables and water boarded in the U.S. are safe for passengers to consume without a second thought. But travelers should be wary of uncooked foods or water supplied to airlines from countries where microbes unfamiliar to the average American stomach are common, or where there has been a recent outbreak of communicable diseases such as cholera. Fruit and vegetables are often grown in soils and with water that can make American travelers sick. This would include food and water loaded in parts of South or Central America, Africa and parts of Asia. Water comes to the plane on a truck, and I have seen some filthy water trucks around the world.

The FAA does not help clarify the problem. There are no federal food and water standards for aircraft supplies.

➤ *When flying on planes provisioned in areas with outbreaks of communicable diseases transmitted by food or water or unsafe handling methods, such as poor hygiene standards, it's safest to avoid uncooked foods, ice cubes and water (unless bottled). If your immune system is compromised or if you are traveling with small children, take your own food and water on the planes provisioned in countries with such diseases or in countries with marginal hygiene standards.*

HOW CLEAN IS A PLANE?

Not very. No regulations require the airlines to launder the blankets, replace the paper pillowcases (much less the pillows), disinfect or even wipe off the tray tables, or ever clean the seats—so they do not. Not surprising, then, that one November 1997 investigation completed by a CBS television station in Columbus, Ohio, took swabbings on twenty-six flights in the United States. The results showed the seats, blankets, pillows, and tray tables to be covered with E Coli, bacteria, or viruses that cause serious staph, strep, lung and bronchial, skin, and eye infections (including pinkeye), and mold, mildew, and fungus.

➤ *Get some small disinfectant towelettes—those little hand wipes sealed in a two-inch-by-two-inch foil pack that you see at doctors' offices, or the new waterless disinfectant hand wash, and wipe off the tray table and arm rests. Keep the blankets away from your nose, mouth, and eyes, and look for a new pillow, or carry your own inflatable neck pillow.*

➤ *For infants and small children, carry your own blankets and pillow or at least pillowcase.*

IN NO SHAPE TO FLY

Airlines used to be required to deny boarding to anyone who is sick unless a physician certifies that the disease is not communicable. The FAA now leaves it up to the airline. A 1996 federal regulation states that in denying boarding to a sick passenger—communicable disease or not—the airline must make its decision based on "reasonable judgment that relies on current medical knowledge or the best available objective evidence." Given that language, do not expect the airlines to reject sick passengers, even if they suspect a communicable disease. Airlines are also supposed to reject anyone who is clearly intoxicated, (14 CFR 121.575 says they are not allowed to let anyone board who appears to be intoxicated) and to ensure that someone who has had too much to drink on board the plane cannot get more. But once again, how are they to make that judgment? I have seen passengers stumble from the airport cocktail lounge to the gate, but I have never seen one refused boarding.

Flying and alcohol do not mix. Someone whose wits are dulled by alcohol presents a hazard to safety. Virtually every case of a passenger assaulting flight attendants or other passengers involved people who had been drinking. The hijackers who commandeered the Air Ethiopia Boeing 767 and forced it to fly until it ran out of fuel and crashed near the Comoro Islands in November 1996 appeared to be drunk. They had downed a bottle of whiskey they took from the service cart on the plane.

I hope that someday booze on planes will go the way of smoking. Planes carry as much as twenty-five gallons of liquor on a flight; a 747 may have over 150 bottles of wine and champagne. I've been told the purpose is to relax the passengers and help make the flight enjoyable. In other words—to dull your senses. It's not much of a revenue source for the airline. But dulled senses are not what you want if you have to get 350 people out of a plane in ninety seconds—especially among those who are responsible for opening emergency exits.

➤ *Object to the boarding of someone who is clearly seriously ill or drunk. If the plane is already airborne, tell flight attendants to move you away from an ill or drunk passenger and suggest they stop serving alcohol to someone who is intoxicated. Remember, the airlines are supposed to exercise their judgment to keep such people off the plane, but did not. You have to help yourself.*

➤ *Regulations should, but do not prohibit, at a minimum, serving alcohol to anyone seated in the emergency-exit rows. The flight attendants come around and make sure you read the safety card, understand the directions, are willing and able to open the door, can see and hear and speak English. Then they say, "Here's your scotch on the rocks—double." How absurd. Speak up. Don't let a soused louse come between you and safety.*

CHAPTER EIGHTEEN

Weather

Pilots must understand every possible weather condition, how it might move or develop, and the impact it might have on an airplane in flight. Weather evaluation is a critical part of all preflight preparation and pilots are required by law to check weather conditions. There are literally dozens of sources of weather reports and advisories available to pilots both before and during a flight.

Passengers are not meteorologists, and cannot second-guess flight crew about weather. But at least one federal court decision says passengers are entitled to be advised of bad weather if the airline knows it will impact the flight.

In the 1973 case of *Fleming v. Delta Airlines,* the carrier knew it would encounter very bad weather but did not warn the passengers before boarding or takeoff. A passenger claimed he was so frightened by the ferocious storm that he had a heart attack. The Federal District Court said Delta should have disclosed the weather before the flight so the passengers could have chosen to skip the flight. (The passenger ultimately lost his case because he could not prove the weather had caused his heart attack.)

Travelers can use common sense to decide whether they want to fly in less than clear blue skies. They can ask the agents at the airport, and the cockpit and cabin crew of a plane, for information about current and developing weather conditions. Passengers usually rely on TV or radio

reports for updates on the weather, and they get the same
weather reports the FAA and airlines do—from the National Weather Service, but they can also check in with
the same service that pilots use. Television and radio stations tend to broadcast general regional reports. Pilots need
more detailed information on weather conditions specific
to an airport's territory, on whether clouds are broken or
how far visibility extends. They get that from the FAA
Flight Service Stations (located across the country). Every
station has a public telephone number that anyone can call.
You can find the number in your local phone book listed
under the FAA.

ICE FOG, DENSITY ALTITUDE
AND JUST PLAIN RAIN

   Pilots can be concerned by many weather conditions—
from the ordinary like fog, wind or rain, to the odd and
unusual like the phenomenon called ice fog. In that case,
the fog is actually ice crystals. This occurs frequently in
Alaska, but can develop anywhere on a cold day when
two planes take off in succession. When the warm vapors
from the first jet hit the cold air, the vapors crystallize
into ice fog, or suspended ice crystals. This fog can blind
the pilot of the next plane, and it can cause ice to form
on that plane as well.
   Another concern for pilots is density altitude. Heat,
moisture in the air and an airport's altitude can make a
plane perform as if it is flying at a different altitude than
it really is. On a hot, muggy day, for example, when the
air is very thick, a plane may perform very sluggishly, as
if it were flying through soup. If a plane is fully loaded,
it may have trouble getting off the ground. It may need a
longer runway to take off. Occasionally density altitude
will compel a pilot to reduce a plane's weight by removing
passengers or cargo. If that is not possible, then the plane
will have to delay takeoff until the temperature drops.
Though this is obviously a great concern to pilots, passengers are usually unaware of it.
   But for scary weather, thunderstorms and snowstorms

top the list for pilots. They are certainly the most common treacherous weather. Both are most threatening during takeoff and landing. Thunderstorms can expose a plane to wind shear, and in snowstorms, snow and freezing rain can cause ice to build up on an aircraft. Of course, hurricanes and tornadoes alarm pilots, too.

SNOWSTORMS

When snow and ice accumulate on a plane, the extra weight and disfiguring shapes can destroy the lift and airspeed created with the wings. Speed and lift are achieved as air flows quickly around the hump of the wing. Piles of snow or layers of ice can break this flow. Naturally this is dangerous for flight, and it can make takeoff lethal. Once the craft is airborne, ice usually can be defeated on large planes by the heating equipment that melts the ice.

Most planes, even small planes without de-icing equipment, are built to fly with light icing for a limited time. As competition among manufacturers and airlines grows, more planes are being built with certification for flight in known icing conditions, and for flying in adverse weather. But the only effective way of eliminating the threat of ice is to avoid it altogether, which requires sophisticated understanding of ice formations and improved ice forecasts.

In addition to destroying lift, snow and ice can block the Pitot tubes found on every plane's wings. These are small protruding tubes, usually on the underside of the wing, through which air flows during flight. This is how the pilot knows how fast the aircraft is moving. The air flowing through the tubes is monitored, its speed registered and relayed to cockpit instruments. If the tubes are clogged with snow or ice, then the plane's airspeed cannot be determined. The pilot, for all intents and purposes, loses several vital instruments.

If snow and ice on the wings interfere with lift and airspeed, then a plane might lose power and altitude. If the Pitot tubes are blocked at the same time, the pilot might be losing airspeed and not even know it. If the plane is taking off, the pilot might not know there is not enough airspeed to generate the necessary lift. That is precisely what happened in 1982, when an Air Florida jet crashed into the Potomac River during a severe snowstorm in Washington, D.C. The plane had been de-iced at National Airport, but had to idle too long in a line of planes waiting to take off. Ice built up anew on its wings and in its Pitot tubes. The pilot did not know that he was getting faulty airspeed readings. When he tried to take off, the plane literally fell out of the sky and into the icy river.

Just as ice on the wings can interfere with lift, ice on a plane's tail can destroy the tail's ability to push down-ward. That downward force in the tail helps keep the plane's nose up, holding the craft level. If ice builds up on the tail, the plane's nose can dive suddenly. In 1991, a USAir Express Jetstream crashed in West Virginia, injur-ing thirteen people, after its equipment failed to keep the plane's tail free of ice. Tail icing is dangerous because pilots do not always think to check for it. The FAA says ice on the tail can sometimes be double the ice on wings. It can also accumulate on the tail when there is none on the wings.

All airports serving commercial passengers have de-icing facilities—either trucks with hoses that travel to indi-vidual planes, or cherry-picker-style "shower" equipment that douses planes from above. Both systems use forms of alcohol, or glycol, sprayed onto wings to melt ice and then prevent buildup of new crystals. The problem with de-icing is that it lasts only a short period of time, and that often depends on the type of de-icing fluid being used. Less expensive fluid is effective for about twenty to thirty minutes, while the more costly chemicals last about forty minutes.

➤ *When flying in winter in freezing weather, keep an eye out for ice and snow on plane wings, tail or fuselage. Remember that the pilot cannot see the wings from the cockpit. Snow buildup on wings is easily visible from passenger windows. Ice is harder to see. It may be dimpled; it may be completely invisible. That is why some planes have small strings attached to the top sur-*

*face of wings. If those strings are immobile, it may be
because of ice. If other planes are de-icing, then your
plane probably needs it, too. If your plane has already
been through the de-icing procedure, be aware of how
long it then sits at the gate or in the takeoff lineup.
Most de-icing compounds are effective for less than
thirty minutes. After that, ice can begin to accumulate
anew. Look out the window at the wing.*

*Speak up. Point out ice or snow to the cabin crew,
and ask them to tell the pilot, "There is visible icing
on the wing." The pilot can look out a cabin window
to decide for himself whether the plane needs de-icing.*

THUNDERSTORMS

All pilots know not to fly into thunderstorms. Strong
storm winds can shift dramatically without notice, and in
thunderstorms a pilot can run into violent wind shifts,
downdrafts, hail or lightning. Air traffic controllers route
pilots around thunderstorms. Pilots know to avoid them.
If a plane is already on the approach to landing when a
thunderstorm springs up, most pilots will wait it out by
circling the airport until it passes. Thunderstorms are fast-
moving and in many cases will cross the airport in a matter
of minutes. The prescription for disaster is written when
harsh weather conditions strike a plane flown by a pilot
with what I call "get-there-itis."

A USAir Shuttle leaving Washington, D.C., in June
1996 had such a pilot. A tornado warning had been posted
in the city, and severe thunderstorms were crossing the
airport. The pilots of every departing plane decided to wait
out the storm—except one. The USAir Shuttle pilot took
off. Wind shear swirled through the air and the plane had
trouble getting off the ground. A wing hit the runway. The
standing-by pilots commented on this lack of judgment
over their radios: "There goes a brave man," the first one
said, to which a second replied, "There goes an idiot."
A third added: "What's the difference?" Right after the
USAir Shuttle took off, the Air Traffic Control tower was

evacuated and National Airport was closed until the tornado warning was lifted.

Later, it was discovered that Air Traffic Control did not have a hazardous weather advisory because the local weather equipment was out of order—particularly, the terminal Doppler radar system. The tower failed to tell pilots this. But that was no excuse for the pilot's continued flight after the wing had hit the ground. The USAir Shuttle flew on to La Guardia Airport in New York, where the wing was found to be damaged. The pilot, who claimed he hadn't realized his wing struck the runway, was fired and the co-pilot was suspended.

I've had get-there-itis myself. I was once on a TWA flight that left St. Louis in a raging thunderstorm, complete with heavy rain and lightning. Many other pilots decided to wait out the weather, but ours chose to take off. Our flight was already hours late, having been delayed by mechanical difficulties. A flight attendant was seated near me, and she was visibly upset, repeating, "This is the worst I've ever seen," throughout our takeoff and climb-out. At least I knew that even in a storm like that, planes are not magnets for lightning. Lightning seeks grounded objects. Besides, the fuselage is rather spherical, so lightning is directed around it. There have been a few incidents of serious damage to planes by lightning strikes, including exploding fuel tanks. Certainly bolts of lightning strike planes, but they almost never knock them out of the sky. Lightning can shut down cockpit electrical systems, like avionics, but there are procedures for landing without instruments, including radios.

You might think that self-preservation would stop pilots from taking risks, but get-there-itis is more common than passengers realize. There have been several notorious accidents as a result of a flight crew's rush to get to a destination—perhaps because the city they are headed for is home.

The crash of an Air Illinois plane is one of the most famous. Right after the plane took off from Springfield, Illinois, it lost all electrical power. But the engines were running fine, so instead of turning back, the pilot decided to run the instruments on the plane's battery to reach their destination of Carbondale, Illinois. Besides, an off-duty crew had traveled all day just to work this flight. The plane's manual clearly said the battery would not last long enough. The Carbondale airport was ten minutes beyond the life span of the battery. The plane should have returned to Springfield. But the pilot was determined to get the plane home for maintenance. Just as the manual stated—ten minutes outside Carbondale—the battery expired. The two pilots had no instruments, and because of rain, could not see the ground. The plane hit a hill and crashed, killing everyone aboard—including the pilot who was in such a hurry.

Get-there-itis may have plagued the military pilot, or perhaps his passengers, who flew Commerce Secretary Ron Brown and thirty-four other people into Bosnia in 1996. Their plane crashed into a mountainside in what was called one of the worst storms anyone in Bosnia could remember. Later that year, an American Airlines crew tried to program new directions into their onboard computer to add a shortcut in their flight plan. But they had already passed the beacon the plane would seek once reprogrammed. The data was input incorrectly, and the plane flew into a mountainside outside Cali, Colombia.

➤ *Air traffic controllers do not have the authority to close airports or deny clearance for departure because of weather (the airport manager does both). The tower's job is to advise pilots of weather conditions—but it is entirely up to the pilot to decide whether or not it is safe to fly because he is "in the front seat looking out the window." So if you're unsure about the weather, ask a gate agent for the latest forecast.*

➤ *Call the local FAA weather station and get the weather report for yourself or just watch the Weather Channel on cable TV. En route, you can ask the airline personnel at the counter. Most can get the weather information from their computer. Then decide whether you want to fly. Be aware that weather can change in minutes if a very fast front is moving through.*

➤ *If possible, avoid flying in thunderstorms, which can spawn wind shear or tornadoes. Do not fly in hurricanes, or in snowstorms, even if the airport is still open. If the pilot is a seasoned, rational professional, then passengers are not at risk. But if the pilot has get-there-itis, he may overlook safety. That is the plane and airline you do not want to be on in severe weather. It can happen to any of the airlines, whether they have good or bad safety records. At least one airline (Valu-Jet) made it hard for even the best pilot to resist takeoff in bad conditions with policies that denied pay for flights not completed.*

➤ *Passengers can be informed and aware. Do not wait for airlines to volunteer information about weather conditions, because they will not. Always bring ice and snow on the wings to the attention of the flight crew.*

➤ *Think of small planes as fair-weather flying and plan accordingly.*

ON A CLEAR DAY: TURBULENCE

There is one weather condition that you can do something about: clear air turbulence. That's those sudden jolts that feel like the plane hit a speed bump while flying through perfectly clear skies. It is nothing more than a moving pocket of air, or up and down drafts, but as you have experienced, they can make a flight very rocky. Pilots, who call turbulence ''chop,'' classify it in four categories:

Light—bumpiness that doesn't affect altitude, or causes only slight, erratic changes in altitude. Passengers may feel a slight strain against their seat belts. Food can be served and people can walk around easily.

Moderate—like light turbulence, but with stronger intensity. The aircraft remains in control at all times. Airspeed will vary. Passengers strain against their seat belts, carry-on bags slide around and food service or walking is difficult.

Severe—large, abrupt changes in altitude and airspeed indications. The plane may be momentarily out of control. Passengers are thrust violently against their seats and seat belts, anything loose is tossed around and serving food or walking is impossible.

Extreme—tosses the plane around violently and makes the craft virtually impossible to control. Structural damage can result.

Clear air turbulence rarely puts a plane in jeopardy, though even moderate jolts can be so forceful that every year many people are hurt. Some end up in the hospital after being knocked over or thrown against the cabin walls or onto the floor. In December 1997, on a flight over the Pacific Ocean, one United Airlines flight hit clear air turbulence so severe that a passenger was killed, and the plane was scrapped by United. Children are especially vulnerable to these kinds of injuries—lap babies in particular. The best way to protect yourself is to wear your seat belt at all times and make sure all children are buckled in, especially infants. This is one ''see no evil'' you can do something about.

CHAPTER NINETEEN

When You Have to Fight

I have seen millionaire businessmen haggle over the price of a tie, and mothers engage in mortal combat over the hottest, must-have toy for Christmas or Hanukkah. Folks buying a used car take it to AAA mechanics and get underneath to take a look themselves. I have seen Department of Transportation and FAA employees argue bitterly over a few hundred dollars of year-end bonus money. Yet virtually everyone is struck dumb and afraid to fight when air safety is in question. Why? Most people have the same answer: "If the airline wasn't safe, they wouldn't allow it to fly." But who is "they"? Most people mean the government. But in a nation so mistrustful of government that more people believe in UFOs than in the Social Security system, it makes no sense that millions leave their health, safety and rights as passengers to chance, to the government or to the airlines. All you need are the regulations, rules and other pertinent facts at your fingertips. Regrettably, some airport staff, airline representatives, crews and flight attendants have no idea what the laws and regulations are, and will warn complaining passengers that their suggestions violate FAA regulations just to shut them up.

This chapter in short summary form will tell you what the laws are, and what your rights are. Where relevant, I have cited the airlines' own rules or the Code of Federal Regulations under Title 14—the Department of Transportation's aviation economic and consumer rules. Rip these pages out if you must (if it's your book) and carry them around with you. Laminate them. Use them to stand up for yourself. You will help bring about changes that in the long run will better ensure your safety and security.

First, two important rules to always follow:

SCHIAVO'S RULE 1

➤ *Always write down the name of the personnel who advised you of the airline's approval, denial or policy that you sought. On countless occasions airline personnel have asked me: "Who told you that?" When I had a name, date and the facts of the conversation, I won the debate. When I did not, I lost. That's because it is often impossible to get the same answer twice from reservations agents, counter agents, gate agents or flight attendants. The reason for the confusion is obvious—the FAA has failed to create certain necessary and reasonable policies, leaving the airlines room to freelance. And freelance they do.*

SCHIAVO'S RULE 2

➤ *Vote with your purse strings. If a plane is shabby and the personnel are unprofessional and uninformed, what do you think that says about the airline? Use your common sense. Is saving $20 on a ticket worth encouraging fly-by-night operations? "They" are not going to make this decision for you. "They've" already admitted as much in the aftermath of the ValuJet disaster.*

Here are the essential facts. Use them to protect yourself, your family and your employees. Use them to force the changes needed in the industry that "they" have failed to make.

BOOKING, BUMPING, CODE SHARES AND EQUIPMENT CHANGES

BOOKING/TICKETS (14 CODE OF FEDERAL REGULATIONS SECTION 253)

Airlines must disclose any code-share arrangements, or whether another airline will be flying you for any portion of your trip. Ask them. (14 CFR 399.88)

Tickets must state on their face any refund restrictions, penalties or fare increases. (14 CFR 253.7)

You can get a refund if the airline offers a lower fare after you purchased your ticket, if you do not make changes to your itinerary, and you meet the requirements of the new fare (advance purchase, minimum stay). Airline Rule 1: Guaranteed Price Rule.

Airlines reserve the right to decline to issue a refund if the reduced fare is for a limited period of time (unfortunately just about all reduced fares). Airline Rule 1.

You do not have to pay any fare increases once you purchase your ticket (and make no changes). Airline Rule 1.

Airlines will not replace lost tickets at the check-in counter. You will have to buy a new ticket. Airline practice, not a federal regulation.

Apply for a refund of the lost ticket, but expect to pay a processing fee. If the ticket is never used, the airline will usually refund your money.

The FAA does not prohibit the transfer of tickets from one person to another. The airlines can change the name on the ticket if they want to.

BUMPING AND OVERBOOKING (14 CFR 250)

Carriers cannot bump people involuntarily unless they first ask for volunteers. (14 CFR 250.2b) They cannot designate volunteers by handing out vouchers. Passengers must have the choice of being a volunteer. (250.2b(a))

If an insufficient number of people volunteer, the carrier can deny boarding to other passengers. (250.2b(b))

If you volunteer, your compensation is determined by the carrier. (Airline Rule 245)

The airlines must tell passengers in advance what they

are offered as denied boarding compensation—like a ticket voucher or money. (250.2b(b))

If you are bumped, you are entitled to comparable arrangements—jet service for jet service, for example—with a confirmed reservation at no extra charge. (250.1) You get no choice of airlines or equipment. An airline can offer noncomparable transportation (a prop plane in place of a jet, a bus instead of a plane) but it must take you to your final destination. (250.5) You can refuse and get a "denied boarding compensation" equal to 200 percent of the value of the remaining flight coupons to your next stopover or, if none, to your final destination, with a maximum of $400.

If bumped and rerouted, and you reach your final destination within two hours of your original domestic schedule or within four hours of your original international schedule, the airline has to pay the cost of your remaining ticket, or $200, whichever is less.

If bumped and you arrive at your domestic destination over two hours late or your international destination over four hours late, then the airline has to pay double the one-way cost of your remaining tickets, or $400, whichever is less.

Bumping rules apply only to jets with sixty or more seats.

Carriers can offer a 200 percent compensation and walk away. They have no obligation to offer you compensation and get you on the next flight.

You have a confirmed reservation if you have a ticket or are in the computer's Passenger Name Record. (250.1) (Of course you still need your ticket to actually *use* the reservation to board a plane, but you have the seat if you are in the computer.)

The rules do not apply to international flights from foreign ports or between two foreign ports. They do apply to international flights leaving the U.S. However, being downgraded or upgraded does not count as bumping—you are still on your flight. Carriers cannot make you pay for an involuntary upgrade, but they do have to refund the difference in the ticket price for a downgrade (first class to coach). (250.6(c))

CHANGE OF EQUIPMENT

Airlines can change equipment as they see fit. All you get is "comparable" arrangements (a jet for a jet ticket— but they can choose which jet). (250.1)

DELAYS, DIVERSIONS AND CANCELLATIONS

Airlines divide cancellations, delays or misconnections into two groups: Force Majeure Events (things that happen that are beyond their control, which includes weather) and Schedule Irregularities (delays, schedule changes, cancellation not due to weather). (Airline Rule 240.)

For Force Majeure Events, you will probably get confirmed on another flight, but airlines don't have to do this—all they have to do is give you a refund. (Airline Rule 240.)

For Schedule Irregularities, airlines offer you another flight—you can demand a different flight on another airline, even if only first class is available. If alternative travel is not acceptable, all you get is a refund. (Airline Rule 240.)

Airlines are not required to give you an airline-paid hotel room if the delay is due to a Force Majeure Event (weather). However, for Schedule Irregularities, most major carriers give you one night's lodging if you are diverted and the delay is over four hours, but they do not have to. (Airline Rule 240.)

Airlines are not required to give meal vouchers, phone calls or other such amenities, but many do for delays or diversions. (Airline Rule 240.)

Every airline is different. Among the majors, Delta and America West are most lenient with hotels, others with food and other courtesies. Even within a carrier's rules, airline personnel have leeway. Ask, cite Rule 240 and you may receive. Do not expect much if the cancellation or diversion is due to weather.

If diverted, whatever the reason, carriers are required to get you to your original destination.

Some discount carriers have no inter-airline ticket exchange agreements with other airlines. So, if your flight is canceled other airlines will not honor your ticket as they would with other major carriers.

GETTING OFF

You may be able to get off a plane if the cabin door is still open and the plane has not pushed back from the gate. In the future, this may change with increased security measures.

Once the plane has pushed back, it is up to the pilot whether to return to let passengers off the plane.

On a domestic flight the carriers do not have to take your luggage off the plane if you get off, and most will not. (But, that may change with increased security—no one wants to be on a plane with unaccompanied bags.) On an international flight, the bags have to come off if you are not on the plane.

BAGGAGE (14 CFR 254)

File a claim immediately for lost luggage and keep copies of the claim. Some carriers have very short windows for filing a claim and the claim must be in writing. For example, America West and Continental require a claim to be filed within four hours (Airline Rules 240 and 95), Northwest's and TWA's limit is twenty-four hours (Airline Rule 95). Bottom line: file the claim before you leave the airport.

The carriers' maximum liability for luggage lost or damaged on a domestic flight is $1,250 per passenger. Airlines are not prohibited from paying more, either. On international flights, it is $9 per pound of luggage. You can buy insurance from the airline for increased baggage coverage when you check in for your flight. The airlines will pay the depreciated value of your possessions.

Most bags are eventually found. Compensation for delayed bags varies widely from nothing, to whatever is reasonably necessary (like a new suit, shoes, shirt, toiletries and coat). Ask (Airline Rules 190, 230 or 95).

Many discount airlines do not transfer luggage to connecting flights with other airlines. They save money; you carry the bags. This is more often the case on international flights because of Customs (going from an international to a domestic flight) or lack of airline agreements.

There is no government regulation that limits your number of carry-on bags, only an FAA regulation that requires airlines to safely stow all carry-ons. (14 CFR 121.589.)

CHILDREN

A child safety seat does not count as one of your pieces of carry-on or checked luggage on the major carriers. Neither does a diaper bag on Continental. (Airline Rule 190.)

You can carry onboard a child safety seat (without buying a ticket for the child that goes with it) if there is space available. (Airline Rule 190 and new airline practice announced in 1997. The FAA may make this a rule.)

There is no regulation requiring adults to place lap babies on the floor in the event of an emergency landing.

No law prohibits the use of an infant sling or Snugli carrier. These strap an infant to an adult's chest (not to the seat of the plane). I have used one on takeoff and landing and in bumpy flights when my babies were not in safety seats.

Children may travel alone at age five, but only on non-stop flights until the age of eight. Direct flights also qualify, but many of these end up requiring a change of plane, so they are unwise for children eight and under. (Airline Rule 50.)

Airlines permit children aged eight to eleven to make connections. (Airline Rule 50.)

After age twelve, children are no longer considered unaccompanied minors. (Airline Rule 50.)

Airlines may charge extra fees for unaccompanied children, such as for connecting flights (currently $30). (Airline Rule 50.)

Request a seat for the child near a flight attendant station.

A child flying alone pays a full adult fare. (Airline Rule 50.)

Booster seats or harness or vest-type child restraints that fasten a child to the airline seat are banned by federal law. (14 CFR Sections 91.107 and 121.311, among others.)

DISABLED PASSENGERS (14 CFR 382)

Carriers cannot refuse to board passengers on the basis

of disability, limit the number of disabled people per flight
or require advance notice of a disabled traveler.

You are entitled to carry a wheelchair on board if it
will fit and can be stowed, and displace other carry-on
luggage (but planes with closets and places where it will
fit are getting rare). Wheelchairs do *not* count as carry-
on baggage.

You cannot sit in an emergency exit row.

SICK PASSENGERS

Airlines have sole discretion over whether to board a
noticeably sick passenger. Some airline personnel may
consider advanced pregnancy as "sickness." Bring a doctor's note.

HUNGRY PASSENGERS

Airlines are not required to serve food—at all.

No law prevents you from bringing food on board, except the federal law that requires items be safely stowed
on takeoff and landing.

AIRPORTS

Names of international airports that fail U.S. security
standards are posted at airports, usually near metal detector
stations or ticket counters.

Do not fly airlines from countries that fail or receive
only a conditional rating on the FAA reviews of foreign
countries' safety standards (see pages 304–308).

PETS

Passengers have no legal right to carry pets into passenger cabins. Airlines that allow them require they be in a
cage that fits under the seat in front of *you*. You may
have to make advance reservations and pay a fee. (Airline
Rule 190.)

Animals ride in sections of cargo holds that are pressurized and climate controlled but only during flight. You
need advance arrangements and have to pay a fee. (Airline
Rule 190.)

You may need a letter from your veterinarian certifying
the animal's fitness to travel. Check with the airline.

PASSENGER ELECTRONICS

The FAA has not yet acted to ban cellular phones, but the Federal Communications Commission has—no use while airborne. Some airlines have rules banning the use of computers and other personal electronics; it is up to the airlines, and you must obey the orders of the flight crew. At least one airline (Quantas) has complained to Boeing that laptops inflight interfered with the plane's controls.

INTERFERING WITH THE FLIGHT CREW/ENDANGERING PASSENGERS/THREATS—REAL OR JOKING

Do not even consider it. Such actions are federal crimes, punishable by fine, imprisonment or even death if someone is killed as a result of your activities.

CHAPTER TWENTY

Silencing the Watchdog

After I resigned my position as Inspector General at the Department of Transportation, the report on airport security that my office had readied for the Secretary, the White House and Congress was suppressed. It didn't matter that the decision had already been made not to classify the report. It was buried for several weeks, until after the Democratic National Convention. When it was finally issued, all the incriminating information about the FAA had been blacked out, including the failure rates and the FAA's response to our findings. That was a first.

Another report that my office was preparing on FAA inspections was also killed. My former staff had documented that many of the same problems that plagued FAA inspections when we examined them in 1990–91 continued in 1996. The 1996 draft report was critical of the FAA because the agency had not made improvements in the terrible inspections system we had previously uncovered. Even though Ray DeCarli, the Assistant Inspector General for Audit, had already testified to Congress about this report, it was not issued.

The Inspector General's investigation of FAA early-retirement buyout abuse was suspended, and turned over to the FAA to handle. Todd Zinzer, the Assistant Inspector

General for Investigations, had worked very hard to put together many of these cases, and the U.S. Department of Justice was already pursuing them. That decision was, as they say, made above his rank.

Larry Weintrob, the Deputy Assistant Inspector General for Audit, had written a magazine article about the importance of the Inspector General's office taking the findings of its investigations to the public. I had approved the article and it was due to be published. Then Larry was forbidden to publish the article.

The Deputy Inspector General, Mario A. Lauro, Jr., resigned.

Inspector General employees were barred from talking to the press.

The Inspector General's office determined it would no longer get involved in Department of Transportation or FAA policy issues, despite the fact that the Inspector General's Act says that is one of the office's purposes.

Safety issues were once again beyond the scope of the Inspector General's office.

For over a year, no new Inspector General was appointed. Finally, a new Inspector General was nominated in 1997. The Acting Inspector General (borrowed from another government agency) was not retained.

The new Inspector General, Ken Mead, was someone I knew and had worked with when he did aviation issues for the General Accounting Office. Occasionally we had tried a "divide and conquer" strategy—his office taking part of an issue and my office the other part. But reforming the FAA seemed impossible.

Midway into my tenure in 1993, Ken, Mario A. Lauro, Jr., Ray DeCarli, and I sat in my office a couple of weeks before Christmas. The FAA was again trying to dodge some troubling reports and a warning to the President of the United States that aviation safety and the FAA were the greatest weakness of the Department of Transportation. We were brainstorming ideas of how to break through the bureaucracy.

"Well, then," I said, "I will simply embarrass the FAA into action. We will make it public."

"You can't embarrass the FAA," Ken said.

"Safety has been compromised, but not once has the FAA ever admitted that anything has compromised safety," I grumbled.

We posed various scenarios of problems, but in every instance someone had an example of aviation malfunction that had actually happened, such as losing engines, inflight shutdowns, uncommanded rolls, near misses, and landing gear collapses, and in every instance the FAA always maintained safety was never compromised.

In late 1997, there were two curious press releases from the Department of Transportation. The OIG and the FAA would be conducting investigations together, first in aviation safety areas and then in hazardous materials cargo on planes. This new togetherness does not bode well for aviation safety, given the FAA's reluctance to find anything a problem. We had tried this joint investigation idea once, on the 1996 security report, and the FAA tried to warn airports and airlines in advance to get compliance up during our review, whitewash our findings, and hide our report through classification. The Inspector General statute requires independence; let's hope they find the fortitude to use it.

I have never doubted that safety was an entirely appropriate arena for the Inspector General. If anyone else did, their uncertainty should have been allayed in November 1996, when the NTSB held hearings on the ValuJet tragedy.

FAA officials admitted then that they had investigated ValuJet the February before the Everglades crash only to avoid being embarrassed by the Office of the Inspector General. My decision to send Larry Weintrob to Atlanta and look into ValuJet's problems myself "was the catalyst" for the FAA's inspection of ValuJet that same month, an agency maintenance manager had told the NTSB. At the time, hearings were coming up in Congress, and the FAA did not want to be outstripped by the Inspector General's office.

"[My boss] said, 'We have to get real sharp real fast on ValuJet,'" the FAA maintenance manager explained at the hearings. He was ordered to prepare a confidential report. He used existing FAA inspection and safety summaries of ValuJet, not secret or previously unknown information. Yet another of his managers, the FAA official who should have acted on his findings, told the NTSB hearings that he never saw the document and knew nothing about the extent of safety lapses at ValuJet until after the Everglades accident.

Still more NTSB hearings brought another explanation. An FAA official said he'd gotten the grounding document in Washington, D.C., before the crash, but it had lain in his In box until after the crash—he just never got around to it.

The NTSB released transcripts of the cockpit voice recorder, and family members read about screams of anguish from their loved ones, the panicky questions of the flight attendants and the confused commands of the pilot. "Fire, fire, fire," the passengers shrieked as a flight attendant said, "We're completely on fire," and the pilot told the first officer, "We're losing everything." One man was said to have called his wife on his cellular phone. Immediately the screams and comments stopped—evidence, the NTSB believed, that many of the people had passed out or died of smoke inhalation as the doomed plane lost all its electrical systems and plunged more than 10,000 feet in less than four minutes.

The crash occurred after oxygen generators on the plane burst into flames. At the hearings, the NTSB revealed that an employee of SabreTech, a ValuJet contractor, had not known what the generators were and thought they were empty when they were loaded into the plane's cargo hold. SabreTech workers were on a seven-day work schedule to finish servicing three ValuJet planes. The contractor faced a $2,500-a-day penalty if the planes were late. And on the day the generators were shipped, SabreTech was scrambling to clean up its Miami facility because another potential airline client was coming by for a visit, and no ValuJet quality control people were on top of the situation. The FAA never inspected the operation.

At the hearings, the NTSB showed a videotape of tests done to re-create the fire. A lone oxygen generator was ignited, and over several minutes sparked a white-hot in-

ferno that produced thick black smoke and 3,000-degree
flames. Other oxygen generators exploded in the heat. The
test fire took long enough to blaze that NTSB investigators
theorized that the real plane might have started burning
even before it left the ground.

Throughout the NTSB hearings, the Office of the Inspector General offered no comment. The FAA had suc-
ceeded in silencing its watchdog—for now. Hopefully
safety will once again rise to the top of the agenda. We
may have to wait some time before the President appoints
agents of change. We may have to wait for another President. We may have to wait for another terrible crash.

Or you, the public, can refuse to wait. You can be the
agents of change. Demand for yourselves what you should
have had all along. Information and safety.

EPILOGUE

If We Really Want
Change . . .

More than just the FAA mandate must change to make
aviation more reliable and effective—the working culture
at the FAA must be radically reshaped. FAA officials must
change the way they think about the purpose of their jobs
and their relationship to the airline industry.

I have several ideas for bringing this about:

1. Give the NTSB more authority. The board should
   have the power to require changes, not just recommend them. Deadlines should be established for the
   implementation of NTSB recommendations that
   have been accepted. Better black boxes, next-gener-
   ation collision avoidance systems, fire-resistant interiors, smoke detection and fire suppression systems
   in cargo holds, and better airplane separation by Air
   Traffic Control are all items the NTSB requested
   years ago. While the FAA dragged its feet, more
   crashes occurred. If the FAA does not respond to
   NTSB recommendations or take acceptable action
   within a reasonable but established deadline—say,
   one year—then the NTSB, by majority vote of its
   board, should be empowered to promulgate new

rules and establish new regulations to address
safety shortcomings.

2. While we did get a change of several top management personnel at the FAA, including the administrator, they continue to waste precious assets and
time in failing to modernize Air Traffic Control, set
more stringent standards for pilots, install terminal
Doppler weather radar and provide airport security.
Congress mandated these programs and taxpayers
have paid for them. But passengers didn't get them.
Those in charge have proved they are not up to the
task and have pledged an even closer relationship
with the airlines and more secrecy. The leaders of
the FAA simply don't get it. Find some who do.

3. Redefine the FAA's Air Traffic Control organization—it's either government or a private business
enterprise. It cannot be both. Controllers cannot decide to strike like private employees and then expect
the protections of government personnel rules. Remove air traffic control from the FAA and make it
a quasi-governmental corporation.

4. Sharpen Congress's oversight of the FAA. After all,
Congress appropriated billions that the FAA wasted.
Responsible congressional committees were inept
and in many cases abdicated their responsibility for
the FAA and the aviation industry. If the committee
and subcommittee chairs do not provide good oversight, a new chairperson must be appointed.

5. Limit the influence of the airline lobby and special-
interest groups, or political action committees
(PACs). They have exploited and compromised the
aviation safety system. These groups should be prohibited from giving contributions to members of
Congress serving on aviation-related committees.
There is just too much at stake for even the appear-

ance of impropriety, as happens when Senator Carl
Levin and Congressman James Oberstar take contributions from Northwest Airlines while they sit on
aviation committees.

6. Require full disclosure of all industry and lobbying
   contacts with the FAA and with Congress, regardless of who initiates the contact. Already there is a
   disclosure requirement for the Department of Transportation to reveal when it has been lobbied. But
   this is a toothless tiger, and the law does not cover
   Congress, where just as much lobbying occurs.
   Every contact should be disclosed in a database
   available to the public. These are our public servants and they are being compromised. Such a mandatory requirement would have disclosed the
   contact by lobbyists on behalf of ValuJet with Congress and the office of the Secretary of Transportation at a time when ValuJet was under scrutiny—
   but well before the Everglades crash.

7. Stop treating the Secretary of Transportation position as a second-class Cabinet post. The country
   holds its breath to see who will be appointed Secretary of State or Defense, but Transportation is often
   a dumping ground for presidential cronies. That in
   part is why you get shocking, shameful responses
   like, ''I did not know,'' or ''They did not tell me,''
   when problems are revealed and political fixes for
   safety lapse.

8. Give aviation industry employees whistle-blower
   protection to eliminate the fear of reprisal in the
   FAA and in the aviation industry if they report
   safety shortcomings. Government employees already have protection; the other part of aviation
   safety should have it, too.

9. Block the revolving door. Stop senior FAA employees and their industry counterparts from moving freely between one another's jobs. Strengthen and lengthen the prohibitions already in place which require a former employee to wait one year before appearing back at his old department.

10. Scrutinize airline work rules so that we never again have a situation like ValuJet's encouraging pilots and others to fly when safety and prudence say they should not take off.

11. Expand the safety data available to the public. Passengers need to know more than on-time arrival rates and raw numbers of accidents and incidents. Revealing safety violation rates for airlines would level the playing field. Right now the public cannot get meaningful information. The FAA still refuses to make any safety comparisons, even internally. How then does it do its job?

12. Stop extending the life of aged planes. At some point, planes are simply too old to survive the strain of regularly scheduled passenger service. Force their retirement. Thirty years is definitely too old. Get the cutoff at twenty-five years and start chipping away from there.

13. Post at airports the FAA list of countries with inadequate or conditional safety oversight. Already the list of countries with inadequate *security* is posted at airports. The safety list should be posted next to it. While we're at it, let's also add the list of countries that require passengers to be sprayed with pesticides.

14. Adopt new passenger rights. If, for example, a passenger declines to travel because of severe weather or a worrisome condition of the craft, he should have the right to immediately reuse his ticket or get a refund. You can take a suitcase back to the store where you bought it if you discover the latch does not work, but you cannot take your plane ticket back if you discover duct tape on the plane door and decide that is not for you.

15. Give children their right to safety. Require airlines to make child safety seats available or make reasonable accommodations for parents to bring their own. In the event of an emergency, throwing kids on the floor with the carry-on baggage is unconscionable; and since there is NO evidence to document its safety, this kind of action is tantamount to criminal negligence by the FAA and any airline that promotes it.

16. Get serious about FAA inspections and oversight. Foreign inspections are nonexistent. Domestic inspections are useless because of the slapdash manner in which many are conducted, and the lack of meaningful tracking, targeting and follow-up. The FAA must either make inspections effective or stop squandering our money and trust and let passengers know that in the aviation industry it is "buyer beware."

17. Get tough with our foreign counterparts. We should not allow planes to land in the U.S. if they do not have comparable safety oversight in their own country. By saying no, we will force improvement. That will include eliminating the State Department from decisions about airline safety. As it stands now, the State Department weighs in on aviation safety decisions by asking the FAA to go soft on some countries, ignoring safety for diplomatic or balance-of-trade reasons. One country that leaps to mind is Greece—which found itself on the security

warning list. After Greece protested, diplomacy in-
tervened and the warning was rescinded.

18. Change the focus of the FAA. Gone should be the
old cost-benefit rule that it is cheaper to have a
crash or two than to fix a costly problem. Empha-
size crash survivability to passengers, rather than
refusing to mention the possibility of a crash. Make
passengers an informed part of the safety team. Let
travelers practice opening emergency over-wing
emergency exits on mock-ups in airports. Put smoke
hoods on board, not just life vests, and teach people
how to use them. Give the public a say in new
regulations. Construct planes with flameproof interiors and ample exits—items that will help prevent
accidents in the first place, and limit casualties if a
tragedy cannot be stopped.

19. Remove the oversight of airport and airline security
from the FAA. They do not do a good job of it
anyway, and security is better performed by law
enforcement. It belongs under the supervision of the
FBI or other enforcement agency. One of the first
things the FBI would do would be to require full
background checks of all personnel in secure areas
of the airport, and that includes all flight crew personnel. A secondary benefit of this transfer of func-
tion would be the elimination of the FAA's ability
to withhold from the American people much of the
information about safety and security it tries to keep
secret. Safety is not a secret.

20. Airports should not be afterthoughts in the aviation
safety triad. The design of our future airports is
every bit as important as our airplanes and airlines.
We must not tolerate ill-equipped and dangerous
airports.

21. The independence of the NTSB is vitally important but is being compromised by two insidious trends. First, the NTSB is hiring personnel and getting board members from the FAA. Since the FAA is often at fault in aviation crashes (over 1,000 deaths are attributed in whole or part to the FAA in the last decade), hiring FAAers is an unconscionable conflict. Forbid the NTSB to hire FAAers. Second, the NTSB must rely on industry to sort out many of the causes of air crashes, including many if not most where the very entity deciding what or who caused the crash will be the entity paying out the claims of the victims. Also, by looking for others on whom to pin the blame, precious time is wasted and in some cases, another crash occurs. The NTSB needs to develop more expertise and independence.

22. When a new airport is built or an existing airport is expanded, often the airport authority or city or county running the airport includes in the bonds and financing a percentage for the arts, such as 2 percent or 5 percent for the arts. Some may find that interesting or amusing, but it does nothing for our safety as passengers. I frequently heard Secretary Peña and his chief of staff Ann Bormolini brag about the money they set aside for art in the Denver Airport. How much did they set aside for safety? Millions went into a fund to buy "art" for the airport. Personally, I would rather see a plain airport wall with a great security system imbedded in it. An airport tower with a computer that works rather than a sculpture (usually indecipherable anyway) in the passenger lounge. For every piece of stupid art I see at an airport, I ask myself, "How much of my airport safety money went into *that?*"

I would prefer to see local schoolchildren's hand-drawn pictures about airport safety or their dreams of becoming a pilot, flight attendant, airport rescue personnel or firefighter, or even an airline president. How about setting aside money to go into a safety research fund? After all, almost all airline crashes happen at or near the airport, and with every new airport expansion or new airport, the airport contributes to the congestion and increased safety issues. Five percent for the arts? Ten percent for safety. The money should go into a research fund under the auspices of NASA's aviation safety research, starting with aging aircraft issues, a huge gap in our aviation safety knowledge. Let's prove twenty-five-year-old planes are safe *before* we let passengers board them.

23. Require airlines to post just inside the door of the plane—the door passengers use to board—the age of the plane (the date the plane first went into service), the date of the last major service checks (such as C and D checks) and waivers pertaining to that aircraft, and the last FAA inspection of the plane. Such a disclosure would be a powerful incentive to retire old planes and avoid getting waivers for safety and maintenance.

24. Airlines with a past should not be able to hide under new identities. The government requires disclosure of code shares so you can know who you are really flying with. Airlines should be required to disclose their past names and identities, for example, AirTran (formerly ValuJet), for a period of three years, because the most dangerous year for new carriers are years two and three, according to a government study.

25. It is time to dislodge air safety research from the FAA. Air safety should be managed—at least for the next few years, to see if the FAA can recover, which I doubt—by a troika: NASA, the FAA and the U.S. Air Force. All conduct and have funding for aviation safety research, and we need the combined talents of all three agencies to stave off the

Boeing and NASA prediction of a crash a week.
We have a drug czar, we just may need an aviation
safety czar. If we canot convince Congress to do
something about safety, how about preserving the
economic preeminence of the U.S. aviation industry? That is clearly what is at stake with deteriorat-
ing safety.

All passengers should join in doing something about
safety. Don't fly on carriers at the bottom of the safety
list; avoid old planes; *ask* when you book your reservation
what kind of a plane you'll be riding on, and ask for other
choices if it's a bad airline or an old plane. Complain
mightily to the FAA, NASA, the Inspector General, Congress and the NTSB about problems you observe on airlines or at airports. Call the media. Get a smoke hood and
carry it. Complain about passengers who appear inebriated
when they board or who are having too much to drink on
the plane. Take your child safety seat on board and if you
can't afford another seat, demand that empty seat on the
plane. Never fly foreign carriers from countries that do
not meet International Civil Aviation Organization (ICAO)
standards. Buy your ticket in the U.S., fly on a major U.S.
carrier; if you have several flight segments, originate the
flights in the U.S. and charge your tickets on a U.S. credit
card. You'll have quadrupled your rights as a passenger.
Ask about the airlines' policy of screening domestic baggage and cargo. They will have no answer or have to lie.
Make them uncomfortable. Start asking about air quality
on planes and cleanliness (remember they don't give you
fresh air or clean blankets, they rarely change the little
paper pillow cases and never disinfect the tray tables—
and they don't have to). Join in a day of shaming the
airlines into safety. Protective breathing devices cost just
pennies a passenger, smoke and fire detection and suppression systems, just thirty cents, yet the airlines and our
government said it was too much money. Let's all pick
one day—say May 11 every year—and on that day, if you
are flying, hand back (nicely, remember the flight attendants are on your side) your thirty-cent can of soda and
your bag of peanuts that cost a few pennies and say, "My

life and yours are worth more than that. Put my few cents' worth toward safety.''

There is no *right* to fly. It is not in the Constitution, the Bill of Rights, or the Amendments. Flying is a privilege to be engaged in only by those who are properly trained, have safe equipment and scrupulously abide by the law. As an Assistant U.S. Attorney, I prosecuted a pilot who landed his ultralight plane in a shopping center. Misguided operators like him often howl that it is their God-given right to fly. If so, God would have given them huge wings, feathers and bird brains. Well, I might concede the last point to them.

Often I wonder whether Washington has abdicated decision-making to the interest groups who ply their trades in the halls of Congress. Influence-peddling has gotten so bad that there are businesses that are paid to gin up fake public opinion. They send massive volumes of letters and place thousands of phone calls to members of Congress, all to create the impression that Americans are clamoring for one policy when, in fact, they may want the opposite. They call this practice ''Astro-Turfing'' as opposed to grassroots. Unless the flying public is heard, the aviation industry will go as far and as high as it wants without having to consider public interest or public safety. They assume the public will never know about this Icarus agenda.

Flight is a public trust, to be engaged in by those who can do it responsibly. People who never set foot in an airport have rights and concerns affected by flight. Thus the right to decide about aviation safety extends far beyond those with a plane or a pilot's license, or the FAA. The President, Congress, the FAA, and the airlines must always remember that. Otherwise, safety promises made after a crash disappear into thin air.

I hope the promises made after the ValuJet and TWA tragedies in the summer of 1996 are kept. As of January 1998, we are still waiting. Congress finally partially eliminated the FAA's dual mandate—giving the agency its best opportunity yet to redirect its priorities and focus on safety. Some of the long-serving officials who for decades conducted themselves as aviation groupies rather than regulatory authorities were forced out of their jobs. The FAA promised to act on several long-standing NTSB safety recommendations—meaning rudders on Boeing 737s will finally be inspected, fire detection systems will be installed in cargo compartments, fuel tanks will be made less explosive and better black boxes will tell what went wrong, but we are still awaiting the rulings.

None of this would have happened without the media scrutiny and the intense outpouring of public shock, grief and anger following the ValuJet and TWA crashes. That's sad, but in the end, it means that air safety has been lifted to the top of the national agenda. I'm happy to see it there. Ultimately, only passengers have the power to force change. The flying public must use common sense and its purchasing power to keep the FAA and the airlines on track. So speak up. Speak up so that rather than flying blind, you'll be flying safe.

HELP YOURSELF

This book is not intended to be your only source of information about aviation safety. Once you've read it, you may want to do further research or to check periodically on the airlines you fly. You may want updates on State Department warnings about foreign airlines or airports. You may be interested in the age of the aircraft you are about to board. There are a number of useful resources that allow you to help yourself. Here are a few telephone numbers and Internet addresses:

DEPARTMENT OF TRANSPORTATION TRAVEL ADVISORY.
1-800-221-0673; recorded information on any threats to security at U.S. or foreign airports.

DEPARTMENT OF TRANSPORTATION WEB SITE.
http://www.dot.gov; news, facts, statistics, laws, biographies of key personnel, even job openings.

FAA WEB SITE.
http://www.faa.gov, or access through DOT site; news and more.

FEDERAL AVIATION ADMINISTRATION CONSUMER HOTLINE.
1-800-322-7873; FAA rankings, reviews of aviation safety

standards in foreign countries. Report consumer complaints to this telephone number, too, but they have no safety information. (To check on the FAA rating of a foreign country, it's faster to check on the Internet at http://www.faa.gov/avr/iasaxls.htm.)

FEDERAL AVIATION ADMINISTRATION SAFETY HOT LINE.
1-800-255-1111; tip line for reporting safety violations.

FEDERAL AVIATION ADMINISTRATION PUBLIC AFFAIRS.
202-267-8521. You get a live person on the line.

DEPARTMENT OF TRANSPORTATION OFFICE OF INSPECTOR GENERAL.
1-800-424-9071; hotline for reports on all facets of transportation, including the aviation industry and the FAA.

NATIONAL TRANSPORTATION SAFETY BOARD.
http://www.ntsb.gov; summaries of 35,000 crashes and the NTSB's annual safety wish list.

DEPARTMENT OF STATE OVERSEAS CITIZENS SERVICES OFFICE.
202-647-5225 or http://www.state.gov; warnings issued for countries to which you may be traveling, or emergencies abroad while traveling.

DEPARTMENT OF TRANSPORTATION BUREAU OF TRANSPORTATION STATISTICS.
202-366-3282 or http://www.bts.gov; data on airline performance, traffic, revenue miles.

LANDINGS.
http://www.landings.com; lots of data on aviation, including one program that allows you to look up an airplane by its tail number or a fleet by its airline. The Federal Aviation Regulations appear here as well, plus news and more.

FLYTE TRAX.
http://www.weatherconcepts.com; select Flyte Trax (a free
option) and you can trace the whereabouts of any plane.
Your screen will show a map with the plane's route, its
location and expected arrival time.

#42 for N-amel

OFFICIAL AIRLINE GUIDE.
— TO send Procure
1-800-342-5624;. diagrams of plane seating arrangements,
flight schedules, equipment rosters and code-sharing details. They now have a website: http://www.oag.com.

AIRLINE RULES GUIDE/AIRFARE REPORT.
1-800-218-9441; rules, by major airlines, concerning passenger rights and courtesies (such as which carrier gives
you a hotel room and meals).

AIR TRAVELERS ASSOCIATION.
202-686-2870 or 1-800-827-2755; member enrollment and
to get the airline safety report card 1-800-247-7233, or
http://www.1800airsafe.com. They also provide other member services.

SMOKE HOODS.
Here are the ones that filter out carbon monoxide: EVAC
U8—Brookdale International (604) 324-3822 or 1-800-
459-3822; PARAT C— Drager Safety (412) 787-8383 or
1-800-922-5518; PLUS 10—Essex PB&R (618) 659-9070
or 1-800-296-7587.

CHAPTER NOTES

INTRODUCTION

Report of Efforts to Improve Airport Security, R9-FA-6-014, Department of Transportation Office of Inspector General, Department of Transportation, July 3, 1996.

Audit of Airport Security, R9-FA-3-105, Department of Transportation Office of Inspector General, September 20, 1993.

Summary, Discussion with FAA Southern Region Flight Standards Personnel on ValuJet, and Office of Inspector General, February 7, 1996.

Federal Aviation Act of 1958, Public Law 85-726.

Safety Issue Analysis, Low-Cost Carrier Safety Record, Safety Analysis Branch, Office of Accident Investigation, FAA, May 2, 1996.

Management Discussion and Analysis of Financial Condition and Results of Operations, ValuJet Airlines.

Department of Defense Commercial Airlift Review Committee Report on ValuJet Airlines, August 25, 1995.

Hearings before the House Aviation Subcommittee, June 25, 1996.

Handbook of Airline Economics (McGraw-Hill, 1995).

Association of Flight Attendants chronology of ValuJet's safety record.

ValuJet Inspections, 1993–1996, Department of Transportation Office of Inspector General, Assistant Inspector General for Auditing.

Wall Street Journal, November 6, 1985.

Report Summarizing ValuJet Airline's Accident, Incidents and Enforcement History, ValuJet VJ6A465W, Atlanta, Ga., February 14, 1996.

FAA Service Difficulty Report, "Examples of ValuJet Planes with Chronic Maintenance Problems," DC-932-#901VJ, July 17, 1996.

U.S. News and World Report, June 24, 1996.

Memorandum on FAA Oversight of ValuJet from A. Mary Schiavo to Ann Bormolini, Chief of Staff, Department of Transportation, February 28, 1996.

Consent Order, in the matter of ValuJet Airlines and Department of Transportation Federal Aviation Administration, Atlanta, Ga., June 17, 1996.

Memorandum from inspectors, Federal Aviation Administration Atlanta Flight Standards District Office, to Lewis Jordan, ValuJet, February 29, 1996.

Memorandum from Rep. John J. Duncan Chairman, House Subcommittee on Aviation Safety, to members, June 20, 1996.

New York Times, June 4, 1994.

New York Times, March 29, 1996.

New York Times, January 11, 1995.

New York Times, January 10, 1997.

Nightline, ABC Television, May 13, 1996.

ABC, NBC and *CBS News,* and *Nightline,* various dates.

Cleveland Plain Dealer, May 19, 1996.

Cleveland Plain Dealer, April 11, May 14, June 12, 18, 19, 20, 23, July 29, August 23 and September 3, 1996.

Dallas Morning News, May 18, 1996.

Washington Post, June 19, 1996.

Washington Post, June 11, 1996.

Hearings before House Subcommittee on Aviation, June 25, 1996.

Hearings before House Transportation Aviation Committee, June 25, 1996.

Safety Recommendation, National Transportation Safety Board Chairman Jim Hall, to David Hinson, Administrator, Federal Aviation Administration, May 31, 1996.

Department of Transportation, Research and Special Programs Administration, May 24, 1996.

Letter to Lewis Jordan, ValuJet Airlines, from Patricia L. Thomas, FAA Chief, Air Carrier Fitness Division, June 21, 1996.

Letter of Retirement, Anthony Broderick, Associate Administrator for Regulation and Certification, June 17, 1996.

Aviation Week and Space Technology, various dates.

Aviation Daily, July 31, 1996.

Metro Dade Aviation Department.

Hearings before Senate Commerce, Science and Transportation Committee, August 1, 1996.

Transcript of Announcement by Lewis Jordan to ValuJet

employees, July 9, 1996, from "Association of Flight Attendants objections to ValuJet Airlines application to U.S. Department of Transportation."

Secretary of Transportation Federico Peña, press release, July 11, 1996: "Peña Voices Strong Support for Bill to Eliminate Dual Mandate."

"Department of Transportation Issues Final Order," *DOT News,* September 26, 1996.

"Department of Transportation Issues Show Cause Order" and "FAA Approves ValuJet Air Carrier Certificate," *DOT News,* August 29, 1996.

FAA Statement on ValuJet, *DOT News,* June 17, 1996.

Memo from the Federal Aviation Administration to the Department of Transportation Office of Inspector General, April 12, 1996.

FAA and DOT statements on ValuJet Charters, *FAA News,* December 18, 1996.

Low Cost Airline Service Revolution, Department of Transportation Report, April 1996.

DOT/FAA/RSPA Initiatives on Air Transportation of Hazardous Materials, *FAA News,* November 18, 1996.

FAA Responses to NTSB Recommendations on ValuJet, *FAA News,* November 18, 1996.

Schedules for Transportation Secretary Federico Peña, advance version and final version for February 27, 1996.

Newsweek, May 20, 1996.

Press Release from Senator Ben Nighthorse Campbell on Mesa Airlines, July 31, 1996.

Various NTSB Accident and Incident Reports.

CHAPTER ONE

Letter to United States Attorney General Richard Thornburgh, from Department of Justice U.S. Attorney for Eastern District of New York, Andrew J. Maloney, July 24, 1990.

Letter to Transportation Secretary Sam Skinner, from U.S. Attorney General Richard Thornburgh, August 2, 1990.

Federal Aviation Regulations for Pilots, September 1973.

Glamour Magazine, August 1975.

Alexander T. Wells, *Commercial Aviation Safety* (TAB Books/McGraw-Hill, 1991), and Alexander T. Wells, *Airport Planning and Management* (TAB Books/McGraw-Hill, 1992).

Business Week, September 16, 1996.

Letter from Chairman Jim Hall, National Transportation Safety Board, to David Hinson Administrator of the FAA, on ''Black Boxes,'' April 29, 1996.

Aviation Week and Space Technology, May 23, 1988.

New York Times, October 2, 1985.

Nightline, ABC Television, May 13, 1996.

Federal Aviation Act of 1958, Public Law 85-726.

National Transportation Safety Board Most Wanted List, 1996.

CHAPTER TWO

Flight International, November 22, 1995.

Flight Safety Foundation, http://rhytech.com:80/~fsf/president.html.

Letter to United States Attorney General Richard

Thornburgh, from Department of Justice U.S. Attorney for Eastern District of New York, Andrew J. Maloney, July 24, 1990.

Hotline Complaint on Travel Abuse, Department of Transportation Office of Inspector General, Department of Transportation, June 10, 1991.

Audit on the Controls Over Access to Aircraft for Free Transportation, Department of Transportation Office of Inspector General, AS-FA-60-004, February 20, 1996.

Aviation Daily, July 31, 1996.

New York Times, October 30, 1993.

CHAPTER THREE

Various FAA Air Worthiness Directives.

Report on the FAA Responsiveness to Suspected Aircraft Maintenance and Design Problems, Department of Transportation Office of Inspector General, April 15, 1994.

Various NTSB Accident and Incident Reports.

FAA Service Bulletin ATR72-27-1039, January 12, 1995.

NTSB Special Investigation Report, "Safety Issues Related to Wake Vortex Encounters" NTSB/SIR-94/01.

Aging Aircraft Safety Act of 1989.

Hearings before House Subcommittee on Aviation, September 17, 1991.

NTSB Most Wanted Transportation Safety Improvements, May 1996.

Letter from Chairman Jim Hall, National Transportation Safety Board, to David Hinson, Administrator of the FAA, on "Black Boxes," April 29, 1996.

NTSB Most Wanted List, Transportation Safety Improvements, Safety Issue: Flight Data Recorders-Expanded Parameters, February 22, 1995, and updated through April 26, 1996.

Revisions to Flight Data Recorder Rules, Notice of Proposed Rulemaking, 61 Federal Register 37144, July 16, 1996.

New York Times, April 28, 1993.

"FAA Implements New Wake Vortex Separation Standards," *DOT News,* August 16, 1996.

Various NTSB Accident and Incident Reports.

Various FAA Air Worthiness Directives.

Seattle Times, October 27–31, 1996.

World Airline News, November 18, 1996.

CHAPTER FOUR

Consent Order, in the matter of ValuJet Airlines, Department of Transportation Federal Aviation Administration, Atlanta, Ga., June 17, 1996.

Hearings before House Subcommittee on Aviation, Committee on Public Works and Transportation, February 6, 1992.

Hearings before House Subcommittee on Aviation, Committee on Public Works and Transportation, June 25, 1996.

General Accounting Office report before the House Subcommittee on Aviation, "Problems Persist in FAA Inspection Program," February 6, 1992.

Government Accounting Office report before the House Committee on Government Operations, "FAA Information Resources: Agency Needs to Correct Widespread Deficiencies," June 1991.

Airport Safety Improvement Act of 1990.

"Air Transport Industry Political Action Committee Contributors, January 1993 through March 1996; Democratic and Republican National Party Committees Transportation, Aerospace and Defense Industry Soft Money Donors of $50,000 or More, January 1995 through June 1996" (Common Cause).

Hearings before House Subcommittee on Oversight of Government Management and the District of Columbia, April 30, 1996.

Letter to United States Attorney General Richard Thornburgh, from Department of Justice U.S. Attorney for Eastern District of New York, Andrew J. Maloney, July 24, 1990.

Audit of Surveillance of Designated Mechanic Examiners, Department of Transportation Office of Inspector General, R9-FA-3-106, September 29, 1993.

Report on Survey of FAA Surveillance of Foreign-Manufactured Aircraft Parts, Department of Transportation Office of Inspector General, R0-FA-4-001, November 8, 1993.

Aviation Week and Space Technology, October 30, 1995.

Roll Call, November 9, 1995, and January 29, 1996.

CHAPTER FIVE

Business Week, June 10, 1996.

Flight Safety Foundation, 1957.

Hearings before the Senate Subcommittee on Oversight of Government Management and the District of Columbia,

May 24, 1995: "Aviation Safety: Do Unapproved Parts Pose a Safety Risk?"

List of Aviation Parts Seized from Around the World, Department of Transportation, Office of Inspector General.

Air Transport World, July 1994.

NTSB Bogus Parts List, August 1984 to September 1992.

Audit Report, Suspected Unapproved Parts Program, Department of Transportation Office of Inspector General, R4-FA-6-026, April 9, 1996.

Memorandum of Understanding between the Department of Transportation, Federal Aviation Administration, Office of Inspector General and the Federal Bureau of Investigation, unsigned, undated.

Hearings before House Subcommittee of the Committee on Appropriations, 1992.

Memorandum from A. Mary Schiavo, Office of Inspector General, to Deputy Secretary of Transportation, regarding OIG Investigation of Chromalloy, November 30, 1992.

Letter from FAA Assistant Chief Counsel for Enforcement Elliott Jacobson to Assistant U.S. Attorney Southern District of New York, December 1992.

Memorandum from FAA Administrator David Hinson to the Secretary of Transportation and Deputy Secretary, August 21, 1992, "Suspected Unapproved Parts."

Hearings before House Subcommittee of the Committee on Appropriations, 1994.

Aviation Daily, August 2, 1996.

FAA Advisory Circular 21-29, Detecting and Reporting Suspected Unapproved Parts, July 16, 1992.

Suspected Unapproved Parts Program Order #8120.10, September 28, 1993.

Replacement and Modification Parts; Enhanced Enforcement, 14 CFR 21, February 17, 1995.

"The Hotline," The Aeronautical Repair Station Association, March 1995.

Anthony Broderick, keynote remarks to Annual Repair Symposium, Aeronautical Repair Station Association, April 4, 1993.

Memorandum from Admiral J. W. Kime, Commandant, U.S. Coast Guard, November 29, 1993.

"DOT Today," Secretary's Awards, November 1992.

Flight International, August 21, 1996.

Condé Nast Traveller, March 1996.

Various DOT News Releases on Bogus Parts Cases, Indictments and Convictions, or Pleas Agreements.

FAA Briefing Memo for Rep. Frank Wolf on Bogus Parts Program, June 1996.

Ft. Worth Star-Telegram, August 26, 1994.

Los Angeles Times, December 15, 1996.

Newsday, February 29, 1996.

Aviation Week and Space Technology, January 27, 1996.

Department of Transportation Office of Inspector General memo on Price of Aircraft Parts, September 27, 1993.

FAA Proposed Memorandum of Understanding with the FBI and Department of Transportation Office of Inspector General.

NTSB Letter to Rep. Frank Wolf, June 14, 1996.

CHAPTER SIX

New York Times, December 21, 1995.

Hearings before Senate Subcommittee on Aviation, May 1, 1996.

Hearings before House Subcommittee of the Committee on Appropriations, April 23, 1996.

Federal Aviation Administration Authorization Act of 1994, Public Law 103–305, August 23, 1994.

Proposed Rules, Federal Register, February 26, 1996.

"Airport Revenue Protection Act of 1998," a proposal from Senator John McCain 3rd, May 20, 1996.

CHAPTER SEVEN

Hearings before the House Subcommittee on Transportation, March 1995.

Department of Transportation Press Release, November 17, 1995.

Department of Justice Press Release, November 15, 1995 and April 22, 1996.

Nightline, ABC Television, February 21, 1995 and March 30, 1995.

Report of Investigation Concerning the Federal Aviation Administration, "Gregory May and Related Training Issues," Department of Transportation Office of Inspector General.

Department of Transportation press release: "Former FAA Training Contractor Sentenced for Role in Fraud Scheme," April 23, 1996.

Analysis of FAA Personnel Actions Regarding the FAA Training Investigation.

New York Times, April 2, 1995.

CHAPTER EIGHT

USA Today, September 27, 1985.

New York Times, June 4, 1994.

Nightline, ABC Television, June 24, 1996.

Government Accounting Office Report to the House Committee on Government Operations: "FAA Information Resources: Agency Needs to Correct Widespread Deficiencies," June 1991.

Various NTSB Accident and Incident Reports.

New York Times, October 16, 1995.

Aviation System Capital Investment Plan, January 1996.

"An AAS Status Report," FAA Administrator David Hinson, March 3, 1994.

Review of Midway Data Submissions, Department of Transportation Office of Inspector General, February 24, 1992.

AAA Cites Worst ATC Centers, August 27, 1996.

General Accounting Office, testimony before the House Subcommittee on Transportation and Related Agencies, "Air Traffic Control: Uncertainties and Challenges Face FAA's Advanced Automated System," April 19, 1993.

Government Accounting Office Fact Sheet for Congressional Committees: "Air Traffic Control, Status of FAA's Modernization Program," April 1993.

Report on Advanced Automation System Program, AS-FA-4-007, Department of Transportation Office of Inspector General, March 3, 1994.

Instrument Flying Handbook, Department of Transportation, 1980.

Aviation System Capital Investment Plan, December 1991.

FAA Administrators Fact Book, "Safety," November 5, 1996.

Audit of Federal Aviation Administration Sponsored Higher Education Programs, AV-FA-3-010, Department of Transportation Office of Inspector General, May 19, 1993.

Audit of FAA Revitalization Pay Program, AS-FA-6-005, Department of Transportation Office of Inspector General, February 29, 1996.

Audit on the Controls Over Access to Aircraft for Free Transportation, AS-FA-60-004, Department of Transportation Office of Inspector General, February 20, 1996.

Department of Transportation press release: "Common Sense Personnel and Acquisition Management Reforms Adopted by FAA," March 28, 1996.

Audit on Management Controls Over Employee Relocations, AS-FA-6-001, Department of Transportation Office of Inspector General, October 27, 1996.

Report on Voluntary Separation Incentive Payments Departmentwide, R6-FA-6-009, Department of Transportation Office of Inspector General, February 9, 1996.

CHAPTER NINE

Government Accounting Office Report to the House Subcommittee on Aviation, "Aircraft Certification: New FAA Approach Needed to Meet Challenges of Advanced Technology," September 1993.

Computer Weekly, May 25, 1995.

Computer Weekly, June 1, 1995.

New York Times, August 28, 1996.

U.S. News and World Report, May 8, 1995.

Hearings before House Subcommittee on Aviation, September 17, 1991.

U.S. News and World Report, June 26, 1995.

New York Times, August 28, 1996.

The Seattle Times, October 27–31, 1996.

Hearings before the House Subcommittee on Aviation, September 17, 1991.

CHAPTER TEN

Secretary of Transportation Federico Peña, press release, July 11, 1996: ''Peña Voices Strong Support for Bill to Eliminate Dual Mandate.''

Report of Efforts to Improve Airport Security, R9-FA-6-014, Department of Transportation Office of Inspector General, July 3, 1996.

Audit of Airport Security, R9-FA-3-105, Department of Transportation Office of Inspector General, September 20, 1993.

Aviation Week and Science Technology, September 18, 1995.

Nightline and *ABC News,* ABC Television, June and July 1996.

Letter to Adrian Pfeffer, Station Manager, American Trans Air, O'Hare International Airport, Chicago, from FAA Federal Security Manager O'Hare International Airport Donald A. Slechta, January 29, 1996.

Letter from A. Mary Schiavo to President William J. Clinton, July 8, 1996.

Hearings before the Senate Committee on Commerce, Science and Transportation, July 17, 1996.

National Transportation Safety Board Comparison of U.S. Transportation Fatalities, Year 1994 vs. Year 1995.

FBI Explosives Unit-Bomb Data Center General Information Bulletin 95-2.

House Resolution 3539 as approved by the House and Senate, Title IV, Aviation Safety, Section 401: Elimination of Dual Mandate.

CHAPTER TWELVE

Federal Aviation Act of 1958, Public Law 85–726.

Airport and Airway Improvement Act of 1982, Title II, Section 201, Public Law 103-305 to amend the term of office of FAA Administrator, 1994.

General Accounting Office Report before the House Subcommittee on Aviation: "Problems Persist in FAA Inspection," February 6, 1992.

New York Times, August 4, 1996.

NTSB Memo: "FAA Is Contributing Factor in 241 Accidents," June 21, 1996.

CHAPTER THIRTEEN

Hearings before the House Subcommittee on Aviation, "Assuring the Safety of the Aging Airline Fleet," September 27, 1989 and October 10, 1989.

Various NTSB Accident and Incident Reports.

Various FAA Air Worthiness Directives.

CNN, November 22, 1996.

Aging Aircraft Safety Act of 1990.

Handbook of Airline Economics (McGraw-Hill, 1995).

Air Transport World, September 1994.

Ed Sternstein and Todd Gold, *From Takeoff to Landing* (Pocket Books, 1991).

Flight International, August 17, 1994.

Aerospace Propulsion, August 18, 1994.

New York Times, March 5, July 12 and September 12, 1989; May 2, 1994; November 2, 1996; January 10, 1997.

Collins/Jane's Civil Aircraft (HarperCollins, 1996).

William Berk and Frank Berk, *Guide to Airport Airplanes* (Plymouth Press, 1993 and 1996).

New York Times, February 25, 1989.

Association of Flight Attendants, November 1996.

Official Airline Guide, 1996.

Richard Taylor, *Understanding Flying* (Thomasson-Grant, 1992).

Handbook of Airline Economics (McGraw-Hill, 1996).

The Seattle Times, February 25, 1995; May 7 and 12, 1995; June 5, 12, 14, 1995; January 19, 1996; October 27–31, 1996; November 22, 1996; December 18, 1996; and January 2, 1997.

Vice President Al Gore on C-Span Television, January 16, 1997.

Allan Edwards, *Flights Into Oblivion* (Paladwr Press, 1993).

Karl Sabbagh, *Twentieth-Century Jet* (Scribners, 1996).

The Economist, January 11, 1997.

FAA Issues Air Worthiness Directive Affecting 737 Flight Procedures, *FAA News,* January 2, 1997.

Landings, via the Internet.

The Washington Post, January 16, 1997.

J.P. Airline—Fleets International (Bucher & Co., 1996–1997).

CHAPTER FOURTEEN

"Safe Skies for Tomorrow: Aviation Safety in a Competitive Environment," Office of Technology Assessment, 1988.

Federal Aviation Administration 90-Day Safety Review, September 16, 1996.

Memorandum from A. Mary Schiavo to Christopher A. Hart, FAA Assistant Administrator for System Safety, "Comments on FAA's Proposed Global Analysis and Information Network (GAIN)," June 10, 1996.

U.S. News and World Report, July 26, 1996 and November 14, 1994.

Wall Street Journal, July 24, 1996.

Washington Post, October 8, 1996.

Federal Aviation Administration Air Carrier Accident and Incident Data.

Department of Transportation Bureau of Transportation Statistics, "Air Carrier Traffic Statistics Monthly" for 1991–1995.

Washington Post, November 13, 1996.

New York Times, May 19 and July 23, 1993; February 24

and December 17, 1994; April 6, September 29, October 5, November 11, 13, and 18, 1996.

FAA Commuter Safety Rule, March 24, 1995; *Business and Commercial Aviation,* June 1995.

Government Accounting Office Report to House Aviation Subcommittee: "Start-Up Airlines," October 22, 1996.

Handbook of Airline Economics (McGraw-Hill, 1995).

FAA Administrator's Fact Book, "Safety," November 5, 1996.

Aviation Week and Space Technology, various, 1996.

Wall Street Journal, November 6, 1985.

FAA News press releases, various, 1996.

FAA Administrator's Fact Book, "Safety," October 31, 1996.

FBI Explosives Unit-Bomb Data Center General Information Bulletin 95-2.

Hearings before House Subcommittee on Aviation, September 27 and October 10, 1989.

Atlanta Constitution, June 20, 1996.

World Airline News, November 18, 1996.

NTSB Accident Reports, various, 1996.

14 Code of Federal Regulations Parts 107 and 108.

General Accounting Office Study: Aviation Safety, New Airlines Illustrate Long-Standing Problems in FAA's Inspection Program, October 1996.

Air Carrier Traffic Statistics Monthly, Bureau of Transportation Statistics, Volume 5, 1991–1995.

Safety Issue Analysis, Low Cost Air Carrier Safety Record, FAA Office of Accident Investigation, May 2, 1996.

Counts of Accident and Incident Data, Near Mid-Air Collisions, and Pilot Deviations, FAA, 1996.

USAir NASIP Report, March 19, 1993.

USA Today, November 13, 1996.

David Gero, *Aviation Disasters* (Patrick Stevens, Ltd., 1996).

Columbus Dispatch, November 24, 1996.

Cleveland Plain Dealer, December 10 and 28, 1995; April 28 and September 4, 1996.

Business Week, July 29, 1996.

Business and Commercial Aviation, June 1995 and October 1996.

Air Safety Week, August 12, 1996.

Aviation Daily, August 9, 1996.

FAA Responses to Various Freedom of Information Act Requests, 1996.

NTSB Annual Review of Accident Data PB 95-261723.

CHAPTER FIFTEEN

U.S. Flight Information Publication: "Airport/Facilities Directory," October 1996.

U.S. Flight Information Publication: "U.S. Terminal Procedures," October 1996.

Airport Facilities Directories, through December 5, 1996.

U.S. Terminal Procedures, through October 5, 1996.

Dateline, NBC Television, November 1996.

AAA Cities Worst ATC Centers, August 27, 1996.

New York Times, October 16, 1995 and March 23, 1996.

NTSB Air Accident Report, Delta Airlines L-1011-385-1, N726DA, Dallas/Fort Worth International Airport, August 15, 1985.

Report of Efforts to Improve Airport Security, R9-FA-6-014, Department of Transportation Office of Inspector General, July 3, 1996.

Audit of Airport Security, R9-FA-3-105, Department of Transportation Office of Inspector General, September 20, 1993.

Aviation Security Improvement Act of 1990.

Aviation Week and Space Technology, January 20 and 29, 1997.

Flight Guide Airport and Frequency Manual, Volumes 1, 2 and 3, 1996.

FAA Administrator's Fact Book, via the Internet.

U.S. News and World Report, June 26, 1995.

Nightline, ABC Television, June 24, 1996.

The Economist, January 11, 1997.

The Washington Post, August 29, 1996.

AIM/FAR (Airman Information Manual and Federal Aviation Regulations), (TAB/Aero Books, 1996).

NTSB Safety Study—Aviation Safety in Alaska, NTSB/SS-95/03.

NTSB Special Investigation Report—Air Traffic Control Equipment Outages, NTSB/SIR-96/01.

Terry Denham, *World Directory of Airline Crashes* (Haynes Publishing, 1996).

David Gero, *Aviation Disasters* (Haynes Publishing, 1996).

The Boston Globe, March 24, 1996.

Newsweek, July 27, 1987.

CHAPTER SIXTEEN

"Fly Rights: A Consumer Guide to Air Travel," Department of Transportation, Tenth Revised Edition, September 1994.

Various NTSB Accident and Incident Reports.

Department of Transportation, Federal Aviation Administration 14 CFR Parts 25 and 121, Miscellaneous Changes to Emergency Evacuation Demonstration Procedures, Exit Handle Illumination Requirements, and Public Address System; Federal Register, August 26, 1993.

Department of Transportation report AM/89/12.

"FAA Tips for Parents Using Child Restraints on Aircraft," Department of Transportation publications.

"Fly Smart: An Air Traveler's Guide," Department of Transportation, 1994.

Hearings before House Aviation Subcommittee, August 1, 1996.

New York Times, July 31, 1988.

Terry Trippler, Airline Rules Guide, The Airline Report, 1997.

Various U.S. Code of Federal Regulations Sections.

USA Today, November 8, 1996.

The Airplane List, via the Internet.

The Washington Post, November 27 and December 16, 1994.

New York Times, March 3, 1991; March 27 and June 24, 1992.

Ed Sternstein and Todd Gold, *From Take-Off to Landing* (Pocket Books, 1991).

Aviation Daily, October 21 and 24, 1996.

Travel and Leisure, August 1993.

CHAPTER SEVENTEEN

Association of Flight Attendants, November 1996.

Aviation Week and Space Technology, January 20, 1997.

Aviation Daily, May 2, 1995.

Consumer Reports, August 1994.

Various U.S. Code of Federal Regulations Sections, and Federal Register Proposed Regulations.

Sunset Magazine, March 1993 (chap. 16).

Virginia Pilot, June 14, 1996.

CHAPTER EIGHTEEN

Fleming v. Delta Airlines 359 F Supp 339, (S.D.N.Y. 1973).

"Pilot's Handbook of Aeronautical Knowledge," Government Press Office.

Various NTSB Accident and Incident Reports.

U.S. News and World Report, June 16, 1995.

CHAPTER NINETEEN

Various U.S. Code of Federal Regulation Sections.

Airline Rules Guide.

Pete Peterson, *Will America Grow Up Before It Grows Old* (Random House, 1996).

"FAA Bans Use of Booster Seats and Harness and Vest

Child Restraints Aboard Aircraft,'' *FAA News,* June 4, 1996.

CHAPTER TWENTY

Aviation Daily, November 13, December 16 and 23, 1996.

Aviation Week and Space Technology, November 4, 1996.

Air Safety Week, November 18, 1996.

''Should Inspectors General Offices Come Equipped With Soapboxes?'' by Lawrence H. Weintrob.

EPILOGUE

Report of Efforts to Improve Airport Security, R9-FA-6-014, Department of Transportation Office of Inspector General, July 3, 1996.

Ralph Nader and Wesley Smith, *Collision Course* (McGraw-Hill, 1994).

Thank you for your help in supporting air safety.

Proceeds of this book are being used to support and fight for aviation safety. After the first edition of the book was published, the outpouring of public response and support, and the effect that the collective effort of the demands of an informed and empowered public had on the aviation industry, compelled me to devote my energies and profit from this book to form an organization dedicated to continuing efforts to change the future of aviation for the better. We are proud to assist in demanding aviation safety improvements, providing support for safer aviation practices, airplanes and airports, and helping air crash victims and their families to obtain truth, justice, and a safer future for all of us.

Schiavo and Associates
A private law firm in the public service
Columbus, Ohio

controls himself. After all, airport air traffic disasters
happen at or near the airport, and with every new